Turning the
World
Upside Down

Also by John Tebbel

The Magazine in America (with Mary Ellen Zuckerman)
A Certain Club
Between Covers
The Press and the Presidency (with Sarah Miles Watts)
Opportunities in Journalism
Opportunities in Magazine Publishing
Opportunities in Publishing Careers
The Media in America
A History of Book Publishing in the United States (4 volumes)
The Battle of Fallen Timbers
South by Southwest (with Ramon E. Ruiz)
The Compact History of American Magazines
Open Letter to Newspaper Readers
Compact History of the Indian Wars
Red Runs the River
From Rags to Riches
Compact History of the American Newspaper
Paperback Books: A Pocket History
David Sarnoff
The Epicure's Companion (editor, with Ann Seranne)
The Inheritors
The American Indian Wars (with Keith Jennison)
The Magic of Balanced Living
A Voice in the Streets (fiction)
George Washington's America
The Life and Good Times of William Randolph Hearst
Touched with Fire (fiction)
The Conqueror (fiction)
Your Body: How to Keep It Healthy
Makers of Modern Journalism (with Kenneth N. Stewart)
The Battle for North America (editor)
George Horace Lorimer and the Saturday Evening Post
The Marshall Fields
An American Dynasty

Turning the World Upside Down

Inside the American Revolution

✝ ✝ ✝

JOHN TEBBEL

Orion Books
New York

Published by Orion Books, a division of Crown Publishers, Inc., 201 East 50th Street,
New York, New York 10022. Member of the Crown Publishing Group.

Random House, Inc. New York, Toronto, London, Sydney, Auckland

ORION and colophon are trademarks of Crown Publishers, Inc.

Manufactured in the United States of America

Design by Leonard Henderson

Library of Congress Cataloging-in-Publication Data
Tebbel, John William,
        Turning the world upside down : Inside the American
        Revolution / by John Tebbel
        Includes bibliographical references and index.
        1. United States—History—Revolution, 1775–1783—Social aspects.
        I. Title.
        E209.T43 1993
        973.3—dc20   92-21080
                                                                      CIP

ISBN 0-517-58955-9

10 9 8 7 6 5 4 3 2 1

First Edition

For Kacy,
who made it all possible

Contents

Contents

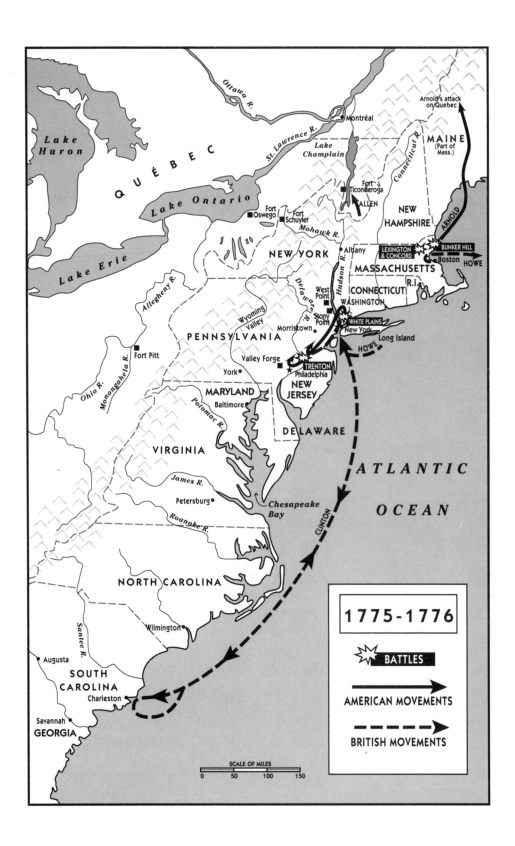

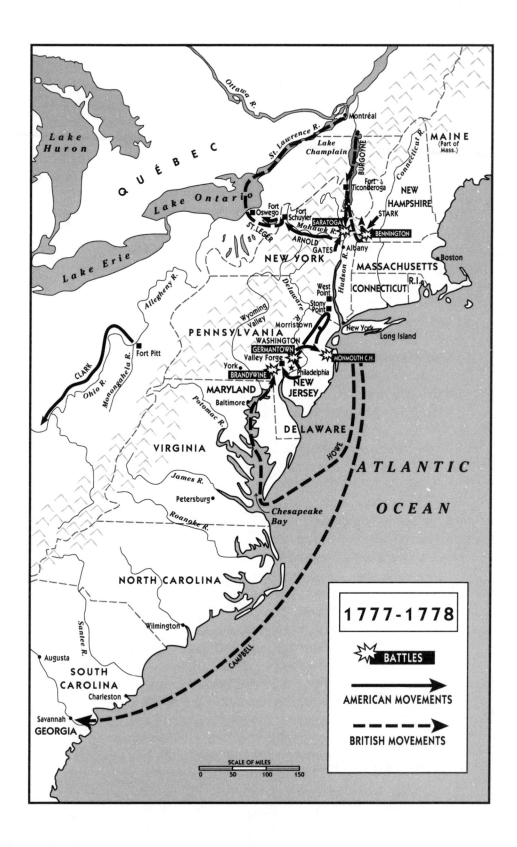

Lake Huron

Ottawa R.

Lake Ontario

St. Lawrence R.

Montréal

QUÉBEC

Lake Erie

Fort Oswego

Fort Schuyler

Mohawk R.

SARATOGA

Lake Champlain

BURGOYNE

Fort Ticonderoga

NEW HAMPSHIRE

MAINE (Part of Mass.)

Connecticut R.

ST. LEGER

ARNOLD

GATES

Albany

STARK

BENNINGTON

NEW YORK

Hudson R.

MASSACHUSETTS

CONNECTICUT

R.I.

Boston

Allegheny R.

West Point

Stony Point

New York

Long Island

Wyoming Valley

Delaware R.

Morristown

WASHINGTON

PENNSYLVANIA

Fort Pitt

CLARK

Ohio R.

Monongahela R.

GERMANTOWN

Valley Forge

York

BRANDYWINE

MARYLAND

Philadelphia

NEW JERSEY

MONMOUTH C.H.

HOWE

Baltimore

Potomac R.

DELAWARE

ATLANTIC

OCEAN

VIRGINIA

James R.

Petersburg

Roanoke R.

Chesapeake Bay

NORTH CAROLINA

Santee R.

Wilmington

Augusta

CAMPBELL

SOUTH CAROLINA

Charleston

Savannah

GEORGIA

1777–1778

BATTLES

AMERICAN MOVEMENTS

BRITISH MOVEMENTS

SCALE OF MILES

0   50   100   150

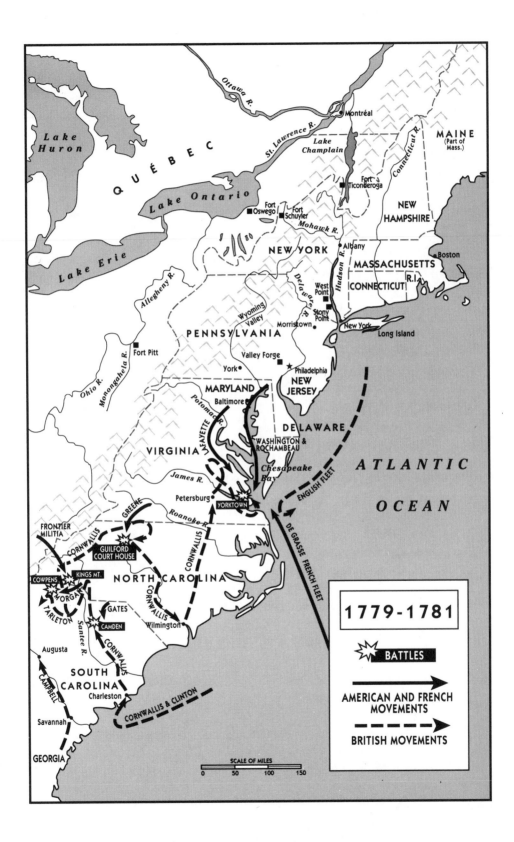

Lake Huron

Lake Ontario

Lake Erie

QUÉBEC

Ottawa R.

St. Lawrence R.

Montréal

Lake Champlain

MAINE (Part of Mass.)

Connecticut R.

Fort Ticonderoga

Fort Oswego

Fort Schuyler

Mohawk R.

NEW HAMPSHIRE

NEW YORK

Albany

Boston

MASSACHUSETTS

Allegheny R.

Wyoming Valley

CONNECTICUT

R.I.

West Point

Hudson R.

Stony Point

New York

Long Island

Morristown

PENNSYLVANIA

Fort Pitt

Ohio R.

Monongahela R.

Valley Forge

York

Philadelphia

NEW JERSEY

MARYLAND

Baltimore

DELAWARE

Potomac R.

LAFAYETTE

WASHINGTON & ROCHAMBEAU

VIRGINIA

James R.

Chesapeake Bay

ATLANTIC OCEAN

ENGLISH FLEET

Petersburg

YORKTOWN

Roanoke R.

GREENE

DE GRASSE FRENCH FLEET

FRONTIER MILITIA

CORNWALLIS

GUILFORD COURT HOUSE

CORNWALLIS

COWPENS

KINGS MT.

MORGAN

NORTH CAROLINA

CORNWALLIS

TARLETON

GATES

Santee R.

CAMDEN

Wilmington

Augusta

CORNWALLIS

SOUTH CAROLINA

CAMPBELL

Charleston

CORNWALLIS & CLINTON

Savannah

GEORGIA

1779-1781

✦ BATTLES

AMERICAN AND FRENCH MOVEMENTS

BRITISH MOVEMENTS

SCALE OF MILES

0   50   100   150

A Note to the Reader:
The Vitality of the Revolution

For nearly two hundred and fifty years, the American Revolution has been at once the best known and least understood major event in our history. "Best known" because it is the fabled center of that American mythology we choose to call our national history, a story well known to generations of citizens in its mythic form, celebrated in every conceivable way. Yet it's "least understood" because the work of whole legions of historians has failed to change successfully a multitude of popular beliefs about it.

No other war in our history has had so much written about it, with the possible exception of the Civil War, but in the popular mind the image prevails of embattled farmers rising in defense of liberty, achieving independence by a series of heroic acts, led by an almost supernatural commander who remains an icon even now for most Americans.

Only in the past fifty years or so have professional historians looked at the Revolution with revisionist eyes, but there have been certain limitations inherent in their work. As scholars, they have been most interested in the intellectual and political origins and progress of the Revolution, contributing greatly to our understanding of the terms of its argument and how it came about. There have been numerous more or less comprehensive histories of the revolution, too, many of them excellent, but they tend to view the unfolding drama from a perspective above the action.

Reading these histories and the abundant literature of the Revolution over the past fifteen years, I have come to believe that the feeling of the war has been somehow lost, in spite of the admirable qualities of so many of the works. Only in glimpses do we see in these narrative histories what it was like for soldiers and civilians, what they themselves were like as people, and what the events of the war meant to them. In short, the view from ground level seems to have been, if not lost, at least so widely dispersed that we don't see the war in terms of the people who lived through it, but rather as an overall view of successive events.

The materials for a more focused view have been available for some time in the superb collections of firsthand accounts derived from letters, diaries, and other memoirs by participants at every level. They are *Rebels and Redcoats: The Living Story of the American Revolution*, edited by George F. Scheer and Hugh F. Rankin; and, in two volumes, *The Spirit of Seventy-Six: The Story of the Revolution as Told by Participants*, edited by Henry Steele Commager and Richard B. Morris. To these must be added *The Revolution Remembered*, edited by John C. Dann from the records of veterans seeking pensions. I have drawn freely on the materials gathered by these scholars, and on occasion quote their views as expressed in the accompanying commentaries.

While these volumes are the foundations on which this book has been built, the framework standing on it is derived from hundreds of other books, the most prominent of which are listed in the bibliography. My view of the war, while it was shaped by these sources, is my own, and it emerges as a cross section of the widely varying opinions and differing conclusions drawn by the scholars.

There is still little consensus about the Revolution among professional historians. Don Higginbotham, one of the most respected specialists on the war, writes: "The view of the military profession, damning American warfare and attributing the outcome almost solely to French intervention and British blunders, has also lost much of its lustre." Yet there is a view held by other scholars that seems to have lost no lustre at all. As the following chapters will show, it seems to me that the facts justify no other conclusion.

Similarly, in reviewing a recent book, *The World Turned Upside Down: The American Victory in the War of Independence*, for the *Journal of American History*, Professor Victor D. Brooks, of Villanova, notes that "much of the patriot success was based more on British incompetence and poor communications than on American genius, a concept that Sylvia Frey develops in a key chapter." In this collection of essays on the Revolution, edited by John Ferling, it is worth noting that eleven of the contributors insist that one particular factor should be accepted as the cause of American victory —but they fail to agree on which one.

So historians differ, as they have always done, and continue to do, from the perennial argument over the role of militias in the Revolution to the true assessment of Washington's role. Having surveyed the literature, I have reached my own conclusions, as readers will see. These readers should keep in mind that this book is not a work of original scholarship, designed to refute previous views or establish new ones, but an attempt to write a narrative history of the Revolution in human terms, which I believe is the best way properly to understand it.

I felt that perhaps the most vital and exciting story in our history had not been told because it was fragmented in so many places, and that mythology had obscured the far more fascinating story of what actually happened. The problem, it seemed to me, was how to make the story real—so real that the reader would be given a sense of immediacy and be able to absorb the sights, sounds, even the smells of this all too human war.

For some time I was at a loss to determine how that could be done, until I began reading a history of the French Revolution written by the French historian Claude Manceron, now in its fifth volume and still unfinished. To give his readers the "you are there" feeling I wanted to create, Manceron used a simple device—the present tense, employing colloquial, even present-day speech (although not anachronistically) in his narrative to make his impressive scholarship serve the general reader's needs. I am well aware that many historians who still scorn the narrative technique (although it appears to be regaining some respectability) will be aghast at not only using this method but embroidering it with the rhythms and colloquialisms of common speech. I can only reiterate that this book is not for them but for the general reader. The professionals will find nothing here they don't already know, but I believe most other readers will discover a story of the Revolution they have never heard before.

My gratitude to M. Manceron for showing me the way so that I could adapt his approach (and a few of his viewpoints as well) to my own purposes. I am also grateful for the insights provided by the work of such specialists as John Shy and John Pancake, among others, whom I have quoted here and there, as well as recent work by Bernard Bailyn and Don Higginbotham.

It is a testimony to the vitality of the Revolution that after more than two centuries scholars continue to disagree with one another on many points, as indeed scholars should do. This simply means that the Revolution is not the cut and dried subject most Americans think it is. We still don't have the answers, and every year bears out the truth of John Shy's 1976 observation that "The American Revolution, possibly like all revolutions, seems fated to be remembered with an endless debate, about what kind of revolution it was, and whether it was a 'real' revolution at all."

For the readers whom I am addressing, I hope that this volume will inform Americans who want to get as close as possible to the truth about how this country was born and what its people were like—on both sides. My further hope is that this knowledge will lead these readers to understand why the Revolution was by far the most unpopular war this nation ever fought, and in some ways the most savage.

From the perspective I have taken, the Revolution turns out to be like other wars—not a glorious, high-minded struggle, but one (for both sides) in which initial enthusiasm quickly fades, the gap between soldiers and citizens widens, and the distance between illusion and reality becomes ever greater. Yet the Revolution produced authentic heroes, and a cast of other characters that would dwarf any Hollywood extravaganza for sheer variety, if nothing more. The War for Independence was a unique event in our history, one that deserves to be understood much better if we are to understand ourselves as a people and as a nation.

1

✛   ✛   ✛

The Boston Massacre—
Or Was It?

On a hot summer afternoon in 1768, the unthinkable begins to happen in Boston. A line of British ships sails into the harbor, and soon from their holds emerge long columns of red-coated troops. They're Lieutenant Colonel William Dalrymple's 14th and 19th Foot, and they've come to occupy the city.

Boston an occupied city? It's unbelievable to the sullen crowds who line the streets and watch the soldiers march by. One of those who watch is Mercy Otis Warren, sister of James "Jemmy" Otis, mercurial leader of the radical Whigs, and wife of James Warren, another strong party man. Writing about the redcoats' arrival years later in her history of the War for Independence, Mercy declares with conviction: "The American war may be dated from the hostile parade of this day; a day which marks with infamy the councils of Britain."

Mercy reminds her readers that until then the citizens of Boston "almost universally breathed an unshaken loyalty to the King of England." Now, standing in the afternoon sun, nearly dumbstruck by the spectacle, these citizens are "filled with grief and apprehension" as they watch the colonel's troops march past. Mercy exaggerates their loyalty more than a little. Those in the Warren family's upper class and those in the more prosperous portion of the middle class have their complaints, but at the moment revolution and independence are still far from their minds. But further down the economic scale lies an untutored, restless mass, easily manipulated by radicals like John Adams's cousin Samuel, who are already talking what can only be considered treason.

Sam Adams and Mercy's brother Jemmy are among the intellectual theorists of the coming Revolution, and they're adept at rabble rousing. Sam has already exhorted the citizens to take up arms. He shouts to a crowd rounded up by the Sons of Liberty: "We will not submit to any tax! We will take up arms! We are free, and we want no King!" But that's not the general sentiment in Boston, or anywhere else in the colonies. Most people are still more or less loyal to George III. They share a general concern about taxes, but they're not ready to give up on the King and his Parliament. Their anger is directed chiefly at the royal tax collectors, and in Boston at the royal governor of Massachusetts, Francis Bernard.

However, it's one thing to object to taxation, quite another to embrace the idea of violence and a call to arms. Bernard is well aware of the incipient revolt that's taking shape under his nose, and he's also read about the pro- and anti-American riots in London and Dublin. It's occurred to him that things could be much worse right there in Boston unless troops are sent in to control this "spirit of sedition," as he quite correctly puts it. An urgent request for help has brought Colonel Dalrymple's troops down from Halifax.

Now that they're here, the governor doesn't know quite what to do with them. No one's thought about where to quarter these soldiers, who have no clear idea of why they're here. Until someone finds a place for them to lay their heads and muskets, the 19th Foot pitches its tents on Boston Common, while the 14th lays out its pallets on the floors of Faneuil Hall and the Town House. Meanwhile, Bernard is beginning to understand that he's taken on a large problem. He isn't naive enough to think that a sufficient number of households will volunteer to quarter the troops. Not knowing where else to turn, he appeals directly to the Boston Town Council for help.

"What do you mean?" the councilmen say, in effect. "We didn't ask for any troops. It's up to you to quarter them, Governor."

Bernard frets, vacillates, and finally turns to someone who has real clout, Major General Thomas Gage, the King's commander-in-chief in America. The general comes up from his New York headquarters, taking his time about it, and with cool October winds already blowing in from the harbor, he meets with the Council. They listen while he tells them it's necessary to do the decent thing by these homeless men. Instead, the Council does a halfway decent thing. It grants permission to quarter the soldiers in a building so decrepit it's in danger of collapsing. Better than nothing, Gage says, and promptly accepts.

But the Council neglects to tell the general that the building is already occupied. A few of Boston's poorest people, huddled in their rags, are living there, and when the first troops arrive, they simply refuse to move. Shabby as it may be, they say, it's the only home they have.

Informed of the impasse, Bernard sends his lieutenant governor to the scene with orders to move the tenants anyway. They listen to the order and give a resounding "No!" Their leader says they've already talked to a lawyer, and they intend to stand on their rights. If the governor means to evict them, they say, he'll have to do it by force.

Very well, then, let it be force, Gage responds, relieving the governor of responsibility. He orders troops to surround the building but gives them no orders to carry out a physical eviction; consequently the soldiers are showered with a barrage of obscenities and shouts of defiance. They absolutely refuse to leave. After a few hours of this, it's clear to both the general and the governor that the situation can easily get out of hand if force is used and violence results. The troops are called off.

That leaves only one alternative: to quarter the soldiers on the townspeople, and fortunately there are enough Loyalists and other Bostonians who want no trouble to accommodate Colonel Dalrymple's men. But it's only a temporary solution. In November, two more regiments arrive from Ireland, and obviously quarters have to be found for them too. Bernard's back at square one in this exasperating muddle, and he gets no help from Gage, who's returned to New York, believing positive results have been achieved. For him it's enough that, with two regiments on hand in Boston, it's now possible for the British customs commissioners who collect the taxes to return from the safety of Castle William in the harbor, where they had taken refuge from the people's wrath a few months earlier.

Bernard has no choice but to find still more quarters among the inhabitants, which elevates the slowly rising tension a few more notches. Now there are nearly three thousand officers and soldiers in Boston, a city of about sixteen thousand. They're mostly rough countrymen, surprisingly well behaved on the whole. But they're soldiers on foreign soil, not called upon yet to fight anyone, and they have a great deal of idle time, since the drawing in of a New England winter precludes all but a minimum of drilling. Dalrymple's men do their best to get along with the inhabitants, especially the girls, as occupying troops have always done. But the Bostonians know they're doing just that—occupying—and increasingly, they find it hard to endure.

It's irritating enough just to know the soldiers are there, but now it's not possible to walk down the street in daylight without seeing their highly visible presence, and at night citizens are challenged directly by sentries. People who live across the harbor in Charlestown, or in other outlying areas, are not only challenged but often searched, and sometimes questioned if the guard thinks there's anything suspicious about them. It's a situation that makes Colonel Dalrymple nervous as well. He's wary of every civilian, and gives strict orders that what amounts to martial law must be observed.

Naturally, the citizens are outraged. Fistfights with soldiers break out so often they're not even reported. These skirmishes often occur in taverns or grog shops when the combatants on both sides have taken in a little too much alcohol. And the redcoats are just as unhappy as the citizens. Here they are, strangers in a strange land, living in uncomfortable quarters for the most part, aware that many of their hosts hate them and that few others make any attempt to hide their dislike. These foot soldiers are also bored, as soldiers are when they're not fighting, and at least some of them discover that they can sympathize with these citizens, especially those who've come from places they know. Others see that Bostonians aren't much different than themselves.

Desertions are not uncommon, and soon it's an epidemic. Those caught are given the brutal British army treatment, adopted by the Americans as soon as they have their own army. Offenders are court-martialed and shot, except for those taken out on the Common and publicly flogged. Much as they might hate their occupiers, Bostonians who witness these disciplinary demonstrations aren't inclined to view them with satisfaction. Most are disgusted, not believing it can ever happen to their own American men.

When no one is being shot or whipped, Sam Adams and other Sons of Liberty aren't above inventing incidents and peddling word of them about town, or even making false charges against soldiers, who are then brought into civil courts and made to answer for their alleged crimes. Most of these incidents, real and fabricated, are spread far and wide by the town's leading newspaper, the Boston *Gazette*, run by two young firebrands, Benjamin Eades and John Gill, who sometimes ornament the stories with a few details of their own.

Through the dreary winter months of 1768–69, tensions continue to build just below the surface of daily life. Boston is like a pressure cooker, needing only a little more steam to blow off the lid. When spring comes, things actually begin to look better. A rumor circulates through town that Gage intends to evacuate two of the regiments. Even better—and no rumor—is the announcement that Governor Bernard has been recalled by the King to give a firsthand report on conditions in the colony.

Never has a departure been hailed with such joy on both sides. For some time, Bernard's been trying to get out of what he sees as an impossible situation; the summons home is like a condemned man's reprieve. As for the Bostonians, they're so happy to see him go that when he sails in late July on H.M.S. *Rippon*, the air is filled with the joyous clangor of church bells, and that night bonfires flare up on the streets of Boston. In many of these the centerpiece is an effigy of the departed governor.

Sam Adams seizes the moment. With the Sons of Liberty, he invades the governor's mansion and finds that Bernard has been careless about his private papers, leaving some of them lying about— small, ticking time bombs. Sorting through them, he finds reports written to the Crown authorities in London, some by Bernard, others by Gage and his naval counterpart, Commodore Samuel Hood, as well as a scattering of missives by various customs officials. Believing themselves free of local prying eyes, these servants of the King have reported what they really think about events in Boston, about the so-called patriots, and about the citizenry in general. It would be hard to find a flattering mention in the lot.

Using these reports as raw material, Sam puts together a document of his own which he calls grandly, "An APPEAL TO THE WORLD, or a VINDICATION of the town of Boston, from many False and Malicious Aspersions." He's really saying to his fellow Bostonians, and a larger audience beyond them, "You see, everything we've been telling you about these British is true." Adams implies that if there are any doubters who are still loyal to the King, or sitting on the fence and think peace is possible, they'd better think again.

Adams presents his broadside to a town meeting on October 4, and it's promptly ordered to be published. The meeting adds a few fiery and self-righteous resolutions of its own. Eades and Gill print the entire text in the *Gazette*, and then, assembling it in pamphlet form, they send it out to circulate through all the other colonies. Adams and his friends hope to convince those remote from the scene of action that the British are indeed, as charged, involved in an evil conspiracy to take away the liberties of all Americans.

While the Americans are reading this document, George III is assuring Parliament that Boston is "in a state of disobedience to all law and government." The House of Commons agrees with him, in spite of opposition. It's ruled that everything done by local and state authorities is condemned, including calls for a provincial convention and elections which have already been held in nearly a hundred towns and villages of the colony. Anyone guilty of treason, says the Commons, must be arrested and brought to England for trial. Wiser heads, however, point out that if people like James Otis, Sam Adams, and Joseph Warren, not to mention John Hancock, the town's leading merchant, are arrested, the result will certainly be spilled blood, and in spite of all the intemperate talk on both sides of the Atlantic, no one except the radicals advocates that fatal step.

In Boston, meanwhile, citizens are trying everything they can think of to get the redbacks out of their houses and out of their lives. First they propose putting the troops in barracks in the remote safety of Castle William, but Dalrymple declares blandly that he has no authority to do such a thing. He'll promise nothing more than to see they're confined to quarters during the forthcoming election.

By this time the colony has a new governor. He's Thomas Hutchinson, whom the historian Bernard Bailyn has called "a conservative in a time of radical upheaval." He's not someone the King has sent over to restore order, but a native American, a fifth-generation New Englander, a man of many talents—merchant, historian, scholar, member of a family who have created more wealth and power than any other in New England. He also happens to be the most feared and hated public official in America, denounced as a traitor, accused of being a potential tyrant, a man for whom almost no one has a good word. Some resent his political and financial power, carefully built up by generations of his family. Others hate him because he simply doesn't understand anything outside his own conservative way of thinking and acting. He plays by the rules and believes his first loyalty is to carry out the duties of the office to which he's been appointed— and he's held nearly all the colony's important offices.

One thing Hutchinson does understand, though, is that he's dealing with a radical movement that will stop at absolutely nothing. He remembers with horror the night of August 26, 1765, when a mob more violent than any ever seen in the colonies attacked his house. He was then chief justice and lieutenant governor of Massachusetts. Eating supper that night with his children (his beloved wife had died a few years earlier), Hutchinson had heard the mob coming and barely had time to flee before axes were smashing in the doors.

Like a feeding frenzy of sharks, the invaders swarmed through the rooms, tearing down the hangings and ripping off the wainscoting, splitting the furniture into woodpiles, even tearing open interior walls and destroying some of them. Finding £900 in cash, they absconded with it, and for good measure stole all the plates, decorations, even clothing. Some drifted outside and ravaged the garden.

Worst of all, this mob, acting in the name of liberty, destroyed or scattered Hutchinson's splendid library, perhaps the best in the colonies, including the manuscript of Volume 1 of a history of the colony that he'd begun to write, as well as a fine collection of historical papers, the result of many years' research, which he had intended to present to the colony as a public archive.

In their savage fury, the mob worked for three hours on the cupola surmounting the house before it came down. If it hadn't been for the heavy brickwork, they would have torn down the entire house, and even so, they worked hard trying to do it until daylight. Then they slunk away, leaving behind streets and lawns littered with money, plate, gold rings, and other loot carelessly dropped as they departed. It says something about Hutchinson's character that he would have stayed and faced this insensate fury alone if his frantic daughter hadn't persuaded him to flee with the other children; otherwise he would almost certainly have been killed.

Next morning he appeared in court without the robes of the chief justice, which had been shredded by the mob. A young lawyer, Josiah Quincy, Jr., reported later that Hutchinson, "with tears starting from his eyes and a countenance which strongly told the inward anguish of his soul," made an apology for his appearance, explaining that he had no other clothes than what he had on, and some of them were borrowed. His family was just as destitute, he said, and their plight was "infinitely more unsupportable than what I feel for myself." In a moving address to the stunned courtroom, he declared himself innocent of all the charges brought against him, especially the accusation that he helped to pass the Stamp Act, when in fact he had done everything he could to prevent it.

A shock of horror ran through the colony that day, embracing every political faction. This was a "savageness unknown in a civilized country," one observer wrote. As though they had to see it to believe it, as many as ten thousand people came to look at the ruins, and there were some who wondered whether their own lives and property might be next. A fear of anarchy hung heavily in the air, and the attorney general, who had also been threatened, thought it prudent to leave town for ten days, a move emulated by a number of other people.

What was the cause of this brutality? many people wondered. Years later, Hutchinson thought he had part of the answer. He wrote in his restored *History* that one of the rioters had reported that he was inflamed to action by a sermon he had heard the day before, preached by the Reverend Jonathan Mayhew, on the text, "I would they were even cut off which trouble you." It was true there were inflammatory figures in the pulpit, as well as in the taverns and back alleys. Nor could the riot be excused as a demonstration for liberty, since liberty was less threatened in America at that moment than anywhere else on earth. Nevertheless, Hutchinson continued to be an object of hatred and verbal attack until he became governor. Now his troubles have really begun.

No sooner has he taken office than the colony's House of Representatives petitions him to withdraw the troops. Hutchinson tells them the truth, which is the wrong answer. He's as powerless as Dalrymple to move the troops, he says, without permission of higher authority. This assertion is widely disbelieved and sets off a frenzy of letter writing to the *Gazette*, along with new and even more fiery speeches by Sam Adams and his friends, all with the same refrain: "Resist this tyranny or submit to chains."

So the pressure in the cooker continues to rise as a tense autumn ends with an early winter and the fateful year of 1770 begins. Boston is filled with hot words, while people shiver in below-freezing temperatures. Under considerable pressure, local merchants have agreed not to import British goods, an act now bankrupting small businessmen. But Sam Adams sees it's enforced by deploying gangs of toughs, headed by an enforcer named Will Molineux. When a few merchants, including Hutchinson's sons, a scattering of Tories, and a few patriots who don't want to see their businesses ruined, defy Sam and his gangs, their shop windows are smashed, with worse promised unless they give in to the boycott.

A nasty piece of business occurs when a mob, composed for the most part of Molineux's ruffians, gather in front of a house occupied by Ebenezer Richardson, a man they believe to be a Tory informer. Richardson, not intimidated, fires into the mob and fatally wounds an eleven-year-old boy. Miraculously, he himself escapes with his life, but he's later convicted of murder. Pardoned immediately by the King, he leaves town secretly and disappears.

The Sons of Liberty, who know something about public relations even if they don't know its name, make a great propaganda display out of the poor boy's public funeral. John Adams writes of it: "A vast number of boys walked before the coffin, a vast number of men and women after it, and a number of carriages. My eyes never beheld such a funeral."

Hearing about these events in New York, General Gage writes to the Home Office that government is at an end in Boston, and as far as he can see, matters aren't much better in New York. For once, he assesses the situation correctly. It's clear that affairs are nearing some kind of climax in Boston, and it arrives on March 5, with the bloody, ambiguous event we still call the Boston Massacre.

This confused drama has a stark setting. Winter still has Boston by the throat. There's a foot of snow in the streets, and eight inches of ice covers the harbor. British sentries suffer from frostbitten feet. Every citizen who can stays as close to the fireside as possible. Nevertheless, the uneasy truce between soldiers and Bostonians strains toward the breaking point every day, and during the first long weekend in March the simmering cauldron boils over.

It begins with fights breaking out here and there. Snowballs, and possibly lethal hunks of ice, are thrown, but these are followed for the first time by clubs. Some fearful citizens wonder whether muskets and bayonets can be far behind.

At night the fighting is worse because that's the time the toughs spill out of the taverns, half-drunk. During the day, young boys shout insults at the soldiers, and the redcoats vow to teach the little rascals respect for His Majesty's uniform. By this time, Hutchinson is so hated that the town decrees a street named for him will be renamed Pearl Street, and so it is today.

Then a small incident touches off a large happening. After a particularly uproarious weekend, filled with incidents of violence, a cold, gray Monday morning dawns on March 5. One of those who ventures out is a private from the 29th who knocks on the door of a journeyman rope maker named Sam Gray. The private is one of those soldiers so badly paid that they're forced to look for odd jobs to get money for small comforts.

"Do you want to work?" Sam Gray asks him, already knowing the answer. "Yes, I do that," the soldier tells him.

For what follows, we have to rely on the redcoat's understandably biased account, but it's believable because it reflects the almost personal antagonism that has grown up between soldiers and civilians. Many of the soldiers are recognized by inhabitants, and the taunts and quarrels often take on a personal tone. In any event, according to the job seeker, Sam Gray tells him what kind of work he can do in language that can't be repeated in mixed company when the story circulates around town.

It's enough to send the soldier flying at Sam, fists flailing, but a few minutes later, he finds himself bruised and bloody on the ground. Getting up, he limps back to the barracks and returns with a few comrades. Some of Sam's friends join in the fight, and the conflict attracts other soldiers and civilians from adjoining streets and squares until this minor quarrel begins to look like a major brawl.

In the end, the soldiers have to retreat to their barracks, nursing their wounds. Further repercussions occur as the story circulates. Sam's employer appears at the shop and, without examining the rights or wrongs of the matter, fires him. He wants to avoid any trouble with the occupiers. At their barracks, the soldiers are reprimanded by their officers and confined to quarters. But it's too late. The damage has been done.

While all this is taking place, another private in the 29th, Kilroy by name, has been caught robbing a respectable Boston woman of most of her exterior clothing, including her muff and tippet. Kilroy's motive is simple. He's desperately cold, but he's forced to give up his illicitly acquired warmth.

As the day goes on, similar street scenes occur here and there in

Boston. Are they as hit and miss as they seem, or are they orchestrated? Later on there will be some who think so. One of them is John Adams, who hates Hutchinson as much as anyone but isn't yet the radical his cousin Sam is, and he thinks Sam is trying to incite violence and push the citizens toward a showdown with the redcoats.

This is the theory. If the soldiers can be provoked into firing on the civilians, public opinion will be so aroused, even among moderates, that the remaining two regiments will have to be withdrawn, all six hundred of them. Sam Adams is on record as asserting that troops can't be quartered on an unwilling population indefinitely without bloodshed. Now it appears he's willing to produce the blood, although preferably not his own.

Through that turbulent, gray Monday, small mobs and individual battlers roam through the restless streets. In the late afternoon, the snow that has been falling since daylight suddenly stops and a wintry sun comes out briefly, illuminating the radicals who are preparing for the night's work. As events are reconstructed later, that means sending gangs to harass the soldiers and stir up trouble at various places, since no one seems certain where the real flash point may be.

John Adams has an aristocratic disdain for these self-styled patriots. He calls them "the lower classes," and certainly no one is going to mistake them for gentlemen. The same can be said for the small bands of soldiers released from the restraint of barracks by their colonels, and now engaged in what they call "sweeping the streets," meaning that they're harassing civilians with insults, shoving, and cursing.

About eight o'clock that night, the anticipated flash point is reached in two places. On Brattle Street, outside Murray's Barracks, Captain Goldfinch, of the 14th, a blameless officer whose fault, as it appears later, is a failure to pay his barber, finds himself observing a young boy being beaten by a soldier. The boy's yelling, "I'm killed, I'm killed," although it's obvious he's far from death. The captain watches as a crowd quickly gathers, blocking the passage of some soldiers who are trying to get back to their barracks from duty.

Seeing himself obstructed, the ensign in command of the returning soldiers orders them to use their bayonets if necessary to get through. At that point, Goldfinch steps forward and admonishes the ensign sternly. He takes charge and manages to get the soldiers into the comparative safety of an old sugar house on the street—but not before they've exchanged blows with some in the crowd. The night has begun to turn ugly.

In the confusion, Goldfinch, with his immediate mission accomplished, attempts to make his way to King Street nearby. He's recognized, however, by the young boy who had been the center of the original incident. He's the son of a French barber named Piemont, whom Goldfinch owes for his haircuts, and apparently this debt has become a family matter because now the boy pursues the captain, crying havoc at his heels as he tries to get away.

With the barber's son bawling insults behind him, Goldfinch emerges at last into King Street. He pauses for a moment in the bright moonlight, near the sentry guarding the Custom House. Piemont's boy has elevated his voice by that time until he's bellowing, cataloguing Goldfinch's sins and going so far as to call him a son of a bitch.

The captain has heard worse words before, and he's trying to pay no attention, but the scene somehow drives the sentry who's watching it past the point of restraint, and with good reason. For hours he's been the target of passing civilians, who have been heaving ice chunks, snowballs, even oyster shells at him, accompanied by choice curses. His tormentors stay tantalizingly out of range of the bayonet he occasionally threatens to use on them.

But now this exasperated private, whose name is Montgomery, leaves his post and does what he never should have. "Show your face," he demands of the boy.

"I ain't ashamed of my face," the boy replies insolently.

Somehow this answer is simply too much for Montgomery. He flings out an arm and strikes the boy, with not even enough force to knock him down, but it's enough to attract the instant attention of a small crowd that's been loitering near the sentry for some time, enjoying his harassment. Now they take quick offense and move ominously toward him. "You bloodthirsty butcher, you're murdering the child!" someone in the crowd yells.

Meanwhile, nearby, a third small gang has been roaming the streets, looking for trouble, incited by a tall man who's been exhorting them in the shadow of Faneuil Hall. Is it Sam Adams? At the time, some people think so, but it's unlikely. For one thing, Sam is short, and besides, the mysterious orator is wrapped in a red cloak and wears a white wig, making it much more likely that it's Will Molineux, the leader of patriotic mobs. What's certain is that, by the time he's finished speaking, his listeners are so worked up, according to contemporary accounts, that they're shouting, "Kill all the lobsters!" and "To the Main Guard!"

This is no ordinary mob, but to this day no one has been able to prove they're a specially selected group whose mission is to produce the decisive blood that Sam and his friends have been calling for. Certainly they're a tough lot, with the general appearance of street fighters—a clutch of sailors, some muscular porters, other brawny types—two hundred of them in all.

This dangerous crowd comes pouring into King Street, linking up with the other two mobs—the original brawlers who had encountered Goldfinch and the barber's boy on Brattle Street, and those who've been menacing the sentry. A full moon, reflecting off the brilliant whiteness of the newly fallen snow, illuminates this historic stage. The angry, shouting crowd mills about until they're packed in from the Old State House to the Custom House.

By this time, the beleaguered sentry and Captain Goldfinch are getting some help. Captain Charles Preston, of the 29th Foot, an officer well liked even by some of the civilians, though grudgingly, has hurried to the scene over the narrow, icy streets, leading a corporal and a six-man squad. As they arrive at the main Guardhouse, across the street from the State House, about nine o'clock the great bells in the Old Meeting House split the night air with a clangorous summons, the kind usually heard when there's a fire.

Windows fly up and doors open all over Boston as alarmed citizens respond. Rumor spreads from tongue to tongue with incredible speed. Conventional people think the town is on fire, but other ideas circulate quickly: the soldiers are slaughtering the townspeople or, more modestly, someone is cutting down that patriotic rallying point, the Liberty Tree. Sounding over the confusion from a hundred throats is that ancient rallying cry of the citizen in danger: "Town-born, turn out! Town-born, turn out!"

While they're turning out, poor Montgomery is rapidly reaching a point of desperation as the menacing mob moves in upon him slowly. Above the cursing, he hears dreadful cries of "Kill him! Kill him!"

"I'll blow your brains out if you come near me," he warns them, terrified.

"Fire and be damned," they yell back.

Montgomery loads his musket, and as he does so, an apparition confronts him, one that's about to go down in history. Crispus Attucks is an intimidating man, more than six feet tall, with the coloring of a mulatto, a hearty forty-seven years old. A former slave, he's possibly the hired hand of a Framingham farmer, but we don't know for sure; he's a mysterious figure, and remains so today. Historians can't do much more than speculate about who he was or where he came from. In any case, no one knows what he's doing there on King Street at this moment, or how he's come to be a part of the mob. A recent investigator thinks he came up from the Bahamas to Boston and was living in Farmingham as an itinerant workman. One thing is certain, he's there on King Street this night with twenty sailors carrying two-foot clubs.

At the moment, Montgomery has no interest in Crispus Attucks's origins. All he knows is that he's about to be killed, and he sings out in a voice loud enough to be heard across the street, "Turn out, Main Guard!" As he shouts, Attucks takes a tentative poke at Montgomery and threatens, "Lobsterback, I'm going to have one of your claws."

But the call for help is heard. Captain Preston and his corporal's guard, eight men in all, come pouring out of the main guardhouse, where they've been standing on alert, and begin working their way through the mob to reach their embattled comrade. It's a struggle, but they make it at last, wheeling in a semicircle, facing the mob. Cold steel flashes in the moonlight as bayonets are leveled. It's come down to eight men and Montgomery against a roaring, boisterous mob of several hundred men and boys. Preston is known as a cool officer, but his judgment is about to be tested. He knows one indisputable fact: he's not about to let Montgomery be clubbed to death.

In a loud, clear voice, Preston orders his men to prime and load. When the mob hears that command, an abrupt silence falls. The moment has come at last for the blood the radicals have wanted. In the ominous quiet, everyone can hear the iron ramrods thrusting down the barrels. Then Captain Preston steps in front of his men, a human barrier against any immediate violence.

A plump young man emerges from the crowd and clutches Preston's arm. It's Henry Knox, a twenty-year-old Boston bookseller, well known and liked by everyone, who in six short years will be commanding General Washington's artillery.

"For God's sake, Captain, take your men away," Knox pleads. "If you fire, you'll answer for it with your life."

"I'm sensible of that," Preston tells him quietly.

Someone shouts from the crowd, "Those guns ain't loaded."

"Are they?" Knox asks.

"They have powder and ball," Preston answers firmly.

"Do you mean to fire on the inhabitants then?" Knox asks.

"By no means," Preston replies, but Knox, as he says later, believes that the captain isn't all that certain about it.

In fact, at this critical juncture, the British are trying to stave off the disaster staring them in the face. Captain Goldfinch and some of the other officers are begging those in the forefront of the mob to go home and avoid bloodshed, but blood is what's wanted. A forward movement begins somewhere at the rear as men push against the backs of those in front of them, even climbing up to see what's happening. The resulting pressure ends with a surge of bodies toward the waiting bayonets.

Crispus Attucks is in the front line. He swings his club at Preston, grazes him, knocks Montgomery down instead, and grapples with him, trying to get his musket. But Montgomery, a strong country boy himself, manages to keep it and get to his feet again.

In this surging wave of human flesh, there are some who've played bit parts earlier in the day. There's Private Kilroy, who only that morning mugged a lady to get her outerwear. He has his eye on one man in the mob, Sam Gray, now unemployed, whom he recognizes. Kilroy has heard about how Sam beat up his comrade who was only looking for an honest day's work.

Suddenly it all comes down to a single fateful moment. Is it Captain Preston's voice that commands above the tumult, "Present!" as the muskets come to eye level? Preston denies it at his trial, and witnesses standing nearby agree. But someone *does* give that order, and follows it with the final stroke: "Fire!"

No one can blame the tormented Montgomery's response to that command. Someone has swept off his hat, and the moon glistens on his half-bald pate as he aims directly at his chief tormentor, Attucks, and puts two musket balls through his chest. Attucks falls, dead. Nor can anyone completely blame Kilroy, who takes dead aim at Sam Gray and kills him with a single shot.

But others are falling, too. There's Isaac Greenwood, a young printer's apprentice, who's been standing there holding the hand of a twelve-year-old boy, his master's son. Isaac's so carried away that he throws up his fists and yells, "Fire away, you damned lobsterbacks!" They oblige him, and a few hours later he's dead. All told, five men die and others are wounded. Kilroy, a bad lot in any case, most agree, shoves his bayonet through Sam Gray's chest, but Sam doesn't feel it. He's already dead.

The scene, hopelessly idealized for propaganda purposes, is frozen for us by Paul Revere, an engraver who's also a radical activist. He gives us the familiar engraving, showing the British soldiers standing in a line and delivering a volley in unison, which was far from the case. Preston is shown holding his sword in the air, obviously having just given the command to fire. But Preston, as it turns out, never removed his sword from its scabbard, never gave the command, never fired himself.

Now the radicals have their blood, which stains the glittering snow in a dark flood. The mob has fallen back in terror and run away in wild disorder, some leaving hats and overcoats behind—black clumps on this unlikely battlefield, hardly distinguishable from those other clumps of clothing beneath which are dead men.

The first blood of the coming Revolution has been shed, and scarcely has the mob melted away down the side streets before another sound fills the night—British drums beating the call to arms. Both regiments, many men still pulling on their uniforms as they come, rush into King Street and swing into their classic formations, which will do many of them so little good later on. Now they fix their bayonets, ready for God knows what. The mob has gone, but the townspeople are gathering from every quarter, summoned by the bells, demanding to know what's happened.

Someone has gone to summon Hutchinson, entreating him, "For God's sake, go to King Street or the town will all be in blood." In an act of great personal courage, he responds and is soon plunging through the crowd in King Street. Reaching Captain Preston, he demands, "How came you to fire without orders from a civil magistrate?" Whatever Preston answers is lost as people push Hutchinson toward the Council chamber, from which he addresses them and manages to gain control. He promises a full, impartial inquiry, and assures them, "The law shall take its course! I will live and die by the law!" Vintage Hutchinson. With that, he urges everyone to disperse, and reluctantly they do so. Hutchinson spends the remainder of the night, until 4:00 A.M., conducting his inquiry. Some Council members take advantage of the situation to urge evacuation of the troops before more bloodshed occurs, but the governor can't make that decision, he tells them once more.

At 11:00 A.M. next morning, there's an emergency meeting at which the Boston selectmen tell Hutchinson bluntly that if he doesn't get the troops out of town there will be "blood and carnage," and "the most terrible consequences [are] to be expected." Characteristically, Hutchinson sticks to the rule book. He has no authority to dispose the King's troops, he tells them one more time, but he points out that these selectmen have the power to control the mob. Why don't they exercise it? One replies that if all of them got down on their knees before these people it would do no good.

Hutchinson continues to pursue a hard line, pointing out that if any attempt is made to drive out the troops, anyone who abets that move, or even advises it, will be charged with high treason.

At this point, Colonel Dalrymple introduces a conciliatory note. He'll take the responsibility for sending the 29th to Castle William in the harbor, leaving the 14th in place, and will do everything possible to forestall any further bloodshed. The selectmen seize upon this tactical error. If the colonel has authority to move one regiment, they say, certainly he can use it to move two, and if the governor no more than expresses the "desire" for him to move the 14th, that should be enough. Thus Hutchinson's options are reduced, as Bailyn says, to "where it seemed the future of Anglo-American relations and the lives of hundreds of innocent people rested on his willingness not to issue an illegal order but merely to express a personal wish, one that everyone knew would have the force of an order."

This impasse sets the stage for an afternoon session of the Council. In the coming months, no one is certain about exactly what happened in that dramatic confrontation. The Council meets under renewed threats of violence, leading the selectmen to maintain their own hard line. If the troops don't leave, they insist, then the citizens must expel them forcibly, and if that means mustering armed civilians from surrounding towns, they're prepared to do just that. If this happens, they add, more blood will certainly be spilled, and it will be on Hutchinson's hands. Then the Council issues an ultimatum. If the troops aren't removed and unless he flees to the safety of Castle William, the governor himself will be seized.

Since it's the constitutional duty of the Council to advise the governor, and since it's just voted unanimously to authorize an insurrection, in effect, Hutchinson appears to have no choice. But through that long afternoon, under inexorable pressure, the governor stubbornly clings to his principles, even though everyone else, including the regimental commanders, tells him he has to surrender.

He's alone, conscious that he stands at a crucial turning point, not only in the colony's affairs, but in the entire system he has sworn to uphold, not to mention his career as a public servant. If he permits the troops to go, how can the British government any longer maintain its authority in America? By this time, he firmly believes that the whole thing, including the event in King Street, has been a secret plot against him. But at the end of the long afternoon, it's clear even to him that he has no choice. "Under duress," he says for the record, he gives in.

Outside the Council rooms that afternoon, the town is buzzing. Captain Preston and his eight soldiers have been arrested and are under guard, awaiting trial, just as Hutchinson promised. The law will prevail. But where in Boston, many people wonder, is it possible to find twelve good men and true who will swear with a straight face that they will be unbiased as jurors? In fact, is there any such thing as an unbiased man in Boston at this point? Further, where can a lawyer be found with enough courage to come forward and defend these British soldiers and their officer?

An answer is immediately forthcoming. One of the friends Captain Preston has made among the citizens is a curious fellow named Forester, whose nickname (no one can say why) is "The Irish Infant." Forester visits Preston in his cell and vows to find a lawyer for him.

At first, the Irish Infant thinks that Tory lawyers will certainly step forward to defend one of their own, but when he calls on them that day, he finds that they're so terrified of the street gangs that not one of them will volunteer, not even the most revered among them, Judge Auchmuty. Increasingly desperate now, Forester turns to Josiah Quincy, Jr., twenty-six years old and dying of tuberculosis, one of the great orators of his time, a splendid lawyer who's been denied the right to put on a barrister's robes because the Supreme Court of the colony distrusts him. He conducts his ample practice in street clothes.

Quincy agrees to defend Preston and the others, but only if John Adams, who's nine years older, agrees to act as senior counsel. The Irish Infant hurries off to see Adams, who hears his distraught plea and answers with an early proof of his greatness. He writes later: "I had no hesitation in answering that counsel ought to be the very last thing that an accused person should want [meaning "lack"] in a free country, that the bar ought, in my opinion, to be independent and impartial, at all times, and in every circumstance and that persons whose lives were at stake ought to have the counsel they prefer."

There's more to it than that, of course. Adams is no Tory, but at this stage he has little sympathy with what the radicals are doing, and he doesn't share Cousin Sam's love for the unwashed. Later, he refers to those involved in the affair as a "motley mob of saucy boys, Negroes, mulattoes, Irish teagues and outlandish jacktars." Adams has gone along cautiously and sometimes unwillingly with the movement toward resistance, but in the wake of the affair on King Street, he means to abandon caution completely for the sake of principle.

He well knows what this decision could mean for him. As he tells us in his *Autobiography*, he understands that defending Captain Preston and his soldiers will mean that he has agreed to "differ in opinion from all my friends, to set at defiance all their advice, their remonstrances, their raillery, their ridicule, their censure, their sarcasm, without acquiring one symptom of pity from my enemies." Adams doesn't say so, but taking on the defense, in a worst-case scenario, might even mean that he will lose his law practice.

Calmly, however, he prepares for trial, trying not to hear the insulting epithets and ridicule hurled at him in the streets when he and Josiah Quincy walk to court. As it happens, Quincy's eldest brother, Sam, will be representing the Crown in these proceedings.

Adams and Quincy are behaving with quiet heroism, but there's another hero who lies slowly and painfully dying in his master's house for four days after the King Street affair, which Colonel Dalrymple is still calling "a scuffle." That's Patrick Carr, the "Irish teague" Adams has referred to. Carr has taken a bullet in the abdomen, and in those days that's a particularly agonizing way to die. Yet he lies there, hour after terrible hour, and under questioning simply refuses to blame the soldiers. Instead, he tells his questioners that the troops were grossly abused and would have been hurt, probably killed, if they hadn't fired. They had done so in self-defense, he says, and he can't find it in his heart and conscience to blame them, not even the man who did him in, whoever he was.

Carr remembers that back in Ireland he's seen the same kind of thing—British soldiers called out to face a mob—but as he's quoted in court, "He had never in his life seen them bear half so much before they fired." He bears no malice toward anyone, the dying man says.

This is extremely valuable testimony for Adams and Quincy, who take it all down carefully and have it attested. It gives the direct lie to the version being circulated by Sam Adams and the radical Whig machine. Sam is infuriated by Carr's testimony, and stoops so low as to charge that Carr is just a poor Catholic immigrant whose word is therefore hardly to be trusted.

But Sam is a complicated man, then as he is today, although he's been dissected by generations of historians. If he's such a howling demagogue, thirsting for the blood of Englishmen, why at the trial and after does he refrain from denouncing Cousin John and Josiah Quincy? Is it because he and his fellow radicals have some dirty linen they'd just as soon not see washed in court, and think that if they keep a low profile, the two young lawyers for the defense won't wash it? At the time, there are those who believe so.

The trial is still months away, however, since John Adams is in no hurry to have it start while passions are still inflamed. Meanwhile, in the immediate aftermath of the "massacre" and the Council's ultimatum, Hutchinson is coming to the end of his rope. On the late afternoon of March 11, silent crowds of people line the streets and watch the two regiments marching ignominiously to the docks, where ships will take them to Castle William. To make the point perfectly clear, they're escorted by the Sons of Liberty's chief enforcer, Will Molineux, and his men.

Exhausted and humiliated, Hutchinson does not watch the evacuation. He pours out his anguish in letters to distant friends, although little real emotion seeps through his always carefully restrained prose. To a former governor, John Pownall, he reports that Boston is ungovernable, and its people do anything they please. Town meetings are little more than mob scenes, he says, where as many as 4,000 people jam the hall, even though it's well known that there are no more than 1,500 legal voters. To his predecessor, Bernard, now safely home in England, he writes despairingly that he has lost any hope of reasoning with the people. If a native American like himself, who has spent forty years serving his country, can be rendered despised and helpless, who can expect anything better? he wants to know. He feels himself at the point of physical and psychological collapse, and is trying to avoid both by taking brief trips to the country and exercising as much as possible.

What's most galling to Hutchinson is that he now has to withdraw that nomination for the governorship (he's only been acting governor since Bernard's departure), a post he's sought so ardently for so long. Instead, he resigns, and while his resignation letter is still at sea, confirmation of his appointment by George III arrives. Now there's pressure of another kind—from London, urging him to stay. Since tension in the months after King Street appears to be lessening, he agrees reluctantly in June to carry on for a time.

It's a decision that doesn't please the radicals, naturally enough, and they're also disturbed by the deliberate slowness with which John Adams is approaching the trial. Sam Adams wants it as soon as possible, before people cool down, and he urges that a new gallows just erected in the city be used at once. That view is endorsed by righteous bellowings from Boston clergymen in their pulpits. But John and Josiah resist pressure, using their legal talents to the fullest. Consequently, it's nearly the end of October before the trial finally gets under way.

Meanwhile, the citizens have had plenty of time to discuss the matter, and as the talk about Sam Adam's political machine and what it might do reveals a bit more detail, the moderate Whigs and many unconvinced fence-sitters become aware that the radicals in reality constitute a semisecret political organization, manipulating town politics, enforcing their demands with terror. It's also becoming clear that the people of Boston have let themselves come under the virtual control of a relatively small group of men, and they find this fact highly disturbing. There's no more talk about using the new gallows.

In court, the trial is carried out in the usual way, without incident, and a much more impartial jury than might have been assembled in March acquits Captain Preston, who joins his comrades in Castle William. A little later, he returns to England, retires from the army, and is given a life pension by his grateful King.

Preston's case had been tried first. A month later, his men come into the dock and do not do quite as well. The jury acquits five of them, but the other two are convicted of manslaughter. They plead what is called "benefit of clergy," meaning in essence that they're sorry for the whole thing. The judge sentences them to the quaint colonial penalty of being branded on the thumb. After the branding, they don't neglect to thank Adams and Quincy, knowing it could have been much worse for them. That's more than Captain Preston did. He expressed no gratitude, publicly or privately. For his work, Adams is paid a total of nineteen guineas, at a time when a day's labor was worth two shillings.

By now, Bostonians are weary of "massacres" and riots and mobs. They pay little attention to Sam's outraged letters in the *Gazette*, in which he refuses to accept the jury's two verdicts and gives his own version of the testimony. But the perverse voters elect both him and Cousin John to the Massachusetts legislature.

In Boston, there's a brief lull, but unrest is still in the air, there and everywhere in the colonies. The bloody night on King Street is only the most dramatic of an increasing number of incidents whose eventual outcome no one can foresee.

2

Boston Has
a Tea Party

When the jury listened to John Adams and Josiah Quincy and decided that no "massacre" had been committed on King Street, the verdict satisfies everyone but the radicals who simply bide their time and wait for the next development.

It's not long in coming, and once more it's an event long since blurred by national mythology. The Boston Tea Party is still celebrated as a patriotic reaction to an onerous tax on tea that Americans refused to pay and, to make their point clear, threw a quantity of it into Boston Harbor. In reality, these duties had been in force for six years, and most of the time were either paid without any trouble or simply disregarded. Nor was anyone forcing the colonists to buy the East India Company's tea.

The Tea Party, then, is no sudden explosion, and its origins may not even have been in Boston, but in Philadelphia, where for years certain merchants have been making handsome profits in smuggled tea and may have organized a quiet conspiracy in the major port cities to prevent any disturbance of their cozy arrangement.

If so, it seems at first they'll be successful. Before the Boston affair, when shipments of East India Company Tea arrive in Charleston, they're seized by customs officers and stacked away in damp cellars, where they will surely rot. This extraordinary behavior by such officials suggests that deals have been made. Other tea ships bound for the ports of Philadelphia and New York are given to understand they won't be permitted to land their cargoes and, taking the hint, return to England.

In Boston, however, already a tinderbox, where the radicals are only waiting for an excuse, it's a different story, and there the unfortunate Hutchinson is caught in a new crisis not of his making. He's opposed the tea duty since it was first imposed, and has frequently urged its repeal, but this exemplary resistance is overshadowed by the fact that he's secretly involved in tea merchandising himself, and in fact has invested much of his liquid capital in the East India Company. Worse, he owes his salary from the Crown (£1,500 yearly) to the income from the tea duty. Since no one has seriously objected to the tax, and because he believes the Philadelphia smugglers are trying to protect themselves from competition, he says the tea ships have every right to land.

The first of them, the *Dartmouth*, bearing 114 casks of tea, sails into Boston Harbor on November 28, 1773, and rides at anchor while the customs officers come aboard next day and the Boston activists demand that she return to England at once. But the *Dartmouth* is formally entered at customs and docks at Griffin's Wharf. When all its cargo, except for the tea, has been taken ashore, a military guard commanded by John Hancock throws a picket line around the ship to prevent any further unloading. In this 25-man guard is the young activist Paul Revere, armed with musket and bayonet.

This situation is shortly compounded by the arrival of two more tea ships, carrying a cargo of tea worth £18,000. Alarmed, "the Body," as the almost continuous mass meetings of citizens is now called, concludes that they'd better warn other ports along that part of the coast not to let in any tea ships. With five other express riders, who have been keeping the colonial Committees of Correspondence informed, Revere sets out on his first recorded ride of warning.

The town meetings, now taking place in Old South Church because Faneuil Hall is too small, are filled with thousands of non-legal voters, of whom Hutchinson has already complained. They mean to vote anyway. Sam Adams brings in more recruits from neighboring towns, and they vote too. Schoolmasters even take their students to watch what is happily considered to be democracy in action, although many citizens, Whig and Tory alike, are shocked by what's going on, and fear the mob has taken over from duly constituted authority.

No one deplores this development more fervently than Hutchinson. To him, the immediate problem is clear. These ships can't leave the harbor legally until they're given customs clearance, and if they don't pay duty on their taxable goods within twenty days of arrival, their cargoes will be confiscated. That's the law. It will have to be enforced on December 17.

Once more Hutchinson stands on his principles and the law, hoping that the presence of British warships blocking the harbor will help him enforce it. Once more he's threatened by the mobs, in the streets and at the mass meetings. The radicals vilify him at every opportunity. At one meeting, Sam Adams roars with the authentic voice of demagoguery, "Is he that shadow of a man scarce able to support his withered carcass on his hoary head? Is *he* a representation of Majesty?"

Another beleaguered man is the owner of the *Dartmouth*, a Captain Rotch. On the late afternoon of December 16, threatened with confiscation of his ship next day, he rides out to the governor's mansion in Milton to plead with Hutchinson to overlook the law for once, and let him leave the harbor with his tea *sans* a customs clearance. Hutchinson refuses bluntly. He intends to enforce the law no matter what happens; the authority of Parliament, which he represents, is legitimate and must be upheld.

Thus the stage is set for the Tea Party, which has already been carefully planned, mostly in a tavern called the Green Dragon, which the radicals have virtually taken over. Someone's even written a rallying song for the imminent Party:

> *Rally, Mohawks! bring out your axes,*
> *And tell King George we'll pay no taxes*
>   *On his foreign tea;*
> *His threats are vain, and vain to think*
> *To force our girls and wives to drink*
>   *His vile Bohea!*
> *Then rally, boys, and hasten on*
>   *To meet our chiefs at the Green Dragon!*

What this ditty lacks in substance, it makes up in inspiration. But the coming "Party" is one of the worst-kept secrets in a city that can scarcely have any. On that fateful December afternoon, while the

Dartmouth's owner is making his fruitless plea, crowds—perhaps as many as seven thousand—pass in ceaseless procession to and from the wharves for a look at the ships. All classes, high and low, are represented; many have come from surrounding towns. Having seen the ships, they roam the streets, peering in the windows of the Green Dragon, waiting for the climax of this drama.

At five forty-five on a gray, rainy afternoon, Captain Rotch appears at the packed town meeting in the Old South and reports his failure with the governor. "If called upon by the proper officers," he reports Hutchinson as saying, he would "attempt for his own security to land the tea." As though it's a prearranged signal—and no doubt it is—Sam Adams leaps to his feet and cries: "This meeting can do nothing more to save the country!" An answering roar erupts from the crowd, there are calls from the gallery, "To Griffin's Wharf," and "Boston Harbor's a teapot tonight!" The mob pours out of the building, followed by Hancock's admonition, "Let every man do what is right in his own eyes." What's right has already been determined in that substantial brick tavern on Union Street, the Green Dragon.

The planning has been a little ambiguous, however. On the one hand, it's been decided that young men not well known in Boston and therefore not easily recognized should do the work. On the other hand, some older conspirators fear looting and send along a few lieutenants to oversee the work, all of them familiar faces, while young Lendell Pitts, son of a rich merchant and well known to everyone, appears as commander-in-chief of the party and makes no effort at concealment.

There are other familiar faces among these barely disguised "Mohawks": Will Molineux; Paul Revere, not disguised and taking a considerable risk since he's been married only two months; John Hancock; and of course, Sam Adams. The remainder of this war party of fake Indians, somewhere between 100 and 150 of them, are journeymen, apprentices, or strangers from other towns. Many of these, too, have failed to disguise themselves. The others jocularly pass themselves off as Indians from Narragansett, since it's customary to blame the Indians for any lawless acts. They carry hatchets, described as tomahawks, as well as clubs, and some have painted their faces and hands with coal dust in a blacksmith shop, looking more like slaves than Indians.

Reaching the wharves, Pitts as leader divides the party into three groups, one for each ship, and leads his own group to the *Dartmouth*, where he sends a note to the mate, with a peremptory demand for the keys and a light to illuminate the dark hold. Without a word, the keys are forthcoming, a cabin boy brings lights, and the "Indians" go to work. They bring up the chests of tea to the deck, break them open, and throw the contents into the harbor. Similar scenes are taking place on the other two ships. At the moment, the tide is low, but when it rises again a windrow of tea will stretch from Boston to Dorchester.

Earlier suspicions prove justified. There are those who attempt to scoop up and conceal a little tea for themselves; they are dealt with quietly and severely. On the dock, thousands of people stand in a strange silence, watching the men at work. They had begun late in the evening, and before dawn they're finished; some claim it took only three hours. To the surprise of these fraudulent Narragansetts, not a hand is raised against them, not a protest is heard. They come off the ships, form in a rude column, and with fife and drum preceding them, march to the State House.

One of the interested spectators of the unloading has been Admiral Montague, commander of the British warships at Castle William, spending the night with a Tory friend whose house is so close to the wharf that the admiral is able to watch the whole affair from a window. As the Tea Party marches by, Montague has the temerity to put his head out the window and shouts "Well, boys, you've had a fine, pleasant evening for your Indian capers, haven't you? But mind you, you've got to pay the fiddler yet."

"Never mind, squire," Lendell Pitts shouts back, "just come out here, if you please, and we'll settle the bill in two minutes." Prudently, the admiral retreats, and he's lucky that nothing worse happens to him.

At the State House, the Party huzzahs and disperses. Betsy Hunt Palmer reports later that she was rocking her baby that dawning when the parlor door opened and "three stout Indians," one of whom was her husband, walked in. Before she could jump up, her husband said, "Don't be frightened, Betsy, it's I. We've only been making a little saltwater tea." But when George Hewes comes home, his wife Sally, a confirmed tea drinker, comes directly to the point: "Well, George, did you bring me home a lot of it?" Another of the conspirators, Thomas Melville, when he reaches his house and undresses, discovers that his shoes are full of tea. Thinking of posterity and the historic event he has just helped to create, he pours it into a glass bottle, labels, and seals it. The tea survives well into this century.

But Admiral Montague was right. The piper will have to be paid, and Hutchinson is about to make the first payment. He's absolutely stunned by what's happened that night. As a conservative, law-abiding man of principle, no matter what others may think, it's simply incomprehensible to him that such valuable property would be so ruthlessly sacrificed by men who obviously care nothing for the law or for property. Why, he wonders, would men like Hancock and his merchant friends be willing to pay for the tea they've destroyed—it doesn't occur to him that they would do otherwise—rather than pay the duty, which would have been much less?

As for his own responsibility, he stands as always on principle and the law. If he'd given in to this "lawless and highly criminal assembly," he says, he would have aided and abetted gross violation of the law. On the other hand, he can hardly escape some responsibility for the Tea Party. After all, he had been responsible for the protection of this valuable property, as well as for enforcing the revenue laws, and in both cases he has failed. When news of this event reaches London, he can confidently expect to be the ex-governor of Massachusetts, and that's exactly what occurs. But the piper will exact a far heavier payment from the Bostonians. Parliament enacts what are called the Coercive Acts, and to enforce them, they appoint General Gage as the military governor of Massachusetts and give him what amounts to eleven regiments as insurance that the acts will be enforced.

Under ominous leaden skies, Gage arrives from England on May 17, 1774, and in spite of the driving rain and a lashing east wind, thousands turn out to see him, wrapping themselves in cloaks and pulling their hats down over their upturned collars. With no protection from the elements at all, the Ancient and Honorable Artillery Company, the Boston Grenadier Corps, are turned out and stand drenched to the skin on the Long Wharf as the drums roll, British vessels in the harbor salute, and Gage comes ashore with his staff, not only as military governor of the colony but in command of all British forces in North America.

Of course he's no stranger in Boston. Was it only four years ago that he'd come up from his post in New York to sort out the argument over how to house the first occupying troops? He'd gone home on leave in 1773, and hoped to stay there, but his American wife, the former Margaret Kemble, daughter of an old and rich New Jersey family and a cousin of Philip Schuyler, was homesick, and when Parliament called on him to return, her yearnings were satisfied.

Some of the older men in Boston remember Gage from earlier days. He had first come to America in 1755, having served a seventeen-year apprenticeship in Britain's continental wars, and fought beside Americans under General Edward Braddock in the battle with the French for North America. He had fought bravely, if futilely, in the 1758 attack on Ticonderoga and, when the war was over, had served for a time as governor of Montreal before he became commander-in-chief of the British army in North America for the first time in late 1763.

What kind of man is this Thomas Gage? A contemporary historian calls him "a good-natured, peaceable, sociable man," but John Shy, a far more perceptive historian of our own time, describes him as "the second son of a noble family known primarily for its lack of distinction and its reluctance to give up Catholicism. His father, Viscount Gage, pursued an erratic course in British politics. His mother had a reputation for social promiscuity. His brother's outstanding trait was absentmindedness. His sister married into a Catholic family, his parents lived as Anglicans but returned to the Church. Wealth came into the family when the eldest brother married a Jewish heiress. . . ."

Aside from this dubious inheritance, Gage is something of a self-made general who used his brother William to get his first commission, rising to lieutenant colonel soon after his thirtieth birthday, having passed through successive ranks obtained by buying vacant commissions. Although he's brave enough, Gage has never shown any particular talent for military leadership; nearly all his attacks in the French and Indian War were failures.

Arriving in Boston, he finds the whole country in an uproar, from Maine to Georgia, but nowhere does it blaze more brightly than in Boston. As he steps ashore, there is another ship in the harbor that is soon to carry away Thomas Hutchinson, who many colonists erroneously believe is the sole author of all their ills. There's some attempt to gloss over the circumstances of his departure. A few merchants, lawyers, and Episcopal clergymen, along with a group of neighbors in Milton, present him on May 30 with some face-saving testimonials. How little these reflect the sentiments of the populace can be seen in the news stories about them. The clergymen are labeled "sycophants in cassocks," the others accused of being betrayers of the people by giving such testimonials to the "disgraced and excoriated traitor."

Hutchinson sails for England on June 1—not going home but into exile, since he's an ardent as well as a native American. On that day, the first of the Coercive Acts, the Boston Port Bill, goes into effect, and all the church bells toll mournfully, the last sound the departing governor hears in America.

Once in England, Hutchinson does what little he can to avoid the coming war, beginning with a futile effort to limit the effects of the Coercive Acts. As time goes on, he grows more and more alienated from life in what is to him an alien country, longs passionately to return to America, and, as Bailyn tells us, his family, "once prominent, disintegrated in defeat, exile, disease, and death." Except for one shining moment. Ironically, on the very day Americans declare their independence, Hutchinson will be awarded an honorary degree from Oxford—the most satisfying day of his life.

Besides the Port Bill, there are other obnoxious acts in the omnibus package of Coercive Acts. One, contrary to the colony's charter, permits the Assembly to function, but the upper chamber, the Council, has to be appointed by the King. The governor—now Gage—is empowered to appoint judges, sheriffs, and other executive officers. Sheriffs can choose juries, but that means little since they owe their offices to the governor. Town meetings, which have been almost continuous, can now be held only with Gage's permission, except for annual elections. Anyone indicted for crimes involving riots or enforcement of revenue laws must be taken to England or another colony for trial. Still another law authorizes the quartering of troops on the town.

All of these acts are oppressive enough, but the Port Act that goes into effect June 1 is a disaster. Enforced by a blockade, it closes the port to all commerce. Salem and Marblehead are the colony's only other ports. Salem now becomes the provincial capital. This means that 25,000 Bostonians are sealed off from the world, effectively bringing their economy—based on shipbuilding, fisheries, whaling, and seaborne trade—to a sudden halt. Rum distillers, for example, can no longer get their supplies from the West Indies. Citizens who work on ships or wharves, in shipyards or sail lofts, are unemployed. With shipyards closed and wharves empty, the streets are full of idle sailors. Food becomes scarce instantly since access to the grazing grounds on islands in the outer harbor are now denied. This is the law to which Gage orders "a full and complete submission."

Even before the blow struck at high noon on June 1, citizens had observed days of fasting and prayer, knowing what was coming, and many wore badges of mourning. Now all who can do so flee to the country or to nearby towns, wherever they have relatives or friends.

The town is living on the charity of the other colonies, or its citizens could well face starvation. Hundreds of sheep are driven in from Connecticut, other New Englanders send flour, cattle, fish, and assorted foodstuffs. Rice and money come up from the Carolinas, while Delaware also sends money, with a promise of more. All the other colonies contribute supplies, and even Quebec ships down by land a thousand bushels of wheat.

All these contributions keep body and soul together, but meanwhile there's a complete breakdown in government. The entire judicial system and other public officials simply decline to function, yet miraculously the 300,000 people in Massachusetts seem able to get along without them. In general, order prevails.

In the fall, Gage moves into Boston from Salem so he can better direct the swelling tide of soldiers, who are creating all kinds of problems. They're temporarily housed in tents on the Common, just as they were before the "Massacre," and in rented warehouses, but building the necessary barracks has become a frustrating problem because no Boston workman will lay a hammer to them. Gage has to bring in carpenters from as far away as New York and Halifax, and even then he has to contend with a continuing campaign of sabotage. Barges carrying bricks to the sites are mysteriously sunk. Wagons carrying building materials somehow turn over. Straw carted in to make beds for soldiers suddenly ignites and burns. It's the end of the year before troops can be moved from the Common.

Gage is getting the distinct impression that he's surrounded by people preparing to do him in if they can. In August, he hears that the provincials in and around Boston have been removing gunpowder from a magazine called "the powder house," on Quarry Hill in Charlestown, that is owned communally by the province and nearby towns. Gage hears that this powder is being slowly removed and taken to people's homes, where it's not hard to guess what they intend to do with it.

Alarmed, the general-governor sends 260 soldiers on September 1 to take away what remains in the magazine, about 250 half barrels. While they're at it, a detachment of these troops seizes a pair of fieldpieces in Cambridge, recently bought by that town's militia. All this booty is taken directly to Castle William.

While there have been incidents accompanying this foray, Gage hasn't counted on the power of rumor, in a place where word of mouth could easily start a war. Wild stories fly across the countryside. People in Charlestown resisted the seizure, it's said, and six of them have been killed. Minutemen from everywhere within a radius of thirty miles of Boston seize their arms and begin to march on the city. There are four thousand of them in Cambridge next day. By that time, the rumors have reached Pomfret, Connecticut, and the ears of Israel Putnam, and they've grown considerably. Now the story is that British ships are bombarding Boston, a most unlikely event, but Putnam believes it. Within three days, as many as thirty thousand men may be on the march toward the city (estimates vary), although many turn back as they near Boston and learn that the rumors are false. Those who had arrived earlier disperse, and relative quiet prevails once more.

It's a deceptive quiet, however. Both sides are preparing for any eventuality, although only the radicals still talk of war. A cat-and-mouse game develops between Gage and the provincials. In September, defensive works are built on the mainland in spite of strikes and sabotage, but other defenses have a way of disappearing. One night a battery in Charlestown is stripped of its guns, which are carried into the country. In an even more daring raid, four cannon from a gunhouse near the Common, under the very noses of the troops, are liberated and disappear. On a daily basis it's impossible to control the arms trade carried on by countrymen whose wagons conveying produce into town also conceal muskets and ammunition when they leave.

To the soldiers, these countrymen are a novelty, and their occasional encounters become the stuff of widely circulated stories. On October 1, for example, a Whig merchant named John Andrews, who had stayed in town to protect his property, writes to his friend William Barrell, a Philadelphia counterpart, about a current incident much appreciated by the citizens. Soldiers, he writes, often spend their idle time, of which they have a great deal, firing at a target fixed in the stream at the bottom of the Common. A countryman watches them one day, laughing heartily while an entire regiment fires and fails to hit the target. Andrews reports the following conversation.

"Why are you laughing?" an officer demands.

"Perhaps you'll be affronted if I tell you," the countryman says.

Assured that this will not be the case, the countryman says, "Why then, I laugh to see how awkward they fire. Why, I'll be bound, I can hit it ten times running."

"And will you?" the officer replies. "Come and try. Men, go bring in five of the best guns, and load 'em for this honest man."

"Why, you needn't bring so many," the countryman protests. "Let me have any one that comes to hand. But I choose to load *myself*."

He does so and asks the officer where he should fire. "To the right," the officer tells him. The countryman shoots and hits the target as far to the right as is possible. Amazed, the officer calls it pure chance and says he's sure this upstart can't do it again. But the countryman simply loads once more and asks, "Where shall I fire?" Told to try the left this time, he does as well as before. There's only one trial remaining. Asked to fire at the center, he does so and hits it squarely. Officers and soldiers stare. They think the devil is in him.

"Why, I'll tell you," the countryman says, enjoying his advantage and pressing it, "I've got a *boy* at home that'll toss up an apple and shoot out all the seeds as it's coming down."

Another story much enjoyed by Bostonians involves the 59th Regiment, which has come in from Salem and is lined up on both sides of the Neck. A countryman comes by, leading his horse and wagon. He's reported to be nearly eight feet high, and from that altitude surveys the regiment so contemptuously, they can't help noticing him. "Ay, ay," he addresses them, "you don't know what *boys* we have got in the country. I'm near nine feet high, and one of the smallest among 'em." The soldiers look uncomfortable and some citizens standing nearby applaud.

But it isn't all fun and games in Boston by any means. Not only is there the usual friction between civilians and soldiers, there is also unavoidable and irritating proximity of Loyalists and Whigs to each other. The Loyalists in Boston and elsewhere are beginning in 1774 to be subjected to a savagery that will last throughout the war, one they return with interest when they have the opportunity.

Describing an early incident, taking place on a freezing January night, a Whig matron, Ann Hulton, writing to her friend Mrs. Lightbody, reports "the most shocking cruelty" exercised a few nights before against "a poor old man, a tidesman, one Malcolm, suspected of being a Tory." One of the street mobs picked a quarrel with him, and although he defended himself for some time, they pinned him down at last, and as Mrs. Hulton describes it: "He was stript stark naked, one of the severest cold nights this winter, his body covered all over with tar, then with feathers, his arm dislocated in tearing off his clothes. He was dragged in a cart with thousands attending, some beating him with clubs and knocking him out of the cart, then in again. They gave him several severe whippings, at different parts of the town. This spectacle of horror and sportive cruelty was exhibited for about five hours.

"The unhappy wretch they say behaved with the greatest intrepidity and fortitude all the while. . . . When under torture they demanded of him to curse his masters, the King, Governor, etc., which they could not make him do, but he still cried, 'Curse all traitors!' They brought him to the gallows and put a rope about his neck, saying they would hang him. He said he wished they would, but that they could not, for God was above the Devil. The doctors say that it is impossible the poor creature can live. They say the flesh comes off his back in stakes. It is the second time he has been tarred and feathered and this is looked upon more to intimidate the judges and others than spite to the unhappy victim. . . . He has a wife and family and an aged father and mother who, they say, saw the spectacle which no indifferent person can mention without horror. These few instances amongst many serve to show the abject state of government and the licentiousness and barbarism of the times. There's no magistrate that dare or will act to suppress the outrages. No person is secure. There are many objects pointed out at this time, and when once marked out for vengeance, their ruin is certain."

As 1774 winds down to its bitter close, such incidents become more common, and it's clear that Boston, now heavily occupied by Gage's eleven regiments, with its economic life in ruins, can't go on much longer without an explosion of some kind. That it occurs outside and not inside the city is a tribute to Gage's iron grip, but that it occurs at all results from his complete misreading of the situation, the first in a long line of mistakes made by British generals that cost them America.

3

✛   ✛   ✛

The Revolution Begins

A *rage militaire*, the French call it, that excessive enthusiasm for high-minded slaughter that afflicts people before the reality of war sets in and the blood begins to flow. In America, it lasts for little more than a year after the initial resistance turns into outright revolution. After that, it declines swiftly until there is not much *rage* remaining, except in the South, and very little that's truly military.

At first, however, it's like a deadly game, played with live chessmen, fueled by the kind of righteous indignation that makes war possible. In the late fall of 1774 and the early spring of 1775, for example, it's a game of "I Spy." Paul Revere and about thirty other radicals have set up an espionage network that works so efficiently there's little they don't know about what the British are doing. In pairs, they patrol the streets at night, these businessmen and tradesmen, all of them well known to the citizenry and consequently feeling no necessity to disguise themselves. They meet regularly at the Green Dragon to plan and exchange notes.

At every meeting they take an oath not to tell anybody about what they're up to—except, of course, John Hancock, Sam Adams, Joseph Warren, and a few others certified as patriots. They also tell Dr. Benjamin Church, Jr., soon to be Director of Hospitals but already a spy himself—for the British. Church *does* have a perverse sense of honor, however; he regularly supplies Gage with information, but he doesn't disclose the names of the Green Dragon gang, or what they know.

What Gage wants to know most is where the Americans are storing their munitions, since obviously, if he can find out and seize them, there will be less chance of open warfare. His own intelligence operatives report that there are magazines in Charlestown, Watertown, Worcester, Salem, Marblehead, Mystic, and Menotomy, as well as several places in Connecticut. They're making gun carriages in Charlestown, Watertown, and Marblehead. In Salem, twelve brass cannon have been stored away. Hartford is laying in large supplies of food and munitions. In Menotomy, tools are being made, and in Mystic it's pickaxes.

Gage believes the largest of these munitions dumps must be in Worcester. He sends out two regulars disguised as civilians to confirm his belief. These would-be spies are Captain William Brown, of the 52nd Foot, and Ensign Henry De Berniere, of the 10th. Stopping en route to Worcester at Jonathan Brown's tavern, the captain is recognized at once by a black serving woman who has worked in Boston. Still, they get to Worcester safely and stay at a Tory inn, but they're so plainly not part of the Whig landscape, where everyone knows everybody else, that they're continually under suspicion and barely escape. They're not captured, and come back to Boston with reports that fail to satisfy the general.

An impartial observer, if there had been one, might have some sympathy for Gage. He's been ordered to round up the rebels and seize their warmaking equipment, but there's no rebel army to round up and seize, and he can't really be sure exactly where the supplies are stored. Constantly, he calls for reinforcements. "If you think ten thousand men sufficient, send twenty," he advises London. Massachusetts is proclaimed to be in a state of rebellion on February 9, but that merely confirms what everyone has known for some time. By April 5, the British have also imposed an embargo on the other colonies, preventing them from trading with Europe and closing the North American fisheries to them.

But Gage believes he has to intimidate the inhabitants, if nothing else, and on Sunday, February 26, he sends Colonel Leslie to Salem, with 240 men, to seize stores and a few brass fieldpieces he's learned are there. The colonel carries his troops in a transport to Marblehead, where they disembark and begin to march on Salem, five miles away. It's hardly a surprise to the inhabitants; Revere's spy network has already warned them.

Recalling that day years later, William Gavett remembers that his "father came home from church rather sooner than usual, which attracted my notice, and said to my mother, 'The reg'lars are come and are marching as fast as they can towards the Northfield bridge'; and looking towards her with a very solemn face, remarked, 'I don't know what will be the consequence but something very serious, and I wish you to keep the children home.' I looked out of the window just at this time and saw the troops passing the house. My father then stepped out and stood at the foot of the yard looking into the street. While there our minister, Mr. Barnard, came along and took my father by the arm, and they walked towards the bridge beside the troops. . . ."

What alarmed the senior Gavett in church and sent him home early was the precipitate entrance of Colonel David Mason, of the militia, in the middle of afternoon services, crying out at the top of his voice, "The reg'lars are coming after the guns and are now near Malloon's mills."

David Boyce, a Quaker who lives near the church, runs out the door, harnesses his team, and helps carry the guns out of reach to a safe place on the road to Danvers. Meanwhile, the troops arrive, and as William recalls, his father walks along beside them, to see if he can recognize any from Fort William, many of whom he knows, but he sees no familiar face. The soldiers resent his inquisitiveness, swear at him, and demand to know what he's looking for. Soon they reach the drawbridge leading into town and find that the northern half has been hoisted up, preventing them from going any farther.

Captain John Felt, commanding the local militia, stands with his men on the far side. Colonel Leslie calls to him and demands that the bridge be lowered, else he will be compelled to fire. If the troops fire, Felt replies, they will all be dead men. Later he remarks that, if actual firing had occurred, he intended to reach Leslie, grapple with him, and jump into the river, for, as he says, "I would willingly be drowned myself to be the death of one Englishman."

On the British side of the bridge, townspeople are busy sabotaging two boats Leslie evidently intends using to cross. One of the saboteurs, a foreman in the local distillery, is ordered by the soldiers to stop, and when they threaten to stab him with their bayonets if he doesn't, he opens his breast, daring them to strike. They prick him enough to draw blood but stop short of killing him. (At least one historian believes this may be the obscure beginning of the otherwise purely mythical story of Barbara Frietchie.)

While all this is taking place, the soldiers stand shivering in the February cold, having come without overcoats. They're made doubly uncomfortable by numerous citizens who climb up on the drawn bridge and toss insults at them. One of them cries out fiercely, "Soldiers, red-jackets, lobster-coats, cowards, damnation to your government!" More conservative neighbors rebuke him, and argue that nothing more should be done to irritate the troops.

Colonel Leslie, however, is already so irritated that he tells the Reverend Mr. Barnard, "I will get over this bridge before I return to Boston, if I stay here till next autumn." Barnard answers piously that he prays to heaven there will be no collision. At this, Leslie threatens to burst into the stores of two merchants on his side of the bridge and make barracks out of them until he can get across, and he adds, "By God, I will not be defeated!"

"You must acknowledge you have already been baffled," Felt tells him.

Leslie tries another tack. He's standing on the King's highway, he says, and therefore can't be prevented from passing over the bridge. Old James Barr, an Englishman himself and a man known to be fearless, replies, "It is *not* the King's highway, it's a road built by the owners of the lots on the other side, and no king, country, or town has anything to do with it."

"There may be two sides to that," Leslie tells him.

"Egad," says the old man, "I think that will be the best way for you—to conclude that the King has nothing to do with it."

It's time for damage control and face-saving. Leslie strikes a bargain with Captain Felt. If the bridge is lowered, his troops will cross it, march fifty rods, and march back again. After some discussion among the inhabitants, it's agreed. The bridge is lowered, the troops do exactly as their commander has promised, and keep on marching along North Street toward Marblehead as the curtain comes down on this *opéra bouffe*. On the way to Salem, their fifes and drums had played "Yankee Doodle." On their frustrated way back, they play "The World Turned Upside Down," an old British melody that will be heard again at Yorktown.

Gage is vastly annoyed by this failure. He's aware that behind his back the troops are calling him "old woman" because he's not doing more to put down the rebellion, but he hardly knows where to strike. He's convinced that the Americans have stored a quantity of guns in and near Worcester, but he needs better intelligence. On April 5, he tries again. This time he sends as spies an unlikely duo, Lieutenant Colonel Francis Smith, an officer as ponderous in thought as he is in weight, and a private, John Howe, who was on the first unsuccessful spying expedition. They're dressed as wandering laborers, wearing leather breeches and gray coats, with blue mixed stockings and handkerchiefs knotted around their throats. Their traveling necessities are wrapped up in what will later be called a bandanna, thrown over the shoulder.

The two stop for breakfast at a tavern in Watertown, six miles on their way, the same one where Brown and De Berniere were spotted before. The same watchful black servant is there; she can scarcely miss recognizing so prominent a figure as Smith. When she greets him by name, the spies hurry out and hide behind a stone wall, where they hold a council of war. Obviously, Smith says, it's pointless for him to continue; he's likely to be recognized, although he vows that if he ever comes down that road again with his regiment, he will "kill that wench." He gives John Howe a journal book and a pencil, ten guineas, and letters of introduction to Tories along the proposed route. Then, casting dignity aside, he makes an unwieldy escape, running through barberry bushes.

On his own, Howe gives up pretending to be a laborer and calls himself a gunsmith. A black man directs him to a tavern in Weston, kept by Joel Smith, a confirmed Whig, or another one half a mile from it whose proprietor is Captain Isaac Jones, equally well known as a Tory, and to whom Howe is carrying a letter from Gage. Inexplicably, Howe stops in at the first tavern, but people regard him so suspiciously, directing him to still another tavern where he might find work, he suspects a trick. He tells this story to Captain Jones, where he stops next, and Jones sees through it too, sending him on to the remote house of a trusted Loyalist named Wheaton, where he's given his own room, writing materials, and the company of the family's daughters, with whom he plays cards. Helped by Jones's hired man, he reaches the Worcester road next day, and then goes on to Marlboro by way of back roads.

Traveling by night, he's unfortunately seen by a woman sitting up with a sick child; she sends out a general alarm, and after a night or two in Worcester, at the house of a Tory named Barnes, Howe has to escape out a back window and down the roof when local patriots come to search the house. Jumping off the roof, he falls into six inches of new snow. He runs blindly through a swamp and takes a long chance by knocking at the door of the first house he sees. A hospitable black man and his wife let him stay the night. Next morning he offers some silver if his host will put him on the road to Concord. There's some hesitation, but at last the man, convinced that Howe is as much a Tory as he is, takes him to the Concord River, where he borrows a canoe from another black man who lives there, takes him across, and walks with him until nearly midnight when they come to a tavern. They drink some brandy and spend the night, Howe going on to Concord nearby next morning.

Once more Howe introduces himself as a gunsmith. He's believed this time, a shop is found for him, and some gunlocks are brought at once to be repaired. Fortunately, Howe is able to do this job quickly and efficiently. Impressed, his new American friends take him on a tour of the Concord magazine, and at last Howe sees at first hand a supply of rebel arms. Claiming he has to go back east and get more tools before he can settle down in Concord, he departs next day and spends the night in Lincoln with a friendly Tory, who takes him to Charlestown, from where he's ferried over to Boston at 2:00 A.M.

Both Gage and Smith are overjoyed with this windfall of information. Smith gives Howe a guinea, the first installment on a bonus of fifty, and says, "Take that, John, and go and get some liquor. You aren't half drunk enough for officers' company." Gage wants to know how many men it would take to capture the Worcester stores. Ten thousand would never do it, Howe tells him.

"Howe has been scared by the old women," Smith says disdainfully.

"But not by a black wench, John," a fellow officer reminds him.

Knowing now that what he presumes must be a major cache of rebel arms is in Concord, Gage plans a quick and what he hopes will be a secret strike. He chooses his best troops for the task, four hundred light infantry and four hundred more grenadiers. They are tough soldiers. The infantry has been taught how to move swiftly, and the grenadiers represent the tallest and strongest of any soldiers of that time. Smith commands them, and second in command is Major John Pitcairn, a Marine not well known to the infantry under him. Pitcairn is not as fat as Smith, but he has pretensions, and he's fifty years old. Perhaps because of these possible drawbacks, Gage places a reserve force of a thousand foot soldiers under a young brigadier general, Hugh, Earl Percy, a descendant of Hotspur and heir to the Duke of Northumberland.

The machinery for Gage's quick strike has been assembled, but the secret is already out. Two days earlier, the Revere intelligence network learned that the British mean to raid Concord and seize the stores. An immediate warning goes out, and as much of the stores as possible are moved to safer places, so that all of John Howe's perilous work goes for nothing, his information outdated.

Gage has an undercover spy in Concord who observes the sudden movements, but for some reason he can't find out what's happening. On April 16, Revere rides out to Lexington, warning Hancock and Sam Adams, who are staying there momentarily on their way to Philadelphia to join the Continental Congress, that the British are coming. The famous ride doesn't occur until two days later, in which Longfellow, preserving it for generations to come, uses his poet's license to bury the facts in order to create the romantic, enduring legend. "One if by land," meaning the lanterns in the Old North Church, would have been enough, but the absurdity of "two if by sea" is added so that "I on the opposite shore will be" completes the rhyme. In fact, Revere isn't on the opposite shore when the lanterns are hung; he's still in Boston. He may even have helped hang them, and they're meant as a signal not to him but to Colonel Conant, of the Charlestown militia.

In any case, it's virtually impossible to keep a secret in Boston. Pitcairn lives almost next door to Revere and, like the other officers, he talks far too freely for a military man. On the night the troops are about to move out, Lord Percy, not yet in uniform, attends a final briefing at headquarters and, walking back across the Common to his lodgings, he comes upon several excited men. "The British have marched," one man says, "but they'll miss their aim."

Percy stops. "What aim is that?" he inquires.

"Why, the cannon at Concord," the man tells him. So much for Gage's secret strike.

Nevertheless, Revere is ready to spread the news to the countryside, as planned. Just as he's about to be ferried across the Charles River, it occurs to him that the oars ought to be muffled, but no material is at hand. One of the two men with him knows a girl who lives nearby, and a whistle under her window brings her in view. After a whispered exchange, she throws down a flannel petticoat. Telling this story to his children years later, Revere likes to say it was still warm, but he's no more given to the facts than Longfellow.

With their petticoat-muffled oars, the men row almost under the riding lights of the sixty-four-gun British warship *Somerset*, and reach Colonel Conant's house in Charlestown, where he's waiting for them, having seen the light in the church steeple that tells him the troops are moving and are coming across the river.

While Revere rides off to alarm the citizens all the way to Lexington, John Howe is doing a fair imitation for the other side. In his proper guise now, he's riding in the same direction to rouse the Tories. The news races ahead of both men. Alarm guns, church bells, and the roll of drums fill the chilly April night. Gage's surprise party is a total flop.

Revere's arrival in Lexington has produced a commotion that rouses Hancock and Adams, who are staying in the house of the Reverend Jonas Clark (Harvard, '52), a farmer who's also pastor of the First Parish Church. His guests are his close friends, and at the moment they're accompanied by Hancock's old aunt, a formidable lady who's playing duenna for John's pretty fiancée, Dorothy Quincy.

The two radical leaders are an odd couple. At fifty-two, Adams looks much older, but his gray eyes are clear and his heavy jaw still firm, although palsy is making his voice and hands shake. He wears the garb of the proletariat—old, faded, patched-up clothes.

Adams despises money because of the power that goes with it, but he manages to make an exception of his fellow leader, Hancock, who has plenty of it, derived from his ships and store, as well as a lucrative smuggling operation. He's considered to be the richest man in New England. Adams seduced Hancock into the radical camp when the young merchant was only twenty-six and had just inherited a fortune, which Sam believed would be useful, along with the prestige of his name. Privately, he subscribes to the common opinion that Hancock is a young man whose "brains were shallow and his pockets deep." For Hancock's part, the alliance has meant future power and immediate excitement, mixed with a certain amount of idealism, his most attractive attribute, offset by a selfish, vacillating nature that arouses deep distrust in Adams, who bears no particular affection for him.

But now, hearing the commotion of Revere's arrival, both men put their heads out of Parson Clark's window, and Hancock calls out, "Come in, Revere, we're not afraid of *you*." They have good reason to be afraid of possible seizure, however, and the house is under guard. In Clark's parlor, Revere tells his story for the first time, and Hancock is so excited by the imminent appearance of the enemy that he vows to arm himself and take the field. Adams tells him not to be a fool. They're both elected representatives to the Second Continental Congress, and the best thing they can do will be to remove themselves quickly and save their talents for more important work.

Meanwhile, the grenadiers and infantrymen have crossed Back Bay with their own oars muffled, though not by petticoats, and have disembarked at East Cambridge, intending to come ashore at Lechmere Point. But they're too heavily loaded. They carry the usual sixty-pound packs, and sink into marsh water up to their knees, giving them a preliminary idea of the long, hard night to come. By that time, it's midnight, and Revere is in Buckman's Tavern, the town rallying point, where all the candles are lit. Some of the militia are already out.

Over a cup of spirits, Revere tells about his ride, how he borrowed a horse from Deacon Larkin and urged it in bright moonlight through the chilly night, passing such local landmarks as the gibbet where Captain Codman's black slave still hangs in chains after twenty years, lynched because he was said to have poisoned his master, and serving now as a warning against any ideas about liberation.

There was one close call along the way, Revere tells his eager listeners. Riding on a sandy road that narrowed as it approached woods, he says, two horsemen appeared just ahead. He recognized them as British troops by their holsters and cockades. Quickly turning his horse around, he spurred toward the Mystic road at full gallop, with one horseman in pursuit. But the pursuer's horse stumbled in a clay pond and Revere was safe. In Medford, he says, "I awakened the captain of the minutemen. And after that I alarmed almost every house until I got to Lexington."

By this time, one of Revere's fellow couriers, William Dawes, has arrived, having completed the same mission but unfortunately he was not celebrated by Longfellow and remains relatively unknown. Meanwhile, the militia, about 130 men strong, have gathered on Lexington green under Captain John Parker, a forty-five-year-old veteran of Rogers' Rangers. There is much discussion of what ought to be done. Two men are dispatched to scout the road toward Boston and find out where the British are. One soon comes back and reports he's seen nothing.

But those in Lexington know that trouble is already traveling the highways. Earlier in the evening, about ten o'clock, several British officers had ridden through town on the road to Concord, and three men on horseback had been dispatched to follow them. Near Lincoln, they unexpectedly caught up, British pistols were pushed in their chests, they were detained for several hours, questioned, abused, and otherwise insulted. It's also learned that innocent civilians passing on the roads that night have been similarly detained, and a few have been seized in the doorways of their own houses.

Revere and Dawes soon have reason to learn about these British reconnaissance parties. Having eaten hastily, they mount again and ride on toward Concord. Along the way, they first encounter a friendly face, that of twenty-three-year-old Dr. Samuel Prescott, of Concord, on his way home after courting a Lexington girl, a Miss Milliken, rather late into the early morning. Prescott comes of conservative stock, but he considers himself an ardent Whig. For what happens next as they ride along, we have Revere's own narrative:

"When we had got about halfway from Lexington to Concord, the other two stopped at a house to awake the man. I kept along. When I had got about two hundred yards ahead of them, I saw two officers under a tree. I immediately called to my company to come up, saying here was two of them. . . . In an instant, I saw four officers, who rode up to me with their pistols in their hands and said, 'God damn you, stop! If you go an inch further, you are a dead man!' Immediately Dr. Prescott came up. . . . We attempted to get through them, but they kept before us and swore if we did not turn into that pasture, they would blow our brains out. They had placed themselves opposite to a pair of bars and had taken the bars down. They forced us in. When we got in, Dr. Prescott said to me, 'Put on!' He took to the left, I turned to the right towards a wood, intending when I had gained that to jump my horse and run afoot."

Prescott, on familiar terrain, jumps his horse over a low stone rail into another pasture and rides hellbent for Concord. Dawes escapes too, and as he departs, calls out as though he's commanding troops, "Halloo, boys! I've got two of 'em!" At that point, he falls off his horse and has to flee on foot.

Revere's break to the woods ends suddenly when six officers ride out of its shelter and seize his bridle. "They put their pistols to my breast," he writes later, "ordered me to dismount, which I did. One of them, who seemed to have command there and much of a gentleman, asked where I came from. I told him. He asked what time I left. I told him. He seemed surprised. He said, "'Sir, may I crave your name?' I answered, 'My name is Revere.' 'What?' said he. 'Paul Revere?' I answered, 'Yes.' The others abused me much but he told me not to be afraid, no one should hurt me."

Having been recognized and feeling he has nothing to lose, Revere tells these British scouts bluntly that he has "alarmed the country all the way up from Boston," so they will "miss their aim." Knowing that his captors have no knowledge of what's happening in Boston, he concocts a bold lie and says the British boats have run aground, delaying them so much that by the time they get to Lexington they will find five hundred men waiting for them.

That produces considerable agitation in the British patrol. They join Revere with four countrymen they've picked up in various roads and turn them all toward Lexington. Along the way, Revere writes later, "I was often insulted by the officers . . . calling me damned rebel, etc., etc. The officer who led me said I was in a damned critical situation. I told him I was sensible of it. After we had got about a mile, I was delivered to a sergeant to lead, who was ordered to take out his pistol and should I run, to execute the major's sentence. When we got within about a half a mile of the Lexington Meeting House, we heard a gun fired. The major asked me what that was for. I told him to alarm the country."

At that the patrol cuts the girths and bridles on the Americans' horses and drives them off. The countrymen are told to start walking, but Revere is held briefly until his horse, too, is driven off, and he walks the remainder of the way through the fields to Pastor Clark's house, where he reports to Hancock and Adams, who are so alarmed by his story that they conclude to start out for a safer part of the country at once. Revere goes with them a way on the road to Woburn, their first stop, to make sure they're safe and then hurries back to Pastor Clark's house, where he watches the unfolding events on Lexington green from the safety of an upstairs window. Unknown to him or anyone else, in another house on the green, a French spy is also watching.

For all its historic importance as the beginning of armed resistance, what transpires that early April morning is brief and bloody, but scarcely even a skirmish. Captain Parker, a tall man with a large head, has been trying to keep his militiamen on the alert after Revere brought the warning, but nothing has developed. The men stomp about in the cold night air, blowing on their fingers to keep them warm for their muskets. About 4:00 A.M. , they disband, some retiring to their houses, others stopping in at Buckman's for a drink to warm chilled bones. Parker's second scout hasn't returned, so there seems to be no immediate danger.

A half hour later, Thaddeus Bowman, the missing scout, races into town with the electrifying news that the regulars are approaching. Parker's drum beats the alarm, a warning gun is fired, and seventy men, nearly half of Lexington's adult males, turn out again. They line up in double file on the green and Parker gives them their orders: "Let the troops pass by, don't molest them unless they begin first." Forty unarmed residents stand in the rear to see whatever may happen.

Within fifteen minutes, the advance guard of six companies under Pitcairn appears. They had stopped just long enough to prime and load their muskets. Expecting to find themselves confronted by a force of anywhere from five hundred to a thousand men, they've been given their own orders by Pitcairn: "On no account will you fire, or even attempt it without orders." The soldiers draw up in line of battle, deployed in three ranks, two platoons of two hundred men each. Pitcairn rides ahead with several other officers and addresses the waiting minutemen.

"Lay down your arms, you rebels, and disperse," he calls out. No answer from the ranks. Other officers take up the chorus of demands, in words that sound melodramatic now but many witnesses hear them: "Ye villains, ye rebels, disperse! Damn you, disperse! Lay down your arms! Damn you, why don't you lay down your arms?" Again there's no response, but the minutemen, on Parker's command to look out for themselves, begin to break for the shelter of trees and stone walls.

Until the day he dies on Breed's Hill two weeks later, Pitcairn will insist that he never gave any command to fire, but none is necessary. Having marched all night, wet and miserable much of the way, the troops and other officers mean to have blood. An officer fires his pistol at the retreating backs of the minutemen, while another brandishes his sword, points it toward them, and calls to his men, "Fire! By God, fire!" The men respond. They fire as long as there's anyone within sight.

Not one of the minutemen fires back in the first volley. Jonas Parker, the captain's older brother, holds his ground for a moment but a bullet brings him to his knees and a bayonet kills him. Jonathan Harrington, dying, drags himself on hands and knees toward his house, but he's dead when his frantic wife bursts from the door and finds him on the lawn. John Brown gets as far as the edge of a swamp and safety before he's cut down. One of his neighbors falls dead behind a wall in John Buckman's garden. Captain Parker himself is another casualty. Through it all, the British troops are going wild, firing at will, screaming invective, out of control. Pitcairn finally gets them in command again just as Colonel Smith and the main body arrive.

The whole affair has taken only a few minutes. Eight minutemen lie dead or dying, most of them shot in the back at the first volley. Nine others are wounded. Their scattered return fire from behind walls and trees has hit one soldier in the leg and two bullets have creased Pitcairn's horse. Later, one of the British officers, Lieutenant Barker, admits that the men had been "so wild they could hear no orders." Vainly, Pitcairn had slashed the air with his sword, trying to command a cease-fire, but no one listened. Now, with the damage done and order restored, the light infantry pulls back and re-forms as Smith and his grenadiers come up. The British give a huzzah and fire off a volley to celebrate the first blood drawn, and with their fife and drum corps playing, set off for Concord in the bright sunshine of early morning.

While all these events have been taking place, Concord hasn't been asleep. After escaping from the British patrol, Sam Prescott, Paul Revere's chance-met companion, rode hard into his hometown to bring the news that the redcoats were on their way. The word spreads rapidly through the town. Parson Emerson hears it two miles away in the Old Manse and he's first on the scene. Militia begin to stream into the center from every corner of the town, assembling at Wright's Tavern under Major Buttrick. They begin at once to remove to safer rural quarters the remainder of the military stores the British are coming after. This done, the men disperse, as they had in Lexington, but now no one goes home. A company from Lincoln appears about 4:00 A.M. to join their Concord neighbors in a chilly vigil.

By this time the alarms of the night, from Cambridge to Concord, have spread with incredible speed not only into the Worcester and Hampshire counties, but as far away as New Hampshire and Maine. The response is instantaneous, as though a live nerve has been struck. All roads lead to Concord. As far away as Bedford, the militia eat their breakfast together at Fitch's Tavern before setting out, and hear their captain say, "It's a cold breakfast, boys, but we'll give the British a hot dinner. We'll have every dog of them before night."

In other places, immediate sacrifice is involved. Isaac Davis, a gunsmith, is the thirty-four-year-old father of four children, all of them ill that morning, but he assembles the local militia company at his farm and prepares to go anyway. Years later, his widow recalls: "My husband said but little that morning. As he led the company from the house, he turned himself round, and seemed to have something to communicate. He only said, 'Take good care of the children,' and was soon out of sight."

Many of those who march toward Concord have either lived there previously or have relatives who still do. Ironically, all those marching to defend the town are carrying muskets that are required by the British law under which they have all been living. Even their militia companies had been decreed by the Crown, and were in fact called Crown militia until this breaking point. It's required that every male from sixteen to sixty must enroll in the militia, subject to drafting if danger threatens. Of course nearly all of them also belong to minutemen companies operated by Whig Committees of Safety.

In Concord itself, with help coming from every direction but not yet there, the minutemen take up a position on Punkatassett Hill, overlooking North Bridge, "the rude bridge that arched the flood," spanning the Concord River. Beyond the bridge lies the farm of Colonel James Barrett, the local militia commander, where Gage believes (mistakenly) there's a major arms cache. As they wait, some of the men grow restive, and without orders (such is the casualness of militia command) they march down toward Lexington for about a mile and a half until, abruptly—there they are, coming down the road, red coats and arms glistening in the morning sun. The British have at last arrived.

The militia detachment holds its ground until the redcoats are about a hundred rods away, then they think better of it, about-face, and march back with drums and fifes playing, their music mingling with their counterparts in the British army. "We had grand music," Corporal Amos Barrett remembers later. The militia resume their position on the heights, about a mile from town, looking down on it as the British enter.

Curiously, historians still differ about what happened when the troops marched into Concord. Some say they behaved well, others that they committed all manner of atrocities; still others declare that the only civilians remaining were a few women huddled in the Old Manse. That there was resistance is verified by a British officer, who writes home: "Even women had firelocks. One was seen to fire a blunderbuss between her father and husband from their windows. There these three, with an infant child, soon suffered the fury of the day. In another house, which was long defended by eight resolute fellows, the Grenadiers at last got possession, when after having run their bayonets through seven, the eighth continued to abuse them with all the beastlike rage of a true Cromwellian, and but a moment before he quitted this world, applied such epithets as I must leave unmentioned. . . ."

Some women who linger after the husbands leave are taken by surprise. Phebe Emerson is upstairs when her black slave, Frank, bursts in with his ax in his hand, shouting, "The redcoats have come." Phebe immediately faints but recovers quickly and goes downstairs to greet her unwelcome guests. Mostly these soldiers who enter private homes are looking for food. They're hungry after the long night's march, and surprisingly, considering their conduct otherwise, insist on paying. Colonel Barrett's wife, Rebecca, at first refuses to take it, saying, "We are commanded to feed our enemies." When an officer throws money in her lap, she says, "This is the price of blood," but she keeps it.

Other encounters in the town are not so peaceful. Ephraim Jones, proprietor of both an inn and the town jail, tries to prevent Major Pitcairn from coming into his tavern—with good reason, because he has three cannon hidden in the jailyard next door. Pitcairn, a nononsense man, throws him to the ground, swears at him, and retrieves the cannon, after which he comes back in and orders breakfast. Jones presents him with the bill, which he pays.

Another officer demands to enter Timothy Wheeler's storehouse, where many casks of flour are stored, and Wheeler lets him in without argument, playing the part of a simple countryman who doesn't wish to offend. "This is my flour," he says, with one hand on a barrel. "I am a miller, sir. Yonder stands my mill. I get my living by it. This is *my* flour, this is *my* wheat, this is *my* rye, this is mine."

"We don't injure private property," the officer tells him curtly.

Those have been the orders, to be sure, but the troops carry out a considerable amount of looting nonetheless, at least 275 pounds' worth of private property. The regulars steal with unrestrained enthusiasm—a quilt and a Bible from the meetinghouse, a book on mathematics from the schoolhouse, along with other books. They would steal the communion silver, but a lady of the church anticipates them and thoughtfully removes it.

Sometimes ingenuity saves the day. Entering Amos Wood's house, an officer notices a locked room and demands to know if a woman is in there. Mrs. Wood says there is, and the gallant officer tells his men, "I forbid anyone entering this room." If they had they would have found a roomful of supplies. Similarly, when Ephraim Jones's tavern is invaded, Hannah Barnes, a black servant girl, tells the officers one room is hers and contains only her own things, although in fact it also shelters the valuable chest of Henry Gardner, treasurer of the Provincial Congress.

The British want to arrest people who might be guilty of hiding military supplies, but that proves to be difficult. Ephraim Wood, the 250-pound town clerk, is a prime suspect but can't be found at first because he's so busy taking supplies out of town. Surprised a little later with a keg of powder on his back, he runs to the river, finds a boat, and gets to the other side just in time.

Farther north, Colonel Barrett's son Stephen has been guiding arriving militia from Harvard and Stow onto safe routes near town. Coming back home, he finds the British there. Hearing that his name is Barrett, they seize him by the collar, kick him, and proclaim triumphantly, "Now we've got you! You must go to Boston with us, and be sent to England for trial." His mother explains their error. Ironically, they completely miss the colonel himself a little later when he walks right by them, dressed in a nondescript old coat, with a floppy hat and leather apron.

Still, the invaders are not entirely unsuccessful. They find five hundred musket balls and throw them into the millpond, break open sixty barrels of flour, ruin Jones's jailyard cannon, and burn up the

Liberty Pole. This fire spreads to the courthouse roof, and threatens the town. An old widow woman, Martha Moulton, begs the British soldiers to call up their men and put out the fire, but they only sneer at her. She persists, and though at first they will only go so far as to say, "Mother, we won't do you any harm," they eventually give in to her pleas and save the courthouse just in time before flames can destroy it and the town.

It's the smoke from this blaze that alarms the militia still waiting on the heights above North Bridge. Reinforcements have arrived by this time and they're four hundred strong now. The British detachment left behind to guard the bridge, under Captain Walter Laurie, numbers less than a hundred men. Laurie is nervous enough to have already sent for help. These two small forces face each other across eight hundred yards of terrain. One militiaman from Lincoln grows tired of waiting, asks a comrade to hold his musket, and walks down to talk with the British. Whatever he's told convinces him to reclaim his musket and go home.

But Lieutenant Joseph Rosman, always eloquent, tells his fellows: "I've often heard it said that the British have boasted they could march through our country, laying waste our hamlets and villages, and we would not oppose them. And I begin to think it is true." Turning to Buttrick, he asks, "Will you let them burn the town down?"

There's a brief debate, and then the men determine to cross the bridge and march into town, prepared to defend their homes or die in the attempt. "Don't fire unless they fire first," Colonel Barrett orders, "then fire as fast as you can." The fifers strike up "White Cockade" and the men move in double file toward the bridge. One of them, David Brown, is passing by his own farm, where the spring grain lies green in the fields and blossoms are beginning to appear on the apple trees.

The moment of collision draws nearer. At the east end of the bridge, some of the British soldiers are trying to pull up the planks. Captain Laurie orders a warning volley, but the Americans march on steadily, and he gives the fatal command: "Fire!" A young fifer, Abner Hosner, and a militiaman fall dead.

At this, Buttrick fairly leaps into the air with rage and excitement, shouting, "Fire, fellow soldiers, for God's sake fire!" They fire, and nearly a dozen British fall, three mortally wounded. Jammed together at the far end of the bridge as the American advance continues steadily, the redcoats panic. They turn and flee toward town. This brief exchange—it takes less than five minutes—becomes the fabled "shot heard round the world," but in fact it's only a small part of a developing British disaster.

Crossing the bridge, about two hundred militiamen take up a position on higher ground, overlooking the main road and the disputed bridge. They watch as Captain Laurie tries to regroup his regulars until the reinforcements he has sent for arrive. Colonel Smith is indeed on his way, but it takes time to move his ponderous bulk; one officer complains he won't reach the bridge in half an hour, even though it's only a half mile away. Meanwhile, Laurie's men are so vulnerable that the militia could kill them all, but they hold their fire. They still believe they're acting in self-defense. When they see Laurie's soldiers march away toward town, their undisciplined ranks simply melt away. Now it's going to be every man for himself. Some take care of the dead and wounded, others go home, and still others decide to carry on the fight.

A few British regulars who had been at Barrett's farm have heard the shots and rush to the bridge, but when they arrive, they see only their dead and wounded comrades. However, the incident has already produced the war's first atrocity story. A twenty-one-year-old minuteman, Amos White, has approached the scene, hatchet in hand, when a dying British soldier tries to rise and frightens him. He lashes out with his ax and strikes the man, who lingers another frightful hour before he dies. But is that the whole story? Not according to Colonel Barrett's daughter-in-law, an eyewitness, who swears the soldier was in such pain that he was trying to drown himself in a puddle of water, and young Amos has simply performed a merciful act when the soldier begs someone to end his life. By the time this incident is embodied in Gage's report to London, the soldier has been brutally scalped, his eyes gouged out, and his nose and ears cut off—a useful propaganda tool.

By now it's almost 11:00 A.M., and Smith has still not made up his mind what to do next. He's ransacked Barrett's farm, expecting to find a large cache of arms, and has come away with nothing of consequence. The town itself has yielded more civilian plunder than war goods. His second in command, Pitcairn, is sitting in Wright's Tavern, so it's said, stirring his brandy with a bloody finger and declaring he will stir "the damned Yankee blood the same way" before nightfall. Smith takes a more realistic view. His troops are both tired and hungry. He can wait for Lord Percy's reinforcements to arrive, or he can start back to Boston and meet them on the way. It takes him until noontime to decide, in his slow fashion, but then he concludes it's best to start the march back, by way of Lexington.

The town militia who have stayed to fight are now being reinforced from every direction. They're lying in wait about a mile from town, hoping to head off the retreat. With men streaming in from Reading, Billerica, and East Sudbury, they're now nearly a thousand strong. They take cover behind stone walls, houses and barns, trees and hillocks, creating the persistent legend that the entire Revolution was fought in this way.

At a fork in the road, a place called Meriam's Corner, the British march into a deadly trap as they cross a narrow bridge over a brook. The militia suddenly open fire, and even though these provincials are poor shots, by and large, enough British bodies lie in the road to wet it down with blood. With considerable courage, the redcoats march on under fire, but the twisting, winding, up-and-down road, crossing and recrossing streams, leads them into one indefensible position after another.

By the time they reach the village of Menotomy, about two miles from Lexington, nearly 1,800 fresh militia are besieging them, and the struggle has become a savage fight at close quarters, from house to house. At Deacon Joseph Adams's place, the deacon is in the barn, hiding in the hay mow, while his wife, recovering from childbirth, lies in bed. Three soldiers break into her bedroom, and one of them parts the bed curtains with a bayonet, then points it at her.

"For the Lord's sake, don't kill me," she entreats.

"Damn you," he says, and another says, "We won't hurt the woman if she'll go out of the house, but we'll surely burn it." Throwing a blanket over her shoulders, Mrs. Adams, who until then could scarcely walk "from my bed to the fire," manages to leave the house and crawls into a corncrib, holding her newborn in her arms. She watches in horror as they set the house afire, knowing that five of her children are in it, but arriving militia extinguish the blaze before it can do any real damage.

Nearby, in Cooper's Tavern, two drinking buddies sit calmly imbibing while the sounds of battle draw closer. Too close, one of them says apprehensively, but the other replies, "Let's finish the mug. They won't come just yet." He's wrong. Soldiers burst into the taproom before they've drained their cups and shoot the man who had made the erroneous prediction. The tavern's owners and two old men have retreated into the cellar, but the latter are discovered and, as one of the owners testifies, were "stabbed through in many places, their heads mauled, skulls broke, and their brains beat on the floor and walls of the house."

As the regulars leave Menotomy in some kind of order and near Lexington, discipline breaks down completely under relentless pressure from the militia. They've been marching and fighting for fifteen hours, and they're hungry and exhausted. Breaking ranks, they begin to run in confusion until their officers outrun them and confront them with bayonets, promising to kill them unless they stop the rout. That's enough to hold the troops together until they come into Lexington, where they find Lord Percy's First Brigade, just arrived from Boston, having been delayed starting out. Seeing them, Smith's harassed troops run forward to the shelter of the brigade's lines and fall on the ground, their tongues hanging out like dogs.

Percy immediately takes command. Swiveling his cannon, he scatters the pursuing militia, meanwhile sending some of his men into houses in Lexington from whose windows sniper fire is coming, with instructions to kill the resisters. So that other militiamen will not take advantage of nearby houses, he burns them while Smith's men rest for the long march still ahead.

That it will *be* a long march is guaranteed by the arrival of a militia general, William Heath, a Roxbury farmer, as fat as Colonel Smith and baldheaded as well, but more talented. When he heard the British were marching on Concord, this veteran officer hurried toward Lexington, picking up Joseph Warren on the way. They arrive only a few minutes after Percy's relief troops. Heath immediately exerts his authority and experience, rounding up the scattered militiamen and forming them into a small army of about three thousand.

After an hour's rest in Lexington, the British set off for Boston. It's an afternoon of sheer horror. Heath's militia pursue from both sides of the road, taking cover behind trees, stone walls, and buildings, as the Concord men had that morning. Musket shots ring out from upstairs windows. Around every bend in the road militiamen are waiting, as well as along the riverbanks where streams have to be crossed. It would have been a slaughter if the militia had been better shots, and hadn't fired too soon, as they so often did.

Percy and Smith do what experience tells them to do. They cover their flanks with light infantry, who inflict some damage on militia unfamiliar with such tactics. These flankers can do little, however, when thick woods close in the road. Worse, the British have to make do with the manpower they have, while fresh militia keep arriving every step of the way. In their rage and frustration, the regulars leave a trail of destruction behind them as they pillage houses, burn many of them, kill unarmed civilians, and yet burden themselves with loot as they continue their dreadful march.

These forays are accompanied by hand-to-hand fighting, the British matching their bayonets against the knives and hatchets of the inhabitants defending their property. Both sides take a few prisoners.

It's nearly dusk when the troops stagger into Charlestown and go on to Bunker Hill, where they camp at last. Heath halts his men at Charlestown Common, posts guards, then sends his troops to Cambridge, where they lie on their arms near the town. In the villages they've left, the dead are mourned. At Lexington, they lie in the meetinghouse, in coffins made of four large boards nailed up, and are buried in a long trench, "as near the woods as possible," their common grave disguised with pine and oak boughs in case the British should find it.

In Acton, Hannah Davis, widowed that day, sits beside the body of her husband in their bedroom. The men who brought him there told her that when Major Buttrick asked Davis whether he was afraid to lead the march to the bridge, he replied, "No, I'm not, and there isn't a man in my company that is." Some of the redcoats who shot him lie buried, hastily, nearby and in various spots along the road.

No one on either side had believed it would end like this when the dawn broke on Lexington that morning. Now the British, who have lost 64 dead, 180 wounded, and 28 missing that day, are lying on Bunker Hill, protected by the guns of their warships in the harbor, their faces still black from tearing open cartridges with their teeth, wondering how everything could have gone so utterly wrong.

They can see below them the campfires of the Americans, in a vast semicircle that runs from Mystic to Cambridge. These militia are not yet an army, but they've been blooded, having lost 49 dead, 41 wounded, and 4 missing. No deserters—yet. That will come later.

Some of the British regulars, who know more about war, have seen enough of it that day. Several of them have defected in Concord, and of eight wounded men left behind, seven will cast their lot with the colonials.

The day of Lexington and Concord has produced one undeniable fact. Blood has been shed on both sides. As Sam Adams pauses in his flight that morning, two miles from Lexington, he hears the first shots and exults, "Oh, what a glorious morning this is." Glory, however, will soon be in short supply.

1775

4

+   +   +

Blood on Breed's Hill

What's next? That's what everyone wants to know on the morning of April 20. For the British, it's a day of bewilderment. Gage looks out upon the militiamen encamped in Cambridge and wonders why they don't go home. His expeditionary force marches into town from their overnight encampment on Bunker Hill, and he can scarcely believe what these provincials have done to his regulars.

In Cambridge, the events of the day before have quickened the emotions of the militiamen, and as word of their actions and inevitable losses spread through the colonies, their spirits are buoyed up by an emotional wave of support. What's needed immediately, however, is some kind of organization. Having come together, they have no intention of going home until some kind of decision has been reached, and meanwhile (although there's a bit of disagreement, as always) they need to become an army.

During the morning, the militia officers meet with Joseph Warren and Timothy Pickering, a register of deeds in Salem who's been a civilian leader, to discuss how to form an army. Pickering writes afterward: "To me the idea was new and unexpected. I expressed the opinion, which at the moment occurred to me, that the hostilities of the preceding day did not render a civil war inevitable, a negotiation with General Gage might probably effect a present compromise and therefore that the immediate formation of an army did not appear to me to be necessary."

Most of the others disagree. Heath presumes that a state of war already exists, and he wants to deal at once with questions of supply, logistics, and strategy. No matter what's decided, these men have to eat, he says, so he sends his sergeants into the countryside to collect anything that's edible. Soon carcasses of beef and pork, intended for Boston markets, arrive in camp, along with some Royal Navy ship's bread seized in Roxbury. Harvard provides the cooks with necessary kitchen equipment.

That afternoon a senior authority figure arrives to take charge. He's General Artemas Ward, commander-in-chief of Massachusetts militia, fully as fat as either Smith or Heath (is there no end to these overweight generals?) who had been ill in bed with gallstones at his home in Shrewsbury when the news of Lexington and Concord was brought to him at daybreak. Characteristically, he hoisted himself into the saddle at once and rode to Cambridge. Ward is a man who moves slowly, and he's deficient in imagination, but he's the kind of leader who can get people to work for him. He calls a council of war at once and, without further debate on the need for an army, proceeds to organize one. He deploys troops, orders fortifications built, and throws up earthworks on the roads leading to Boston.

The war has scarcely begun, but already there are refugees. Mercy Warren, still in Boston, gets an anguished letter from her friend Hannah Winthrop, describing how she and her ill husband fled Cambridge when the troops arrived and, with eighty or so others, had spent a most uncomfortable night in a house about a mile out of town. Some of them were "nodding in their chairs," she writes, "others resting their weary limbs on the floor."

Next day the roads out of Cambridge take on the aspect of all landscapes invaded by war—frightened women and children pulling or pushing carts loaded with household goods, some people seeking shelter in the woods, others walking or riding alternately. Those who pass through Menotomy view with horror a field strewn with bloody forms not yet removed. Hannah writes: "We met an affectionate father with a cart looking for his murdered son and picking up his neighbors who had fallen in battle in order for their burial."

While the Charlestown civilians are seeking safety, other villages are being urged to send more men to form the army at Cambridge. The call goes out not only to Massachusetts but to Connecticut and New Hampshire. How fast the news of bloodshed spreads can be seen in the tale of a post rider named Israel Bissel, who starts out from

Watertown and rides hard until his horse falls dead in Worcester, thirty-six miles away. Unable to find a fresh mount, he has to spend the night there, but he's off at seven next morning, and by evening he's reached New London.

Along the way he's stopped to give Israel Putnam the news. This remarkable character in an army soon to be full of them is "in leathern frock and apron . . . assisting hired men to build a stone wall." Without changing clothes, he saddles his horse and rides toward Cambridge, giving the alarm to militia officers along the way, and gallops into the village at sunrise next morning, having traveled a hundred miles in eighteen hours—on the same horse.

As for Bissel, he rides all night after reaching New London, arriving in Lyme at 1:00 A.M., Saybrook at four, Guilford at seven, Branford at noon, and New Haven in the evening. Resting overnight, he's off again next day, reaching Fairfield at 4:00 P.M., and riding at last into New York City on the twenty-third, where his news is greeted with a civic eruption, Whigs "parading the town with drums beating and colors flying, then overwhelming a sloop ready to sail for Boston with British provisions, and seizing a thousand muskets from an arsenal." Until then, New York had been sitting on the fence.

Among those aroused to action in New Haven when Israel Bissel rides through is Benedict Arnold, a young man whose life so far has been a series of disappointments. Born to wealth, he watched his father lose a fortune. He married the handsome daughter of a New Haven merchant and became his father-in-law's partner, but trade was not for him, and Peggy Mansfield proved to be a cold and unresponsive wife, although she bore him three sons. Arnold is moody and sometimes violent to the point of fighting duels, and so enjoys little respect from others. The fact is that young Arnold's a born soldier, who hopes to gain on the battlefield what's been lost to him at home.

As a member of the elite Governor's Foot Guard in 1774, Arnold was a part of the best-dressed militia unit in a system known for its nondescript uniforms. Elected captain of this group, he had the satisfaction of giving orders to the sons of families who despised him.

The news from Lexington and Concord fires Arnold's military zeal and he's ready to leave at once. But a conservative, frightened town meeting votes neutrality and forbids warlike acts. Arnold isn't deterred. He asks his militia company if they want to fight, and sixty of them shout their desire. Arnold parades them before the tavern where the committee to prevent warlike acts is sitting, knowing they have the keys to the town's powder house. Getting no response, Arnold bursts into the meeting and demands the keys. His superior, Colonel David Wooster, is a member of the committee and points out that the town meeting has voted neutrality. Damn the town meeting, Arnold says. Trying to restrain him, Wooster advises him to wait for orders, but the young captain won't listen. Instead, he threatens to break open the door of the powder house, and proclaims grandiloquently, "None but Almighty God shall prevent my marching!" Not wanting to deal with possible divine intervention, the committee gives him the keys, and soon the company, dressed in its dazzling uniforms and fully equipped for battle, marches off toward Cambridge. For the first time in his thirty-four years, Arnold is completely happy.

When the company arrives in Cambridge, they make such an impression that Ward has them quartered in a mansion. The new arrivals find themselves in a scene of utter confusion. Thousands of amateur soldiers like themselves are arriving, but their leadership is inexperienced when it isn't incompetent, and Ward has not been able to impose any real organization on this motley crowd. They drift in and out of camp as they please, and Ward, well liked as he is and given to quoting the Bible for inspiration, finds he can't create an army on short notice.

Inside Boston, the situation is much worse. Isolated from the rest of the colony, there's an immediate problem of how to get fresh meat and vegetables for the troops, not to mention the citizens. Thousands of Whigs want to get out, and thousands of Loyalists who live outside the town want to get in for protection, so an exchange agreement is negotiated.

Otherwise, an impasse prevails. The chief problem for the Cambridge besiegers is their lack of cannon and ammunition to bombard the British. It's well known that the largest stock of this equipment is in British-held Fort Ticonderoga, on Lake Champlain. Boldly, Arnold convinces the Massachusetts legislature that he knows where the guns are, and how to get them. Impressed, they give him a colonel's commission and authorize him to raise four hundred men for an expedition to seize the fort and its armaments. At the same time, New Hampshire, independent as always, dispatches an American original, Ethan Allen, and eighty-three of the men he calls his Green Mountain Boys to carry out the same mission.

When he hears of this action, Arnold races to get there first and exert his authority as head of the operation, perhaps sensing that he's about to confront a man whose monumental ego is even greater than his own. The difference is that Arnold has given the Massachusetts legislators a detailed report and plan of how to overcome the forty-two-man garrison, under Captain William Delaplace. Allen claims to have a commission from the Connecticut Assembly, of all places, and some of his "Boys" come from that colony as well as from the Green Mountains of Vermont and New Hampshire.

When the two men meet, these prima donnas agree on a joint command after a hot argument, although the Boys, and no doubt Allen himself, consider Arnold just another volunteer, like themselves.

On the night of May 9, this uneasy alliance arrives at Hand's Cove, finds some boats, and crosses over in the early dawn. The assault on Ticonderoga is a complete surprise. Allen orders the barracks secured, while he menaces the sentry with his sword, cutting the man's cheek, and demanding to know where the commander is. "Come out, you damned skunk," he shouts, "or I'll sacrifice the whole garrison!"

His stentorian voice is heard by Lieutenant Jocelyn Feltham, of the 26th Foot, who stumbles out of bed naked and, going to Delaplace's room, tries to wake his snoring superior. He's not successful, so he hastily puts on a waistcoat and coat, and still without his trousers, opens the door to the parade ground. He's confronted by Allen and Arnold, backed by "an armed rabble," as he says, waving muskets and tomahawks. When silence is obtained, Feltham inquires by what authority they are there, and Allen gives him the famous and erroneous answer, "By the authority of Almighty Jehovah and the Continental Congress." Whatever God may have decreed, the Congress has given him no such authority.

With the fort subdued and captured—Allen claims it fell because the British were terrified by his men—the Boys take advantage of the garrison's store of spirits, notably ninety gallons of rum. By the middle of the morning most of them are drunk, and they've begun to plunder the fort, terrifying the wives and children. Whatever is too heavy to lift and steal they smash with their hatchets. Arnold is furious over this outrageous unmilitary behavior. He strides about, quoting military law and trying to wrest possessions from the looters.

In the process he's confronted by Allen, now as drunk as the others and even more belligerent. The patchwork alliance falls apart immediately. Allen denies he ever agreed to a joint command and orders Arnold out of the fort. Arnold displays his commission from Massachusetts, and Allen has one of his own drawn up on the spot. Meanwhile, the loyal, drunken Boys are joining in the argument, even taking random shots in Arnold's direction. One, putting his musket against Arnold's chest, tells him he'd better submit to Allen's authority or he'll be shot. But Arnold stands his ground fearlessly, and the two men face each other toe to toe for a moment. It's Allen's man who backs down. He turns away and the rioting goes on, while Arnold continues to give orders to which no one pays any attention. Arnold reports back to Cambridge that the troops are "in the greatest confusion and anarchy."

That's the situation for the next four days, until the officers and men Arnold, in his anxiety to head off Allen, left behind to recruit arrive aboard a schooner they've seized from a Tory trader. Some of these fifty or more men are New Yorkers and that leads to a new confrontation with Allen's Boys, who have land claims against New York and think they might now get them by force.

At this point, Arnold makes a strategic error by going beyond his commission. In his eagerness to wrest a little glory for himself from this mess, he decides to arm his schooner with cannon from Ticonderoga and sail up the lake into Canada, to St. John, where he's learned a British naval sloop is lying. Invading Canada, of course, will be an act of war, but no war has been declared. Nevertheless, he decides to go by rowboat instead, and packing thirty men into two of them, he crosses the border, surprises the fort at St. John, and takes it without loss on either side, capturing a sergeant and a dozen men, and the big prize—a seventy-ton sloop with two cannon. He sails back in it, the rowboats trailing behind.

On the way, he encounters some of the Boys, who have paddled after him in bateaux, hoping to prevent him from getting any credit. But Arnold can now afford to be magnanimous. He gives them a salute and goes so far as to invite them on board to drink the rum he's captured. But the Boys say they're going on to St. John and occupy it. Four days later, however, with Arnold already back at Ticonderoga, the Boys come paddling home in terror. Having fallen asleep near St. John, they've been attacked by two hundred British regulars and barely escaped, leaving one prisoner behind. This event has had a salutary effect on them. Many remember urgent business on their farms and depart. Allen himself, much subdued, publicly hands over the leadership to Arnold.

This is to be the pattern of Arnold's life. He wins in the field but he loses at home. His enemies in Connecticut tell the Massachusetts legislature that this presumptuous officer has interfered with the expedition they had planned. Since there's now a stir in Congress over Arnold's invasion of Canada, the Massachusetts lawmakers are quite willing to pass on responsibility for him to Connecticut. They call him a captain now, denying their own commission, and Congress sends him an official letter giving him no rank at all. It's even suggested that Ticonderoga ought to be returned to the British, since its capture has threatened any hope that peace might still be possible.

Caught in this witches' brew of provincial politics, Arnold resigns his commission (if he still has one) and goes home, where he finds that his wife has died while he was gone. Moreover, he's spent hundreds of pounds of his own money to help supply the expedition and doesn't know where to turn. After only two months in the army, he's already well known and controversial, but he's gained nothing of what he'd hoped for except experience.

While these events were taking place, the three principal British actors in the great drama about to unfold have arrived in Boston on May 25, aboard the frigate *Cerberus*. And what actors they are—complicated men whose faults and virtues are still being argued. They are all major generals, but otherwise they're quite unlike. Their senior in command, at forty-five, is William Howe, a tall, dark man with a face already ravaged by too much high living, including not only good food and wine but incessant gambling and a long succession of willing ladies. Oddly enough, this man who is supposed to scourge the disobedient Americans is a Whig who has, from the beginning, opposed the Crown's coercive measures. Nor is he a stranger to America. He fought in the French and Indian War, and led an advance unit of twenty-four men up the Heights of Abraham in advance of Wolfe.

Henry Clinton is his exact opposite, the only son of a British admiral, who had been colonial governor of New York at the time of the affair on King Street. Clinton has a bland personality, and sometimes it's hard to understand his actions—or inactions. Some think he exhibits an unusual sympathy for handsome young officers but, if true, no scandal has ever developed.

John Burgoyne is the son of a Lancashire family whose roots are embedded in ancient times, and whose wealth matches its reputation. At fifty-three, "Gentleman Johnny," as his men like to call him, is the veritable epitome of the British ruling class, a solidly built man known as a wit, a playwright, a Beau Brummell of sorts, and a member of Parliament. Moreover, he's an admired military leader, popular with his men, who's astonished as soon as he arrives by what he considers Gage's incompetence, which he does not fail to report back home.

These men have been sent to bring the rebellious Americans under control and save the colonies for the Empire. Instead, they will prove to be, in different ways, the losers of a war they will have it in their power to win a half dozen times. As though to demonstrate that already they don't understand the situation, their first act is to promise pardons for everyone except Hancock and Sam Adams, if the militia will lay down their arms. As a preliminary, they declare martial law—the worst way to win over the colonists. Less than a week later, the war begins in earnest.

All the generals urge Gage, who's still in command, to take the offensive immediately. At a council of war, it's decided to seize Dorchester Heights, south of the city, with an amphibious attack. The British allow themselves five days to prepare for the assault, but they haven't reckoned with the American intelligence network, still operating brazenly in Boston. In less than twenty-four hours, Ward knows what is planned and a countermove is under way. The Americans will occupy Dorchester Heights, and Charlestown too, making Boston a precarious place to be. But the British have equally efficient intelligence and that plan also leaks. Ward then makes a new decision: to occupy and fortify Bunker Hill. This is one of three hills on the Charlestown peninsula. Bunker, at 110 feet, is the highest, and lies just inside Charlestown Neck. Connected to it by a ridge is Breed's, steeper but lower at 75 feet, with brick kilns and clay pits to the east and Charlestown in the opposite direction.

On the night of June 16, Captain Samuel Gridley conducts a detachment ordered to work furiously all night and throw up fortifications on Bunker Hill. For reasons still unknown, Gridley leads his men right over Bunker and down to Breed's, where they go to work.

In the end, this is a fatal error. The advantage of greater height is lost, and although Breed's is closer to Boston, near enough for cannon to reach the town and harbor, it's equally vulnerable to British guns.

Gridley's men work hard, but when they're discovered, about 5:00 A.M., their fort is still only half-finished. The discovery has been made by sailors on H.M.S. *Lively*, and before long, the whole British fleet is bombarding the American position, helped by a battery on Copp's Hill. At that point, if the British had landed in the Americans' rear, they would have "shut them up in the Peninsula as in a bag," a British officer observes later. But Gage goes by the book, which calls for a frontal attack, although Howe protests that this is not good practice in the present situation, and in any case, it's only necessary to teach this rabble a lesson and punish them, not annihilate them.

The British firing stops for a time until about 11:00A.M., and when it begins once more, some of the younger militiamen begin to desert, or at least leave the field of action. One of them, Private Peter Brown, a company clerk in Colonel William Prescott's Massachusetts regiment, writes home later: "We began to be almost beat out, being tired by our labor and having no sleep the night before, but little victuals, no drink but rum."

By 2:00 P.M., the cannonading from ship and shore batteries is incessant. About this time (historians don't agree exactly when) Gage sends nearly three thousand men in rowboats over to Charlestown, which they set afire to deny the Americans any refuge. This move demonstrates how unreliable a militia army can be. When the Americans see what the British are up to, they order the artillery, such as it is, to prevent the landing if possible. Earlier in the day the captain in charge of this artillery has been called on to reply to the British cannon, but he fired only a few times, "then swung his cannon around three times to the enemy, then ceased to fire." Now, faced with an invasion of regulars, the captain collects his pieces and hurries off to Cambridge, "for which he is now confined," Private Brown reports, "and we expect will be shot for it."

After this diversion, the British are now prepared for their frontal assault. With his flair for theater, Burgoyne watches the vast stage before him from a vantage point on a hill, as Gage is doing from the steeple of Christ Church, both generals joining hundreds of Bostonians sitting on roofs and even clinging to precipitous church steeples on this brilliant, cloudless day, while the bloody pageant is played out.

Burgoyne writes home a few days later: "And now ensued one of the greatest scenes of war that can be conceived. If we look to the height, Howe's corps ascending the hill in the face of the entrenchment and in a very disadvantageous ground was much engaged. To the left the enemy pouring in fresh troops by thousands over the land, and in the arm of the sea our ships and floating batteries cannonading them. Straight before us, a large and noble town [he means Charlestown] in one great blaze. The church steeples being of timber were great pyramids of fire above the rest. Behind us, the church steeples and heights of our own camp covered with spectators. The enemy all in anxious suspense. The roar of cannon, mortars, and musketry, the crash of churches, ships upon the stocks, and whole streets falling together in ruins to fill the ear; the storming of the redoubts with the objects above described to fill the eye, and the reflection that perhaps a defeat was a final loss to the British Empire in America to fill the mind, made the whole a picture and a complication of horror and importance beyond anything that ever came to my lot to be witness to."

Down in the trenches, the view is considerably less romantic. The cannonade from British ships is doing little damage, but one shot does kill a soldier, whose brains spatter out on Colonel Prescott, who's standing beside him. The colonel calmly brushes off the blood, wipes his hands with a handful of clay, and jumps up on the parapet, looking down and encouraging the soldiers, even joking with them. But Prescott is under no illusions. He commands less than 1,700 men and boys, as against nearly 2,500 British regulars under Howe, an experienced general.

As usual, however, the British troops have gone into battle on a stifling hot day with 125 pounds of equipment dragging on them as they try to advance up a steep hill, which quickly becomes slippery with blood. Moreover, there are natural obstacles like high grass and many fences. As they advance for the first time, Prescott and his fellow officers are doing their best to prevent their men from shooting too soon. When they do fire, it staggers the British line, but many of these redcoats are still suffering from the humiliation of Concord. They're not about to retreat.

As they come on, Putnam tells his troops he will shoot anyone who fires without orders, and adds his famous command, "Men, you are all marksmen—don't one of you fire until you see the white of their eyes." They're not marksmen, as he well knows, and he doesn't give the order to fire until the British are only fifty yards away. Those who are out of buckshot use rusty nails and pieces of glass. A sheet of flame suffuses the British line, and it falls back in retreat. At the foot of the hill, they regroup.

Doggedly, the thin red lines come up the hill for a second time, stepping over dead comrades, slipping on the blood-soaked grass and clay, sweat pouring from them. But now the American fire is deadly at close range. There's a wavering, and then a break as men turn and run back down the slope. Frantically, their officers try to rally them, but they too are cut down. Every man on Howe's personal staff is killed. It's not exactly a rout, but as Howe says later, "There was a moment that I never felt before." Some historians believe that moment changed his military life, and led him to make otherwise inexplicable decisions later in the war.

But Howe is a thorough soldier, in spite of his faults. His uniform splattered with blood and dirt, his face streaked with grime, he calls on seven hundred men held in reserve, and orders a third charge. As they come up once more, says one account, they face "tall, blue-eyed, Pepperell farmer, William Prescott, in homespun clothes, a sword buckled to his side, a light, loose coat about his shoulders, and a broad-brimmed hat shading his eyes."

Now, however, Prescott is commanding an army falling into confusion. It's hard to see what's happening through the thick smoke swirling about, and it's clear that ammunition is nearly gone. Reinforcements have been sent, but those who come by way of the Neck refuse to cross it in the face of cannon fire from the British ships, while those coming by way of Bunker Hill stay there. No one has told them where to go. With their powder gone, Prescott's men have no option but to retreat. Captain John Chester's company from Wethersfield, Connecticut, covers the retreat, and as he recalls, "The dead and wounded lay on every side of us. Their groans were piercing indeed, though long before this time I believe the fear of death had quitted almost every breast. They now had possession of our fort, and to tell you the truth, our reinforcements belonging to this province, very few of them came into the field, but lay skulking the opposite side of the hill. Our orders then came to make the best retreat we could. We set off almost gone with fatigue and ran very fast up Bunker Hill leaving some of our dead in the field."

That last assault, with slashing bayonets, ends the life of Joseph Warren, who only three days ago was commissioned a major general. He's fought with icy courage until a musket ball catches him in the back of the head just as the British overrun the fortifications. A red-coated officer who witnesses his death says admiringly, "He died in his best clothes, everybody remembered his fine, silk-fringed waistcoat."

There have been other brave individuals too, men fighting with empty muskets against bayonets, while others panic and try to escape through the smoke. Prescott, thrusting away bayonets with his sword, manages to get clear, his clothes in ruins. It galls him to hear the British cheering as they take over the entrenchments, immediately opening a heavy fire on the retreating Americans. As Prescott and his men reach the crest of Bunker Hill, they encounter Putnam, riding up and down, hurling invective, and entreating, "In God's name, form, and give them one shot more!"

On the enemy side, colonial revenge for Lexington and Concord comes to Pitcairn, who's wounded twice, then falls with four bullets in his body, dying in his son's arms. Death comes, too, for the veteran Lieutenant Colonel James Abercrombie. Carried away with a mortal wound, he still has strength enough to plead with his fellow officers not to hang his old friend Israel Putnam. They had fought together in the French and Indian War.

The entire affair has taken only two hours. It's five o'clock of a bright summer afternoon and there's plenty of daylight left. Clinton urges Howe to pursue the disordered Americans. It will be easy to take Cambridge, he says, scatter the troops, kill or capture as many more as possible, and end the rebellion that day. In any case, it would be a devastating blow to further resistance.

But Howe displays for the first time his reluctance to pursue a visibly beaten enemy. In his report to Gage, he argues that his troops "were too much harassed and fatigued to give much attention to the pursuit of the rebels." This is palpably untrue, since the British still have reserves and overwhelming firepower against an enemy almost without gunpowder and unable to defend itself. But Howe prevails.

On the other side, there is bitter recrimination. Prescott bursts into Ward's headquarters and demands to know why there had been no support. He promises his commander that, if Ward will give him

1,500 fresh and well-equipped troops, he will retake Breed's Hill. The general does not take this idea seriously.

Line officers are equally outraged. "Our retreat," Captain John Chester writes, "was shameful and scandalous and owing to the cowardice, misconduct, and want of regularity of the province troops. . . . Some did honor to themselves by a most noble, manly, and spirited effort in the best of the engagement. . . . Some say they have lost more officers than men."

One of Chester's soldiers is less charitable. His captain, he says (not Chester), "had mustered and ordered them to march and told them he would overtake them directly, but they never saw him again till next day. . . . If a man was wounded, twenty more were glad of an opportunity to carry him away when not more than three could take hold of him to advantage. One cluster would be sneaking down on their bellies behind a rock, and others behind haycocks and apple trees."

Chester himself had nearly precipitated a miniature civil war on the way to the fighting. "I imagine we arrived at the hill near the close of the battle," he writes to his friend, the Reverend Joseph Fish, in Stonington. "When we arrived there was not a company with us in any kind of order. . . . At last I met with a considerable company who were going off rank and file. I called to the officer that led them, and asked why he retreated. He made me no answer. I halted my men, and told him if he went on it should be at his peril. He still seemed regardless of me. I then ordered my men to make ready. They immediately cocked, and declared if I ordered they would fire. Upon that they stopped short, tried to excuse themselves, but I could not tarry to hear him, but ordered him forward, and he complied."

No one is more painfully aware of American inadequacies than Ward himself; after all, he's responsible. He can see that his staff is inadequate, that many officers are not equal to what they're called upon to do. Yet Burgoyne, who has watched the whole affair, declares, "The retreat was no flight; it was even covered with bravery and military skill." Like Clinton, he thinks Howe made a grievous mistake in not taking the Neck, thus cutting off Prescott's troops. Other recriminations are passed around freely in the British camp. One of Gage's officers says the general was overconfident and failed to reconnoiter before the troops were committed, and hadn't used the firepower of the ships properly. Howe is also blamed for permitting his men to fire as they came up the hill, wasting ammunition, and for sending them up in lines rather than columns.

The postmortems aren't without their grim humor. At one point, twelve-pound cannonballs were brought up to six-pounders on the British side. Explaining this astonishing error, an officer writes: "The wretched blunder of the oversized balls sprung from the dotage of an officer of rank in that corps, who spends his whole time in dallying with the schoolmaster's daughter. God knows, he is old enough. He is no Samson, but he must have his Delilah." At the end of a long list of complaints, he adds: "We are all wrong in the head. The brave men's lives were wantonly thrown away."

So this first full-scale encounter of the Revolution, erroneously called the Battle of Charlestown by contemporaries and known just as wrongly today as the Battle of Bunker Hill, passes into history. The historian Willard Wallace has called it "the bloodiest conflict on the continent until the Battle of New Orleans, in 1815." The casualties are heavy: of the 2,500 British troops involved, 1,054 are killed or wounded, an unacceptable 42 percent. The Americans lose 144 killed, 271 wounded, and 30 taken prisoner.

Charles Francis Adams sums it up later: "A more singular exhibition of apparently unconscious temerity on one side, and professional military incapacity on the other, it would be difficult to imagine." The Americans can say they've won a moral victory, and there will be a good many other such inconclusive victorious defeats during the war. Most of all, however, they've been lucky. They've escaped annihilation by virtue of British incompetence, and they've so shocked their enemy that it will be fourteen months before any new offensive is launched.

5

✢   ✢   ✢

Boston Besieged

Two days before the first real blood of the war flowed on Breed's Hill, the Continental Congress in Philadelphia appointed George Washington "General of the American Army," a body which has existed on paper since May 31. It's an appointment full of booby traps. For one thing, few people in New England, whose citizens are doing the fighting, have ever heard of him. By the few who do know him, or know of him, he's remembered as a colonel of Virginia militia in the French and Indian War who nearly lost his commission as a result of serious errors on the battlefield, and who served bravely but with no particular distinction under General Edward Braddock, who presided over the destruction of his own army. Since then, Washington has been serving in the Virginia House of Burgesses and quietly getting rich on his Potomac plantation.

New Englanders also suspect, with reason, that the Southerners who dominate the Continental Congress have been careful to choose one of their own rather than John Hancock, who positively yearns for the job. Washington hadn't actually sought the honor, but he'd been highly visible around the Congress, dressed in his carefully pressed militia colonel's uniform and looking military. To some, his rather glum acceptance is not convincing.

From hindsight, we understand better than Washington did at the time what a formidable task he's undertaken; to create out of provincial raw materials an army capable of fighting against British regulars and, as it turns out, professional Hessian mercenaries. To judge by the exciting events around Boston, it seems that the entire population of the colonies is about to be up in arms. But as the historian Linda De Pauw reminds us, most of the colonial population, about 80 percent, was made up of indentured servants, slaves, boys and girls under sixteen, and women, and none of these could join the army legally, although some in each class did. What Washington has to work with to create an army of officers and soldiers is the small percentage of the population that's free, white, and male.

As Professor De Pauw observes, "Women, fourteen-year-olds, blacks, and runaway servants do not make strategy. They may be called upon to implement it, they may be its victims, they may louse it up, but they do not make it."

Obviously, necessity makes some compromises essential. According to Benjamin Quarles, the authority on this subject, about five thousand black men will serve under Washington, in spite of the usual discrimination. There are also a large number of boys, some no older than eleven or twelve, who do the drumming and fifing and sometimes fight as well. Very few women will ever carry a musket, in spite of notorious exceptions like Deborah Simpson and Sally St. Clair, who disguise themselves as men and serve undetected with the infantry.

The new commander is quite grumpy about women. By August 1777, he will complain that "the multitude of women, especially those who are pregnant or have children, are a clog upon our every movement." Yet without women the army can't survive. As soon as it begins to take shape, it's clear that soldiers don't intend to do any cleaning and only a minimum of cooking. That's women's work, they say, and that's what female camp followers do, most of them wives of enlisted men and lower-ranking officers. They cook, launder, and do their best to keep the camp and the soldiers clean, a losing battle since these boys and men away from home let themselves become filthy often enough, and that leads to disease. But the healing arts in the eighteenth century are also mostly left to women, and they do more good than the few doctors available, who give treatments they've been taught to do which more often than not result in the patient's death. So, in most battles, the camp women are also the medics; they do the best they can under impossible conditions.

On the home front, they're equally indispensable. With so many men away, women take over in family businesses and in every kind of occupation. It's women who make the clothing and shoes the soldiers wear, although, through no fault of these workers, those who fight the war are half-naked a good part of the time. The government is perennially short of cash to buy such basic equipment, but even if it were rolling in wealth, the labor shortage is so acute that there simply aren't enough women to produce the cloth needed, or to sew the shirts. Women can and do produce saltpeter for gunpowder, as well as shot. It's heavy work, but colonial women are used to that.

None of these gloomy conditions are yet in the thoughts of the freshly minted general as he prepares to go to Cambridge and assume command. He rides out of Philadelphia on the morning of June 23, 1775, but soon has to abandon his horse because it appears that everyone along the way wants to greet him. He switches to a light carriage drawn by a pair of white horses, and makes a kind of royal progress, of a sort that will irritate John Adams when Washington employs a splendid equipage during his presidency.

His companions are the first young men to become a part of his official "family," a band of "writing" and "riding" aides who will number thirty-nine before the war ends. "They wrote long dispatches and they rode on long errands," says one historian, "and when opportunity arose, they danced and flirted and courted. They were young—young in their enthusiasm, in their lightheartedness, in their impatient ambition."

The entourage includes some other new actors in the coming drama. Here is Thomas Mifflin, thirty-one, a Pennsylvanian who will not be the commander's friend much longer, an elegant man of considerable promise and patriotic fervor who changes progressively in a way that shocks those who know him. Then there are a pair of new major generals, Philip Schuyler and Charles Lee. Schuyler, forty-two, son of a rich Albany family, is difficult in another way. His critics think he's more suited to business affairs than to leading men in combat, but in his relationships with people of his own class, including the commander, he gets along extremely well. There are some things he considers beneath his dignity, and he instantly resents any challenge to his integrity, or any assumption of authority that interferes with his prerogatives. Schuyler has a natural air of superiority he can't help, and it's quickly resented by the New England men at Cambridge.

Charles Lee fits in with none of the above. At forty-four, he has had much more military experience than any of the other American generals, including Washington, but his personality borders on the psychotic. Tall, lanky, ugly, customarily trailed by two or three dogs, whom he likes to say he admires more than humans, Lee is restless, enormously ambitious, and if the commander hadn't suffered a curious blind spot about Lee, he would have recognized him at once as Trouble.

The fourth member of Washington's little band riding out into the rainy countryside is Joseph Reed, thirty-four, another elegant Pennsylvanian, and another close friend of the commander whose loyalty will be in question before the war is over.

For now, this rather ill-assorted party is intent on simply getting to Cambridge. They haven't gone far before they encounter an express rider carrying to Congress an account of the action at Breed's Hill, written by Captain Elijah Hide. A short time later, another express comes clattering after the first, with a masterpiece of anguished ambiguity from the editor of the Watertown, Massachusetts, paper, who regrets his inability to give a comprehensive account of the battle, declaring that "the confusion of the times renders it impractical to give a particular account of what has already occurred but hope to give a good account in our next."

The travelers spend their first night in Trenton, reach Brunswick next day, and push on to Newark. Washington likes to get up before dawn and make a good start without breakfast, to cover as many miles as possible before the heat of the day begins to affect the horses, so they reach Newark at 9:00 A.M. on the twenty-fifth, where a committee from the New York Provincial Congress meets them and reports that Governor William Tryon, an eminent Tory, is returning to New York that day from a trip, and if both men arrive at the same time, partisan passions may boil over. It's Sunday, and the streets will be full of people. The committee advises Washington to go up the Hudson's west bank to Hoboken, take the ferry to Powles Hook, and come in by the back door, so to speak. The commander agrees, and with his usual attention to appearance, he dresses for the occasion before he climbs on the ferry, wrapping a new purple sash about his blue uniform and putting on a hat with a plume.

As the ferry carries him toward the broad green lawns of Colonel Leonard Lispenard's estate, sloping down to the river, with the edge of the town about a mile south, Washington can see a huge crowd gathered at the landing. Blue uniforms of the city's nine militia companies mingle with the Sunday-best colors of men and women who have walked out from the city to see him. It's like nothing he's ever faced before. Stepping off the ferry, he raises his hat and bows, is huzzahed, and makes his way to Lispenard's house, where he's to have dinner.

A cheering, optimistic crowd mills about outside, but inside, a courier has arrived from Boston with the latest news. Charlestown is utterly destroyed, and the army faces a desperate shortage of powder. Washington takes the news with his usual calm. When he walks outside, he presents a confident face to the citizens, and then joins in a grand parade, the largest the town has ever seen, which moves past "the Fields," a public meeting place, where City Hall stands today.

Not all who watch have their spirits raised. Judge Thomas Jones, a Loyalist, writes disgustedly of the "seditious and rebellious multitude." The parade breaks up at Hull's Tavern, near Trinity Church. Tradition says that Tryon sees the end of it and nearly faints at the sight of so much public support for Washington, but that's most unlikely. Tryon is not given to fainting spells.

It's 3:00 P.M. next day before the commander can finish official business and start off again, traveling through places he will revisit in worse circumstances. In New Haven, a military company of Yale students turns out to be reviewed and ushers him from town next day in style. Then it's up the Connecticut Valley to Wethersfield, to stay overnight with Silas Deane, his friend and admirer in the Congress, and off again to Springfield for more pomp and ceremony. As he travels, he has to pause long enough to meet the principal gentlemen of all the larger towns from there to Cambridge, so it's Sunday morning, July 2, before he arrives in Watertown, where he meets the committee from the Massachusetts Provincial Congress in charge of his last leg, a two-man delegation consisting of Moses Gill and Benjamin Church, already a British spy.

These gentlemen conduct him the remaining three miles to Cambridge, where it's been raining all morning. Their arrival is something of an anticlimax. No one appears to be expecting them. In fact, he'd been expected the previous morning and the troops had been turned out to welcome him. Then he was expected earlier this morning, and the soldiers assembled again, grumpily, getting themselves wet before being sent back. By 2:00 P.M., when the cavalcade finally appears, the soldiers are asleep, having lost several hours of it after 4:00 A.M., when the British carried on a three-hour bombardment of Roxbury.

Without fanfare, Washington goes directly to the house of Harvard's president, Samuel Langdon, which has been appropriated for him by the Provincial Congress, leaving one room for its owner. However, a Virginia gentleman feels uneasy about appropriating the home of a man still living in it, especially a man distinguished in his own right who's now confined to a single room while his wife and five children have been compelled to move elsewhere. The commander lets the Massachusetts legislators know how he feels, and they tell him he can choose any house he likes. He chooses the home of John Vassall, a departed Loyalist (it's now the Craigie-Longfellow House), and he and Lee occupy it about the middle of July. But Lee is equally uneasy living with the commander and leaves a few days later to take over General Isaac Royall's house in Medford, which he characteristically renames Hobgoblin Hall, installing himself and his dogs.

Unfortunately for legend, Washington doesn't take command of the army under a tree on Cambridge Common, later known as the Washington Elm, while the troops parade before him. There's no ceremony. He simply takes over and begins to examine the ten miles of encampments, one by one.

As he rides with Lee, Putnam, and other officers, the commander views an incredible scene of a kind no one has ever witnessed before, or will see again in America. The militia represents a cross section of colonists, who shelter themselves according to their individual ideas. Their huts are made of boards, sailcloth, a mixture of both, stone and turf, birch and similar brush. Some have obviously been thrown together in a hurry; others, as described by the Reverend William Emerson, visiting from Concord, are "curiously wrought with doors and windows, one with wreaths and withes in the manner of a basket." There are a few tents and marquees in accepted military style, particularly those of the Rhode Islanders, who've brought their own. A few of the troops are quartered in Harvard dormitories and private houses.

The men look curiously at their new leader and they're impressed. At six foot three and a half, he towers over nearly all of them (average male height at the time is five foot six), until the wilderness giants get there. But he also exudes an aura of confident power that commands their respect. Gazing back at this motley assortment of colonists, the commander must have a few doubts that this assorted mass of militia will be able to hold the British in Boston until he can make them into an army able to fight there and elsewhere.

Everyone's discovering everyone else in these early days at Cambridge. Most of these men have never been outside their own colonies, and they're novelties to one another. Washington himself has been in Boston only once, and that briefly during the French and Indian War. Taking a countryman's pleasure in the lush flowering of full summer, he writes home: "The village I am in is situated in the midst of a very delightful country, and is a very beautiful place itself, though small. A thousand pities that such a country should become the theater of war."

Many of the volunteer army appear to feel the same way. Now that they're in Cambridge, some begin to worry about their affairs back home, and chafe even under the minimal discipline of the camp. Guards are often found asleep, and there are frequent courts-martial for drunkenness, abusive language to officers, insulting sentries, theft, and a variety of other offenses.

Already there's graft in the supply department. A Massachusetts quartermaster draws more provisions than there are men in the regiment. A captain takes home large quantities of food intended for his command. Other officers abscond with the men's pay. In his journal, Lieutenant Benjamin Craft writes: "Stephen Stanwood for saucy talk to Gen. Lee had his head broke. The General gave him a dollar and sent for the doctor."

What horrifies Lee, Washington, and the other generals with experience is the "leveling spirit" of the New Englanders, their stock in trade for generations. Gentlemen like the commander and Schuyler are aghast. Joseph Reed writes to his wife: "You may form some notion of it when I tell you that yesterday morning a captain of horse, who attends the general from Connecticut, was seen shaving one of his men on the parade near the house." To his brother Lund, Washington writes: "The people of this government [meaning Massachusetts] have obtained a character which they by no means deserved; their officers generally speaking are the most indifferent kind of people I ever saw. . . . I daresay the men would fight very well (if properly officered) although they are exceedingly dirty and nasty people."

But all the other camp discipline problems are overshadowed by the arrival in July of the first backwoods riflemen militia from Virginia and Maryland. These men are magnificent specimens, tall and rugged-looking, dressed in hunting shirts, buckskin leggings, moccasins, and round wool hats. To their fellow soldiers, who regard them with some awe and more suspicion, they're "shirtmen." On their shirts is stenciled "Liberty or Death," but in this there is far more bravado than patriotism. They have only a rudimentary idea of the complex argument between the colonies and the mother country; they only know that the British are threatening them as the Indians are still doing, and they believe their mission is to stalk and kill the invaders.

They're ideal guerrilla fighters and expert marksmen. The contingent of ninety-five men who arrive in camp have made the long march from the backwoods of Virginia in three weeks without losing a man. They carry tomahawks and long knives, but their real weapon is the rifle. When more marksmen volunteered in the recruiting camps than could be accommodated, they shot it out for places when a captain chalked a human nose 150 yards away from a firing line and said he would accept those who came closest. The nose was blown to pieces by the first forty or fifty who qualified and the board itself had disappeared by the time the ranks were filled.

The leader of these first arrivals, Captain Daniel Morgan, is about to become one of the war's truly heroic figures, known from Canada to South Carolina. Nearly illiterate, unable to do simple sums, this backwoods giant is clearly made for soldiering. He grew up a rowdy, rum-drinking young man, frequently involved in fights, who saw his first military service as a wagoner with Braddock. Once a British officer struck him with the flat of his sword, for insubordination, and Morgan knocked him out, after which he was court-martialed and sentenced to 499 lashes, leaving him with a back scarred for life and an abiding hatred of the British. He hates the French and Indians too. During the war, they ambushed him and shot him through his left cheek and neck, again leaving him marked, with a gashed cheek and a left lower jaw without teeth.

By the time he was twenty-three, Morgan had seen more of violent life than most men would in a lifetime. He's celebrated for his ability to hold more liquor than anyone, and ruled as King of the Hill in the little tavern center aptly named Battletown, ten miles east of Winchester, Virginia, where he amused himself by fighting his neighbors. Morgan loves Battletown. When the French and Indian War ended, he chose to take his pension land there, married the daughter of a local farmer, and began to be a little more respectable. Obviously, he's a born leader of men in wartime. In 1771, he was captain of militia in Frederick County, and after Concord, he's been chosen unanimously to be captain of one of the ten companies of riflemen Congress is raising in Pennsylvania, Maryland, and Virginia.

The commander comes to admire and respect Morgan, but there isn't much he or any of the generals can say for the freewheeling backwoodsmen who continue to arrive. They have little if any discipline. Without orders, alone or in pairs, they stalk British sentries at night and take a few shots, doing little damage because they're too far away, and wasting precious powder. By August, Washington has to issue a stern order restraining them, which they accept sullenly. They continue to go where they please, however, and progressively alienate the other troops, who remain skeptical of the mountain men's celebrated marksmanship. Some desert, taking their rifles with them; for a time, scarcely a night passes without at least one desertion. Otherwise, as Benjamin Thompson puts it, "There never was a more mutinous and undisciplined set of villains that bred disturbance in any camp." Insolent and arrogant, they're almost impossible to control.

A hundred or so of them are touring Harvard one day, examining the buildings with some wonder, when they're confronted by a crowd of New England militiamen, mostly from the Marblehead regiment, who begin shouting words of ridicule and derision at them. The riflemen are patient about it, but then a fight begins and soon degenerates into a general pitched battle, the men biting and gouging each other and squaring off in individual fights. Hearing the commotion, friends of both sides come running, and in a few minutes more than a thousand men are involved.

Ten-year-old Israel Trank, who's enlisted that year from Essex County, sees it all, and many years later, testifying to get his pension, he remembers how Washington suddenly appeared on the scene, accompanied only by a black servant, both of them mounted. "With the spring of a deer," Trank recalls, "he leaped from his saddle, threw the reins of his bridle into the hands of the servant, and rushed into the thickest of the melee, with an iron grip seized two tall, brawny athletic, savage-looking riflemen by the throat, keeping them at arm's length, alternately shaking and talking to them. In this position the eyes of the belligerents caught sight of the general. Its effect on them was instantaneous, flight at the top of their speed in all directions from the scene of the conflict. Less than fifteen minutes' time had elapsed from the commencement of the row before the general and his two criminals were the only occupants of the field of action."

The day comes soon enough when the commander is heard to say he wishes they'd never come, that he has no choice but to exert his authority. In late September, the mountain men go too far. They've released their comrades from the guardhouse on more than one occasion, and if they're brought out to be whipped for insubordination, they damn their officers. Mutiny is in the air. When a rifleman is held one day in the Main Guard for some offense, twenty-two of his comrades load their rifles and vow to free him. The commander orders the Guard reinforced to five hundred men, who surround the prison with fixed bayonets, while other units are ordered under arms in case they're needed.

Inevitably, there's a confrontation—Washington, Lee, Greene, and their five hundred men against the twenty-two rebels, who no doubt see the disparity and ground their arms when ordered. Other troops surround them with fixed bayonets and the ringleaders are secured. A unique punishment is devised. The rebel's regiment will be compelled to do what they hate most—fatigue and K.P. duties. They are also tried and convicted of mutiny by a court-martial and fined twenty shillings each, an extraordinarily light punishment.

That doesn't help Washington with the sectional antipathies that divide the camp. He's ashamed that the only full regiment from the South happens to be the rebels, but nevertheless he's criticized for being too partial to Virginians. Massachusetts men accuse him of court-martialing their officers so he can put Virginians in their places. For their part, the Southerners think there are far too many New England officers in the army, especially those from Massachusetts. The militia from Connecticut and New York regard each other with deep suspicion.

Southerners, and even those from the middle colonies, see things they haven't seen before. Alexander Graydon, a militiaman from Pennsylvania, deplores New England's "miserably constituted bands," from which he would have excepted John Glover's Marblehead men until he sees among them "a number of Negroes, which to persons unaccustomed to such associations had a disagreeable, degrading effect." Another militiaman, Jesse Lukens, lumps everyone together in one disdainful package: "Such sermons, such Negroes, such colonels, such boys, and such great-great-grandfathers. Such a cursed set of sharpers cannot be matched."

But when you look at them closely, the men in the Cambridge camp are distressingly like everyone else—that is, human beings, in wide variety. Here, for example, is Amos Farnsworth, a young corporal from Groton, Connecticut, who's serious about the war and about his religion. Wounded twice at Breed's Hill, he writes in his diary: "I did not leave the entrenchment until the enemy got in," and in eight weeks he's back in the army again.

On the other hand, there's David Howe, a seventeen-year-old leather worker from Methuen, who perfectly exemplifies General Nathanael Greene's defense of his countrymen as "exceedingly avaricious; the genius of the people is commercial from their long intercourse with trade." Certainly David Howe is always on the lookout for a profitable deal, even in the Cambridge camp.

Among the colonial aristocracy, whole families are often involved in the war, a kind of *noblesse oblige.* The multifaceted Trumbulls of Connecticut are a good example. Jonathan Trumbull, the patriarch, doesn't serve in the army because he's governor of the colony and will be for fifteen years, including all the war years. His son Joseph will be commissary general of the Continental Army when it's formed. Another son, Jonathan, Jr., will be paymaster general in the Northern Department, and later Washington's military secretary. A third son, John, best known to us as a talented portrait painter, will also be one of Washington's aides before he becomes a brigade major. The sister of all these brothers is Faith Trumbull Huntington, called Faithy in the family, who is married to Colonel Jedidiah Huntington, commander of the 8th Connecticut Regiment, and in 1775, at thirty-two, is the mother of an eight-year-old son.

Faithy, in fact, was a spectator at the Battle of Breed's Hill, drawn by the same curiosity that impelled a good many other citizens to take a little lunch and watch the spectacle from a safe place. Utterly ignorant of war, she expected, along with the young friends who came with her, to see a kind of pageant. Instead, she saw men slaughtered and Charlestown burned to the ground. Realizing for the first time what might happen to her husband and brothers, she fell into a depression so deep that by October she's an invalid. Taken by her mother-in-law to live in Dedham, she appears to be recovering until Thanksgiving Day (that movable feast fell on November 23 in Massachusetts in 1775), when all the Trumbulls hoped to be present with the Huntington in-laws in Dedham for a reunion.

On the morning of the holiday, the men in the army aren't certain they can come, since there's a rumor the British might be attacking Cobble Hill; after all, it isn't *their* holiday. Only Jedidiah arrives to see his wife the next morning, and finding her seemingly much better, he leaves. An hour later she hangs herself in her bedroom, another civilian casualty of the developing war. Huntington's regiment sends four junior officers to attend the funeral. They walk all the way from Roxbury, and it's entirely natural for these New Englanders that they spend the two and a half hours it takes them discussing whether it's worthy of human nature to mourn the dead, which leads them to talk of predestination and free will.

Casualties with less reason keep occurring in the Cambridge camp. The problem is boredom and guns, a dangerous combination. Without an enemy to attack, the men use their muskets to start fires, to shoot at wild geese flying overhead, or simply to empty their muskets. Intermittent firing can be heard day and night. There are numerous accidental firings, with predictable results. "Seldom a day passes but some persons are shot by their friends," the commander writes unhappily.

These men are their own enemies in other ways. Large numbers of them are unfit for duty at any one time because they're sick, the result of poor sanitation. Thousands of men use open latrines, and if these facilities are not immediately available, they "sit down and ease themselves" whenever the urge comes. The uneaten remains of cattle are unburied. In the air is a malodorous blend of smoke from greenwood fires, urine, feces, and animal offal. In this depressing atmosphere, there's the occasional suicide, along with a steady stream of deserters, and a nagging homesickness among men, many of whom have never been more than twenty miles away from their hearths.

One result of this discontent is a persistent, random vandalism. Nothing is safe, private houses and Harvard buildings not excepted. In the struggle to get enough firewood, soldiers demolish fences and cut down trees in a mile-wide swath around Cambridge, and they would move against every house in sight if the legislature hadn't appropriated woodlots belonging to Loyalists. Stealing is still another problem. The men steal from the camp and from each other, and they persist in spite of floggings. One literary soldier even absconds with a copy of Johnson's English Dictionary belonging to a Harvard senior.

For a country supposed to be engaged in a war full of high moral purpose, there's a conspicuous lack of even elementary morality in many of these Cambridge soldiers. Where the British plunder because they hate the "rebels"—a word the soldiers dislike—Americans have no such excuse. Many steal in the hope of making a quick profit by selling the stolen property. If they're afraid of being caught pillaging a house, they simply burn it down when there's nothing more worth stealing. Nor is any shame attached to what they're doing. On the contrary, stealing is a standard joke and some of the spoils are shared. It seems scarcely to matter even when they steal from each other, although it appears some kind of limit is reached when those least sick in hospitals steal from those too ill to defend themselves. Stealing and drinking often lead to fights, occasionally ending in death. A private explains apologetically that he really didn't intend to kill a fellow soldier, it was the company commander he meant to do in.

For those whose morality is on a higher plane, there's the problem of profanity. The commander is against it at this point, but the frustrations of this war will cause even him to explode. With their praying parsons always in attendance, the Connecticut and Massachusetts men fight Satan on linguistic grounds every day. While armies of our time would be struck dumb without four-letter words, these colonials are only mildly blasphemous, as far as we know, but they're free with it. A story is told of how an officer came to a jail where one Eli Showall was languishing for failing to enlist, and drawing his sword, said, "Eli, now God damn your soul, but your life is your own. If you don't enlist, I'll run you through." He then ordered two sergeants to "work the son-of-a-bitch over," after which Eli enlisted.

In this contentious Cambridge, even punishment becomes a matter of controversy. The most common penalty is flogging, borrowed from the British army, where this brutality runs as high as 1,000 lashes. The pious Americans follow Mosaic law at first, with 39 lashes as the maximum, but then they go up to 100. In common with his contemporaries, Washington believes that witnessing the punishment defers crime, so the soldiers are called out to observe the floggings, usually performed by drummer boys or by adjutants. On occasion, the offender is made to run the gauntlet, with a soldier preceding him, bayonet pointed at his chest to keep him from moving too fast. A refinement of the flogging torture is to spread it out over four days, with salt rubbed into the wounds between occasions. Long before the first session ends, a man's back will be "like jelly." To the soldiers, the whipping post is known as "the Adjutant's Daughter."

Whipping, even a hundred lashes, appears to be having little effect, so it's proposed to raise the limit to five hundred. There are some protests, but Washington himself, ordinarily not a bloodthirsty man, approves—a measure of his desperation over the discipline problem. Still, he does his best to curb sadistic officers who beat men for no reason, and in one case even behead a victim.

As the Americans settle in for a siege that autumn of 1775, the commander worries not only about discipline and the shortcomings of his new army, but about his inability to conduct military affairs in secret. British spies wander in and out of camp as they please, observing, counting when troops are assembled for prayers, noting positions.

Since Washington and his generals are unaware of how closely they're being watched, the betrayal by one of their own, Benjamin Church, is all the more shocking. On an evening in late September, Israel Putnam rides up to headquarters on Brattle Street with a young woman. She's been caught trying to deliver a letter in cipher to a British staff officer. Disheveled and defiant, she resists at every turn the interrogation that goes on into the early morning. But at last she breaks down, and what she tells the commander and his staff appalls them. Benjamin Church, Director of Hospitals, trusted member of the Committee of Public Safety, is a spy and, it turns out, has been one since long before the war broke out.

Paul Revere knew as early as November of the previous year that there was a leak somewhere in the spy ring, but neither he nor anyone else suspected Church, although it had to be someone in the network itself since it's been reported anonymously that Gage knows everything that's going on in the ring's meetings. It doesn't matter that American spies inside and outside Boston also know everything the British are doing. The idea that Church has been working both sides of the street is insupportable.

As the captured woman unfolds her story in the early dawn hours, it appears that sex, not ideology, is at the bottom of this mess. She has been Church's mistress, and he's used her as a go-between. A month ago, he sent her down to Bannister's Wharf, in Newport, to see Godfrey Wenwood, proprietor of a bakery and bread shop there (famous for its butter biscuits), and to ask him to arrange a meeting for her with Captain Sir James Wallace, commanding the warship *Rose*, lying in the harbor. If that wasn't possible, then Charles Dudley, the Royal Collector of Customs, would do, or George Rome, a Tory merchant and shipowner.

Wenwood has a connection of his own with the lady. She was his mistress at an earlier time, but since he hadn't taken sides in the conflict, he wanted to know what his former light of love was up to. Someone in Cambridge gave her a letter, she said, to be delivered to any one of the three men she has named, then to be forwarded to one of Gage's officers in Boston. Wenwood took the letter but didn't open it. Finally he decided to tell his friend Adam Maxwell, the schoolmaster, about it. Maxwell, a firm Whig, read it, but he and Wenwood decided to put it away.

Now Church provided the rope that will hang him in this tale of clumsy espionage. Realizing that the letter had not been delivered, he told his mistress to find out what was happening, and she in turn wrote to Wenwood. With a premonition that something must have gone terribly wrong, Church was already trying to resign. He was entirely correct. When Wenwood got the lady's inquiry, he realized, belatedly, that if she knew the letter hadn't been delivered, she must somehow be in touch with the British. Talking it over with Maxwell, he decided to take the matter to Henry Ward, secretary of Rhode Island and a committed Whig.

More sophisticated, Ward saw through this awkward piece of business at once. He told Wenwood to take the letter to the Cambridge camp, which he did, carrying with him another letter, from Ward to General Greene, summarizing the story. Greene needed only one look. He took Wenwood and the cipher to Washington, who sent the maker of butter biscuits to find the girl. He had no luck, an order went out for her arrest, and it's Putnam who finally takes custody of her and brings her in.

What a shock as her story circulates. Church is supposed to be an American spy, along with his official duties, and certainly he's been a Whig pillar. Moreover, he is (unthinkable!) a Harvard man. Taken to headquarters, he tries to brazen it out at first, admitting the letter is his but declaring he doesn't know why it's in cipher. He scores a telling point by reminding his interrogators that General Lee has been in constant touch by letter with his old friend, Burgoyne.

A score point indeed. Lee had served in the British army with Burgoyne and, before he came up to Cambridge, was already corresponding with his old friend. Since Burgoyne's arrival in Boston, Lee has continued the exchange under flags of truce. There's nothing seditious in his letters. He has no kind words for George III, and advises both Burgoyne and Howe to stop inflicting themselves on the colonies. Seeking a wider audience for his views, and careless as usual, he has his first letter published before Burgoyne has had a chance to read it. He wants a reunion between the lines with his old comrade, but Congress puts its foot down.

Church is no Lee when it comes to letter writing. He's made a mistake by putting his information in code, which is easily deciphered while he's being held in prison. True, personal letters are often in cipher because it's so easy for seals to be broken in those days; the commander himself played dangerously with this fact when he wrote ill-concealed love letters to Sally Fairfax in his youth while he was engaged to Martha. But if Church is truly innocent, as he keeps insisting, he would give the key to his inquisitors. Deciphering convicts him as a spy. Washington orders all his paper seized, but ironically, another British spy, who is following the case closely, has removed anything that might be incriminating before the colonials get there.

In Massachusetts there's no law to punish spying, but that doesn't prevent the authorities from sending Church to prison in Connecticut anyway. They leave him in Norwich Jail, his windows boarded up, with no writing materials, forbidden to talk with anyone alone. When he's finally given pen and ink, he appeals to Congress, declaring the jail is giving him asthma and he might die. Congress orders him taken to another jail, but the military authorities do nothing about it and he has to petition Congress again. He will be freed, Congress replies, if he posts a £1,000 bond and agrees not to correspond with the British. He must also stay in Massachusetts.

Church is willing, but his jailers are afraid to let him go because the patriots have promised to hang him if they do. They've already tried to break into the jail. After another year, Howe offers to exchange a captured American surgeon for him, but a mob of liberty-loving patriots threaten such violence when he's already aboard the vessel sent for him that he has to be spirited back to jail in Boston, now in American hands.

Thwarted and unsatisfied, the mob invades his house, robs it of everything movable, and destroys the rest, leaving his wife and children destitute. Church finally finds the money and the means to escape to England, but before he can sail, Congress in 1780 exiles him to a small island in the West Indies, and advises him that he will be killed if he ever tries to return. Nemesis pursues Church to the end. En route to exile, the small schooner carrying him is lost in a storm at sea.

Church's removal from the scene in September 1775 causes scarcely a ripple in besieged Boston, where the British have a number of other things to think about. This occupied city is suffering. In late summer, its population dropped to less than seven thousand from seventeen thousand. Food and fuel are in short supply. The Americans keep up an intermittent bombardment, and that means fires. As far as the citizens are concerned, the occupying troops are as much enemies as the forces in Cambridge, since they make few distinctions between Loyalists and Whigs.

Writing to a friend in Philadelphia, John Andrews describes the realities of daily life: "We have now and then a carcass offered for sale on the market, which formerly we would not have picked up in the street; but bad as it is, it readily sells for eight pence lawful money per lb., and a quarter of lamb when it makes its appearance, which is rarely once a week, sells for a dollar. Wood not scarcely to be got at twenty-two shillings a cord. Was it not for a trifle of sale provisions that we have, 'twould be impossible for us to live. Pork and beans one day, and beans and pork another, and fish when we can catch it. . . ."

Abigail Adams, writing to John, declares, "The present state of the inhabitants of Boston is that of the most abject slaves, under the most cruel and despotic of tyrants. . . . Upon the fifth of June, printed handbills were posted up at the corners of the streets and upon houses, forbidding any inhabitants to go upon their houses, or upon any eminence, on pain of death; the inhabitants dared not to look out of their houses, nor to be heard or seen to ask a question. Our prisoners were brought over on the Long Wharf, and there lay all night, without any care of their wounds or any resting place but the pavements, until the next day, when they exchanged it for the jail, since which we hear they have been civilly treated.

"Their [meaning the British] living cannot be good, as they can have no fresh provisions; their beef, we hear, is all gone, and their own wounded men die very fast, so that they have a report that the bullets were poisoned. Fish they cannot have, they have rendered it so difficult to procure, and the admiral is such a villain as to oblige every fishing schooner to pay a dollar every time it goes out. The money that has been paid for passes is incredible. Some have been given ten, twenty, thirty and forty dollars, to get out with a small proportion of their things. . . ."

That was the situation in summer. By November, the British are equally disenchanted with their unwilling hosts. A British officer writes home: "The workmen at Boston were so mulish that the general was obliged to send to Nova Scotia for carpenters and bricklayers to fit up barracks for our accommodation. The inhabitants of this province retain the religious and civil principles brought over by their forefathers, in the reign of King Charles I, and are at least a hundred years behind hand with the people of England in every refinement. They are destitute of every principle of religion or common honesty, and are reckoned the most arrant cheats and hypocrites on the whole continent of America. The women are very handsome, but, like old mother Eve, very frail. Our camp has been as well supplied in that way since we have been on Boston Common, as if our tents were pitched on Blackheath. They [the militia] are numerous, they are but a mob without order or discipline, and very awkward at handling their arms."

On both sides of the lines, the troops are bored and frustrated with this relatively uneventful siege. The officers entertain themselves with amateur dramatics and, to the horror of the natives, make a riding academy out of the Old South Church. The other ranks have no such pleasures. Like the men in Cambridge, they struggle against disease, and the constant hunt for fuel and food. They, too, tear down houses, barns, fences, even the Old North Church steeple, to get fuel. Harvesting the trees, they take particular pleasure in cutting down the Liberty Elm. Always they're waiting for supply ships to arrive from England, bringing oxen, sheep, beer, oats, hay, flour, and other goods.

But crossing the Atlantic is an uncertain business, and storms scatter or sink many ships, while American privateers pick off others.

At any moment, there is the possibility that the Americans may attack and, informed by spies of what's going on in the enemy camp, the colonials take advantage of their uncertainty. One night the British officers are enjoying a farce, *The Blockade of Boston,* written by Burgoyne himself, when an orderly sergeant, standing on watch outside the playhouse and hearing shots from the direction of Charlestown, rushes onto the stage as the play is just beginning, and shouts, "Turn out! Turn out! They are hard at it, hammer and tongs!" The audience thinks he's part of the play and give him a generous round of applause. When he can be heard again, he cries out, "What the deuce are you all about? If you won't believe me, by Jesus, you need only to go to the door, and there you will see and hear both!" At that, the officers rush out to join their regiments and the evening's entertainment ends.

The Americans have timed their own act perfectly, arriving at a mill dam still standing in Charlestown at the hour they know the play is beginning. They fire off several volleys to alarm the British, capture the guard at the mill, and go home. The satisfying result in Boston is a general alarm, with all the troops turning out under arms.

Before the year is over, many of the occupiers become utterly disillusioned about where they are and what they're doing. A disgusted officer writes home: "Boston, the metropolis of North America, may very justly be termed the grave of England and the slaughter house of America. Nothing is to be heard in it but execrations and clamor; nothing is to be seen but distractions and melancholy, disease and death. The soldiery, and inhabitants likewise, I am sure, have done sufficient penance here for the sins of their whole lives. The latter are all ruined; many that were worth sixteen or twenty thousand pounds have not a sixpence left; and if any one of them in the anguish of his heart, or the bitterness of his soul, dares mutter anything like resentment for the loss of his fortune, a distressed family or a murdered friend, he is immediately thrown into a loathsome prison. If we hear a gun fired upon the Neck, we are all under arms in a moment, and tremble lest the Provincials should force their way into the town and put us all to the sword for our cruelty at Lexington and setting fire to the large, ancient and flourishing town of Charlestown. Certainly our conduct in both cases was alike inhuman and unjustifiable; and if heaven punishes us for it, it is no more than we deserve.

"Could you view our hospitals and see how fast we drop off, your very heart would bleed within. Thirty bodies are frequently thrown into a trench at a time, like those of so many dogs, no bell being suffered to toll upon the occasion. But the glorious expedition we are upon is approved of by an all-wise, all-merciful ministry; and therefore all must be right. 'Tis well for our generals that we have nowhere to run to; for could the men desert, I am of opinion that they would be left by themselves but situated as we are, we must unavoidably live and die together."

In Cambridge, the commander tries to avert such despair by keeping his men constructively occupied. If there's one thing these provincials know how to do, it's build or repair. They construct revetments, build more shelters, repair bridges, and lay out works facing Boston Neck. The problem, however, is manpower. Spring militia enlistments begin to run out in the fall, and while the *rage militaire* still flourishes, it's beginning to fade. Obviously, a Continental Army is needed, and indeed Congress authorized one in May, with officers to be appointed, not elected, correcting a major militia defect, but recruiting is slow. On paper, at least, these twenty thousand authorized Continentals are going to be the best-paid army in the world, but as autumn deepens toward winter, only half that number can be found. They have to bring their own muskets, and since there are only two hundred or so gunsmiths in the colonies, many of them Loyalists, that creates still another, even more desperate shortage.

As in all wars, both sides fear signs of fraternization, when men engaged to kill each other learn inadvertently that those on the other side are people like themselves, not monsters. Thus, as Governor Nicholas Cooke, of Rhode Island, reports, two or three of Putnam's officers are down examining the works thrown up by the Americans when they see two or three officers from the British camp on Bunker Hill approaching. Each side edges cautiously toward the other, until they're near enough to talk. "Then," says Cooke, "they laid down their swords and walked up together. The gentlemen that were officers in the regular army seemed to lament much of the unhappy contest and asked the other if there was no way that could be hit upon to settle matters, and asked if the Congress was not sitting and if they would not find out some means for a cessation of hostilities. They made no doubt, if taxation was all we were contending for, it would be given up."

This is no isolated exchange. Lieutenant Jabez Fitch, who has carried four successive truce flags, tells of British officers who pass along news from Boston civilians to relatives on the other side, and Fitch performs the same service for Loyalists. At the meeting to which Cooke refers, Fitch even proposes, half-seriously, that it might be a good idea to build a coffeehouse midway between the lines, "upon which," he says, "we held a considerable banter with good humor on both sides, and we finally parted with great appearance of friendship."

Gage would never approve of such exchanges, but he's gone home, happily recalled in October, leaving Howe in charge, a man who also doesn't see much sense in this war. And at this juncture it *is* a desultory affair. As one civilian writes, "Both armies kept squibbling at each other, but to little purpose. At one time a horse would be knocked in the head, and at another time a man would be killed or lose a leg or an arm. At some times, a shell would play in the air like a skyrocket, and then burst without damage; and now and then, another would fall in the town, and there burst, to the terror or breaking of a few panes of glass. . . ."

Getting those shells and the guns to fire them is a continuing problem for the Cambridge camp, but there's a real windfall in November when privateers capture a royal ordnance brig, the *Nancy*, loaded with 2,000 muskets, 100,000 flints, more than 30 tons of musket shot, 30,000 round shot, 11 mortar beds, and a brass mortar. When this treasure arrives in Cambridge, Putnam climbs up on the mortar, holding a tankard of rum in his hand, and while the troops roar their approval, christens it "Congress."

But more firepower is desperately needed for the siege, and in November, the commander sends his new chief of artillery, Henry Knox, up to Ticonderoga to get the armaments stored there. This is the same rotund Boston bookseller who did his best to stop the killing on King Street. At twenty-five, Knox scarcely looks like a military man. He's one of the old Green Dragon gang, married to Lucy Flucker, daughter of a well-known Tory, and his early bookselling revenues came from the pockets of British officials and officers, who frequented his shop to buy not only books but shoes, drygoods, utensils, linens, and other useful items. One of the attractions for the visiting officers had been his stock of books on artillery and the arts of war, a subject that interested young Knox intensely, and on which he became an expert. After the commander discovers how much he knows, Knox's rise is rapid.

His recovery of the fifty-odd pieces of heavy ordnance from Ticonderoga is an epic tale of sheer persistence against impossible odds. These big guns have to be dismounted, then floated down Lake George on scows and other boats, transferred to sleds, and dragged nearly three hundred miles across the Berkshire Mountains, crossing the Hudson four different times. It takes forty-two sleds and eighty yoke of oxen to get them as far as Springfield, where fresh animals are available to take them the remainder of the way. In the deep snow and bitter cold of a New England winter, it also takes extraordinary courage on the part of Knox and his men, who pull and haul with the ox teams.

In spite of this remarkable December accomplishment, it's a bleak month. There's some solace for the commander with the arrival of his wife, who comes up from Williamsburg (she's never been outside Virginia) with her son, Jack Custis, and his wife, Nelly, General Horatio Gates's wife, and George Lewis. Seeing them off as they pass through Philadelphia, Joseph Reed remarks, "Not a bad supply, I think, in a country where wood is scarce."

Martha's arrival injects new vigor into what there is of social life in camp. John Adams, who comes calling a little later, is quite impressed. In his diary, he writes: "Dined at C[olonel] Mifflin's, at Cambridge, with G. Washington and Gates and their ladies, and half a dozen sachems and warriors of the French Caughnawaga tribe, with their wives and children. . . . There is a mixture of white blood, French or English, in most of them. . . . It was a savage feast, carnivorous animals devouring their prey; yet they were wondrous polite. The general introduced me to them as one of the Grand Council Fire at Philadelphia, upon which they made me many bows and a cordial reception."

Lee gets a more mixed notice from his guests at Hobgoblin Hall. After dinner there, Jeremy Belknap, a historian and minister (a Harvard University Press imprint is named for him) writes: "General Lee is a perfect original, a good scholar and soldier; and an odd genius, full of fire and passion and but little good manners; a great sloven, wretchedly profane, and a great admirer of dogs, of which he had two at dinner with him, one of them a native of Pomerania, which I should have taken for a bear had I seen him in the woods."

The commander isn't enjoying his new social life, however. Enlistments of all the Connecticut and Rhode Island troops expire on December 10, and by the end of the month, all the other New England enlistments are due to run out. Worse, some Connecticut militia believe their enlistments end on December 1, and they prepare to leave. Washington sends out a hurried call for five thousand militia, meanwhile trying to prevail upon the Connecticut troops to stay until help comes. When the regiment is drawn up, those who refuse to stay four extra days are told to step out, and nearly three-quarters of them do. Lee is nearly incoherent with rage. "Men," he says, "I don't know what to call you, you are the worst of all creatures." He follows this with a burst of creative profanity, and threatens to send them against the British encampment on Bunker Hill; if they refuse, he says, the riflemen will be ordered to fire on them, an assignment they would no doubt relish. Other officers take a more moderate tone and beg them to stay; reluctantly they agree to four more days. As a reward, they're given a dram of rum and promised another next morning. After they're dismissed, Lee notices one man trying to persuade others to leave with him. Stepping forward quickly, Lee seizes the recalcitrant's gun and strikes him on the head with it, then puts him under guard.

When all the Connecticut militia finally leave, they depart under a barrage of hisses, groans, and a few objects thrown at them. It's not much better when they reach home. Their old friends and neighbors are happy to see them, but think they should reenlist. Public pressure drives some of them to do so.

Things improve briefly as fresh militiamen respond to the commander's call. But enlistments for the new Continental Army are going slowly, and militia reenlistments are slower still, although Massachusetts sends five thousand fresh troops and New Hampshire two thousand more. "Our situation is desperate," Washington informed Congress as early as November, the first of many letters that begin the same way, as recruiting for the army looks to be perennially inadequate, and the gaps have to be filled with militia, whom the commander doesn't trust.

A rich man himself, although he frequently cries poverty, Washington doesn't understand what a tremendous sacrifice enlisting means to citizens. For many, the farms that represent their livelihood will be left untended, except for what wives and children can do. The same can be said for other occupations. Enlistees face extreme hardship and uncertain pay in the army, so it's all the more surprising that their diaries and letters often exhibit feelings of loyalty, and a purpose more religious than merely patriotic.

On Christmas Eve there's a heavy snowfall, followed by a day of bright sunshine. Both sides cease fire for the holidays, while officers call on each other according to custom, and the soldiers make do with whatever cheer they can. Some of them wade through the snow to country farmhouses, where they can buy fruit and fowl for their dinners.

On New Year's Day, a new flag is raised over the Cambridge camp, "in compliment to the United Colonies." It has thirteen red and white stripes, with British colors in the center. Observing it, the redcoats think it must be some kind of surrender flag.

Not surrender, of course, but it appears on a day of extreme peril as Washington literally exchanges one army for another, the old regiments leaving for home by the thousands, their enlistments run out, and new regiments arriving. You can "search the vast volumes of history through," the commander writes, almost with disbelief, "and I much question whether a case similar to ours is to be found; to wit, to maintain a post against the flower of the British troops for six months together, without powder, and at the end of them to have one army disbanded and another to raise within the same distance of reinforced enemy." If anyone but Howe had been in command on the other side, this vast confusion could well have ended in complete disaster.

On the first day of 1776, the news from Canada has not yet reached Cambridge, and just as well. An army with inadequate manpower, no powder to speak of, little ammunition, and without an adequate supply of guns might lose what confidence they possess when they hear this tale of heroic folly.

6

✢   ✢   ✢

Two Roads to Quebec

Why would any commander in his right mind contemplate invading Canada when he can barely maintain a siege against Boston? Ignorance on the one hand, and illusion on the other. Since few Americans, with the exception of veterans of the French and Indian War, have ever seen Canada, they have no idea of the extreme difficulties an invasion involves. But popular sentiment, faithfully reflected in Congress, simply advocates making Canada a fourteenth colony, thus unifying the continent and preventing further attacks from the north on the lower thirteen. This curious delusion will persist long after the Revolution. Annexing Canada will become a motivating factor in that bizarre conflict we call the War of 1812, and some Canadians today believe the idea isn't dead.

As early as June 1775, Arnold submits to Congress plans for an invasion of Canada, and as usual, he's ignored, although his blueprint becomes the basic plan. Speed is essential, he tells them, and that's ignored too. It's nearly the end of August, much too late in the season, before an expedition finally gets in motion. The man selected to lead it is also the wrong choice. General Philip Schuyler, that tall, dark-eyed aristocrat, has many good qualities but he's not a natural military leader. He's always too courteous and tolerant when aggressive action would serve him better. Chronic ill health also makes him moody and indecisive. Fortunately for the expedition, his health problems catch up with him soon after the expedition pushes off for Montreal on August 28, and he has to return to Albany.

That leaves the command in the hands of one of the war's authentic heroes, Brigadier General Richard Montgomery, whom a fellow officer describes as "well-limbed, of genteel, easy, graceful, manly address. He had the voluntary esteem of the whole army." Only forty, two years younger than Schuyler, he's strong, vigorous, a born leader.

Montgomery has a few well-nourished prejudices. As the son of an Irish M.P., educated at Trinity College in Dublin, he has a low opinion of New Englanders, who are too recently British to suit him. As a lieutenant under Lord Jeffrey Amherst in the battles at Ticonderoga, Crown Point, and Montreal, in the French and Indian War, he somehow also acquired a dislike of New Yorkers, and now, retracing the route he followed in the earlier war, he encounters a large detachment of these forces when he gathers his army at Ticonderoga.

These New York regiments, with which General David Wooster's Connecticut troops are intermixed, present a disappointing spectacle. It's not entirely their fault. After a long trip up the Hudson, many of them are ill, and some have already deserted. For soldiers intending to invade the North Country, they're hopelessly ill equipped—without tents, many missing shoes, stockings, and underwear. Supplies are so short that one detachment has to be kept on board the boat until help comes. There's already bad blood between the New Yorkers and the pious Connecticut men, as we've seen before. The latter have come as usual with their praying chaplains and officers, and they consider their neighbors a wicked, blasphemous lot. As one of them puts it, "I don't see how any of us can expect the blessing of God when His holy name is so often profaned."

Setting off from Ticonderoga for Montreal, Montgomery pushes up Lake Champlain and lays siege to St. John, which Arnold had successfully raided and Ethan Allen's Green Mountain Boys had unsuccessfully tried to occupy. Allen himself is with this new expedition, not much subdued but not involved in any battle for command, although he still feels himself a free man.

At first, the siege does not go well. For one thing, the Americans are dealing now with a general who knows what he's doing, Sir Guy Carleton, a British officer who comes from an old Irish family. This extraordinary soldier and statesman has made one serious mistake in 1775 by sending many of his Canadian regulars to Boston in the belief they would fight for the Crown as they have for Canada. That leaves him with only eight hundred regulars, plus Indian allies, to hold the country.

The provincials lying outside St. John are rapidly losing what little enthusiasm they came with, trying to exist in a forest heavy with early-fall rain. One writes, "We have been like half-drowned rats crawling through a swamp." Nearly half of them, more than six hundred men, fall sick in a week. Montgomery feels the rising tension keenly. "The privates are all generals," he says of the constantly grumbling New Englanders, and the New Yorkers are "the sweepings of the York streets."

Montgomery's state of mind can be judged by the letter he writes his wife Janet; they've been married less than two years and are deeply in love. "I must entreat the favor of you," he pleads irritably, "to write no more of those whining letters. I declare, if I receive another in that style, I will lock up the rest without reading them. I don't want anything to lower my spirits. I have abundant use for them all, and at the best of times I have not too much."

Eventually, Montgomery is able to establish a battery of guns on a hill overlooking the fort, and Carleton slips away to Montreal, leaving the fort to give itself up. Among the prisoners is a young officer named John André, of whom much more will be heard later. Now the march toward Montreal can be resumed, and Montgomery decides to send Ethan Allen on ahead with Major John Brown and a small force to enlist Canadians who might favor the American cause. Naturally, Allen has grander plans of his own. He means to forge ahead and capture Montreal himself, with whatever forces he can muster. No one else could have plotted his own downfall better.

According to Allen's narrative, written years later, he and Brown planned to meet at a rendezvous point, but the major fails to appear. Instead, the intrepid Vermonter encounters a larger party of British regulars and Indians. There's no alternative but to surrender his sword to an officer. As soon as he lets it go, he's attacked by one of the Indians and has to use the officer as a shield until a one-eyed Canadian and an officer with fixed bayonet rescue him.

He and his captured men are marched two miles to Montreal, where Allen is confronted by the garrison commander, General Richard Prescott, who asks if he's the man who took Ticonderoga. Assured that this is the case, Prescott, as Allen writes, "shook his cane over my head, calling me many hard names, and put himself in a great rage." With his usual temerity, Allen advises Prescott not to use the cane, and a captain whispers to the general that this isn't what one does with prisoners.

Frustrated, Prescott orders a squad to kill thirteen Canadians who had been fighting with Allen. Ethan stands in front of his comrades and, as he writes, "opened my clothes, and told General Prescott to thrust his bayonet into my breast, for I was the sole cause of the Canadians' taking up arms." The general hesitates, then says, "I will not execute you now, but you shall grace a halter at Tyburn, God damn you!"

Allen is thrown into the guardhouse, and further secured by thirty pounds of leg irons in addition to handcuffs, with an eight-foot-long bar. Plainly, he's a dangerous man, not to mention extraordinary. After the war, his friend Alexander Graydon writes of him: "I have seldom met with a man possessing, in my opinion, a stronger mind, or whose mode of expression was more vehement and oratorical. His style was a singular compound of local barbarisms, Scriptural phrases, and oriental wildness; and though unclassic and sometimes ungrammatical, it was highly animated and forcible." Ethan has an opportunity to exhibit all these facets of his remarkable character in the next two years, an odyssey related in a later chapter.

Meanwhile, Montgomery and his men are slogging toward Montreal. The sheer misery of this march is recorded by Benjamin Trumbull, the 1st Connecticut's chaplain, in his diary for November 11: "I marched the whole of the day in mud and water sometimes middling and in general over shoes, carried a small pack, a case of pistols by my side, with my gun, cartouche box, etc. The whole day was stormy; it rained and snowed till about sunset, when the snow and rain ceased and the wind blew up raw and cold at northwest. Under our feet was snow and ice and water, over our heads clouds, snow and rain; before us the mountains appeared all white with snow and ice. It was remarkable to see the Americans after almost infinite fatigues and hardships marching on at this advanced season, badly clothed and badly provided for, to Montreal. . . ."

Two days later, these hardy souls march into their goal. It isn't necessary to capitulate, the inhabitants say, since they have no way of defending themselves. The general had promised to protect them and prevent plundering, which is somewhat after the fact since Carleton destroyed everything that might be useful before he departed for Quebec with the garrison's eighty men.

While Montgomery has been making his way through the Canadian wilderness, a new actor has appeared in this Northern drama. Rather, the same old actor looking for a new role. During the autumn, Arnold stopped sulking in Providence and New Haven, and came up to Cambridge, anxious for another try at glory. He meets with the commander, and it's clear they approve of each other. Arnold sees the fine patrician gentleman he aspires to be, and Washington sees a man who, in spite of his embarrassing past, is clearly a brave and energetic leader of men who can be useful in these critical days. Consequently he gives Arnold a task that turns out to be impossible—advance on Quebec through northern New England and eastern Canada, rendezvous with Montgomery at Quebec, and take the city.

It's just the kind of assignment Arnold is looking for, one that will test him to the limit and, if successful, will compel Congress and his other enemies to recognize his military genius. It's also the kind of expedition that appeals to adventurous militiamen who are as ignorant of its perils as Arnold. When volunteers are called for at Cambridge, two battalions are enlisted immediately, including three companies of riflemen and their indispensable Captain Daniel Morgan. Arnold is in command, and under him are Lieutenant Colonel Roger Enos, who has seen service in the British army, and Lieutenant Colonel Christopher Greene, whose father is a justice in the Rhode Island Supreme Court. Almost unnoticed in this assemblage of talent is nineteen-year-old Aaron Burr, son of Princeton's president. There are, all told, 1,050 prepared for the march to Quebec.

This is a campaign like no other in the Revolution, so incredible in its display of courage and endurance that its failure is doubly hard to take. At first it's a saga of man against the wilderness. Arnold proposes to ascend the Kennebec River in Maine, carrying 400-pound green pine bateaux around a succession of falls. First come the Titonic Falls, then the Five-Mile Falls and its gorge at Skowhegan. By the time this passage is completed, exhausted men are falling to the ground, their clothes frozen to their sweaty bodies. At Norridgewock Falls, where the river drops ninety feet in a mile, with an abundance of white water above it, the boats emerge battered and leaking, earning the curses of soldiers on the workmen who made them. Water seeping in has ruined much of the salt fish, salt pork, salt beef, dried peas, and biscuit the army relies on.

Worse is to come. After Carritunk Falls comes the aptly named Great Carrying Place, requiring four portages of eight miles through muddy trails and under weeping skies, which keep progressively raising the level of the river. Supplies are now extremely short, and more are lost when the flooding river overturns some of the boats.

It's now the twenty-third of October and Arnold stops long enough to hold a council of war. His half-starved army is still willing to go on, but there are defections among the officers. Colonel Enos, in particular, has had enough. He turns his men around and heads back down the river toward home, leaving behind the contempt of their fellows. Henry Dearborn, who will become Jefferson's Secretary of War, writes: "Our men made a general prayer that Col. Enos and all the men might die by the way, or meet with some disaster, equal to the cowardly, dastardly, and unfriendly spirit they discovered in returning back without orders, in such a manner as they had done."

Instead, Enos gets away with it. When he reaches Cambridge, an indignant Washington puts him under arrest and has him court-martialed, but the court acquits him, saying the evidence is not convincing.

At this point, Arnold is left with only seven hundred of the faithful. Dr. Isaac Senter records their misery in his journal: "Our greatest luxuries now consisted in a little water, stiffened with flour, in imitation of shoemakers' paste, which was christened with the name of Lilliput. Instead of the diarrhea, which tried our men most shockingly in the former part of our march, the reverse was now the complaint, which continued for many days. We had now arrived, as we thought, to almost the zenith of distress. Several had been entirely destitute of either meat or bread for many days. The voracious disposition many of us had now arrived at rendered almost anything admissible. Clean and unclean were forms now little in use. In our company was a poor dog who had hitherto lived through all the tribulations, became a prey for the sustenance of the assassinators. This poor animal was instantly devoured, without leaving any vestige of the sacrifice. Nor did the shaving soap, pomatum, and even the lip salve, leather of their shoes, cartridge boxes, etc., share any better fate."

Walking and rowing, whatever they are able to do, the little army crosses that spine of the Appalachians called the Height of Land and pushes on through interconnecting ponds until they reach Lake Megantic. Using British ordnance maps which prove to be faulty, they lose their way at one point and nearly succumb to cold and exhaustion. But at last they're in Canada, on the Chaudière River, where there is so much water they have to abandon most of their boats. By this time, men who fall exhausted simply lie there, since none of the others has strength enough to pick them up. It's all they can do to climb over fallen trees or claw their way up hills, like a column of half-paralyzed ants.

Arnold can see his entire force vanishing before his eyes, and in desperation he races on ahead with a few of the ablest men to find a Canadian settlement and get help. Almost drowning along the way, he reaches a village at last and assures the Canadians he means them no harm. When curious Indians from the forest gather around, he convinces them, too, of his peaceful intentions. These hospitable people send him back with all kinds of provisions, including pieces of bullock which the men fall upon and eat raw. Food is carried back along the trail to find and revive those who have fallen on the way, some of them lying unconscious in the snow. It's the end of a march never since equaled in American military history.

Yet not the end, because now the real business of the expedition lies just ahead, the ramparts of Quebec. On November 8, they reach Point Levis, and there the Lower Town lies, just across the river. Quebec's garrison contains only a few militia and a small force of Marines and regulars, but on the calm waters of the St. Lawrence just below the walls lie the *Hunter*, a sloop of war, and the *Lizard*, a frigate. Clearly, taking the city will not be easy in spite of its otherwise weak defenses. Arnold decides it will be best to cross over at night, and he musters some canoes and dugouts for the move.

But now Arnold's bad luck, the successive misfortunes that ruin his life, catches up with him again. First, a strong wind rises and blows so hard for two days that he has to postpone the crossing. Then he writes a letter to Montgomery, who is presumably closing in on Quebec from the west, entrusting this communication to an Indian who unfortunately encounters a Highland officer, Allan MacLean, making his way with 200 men toward Quebec. Not knowing one white officer from another, apparently, the Indian courier hands MacLean the letter, which he reads with great interest. While Arnold is still waiting for the wind to die down, MacLean hurries up to reinforce Quebec.

When it's calm again, Arnold makes his crossing at night, landing

500 of his 650 survivors on the very spot where General Wolfe, already dying, came ashore to scale the Heights of Abraham at the climax of the French and Indian War. He has to leave 150 others behind temporarily because the moon comes out, ending any hope of secrecy.

With more courage than good sense, under the circumstances, Arnold leads his little army up the steep slopes to the Plains of Abraham and to the very walls of the city, where he dares MacLean to come out and fight. MacLean is having none of such rashness. Under a white flag of truce, Arnold sends a messenger to demand that the city surrender, but the messenger's progress is halted by a fusillade of shots, to which the Americans don't dare respond because they have little more than five rounds of ammunition each. Moreover, it's learned that Carleton is nearby with reinforcements, so it seems sensible to retreat to Pointe aux Trembles and wait for Montgomery.

But that beau ideal of generals is having his own troubles. He's suffering from the plague of the Cambridge camp—enlistments running out and militia only too eager to leave before their lives are threatened any further, and before winter makes escape virtually impossible. Montgomery tries bribery, but not even money will make them stay. His force is down to only 800 men as he sails down the St. Lawrence toward Quebec with an advance guard of 300, a supply of food and other stores, and best of all, some warm clothing gathered up at St. John and Montreal.

Arriving before Quebec on December 3, he and his goods, especially the clothing, are enthusiastically welcomed by Arnold and his men, who view with dismay the early arrival of the bitter Canadian winter. The two leaders hit it off perfectly. Montgomery says the only way to capture Quebec is to storm it, taking the words right out of Arnold's mouth.

Siege is laid, since Carleton, who's arrived meanwhile and taken command, absolutely refuses to negotiate. But if he's the chief enemy, weather is his strong ally. In Quebec, snow piles up as high as the second stories of houses, and the ground is so hard that the besiegers have to construct their entrenchments out of ice and snow. As December wears on, smallpox breaks out and the food begins to vanish once more. Arnold's men are a little better off in the subzero temperatures since they've seized a monastery, a nunnery, and some suburban houses for quarters.

Montgomery writes home to Janet: "I wish it were well over, with all my heart, and sigh for home like a New Englander." He tells her that as soon as this campaign is over, he'll resign his commission and in the future will serve only if the country is in real peril. It will have to be in a "much worse" situation than it is now, he adds. It's the last letter Janet will ever get from him.

The climax comes suddenly. Arnold and Montgomery have agreed to storm Quebec on the first night of heavy snow, and when they stir up the troops on Christmas night with a call to the colors, they're rewarded with cheers from men who are glad to get it over with at last.

On the last day of the year, the strategic snowstorm arrives, the wind-driven downfall piling up drifts, with a little hail mixed in. It's to be a surprise attack, but in this Revolution of virtually no such surprises, deserters betray the secret so that just before five in the morning, as the men start creeping toward the walls, rockets go up to signal an attack, and as one spectator writes later, "The bells were all set on ringing, cannons playing, bombs flying, small arms constantly going, drums beating." There are two palisades to breach, and an advance unit of carpenters works hard to clear the way.

Montgomery's part of the attack is brief and tragic. At the head of his column, he leads fifty or sixty men past the second palisade and toward a house directly in front of him. He doesn't know that inside it are four cannon and a contingent of sailors and Canadians. There's a sudden explosion of fire from the house, less than forty feet away, sweeping into oblivion Montgomery and twelve other officers. Instant panic. Aaron Burr tries to rally the troops, but they run for their lives, leaving Arnold and his men to face the enemy alone. Later, the Canadians find Montgomery's body in a snowdrift, one hand raised, frozen in a grotesque gesture of protest at this ruin of all his plans and hopes.

For Arnold, it's even worse, except that he himself escapes death. He's led six hundred men around the city's northern wall into the Lower Town, hoping to enter the city from that direction. They get as far as the Hôtel Dieu before they're discovered, and by then Arnold finds that he's boxed in on a narrow street, facing cannon at the end of it, and continuous volleys of muskets from the windows of houses.

With his customary contempt for odds on the battlefield, he leads the charge, shouting encouragement, but a bullet strikes him in the leg and he falls. Two men help him get up, and he tries to stumble onward, but the pain is too great. He's carried back to the hospital at St. Roche, where he's soon told that the enemy is nearing the place. The doctor attending him, and the aides who've accompanied him, plead with Arnold to let them move him back into the country but, as the doctor reports later, "He would neither be removed, nor suffer a man from the hospital to retreat. He ordered his pistols loaded, with a sword on his bed, etc., adding that he was determined to kill as many as possible if they came into the room. We were now all soldiers, even the wounded in their beds were ordered a gun by their side."

Back in the Lower Town, Morgan is in command. Private George Morrison, who's with him, recalls later: "We are now attacked by thrice our number. Betwixt every peal the awful voice of Morgan is heard, whose gigantic stature and terrible appearance carries dismay among the foe wherever he comes. . . ."

But it's a lost cause. Morgan and his men storm through one barrier, the leader emerging with a bruised knee and powder burns on his face, but then a second barricade faces them. There's a council of war, and Morgan says, not knowing the general is dead, that his orders are to wait for Montgomery. His officers advise advancing no farther, and that's the wrong decision, one that Arnold would never have made. He would have taken the entire Lower Town, which was possible at that point, and the barrier could have been bypassed.

Carleton sees his opportunity. He places troops on the barrier and sends them into houses on the street until the Americans are at the center of a ring of fire. Morgan's command fights with raw courage for nearly three hours, firing at the windows, storming the barrier, at last trying to retreat, but they're surrounded. Wherever the action flows, there's Morgan, exhorting the men, leading charge after charge, until by early morning the exhausted Americans, realizing they have no alternative, agree to surrender on the promise of good conduct.

All except Morgan. Tears of rage flowing down his cheeks, he stands with his back against a wall, waving his sword, defying the bastards to come and get him. The British threaten to shoot him and he dares them to do it. They don't quite dare. His own men plead with him to give up, but he's adamant until, seeing a priest in the crowd pressing around, he surrenders his sword to this noncombatant, vowing bitterly that "not a scoundrel of these cowards shall take it out of my hand."

The battle is over and the cost is high: a hundred Americans killed and wounded, four hundred taken prisoner. British and Canadian losses are no more than twenty. Surveying the prisoners, British officers are struck all over again by the audacity of what they would consider "other ranks" in *their* army passing themselves off as officers and gentlemen. Particularly gentlemen. One writes home: "You can have no conception what kind of men composed their officers. Of those we took, one major was a blacksmith, another a hatter. Of their captains, there was a butcher, a tanner, a shoemaker, a tavern-keeper, etc. Yet they all pretended to be gentlemen."

Guy Carleton is an authentic gentleman himself. He treats his prisoners as though they're what they say they are, has their baggage brought in from the American camp, sees to it that they have their own cook and plenty to eat, and as soon as the weather is warm enough, arranges for them to walk in the sun. It's the most humane treatment of prisoners on either side in the entire war.

Orders come from Arnold's hospital bed to what remains of his army, a few hundred half-starved wretches, shivering in the cold, trying to maintain a camp. Continue the siege of Quebec for the rest of the winter, he commands. Is Arnold insane, as some think he might be? Or is he just indomitable? In any case, his reports to Washington and Congress on the fiasco that has just taken place are honest enough and thoroughly alarm everyone. Schuyler is frantic. He sees his first major enterprise collapsing. As a result of his urgent appeals, Massachusetts, Connecticut, and Rhode Island agree to send a regiment each for service in Canada.

Arnold, meanwhile, is still being pursued by his nemesis. Trying to recover too rapidly, he falls from his horse, reinjures his leg, and has to ask to be relieved. He goes off to take the command in Montreal, changing places with poor old alcoholic, aging General Wooster, who shouldn't even be in the field. Fortunately, Wooster too is relieved by General John Thomas, a vigorous six-footer who finds himself commanding the recently arrived forces Schuyler has summoned.

Assessing the situation, Thomas does the sensible thing and raises the siege. Not quite soon enough, however. Four days later, before any kind of retreat can be organized, three British men-of-war push their way through the river ice and cast anchor at the Lower Town. Carleton, knowing they're coming, has decided not to do anything about the virtually helpless Americans until these reinforcements arrive. Now that they're here, he throws an army of 900 men against Thomas's troops on the Plains of Abraham, and the result is a wild rout. The Americans leave everything behind them—cannon, clothing, food, even the sick.

Retreating—if that's the word for this flight—as far as Chambly, they have some hope of being saved by a rescuing party from Montreal, but the rescuers are set upon by a few Canadians and a party of Indians under Joseph Brant. The rescue turns into a killing field.

Congress, safe in Philadelphia and as ignorant as everyone else about the intractable problems of Canadian conquest, sends a commission up to find out what's going on—a distinguished assemblage that includes Benjamin Franklin, Samuel Chase, Charles Carroll, and his brother, Father John Carroll. These gentlemen see a ragged, half-starved collection of men scarcely worthy of being called an army, stricken with smallpox, and with but one thought: to survive and go home. Unused to such rigors as those prevailing, not to mention the long trip into Canada, Franklin falls sick almost at once and Father Carroll has to take him home; the trip nearly kills old Ben. The remaining commissioners are only an embarrassment to General Thomas, who is also stricken with smallpox and dies. The commissioners get away as soon as they can decently do so.

General John Sullivan, another bad choice, is sent to succeed Thomas. Like Arnold, he's unlucky and prone to take on more than he can accomplish. Sullivan, the son of indentured servants who nevertheless enabled him to study law, is an adroit politician but an uncertain military commander. He's willing enough, always ready for the battle, never turning down an opportunity when the commander offers it to him, always believing he will be successful. If matters turn out the other way, he's the first to offer to die on the barricades. The plain truth is that Sullivan wants desperately to be liked, to be recognized, to have the kind of goodwill a politician needs. Unfortunately, events are always thwarting him.

Taking over this decrepit collection of sick, dispirited Americans, Sullivan makes one of his worst blunders. Knowing that Carleton has heavy reinforcements of British and Hessian troops, and that Burgoyne himself has come up to Quebec, he nevertheless throws what remains of his forces against the fort at Three Rivers on June 7. Having been warned by deserters, Carleton puts Burgoyne in command, and although the American troops, mostly Pennsylvanian reinforcements by this time, fight as well and as bravely as they can, they too have to flee, leaving 25 killed and 200 prisoners behind them, among them their commander, General William Thompson.

When he hears this news, Arnold writes a despairing, somewhat sarcastic letter to Sullivan, advising him to leave Canada and prepare to defend his own country, since that now seems to be in some danger. Sullivan takes this as a command and brings the remnants of his tattered army to St. John, where he meets Arnold, who has brought his 300 survivors down from Montreal. Only the fact that the British have no boats prevents a further calamity.

As it is, matters are close to desperation. Huddled on the low, humid shores of Isle-aux-Noix, below St. John, the survivors are literally melting away from smallpox, malaria, and dysentery. Pits have to be dug in the center of each regiment's camp, and every day new bodies are thrown into it. Arnold decides on a quick evacuation, but that's difficult. The sick go first, floating off on rafts which are sometimes washed over by waves, drowning a few more soldiers and making the sick even sicker. Those who are well follow, and by June 26 every survivor is at Crown Point, where Arnold leaves the 6th Pennsylvania as an advance guard, and by early July most of the three thousand men still living, the residue of the Northern Army, are in quarters at Ticonderoga.

Much else has been happening in that first half of 1776, but the total failure of the Canadian expedition outweighs nearly everything else in the public mind when the news becomes generally known. It's cost a great deal of money, much more than the government can afford, and the total casualties have been at least five thousand.

One popular hero has emerged: Richard Montgomery. He and his wife Janet are the subject of songs, poems, and plays, and he's compared with the great heroes of antiquity, held up as a patriotic example to be followed. The public never learns of his disaffection with the whole affair. Janet becomes a public figure herself, wearing mourning for the rest of her life, which extends into her eighties, and never remarrying, although she does have the pleasure of rejecting General Gates—"a pompous fool," she says—who salves his wound by marrying a merchant's daughter worth half a million only a year later.

The Canadian fiasco casts a gloomy pall over the colonies, not alone because of the failure of all those generals and the appalling loss of life, but because the *rage militaire* is rapidly sliding away. People have begun to realize they're in a war whose outcome is highly uncertain.

1776

7

✚   ✚   ✚

How We Lost Long Island

In the early months of 1776, spies and deserters from Boston report that the British are fitting out ships, and it looks as though they mean to leave town. Washington still wants to attack, but there's that old problem—lack of soldiers. He had expected 10,500 by January 10, but only 8,212 were available. So he has to swallow hard and literally beg the New England colonies to send thirteen regiments of militia who will agree to serve until April.

By the first of March, in spite of shortages in both manpower and powder, Washington feels justified in attacking. His plan is to seize Dorchester Heights and give the Americans a commanding position. On the night of March 4, when tides and weather seem right, he makes his move. Two nights earlier a diversion had confused and alarmed the British—a cannonading full of sound and fury that did little damage. But about 7:00 P.M. on the fourth, General John Thomas and three thousand men march out of Roxbury toward the Heights, with more than three hundred ox teams toiling along behind, hauling the materials for fortification.

All night Thomas's men work hard, in mild weather under a full moon, finishing their task next day without a shot being fired by the British. They've added a diabolical touch, suggested by a Boston merchant—barrels filled with earth, to be rolled down the hill in case of attack, projectiles guaranteed to kill and maim. But nothing happens all that day. In the evening, Washington inspects the works, and soon after, a gale of near hurricane force blows up. In the morning light, it's clear that the British meant to launch an attack that night, but the ships they had intended to use are now hopelessly fouled up with each other, some adrift from their anchorages.

Washington seizes the opportunity. Thomas's men quickly build up the fortifications to the point of being unassailable unless Howe is willing to accept unacceptable losses. He has no such intention. In fact, looking out on the fortifications the next morning, he exclaims, "Good God! These fellows have done more work in one night than I could have made my army do in three months. What shall I do?"

He does what he's been advised to do for months: abandon Boston. Some troops embark hastily on the ninth, and on the seventeenth, a bright Sunday morning, the remainder of his seven thousand men are boarded. Several of his officers find this retreat hard to understand. With overwhelming firepower and manpower at his command, he could have bypassed this colonial Maginot Line, rendered it useless, and destroyed the enemy.

But that's hindsight. The redcoats are gone and the American militia march into Boston while the British ships are still leaving the harbor. Almost at once, the spirit of insubordination that has been festering so long in the Cambridge camp boils over in a mutiny. With Boston captured, some of these reluctant soldiers believe their mission is over. It's not much of a revolt, however. The ringleaders are tried and convicted by a court-martial, two of them are shot, both from the otherwise admired Marblehead regiment. Others are in prison, awaiting the same fate. Their wives come to live with them, there's a constant stream of visiting friends, and floods of repentant tears—it's all too much for the commander, who gives them a last-minute pardon, as he will often do during the course of the war. But he does nothing to prevent the flogging of others, and he won't excuse Putnam's son, a drummer boy, from his duty of applying the lash, although attempts are made to relieve him of the job.

Insubordination is now a constant problem, infecting the army at every level. On Dorchester Heights, Lee had threatened to whip an officer of high rank with his cane because of what the general considered unsoldierly conduct. That incident had created an excited wave of revolt among other officers.

But now all this is momentarily forgotten as the militia occupy a Boston regained, accepting the wild joy of the Whigs, who hail them as deliverers. The town itself is a shambles. Before they left, the British troops pillaged the houses they'd been living in, breaking up the furniture, damaging the buildings, carrying off all the linen and woolen goods they could find, and destroying stores of salt and molasses. Oddly enough, the British left behind a good deal of intact military equipment—heavy cannon, large mortars, cannon shot, shells, small arms. And also about twenty disillusioned Tories, who had been told all along that reinforcements would arrive and the rebels would be put down. Some of them committed suicide, others have given themselves up to the doubtful mercy of the colony.

As he peers through his glasses into the farther reaches of the harbor, Washington can't understand why Howe hasn't sailed away instead of simply standing off the coast. He believes the fleet's destination has to be New York, whose capture would split the colonies. And that, in fact, is exactly what Howe intends to do—eventually. His plan now is to take New York, and then move up the Hudson to meet a British force coming down from Canada. Meanwhile, however, he misleads everyone by sailing for Halifax, where he hopes to meet large numbers of reinforcements from England.

Howe carries with him some interesting human cargo. Here is Dorcas Griffiths, daughter of an old Boston family, a charming little blond opportunist who married at twenty-two and raised a family before she became the mistress of her younger landlord, no less than John Hancock—until, that is, he cast her out in 1775 to get married himself. That insult made a Tory out of Dorcas. By the time Howe's fleet sails, she's become first the mistress of Captain David Johnston and then his wife after he was wounded on Breed's Hill. Now she goes along with him to Halifax, emigrating later to England.

Another Tory refugee is fifty-five-year-old Lady Agnes Frankland, now near the end of her fascinating life, begun when she was a barefoot serving wench in the Fountain Inn at Marblehead. There her charms were observed appreciatively by a young, dissolute Englishman named Henry Frankland, who was so struck by her beauty that he bought her some shoes on the spot, after which, with her parents' consent, he took her to Boston as his ward. There, having grown accustomed to her face while he was having her properly educated, he arranged for her imperceptible passage from ward to mistress, outraging Boston society. Made a baronet in 1747, and being extremely rich besides, Henry did not care. He installed Agnes in a replica of a great English country estate near Hopkinton, not far from Boston, fathered a son by her, and eventually took her on a visit to

England, where his family was even more outraged than the Bostonians had been.

They fled the family's wrath to Lisbon, just in time for the great earthquake of 1756, where Henry was buried in rubble but survived, whether dug out by Agnes, as legend has it, or through his own efforts, we can't be sure. In any case, the experience had a profound effect on Henry. He married Agnes—twice—once in a civil ceremony, again in the Church of England. They returned to Boston, where Lady Agnes, like it or not, was now a social leader. The Franklands lived regally, in the British manner, until Henry sickened and died, leaving Agnes a very rich woman. She lived on at the Hopkinton estate until Boston was besieged, when she fled with other Loyalists to its presumed safety. Here Benjamin Church personally escorted her to the roof of a four-story mansion so she could watch the action on Breed's Hill. Now she's left Boston for good, bound for England, where she marries again but lives only two more years. Always a decisive woman, she orders her will brought to her one day, signs it, and dies.

If the liberation of Boston means the departure of these lively ladies, it also signals freedom for obscure Americans who had been snatched up by the occupying forces on frivolous charges and thrown into jail. Their sufferings have been great. John Leach, an English-born mariner who went around the world three times and wound up teaching a school of navigation in Boston, tells his deliverers how he was thrown into jail on a trumped-up charge of spying, and there suffered the extreme cruelty of the provost marshal, his deputy, and the soldiers on guard.

Leach's prison diary is still shocking today. He tells of a poor printer who was made to get down on his knees in the yard and say, "God bless the King." Leach himself suffered much worse. "We had some of the worst women for our neighbors," he writes, "they acted such scenes as was shocking to nature, and used language horrible to hear, as if it came from the very suburbs of Hell." Leach got his moldy food not through an open cell door but through the bars, accompanied by insults and threats. When his wife came, the provost told her that her husband was "a damned rebel" and "his family the damnedest rebel family in the country," and told her not to come again. When his son brought him breakfast, "the provost said to the soldiers on guard, 'Goddamn that dog (meaning my child), don't let him come up the yard. That dog deserves to be shot.'"

In the midst of his own misery, Leach was conscious of others. An old Dutchman lay in jail because he complained that soldiers burglarized his garden, "which was his whole living, and because he had not a dollar to pay his fees, the soldiers on guard were ordered, each, to give him a kick as he went away." The sick and wounded were treated as badly as the others. Advised that they hadn't been given bread for two days, the provost told them they could eat the nailheads and gnaw the planks and be damned. A British sergeant and a corporal found themselves in jail for giving the prisoners a little air and fresh water while the provost was away and they were nearly suffocating from the heat. This was only a mild prelude to the war's prison cruelty in other places.

It's a long time before order is restored in Boston and life returns to something approaching normality. At least it's never attacked again during the war, and meanwhile the scene shifts.

Washington will leave Boston on April 4, pausing just long enough to be awarded an honorary degree by Harvard (Doctor of Laws). Two months ago, he had sent Lee on ahead to New York with an advance column, and the former master of Hobgoblin Hall arrived there at a critical moment. As the historian John Shy tells us, "Many people were caught up in a shadowy state between war and peace, loyalty and treason, and making small compromises with British officials, talking to Loyalist neighbors, postponing any violent action as long as possible—Lee moved through this murky world of indecision like a flame. In Newport and New York, he made suspected Tories swear an elaborate oath. In New York and Virginia he disarmed them or moved them from sensitive areas. When those living under the guns of British ships used this as an excuse for inaction, Lee told them to move out to safer places. He demanded that the Revolutionary authorities in New York, Maryland, and Virginia stop communication with their royal governors. He antagonized and upset civil officials wherever he went, but also shocked them out of lethargy. He had advocated a Declaration of Independence since October 1775."

But the task of whipping up patriotic fervor is too much even for Lee in these days of recovery from the *rage militaire*. Congress has done its part with an address, in February 1776, explaining grandly that "our troops are animated with the love of freedom. . . .We confess that they have not advantages rising from experience and discipline. But facts have shown that native courage warmed with patriotism is sufficient to counterbalance those advantages." Dream on, gentlemen in Philadelphia! By the end of the year, there will be a general reluctance to fight full time, if at all.

As in most wars, there's an abundance of government propaganda, assiduously distributed by the Whig newspapers, and after more than two hundred years it has a familiar ring. Mothers, wives, sisters, and lovely women are portrayed as eager to send their men out to battle, there to win or die, although not much is said about death. Soldiers and potential recruits are urged to protect these waiting women, some of whom have joined groups proclaiming that they will have nothing to do with men who avoid service. It isn't long, though, before the number of such men becomes too large to handle. Groups of mothers assert they have sent all their sons to the army with instructions not to let them (the mothers) hear of their deaths unless these occur while facing the enemy, although in the end more are going to die of disease than in combat. Other women form military-style companies and do a bit of drilling, but they're not going any farther than the village green.

Intellectuals know better. "We must all be soldiers," John Adams writes in a well-publicized letter to a Boston minister in May 1776, but only seven weeks later he's telling a clerk in his law office who wants to enlist, "We cannot all be soldiers."

Eventually Lee knows better, too, but the revelation comes late. He actually believes that these Americans are engaged in a popular uprising, in the most idealistic sense, fed by the burning flame of liberty. The Cambridge militia began his disillusionment, and it won't be long now before it's complete. Meanwhile, however, he's all restless energy.

Coincidentally, he's arrived in New York on February 4, the day the British warship *Mercury* carrying General Henry Clinton arrives, anchoring safely out of reach in the harbor. Those viewing Lee for the first time think him "plain in his person to a degree of ugliness," and at the moment, he's even more unimpressive because a severe attack of gout has compelled him to be carried about in a litter. But they treat him with due deference and escort him to his lodgings at Mrs. Mantagne's Tavern.

Clinton's arrival is much more spectacular than Lee's, although not what he intended. The Loyalists in New York had expected him to arrive with a large fleet, and when they see only the *Mercury*, there's a dramatic dash to get out of town before more Americans arrive. Many families make desperate passages across the rivers to Long Island and New Jersey, dodging the cakes of ice that threaten their boats. They take with them every cart, horse, and wagon they can find, as well as whatever of their worldly goods they can load in them. Most have no idea where they're going, or how they're going to live. Only the rich have the means to buy or rent safe havens, if there are any.

Lee's gout improves and he takes firm command. He knows that the Tory Governor William Tryon has made dire threats against the rebellious Whigs if they try to move the cannon and stores from the Battery and the yards nearby, but early in February, Lee musters a gang of willing men and boys who spend all day dragging the guns up Broadway to the Common. By this time there are other British warships in the harbor and Tryon wants to know, with some irritation, why they don't fire on this nest of rebels. Captain Hyde Parker, commanding aboard the *Phoenix*, tells him sensibly that there is so much ice in the harbor and rivers that it's impossible to get close enough for a focused fire, and anyway, the British guns wouldn't be able to distinguish between Whigs and Tories. In any case, he adds, the town will be occupied eventually and used as a British base. Why destroy it?

Knowing nothing of this decision, and fearing the worst, the inhabitants are moving out in large numbers. On Sunday the churches are nearly empty, and in the few where services are held, the noise outside is so great that the pastor's words can scarcely be heard. But not all the locked doors and closed shutters mean houses are empty. Some Tories have elected to stay, out of necessity or stubbornness, and that proves to be a mistake when Lee's reinforcements begin to roll into town. It's the old Boston story: soldiers have to be quartered and there's Colonel David Waterbury with eight hundred New Englanders, and William Alexander, who calls himself Lord Stirling and has ferried over a thousand men from New Jersey. Existing barracks can't possibly accommodate them all, so they begin breaking into any house they find empty, and when these run out, the mansions of the rich Tories are appropriated, with the inhabitants still in some of them. It's a shock to see rough provincial soldiers in oak-paneled drawing rooms, surrounded by luxury. "Oh, the houses in New York," an observer writes, "if you would but see the insides of them, occupied by the dirtiest people on the continent."

Outside, the troops are busy converting what had been a handsome city into a heavily fortified military camp. Only a few months before, passing through on his way to Ticonderoga, Henry Knox had written to his Lucy that the houses were "better than Boston, generally of brick and three stories high with the largest kind of windows. Their churches are grand, their college, workhouse, and hospitals most excellently situated and also exceedingly commodious, their principal streets much wider than ours."

But then, conscious that he was in a mare's nest of Tories, Henry had to add: "The people—why, the people are magnificent: in their equipages which are numerous, in their houses furniture which is fine, in their pride and conceit which are inimitable, in their profaneness which is intolerable, in the want of principle which is prevalent, in their Toryism which is insufferable, and for which they must repent in dust and ashes."

They're already repenting. Oliver De Lancey, one of the town's leading merchants, has been nursing a handsome stand of trees for forty years but, looking out the window one morning, he sees Connecticut militia cutting it down for firewood. Rushing out, he makes a pathetic effort to stop them by informing the men that the Earl of Abingdon, a notable champion of their cause, and married to De Lancey's granddaughter, owns a third of those trees. "Well," says a militiaman, "if he be such a great liberty-boy, and so great a friend of our country, he will be quite happy that his wood was so happy for our use."

On Horne's Hook, soldiers invade Jacob Walton's elegant mansion to fortify it and they order Mrs. Walton to leave. Bursting into tears, she cries out, "By what uncertain a tenure do we hold the good and desirable possessions of this world." (This unlikely response was no doubt made in a letter.) It's a scene—and a reflection—that will be repeated a thousand times up and down the coast on both sides before the war is over.

Meanwhile, New York is in a nervous guessing game for a while. What are those British ships up to, anyway? Actually, they're waiting for Howe, but since he's nowhere in sight, they start to move out. One of them, the *Asia*, runs aground off the foot of Broad Street, and

Lee tries to get cannon close enough to fire on her, but the tide comes in and floats her again. For a while all the ships anchor off Bedloe's Island, where Tryon sits in the flagship and tries to run a city he no longer controls. By the time Washington arrives in April, all the ships have gone to sea again except for the *Asia* and a few others off Sandy Hook.

Lee isn't there to greet the commander. In March, he was sent south, where the British are opening up a new theater of war, a "Southern strategy." He has left the city in command of a freshly minted brigadier, Lord Stirling, a character nearly as odd as Lee himself. In spite of his bogus title, he's an American, but at fifty he looks like the upper-class Britisher he claims to be—handsome, ruddy-cheeked, a hard drinker. The House of Lords has already denied him the ancient earldom he claims to have inherited from his rich lawyer father, but he blandly insists to his friends and neighbors in Somerset County that he is indeed a lord and they let him get away with it because they like him. He also claims to be versed in astronomy and mathematics, and has a large library to prove it, but he can't manage his own affairs. By the time the war began, everything he owned was mortgaged, and maybe that's why he suddenly dropped his lifelong conservative views and claimed to be an ardent Whig: in order to avoid bankruptcy.

Lord Stirling takes his title seriously. When a soldier on the gallows, about to be executed for desertion, cries, "The Lord have mercy on me!" Stirling shouts back sternly, "I won't, you rascal, I won't have mercy on you." Yet this amiable fraud fought with some distinction in the French and Indian War, and both the officers and men respect him. Anyway, he's in command for only a month, until Washington arrives, and he spends it putting everyone to work on fortifications.

Provincial troops continue to pour into the city, and the Whigs make life miserable for the few Tories remaining, riding them on rails through the streets, tearing the clothes off their backs. As for the soldiers, some of them think they've entered paradise, finding themselves in a place full of whores, unlike anything they've ever seen before. What a selection of picturesque bordellos! Around King's College you can find the business places of Katie Crow, Quaker Fan, and Man-of-War Nance while, polluting the piety of the St. Paul's area, the streetwalkers congregate on—what else?—the Holy

Ground, as everyone calls it, filled, one appreciative observer says, with "bitchfoxly jades, jills, haggs, strums."

These districts are so notorious that Colonel Loammi Baldwin feels compelled to write and reassure his wife that he has not so much as spoken to any of these women, but he draws a grim picture of the fighting that seems to go with sex on the Holy Ground. As officer of the day, making his rounds with an escort guard, he's been compelled to break up "the knots of men and women fighting, pulling caps, swearing, crying, 'Murder!' etc., hurried them off to the provost dungeon by half dozens, there let them lay mixed till next day. Then some are punished and some get off clear—Hell's work. . . ." Another soldier writes: "Several limbs and heads of men were found at the Holy Ground which was supposed to be killed by the whores. . . . No man is suffered to be there after nine o'clock at night."

Much of this violence is attributed to strong spirits, and Washington issues one of the first "off limits" notices in the country's military history. Not only are troops forbidden to patronize any shop selling liquor, but the owners are warned not to sell, under penalties. Drunkenness is punished severely.

More serious matters lie beneath the turbulent surface of the city. Isaac Ketcham, in jail and charged with one of the colonies' most popular crimes, counterfeiting, hears Tory prisoners hatching dark plots, and it occurs to him that he can get out of jail and resume his profitable work by turning stool pigeon. A group of Tories, he tells the authorities, intend to kidnap Washington and as many of his guard as they can. The leader of this gang is no less than the Tory mayor of New York, David Matthews. After the kidnapping, a small and secret Loyalist army will attack the American rear, while the British in the harbor will move in frontally.

Magazines are to be blown up and artillery seized, to pound the Americans from behind with their own guns. Matthews has organized a force of seven hundred men on Long Island and nearly as many at Goshen. New militia are being recruited, spies are everywhere, and there's even one in the commander's own guard. The plotters meet in taverns (always the best place), at the Sergeant's Arms and Corbie's Tavern, almost in the shadow of headquarters. A mulatto dressed in blue shuttles back and forth with messages between the plotters and Tryon, who is aboard the *Duchess of Gordon*, lying offshore.

One of these letters is discovered and the plot fails—or perhaps a patriotic waiter overhears the conspirators, who knows? Anyway, Matthews is arrested, and so are two members of Washington's guard, Michael Lynch and Thomas Hickey. Other informers bring on more arrests, and soon they're all informing on each other, trying to save their skins. Three more Guard members are snatched up—a drummer, a fifer, and a soldier.

The news leaks and wild rumors spread: Hickey was ordered to stab Washington, or maybe he was to poison a dish of green peas, one of the commander's favorites, and only a warning from his house-keeper saves him. She throws the peas into a chicken pen and all the chickens die.

How much truth there is in any of this is hard to discover, since everyone involved is willing to say anything to save himself. Only Hickey, singled out, for no discernible reason, to be court-martialed, rats on no one and protests his own innocence to the moment he steps on the gallows. None of his alleged accomplices is ever tried, and the three conspirators who testify against him cop a plea and get off. Strangely, no charges of kidnapping or assassination are made against Hickey, but they hang him just the same, as an example.

New York has never witnessed such a scene as his execution. Asked if he wants a chaplain, he says, "They're all cutthroats." At 11:00 A.M. on June 28, on a gallows near the Bowery, eighty men escort sullen Hickey to the rope, while twenty thousand people turn out to enjoy the hanging. Only when the chaplain shakes his hand and says good-bye does the doomed man's defiant mask slip, and he begins to cry. But he recovers quickly, wipes his eyes, and turns a scornful, indignant face to the rope. As he swings free, there is a bizarre incident in the front row: Kip, the moon-curser, sinks to the ground and dies with Hickey. (A moon-curser is provincial slang for a smuggler who likes dark nights.)

Next day everyone forgets about poor Hickey. A rifleman named Daniel McCurtin writes that he was "upstairs in an outhouse and spied, as I peeped out, in the bay something resembling a wood of pine trees trimmed. I could not believe my eyes, when in about ten minutes the whole bay was full of shipping as ever it could be. I declare that I thought all London was afloat." Not all London, but more than a hundred ships are anchored in the Hook before the day's end.

Howe has come down from Halifax at last with nearly thirty thousand troops, three-fifths of them mercenary Hessians. Loyalist spies tell him that Washington has barely twelve thousand men fit to fight, and they also disclose the placement of batteries and men in an arc from Brooklyn across Long Island.

It isn't long before news from another quarter emerges in New York. From the beginning, the British have thought of the South as a promising theater of war, primarily because it is full of ardent Loyalists and well removed from troublesome Yankees. As early as October 1775, about three hundred Whig militia, authorized by the patriot government in Williamsburg, were dispersed by Royal Governor John Murray, Earl of Dunmore, with a force made up of a few regulars, Scottish clerks, and blacks. The governor was aware that he had human resources in the black community. He promised freedom to slaves who deserted their masters and fought for him, and of the two regiments he was able to raise, one was entirely black. Of course, the Tidewater aristocracy takes an exceedingly dim view of all this, as do the Whigs, for different reasons.

A Whig army under Colonel William Woodford attacked Dunmore's troops on December 11 with a force of seven hundred Virginians and two hundred North Carolinians, driving him into Norfolk, which he evacuated by sea. In their zeal to obliterate the Loyalists, Woodford's men and civilian supporters set fire to nearly nine hundred houses in Norfolk on New Year's Day 1776. A month later, they destroyed the four hundred houses remaining and this little port was out of the war.

In neighboring North Carolina, the Whigs have thrown out their royal governor, Josiah Martin, who tried to emulate Tryon for a time by attempting to rule from a British warship; the governor of South Carolina joined him in this ineffective pastime. Georgia's governor was captured, but he escaped.

Obviously, this kind of rebellion requires response, so Clinton sends Charles Cornwallis, damage control expert, with an Irish force, but by the time he arrives in North Carolina the Whigs are in charge. What next, then? Clinton decides to make a sudden assault on Charleston. He puts together a formidable attack force: three regiments and seven companies from other regiments, supported by two 50-gun ships and six frigates under command of Sir Peter Parker. Enough to strike by land and sea, converting Charleston into a strategic base of great value, with its superb harbor and rivers leading to the interior.

Charleston is ready for the blow. It has a lengthy Whig tradition, ornamented by the choleric figure of Christopher Gadsden, the Sam Adams of the South, a tall, violent man much loved by the good old boys of his time. But there are also more respectable figures like John Rutledge and Henry Laurens to boast about. Like their New England compatriots, the Whigs have long been storing up gunpowder and arms, and have raised two regiments of a thousand men each, besides a company of rangers for frontier fighting in the interior. These rebels have taken possession of the harbor fort, set up their own government, and made Rutledge president.

They need a military leader, however, and in March, Congress sends them one, the peripatetic Charles Lee. He leaves New York in a cloud of unpaid bills to become commander of the new Southern Department, stopping first in Williamsburg to organize the colony's defenses. He's no more than started on this task when an intercepted letter informs him that a British fleet is offshore, sailing for the North Carolina coast. For once, Lee doesn't have a ready answer to this "damned whimsical situation. I know not where to turn. I am like a dog in a dancing school. I may be in the north when, as Richard the Third says, I should serve my sovereign in the west."

Further intelligence provides the answer. The British are heading for Charleston, so Lee sends Brigadier General John Armstrong on ahead and soon follows with 1,300 Virginia troops, picking up 700 North Carolinians along the way.

In Charleston, Lee finds that Colonel Gadsden is attending the Continental Congress, leaving the direction of defenses in the hands of another American original, Colonel William Moultrie, of the 2nd Regiment. At first they hardly know what to make of each other. Lee is certainly a shock to anyone, but Moultrie is a character too, a man from the Low Country, florid and stout, a militia veteran and a frontier fighter of Cherokees. He has bold features and a steady gaze that cuts like a knife. His jaw is heavy and he parts his thin hair on the right-hand side, with a lock of it falling down over his left eye. Unfortunately, he reminds the general of old Artemas Ward, back in the Cambridge camp, an officer Lee frequently said should have been a churchwarden. There's one difference, though. Moultrie speaks his mind, without fear or favor, and he's not afraid of anything, animal or human.

On June 1, the British ships appear off Charleston Bar, fifty of them, greatly alarming the populace. Lee doesn't get there until three days later. Trailed by his dogs, he examines every inch of the terrain he's about to defend, indifferent to the fact that the other officers are having trouble getting used to him. Lee doesn't like what he sees in the defenses. He inspects the unfinished fort nestled in the sand dunes and myrtle of Sullivan's Island and tells Moultrie it won't do, because there's no way to retreat. It's a slaughter pen, he says, and advises withdrawing from it. Rutledge insists otherwise. Lee then says all right, but it will be essential to have a bridge of boats as a retreat exit. Rutledge points out that the distance is more than a mile and there aren't enough boats in Charleston to cover it. Moultrie chimes in and says not to worry about retreating because he can't imagine it.

Nothing shakes Moultrie's optimism. When a former master of a man-of-war comes to inspect the fort, he says bluntly, "When those ships come to lay alongside your fort, they'll knock it down in half an hour." Moultrie is unimpressed. "Then we'll lie behind the ruins and prevent their men from landing," he says calmly.

Lee regards all this as nonsense. He has no faith whatever in the entire strategic concept, and Moultrie simply annoys him. Meanwhile, the British fleet is having its own problems. Several days go by because unfavorable winds prevent the ships from getting over the bar. This is followed by such stormy weather that even the anchorages are in doubt, but at last Clinton is able to land troops across from Sullivan's Island on neighboring Long Island and three more tense days go by while both sides prepare. Moultrie spends a restless, hot night, suffering with gout, on June 27, but soon after dawn he leaves the fort to inspect his advance guard facing Long Island. He's just in time to see the British boats about to descend on him. Hurrying back to the fort, he has no more than a few minutes to man the guns before Clinton's ships appear.

Now we're going to see who's right, Lee or Moultrie. The colonel fires on the British as soon as they're within reach, and Clinton responds with a furious attack of his own. But he's made a slight error. Mortars have been deliberately overcharged with powder to make the shells go farther, and they go too far. Most fall within the fort, but they sink into a morass in its middle and do no damage. Other projectiles fall in sand and disappear.

The bombardment goes on from ships now little more than a musket shot from the fort and the sound seems to fill earth and sky. In the midst of it, Lee comes to inspect, cool as ever, and Moultrie generously permits him to point two or three guns, after which Lee makes what amounts to an apology. "Colonel," he says, "I see you're doing very well here. You have no occasion for me. I'll go up to town again." Moultrie has reason to be proud of his defense. He writes later: "Never did men fight more bravely and never were men more cool. Several of the officers as well as myself were smoking our pipes and giving orders."

Lack of powder, the perennial American problem, is the only complaint, making it necessary to conserve by slowing down or stopping the American fire. Clinton can't retreat because wind and tide are against him, but neither can he go forward. The fort's palmetto logs, filled with earth, sixteen feet thick and very high, are simply too formidable.

On this intensely hot day, grog is carried along the firing platform in fire buckets to cool the men. There are acts of individual courage. A drawling Georgia sergeant, William Jasper, sees the fort's flagstaff shot down and falling outside the walls. "Colonel, don't let us fight without our colors," Jasper calls to Moultrie. "How can you help it?" the colonel answers. "The staff is gone." Replying, "Then I'll replace it," Jasper climbs over the wall, finds the flag and ties it to a sponge staff, and sticks it in the fort's wall where the British can't miss seeing it. Then he goes calmly back to his gun.

Not since Breed's Hill have so many civilians watched a battle. In Charleston, they've occupied windows, heights, steeples, even the wharves, and though they're six miles away, they get a good idea of what's happening. Clinton's fleet is in bad shape, but firing continues through the sultry afternoon and into the darkness, the flashes of big guns lighting up the night sky. About nine-thirty, everything stops. By eleven o'clock, the British have silently stolen away. In bright morning sunlight, the fort displays its wounds—shell holes, debris, some timbers shattered, and a few guns blasted away from their swivels—but only 10 men have been killed and 24 wounded, out of 380 officers and men. One British ship has heeled over and exploded after the crew set her on fire. Four deserters report that there has been great damage on the other ships, providing plenty of work for the carpenters. They also report that an American volley struck Admiral Parker's flagship and blew off his breeches.

On the whole, there's cause for celebration. Lee reviews the troops, and the wife of Major Bernard Elliott, of the artillery, presents them with a splendid pair of embroidered colors to replace the tattered flag Jasper rescued. Lee doesn't want to say anything to spoil the occasion, but he is certain that, if the British hadn't lost three of their best ships in an accident before the battle began, he would have been proved right about the fort after all. In any event, the British are now spending a few uncomfortable days on Long Island, swatting mosquitoes, and short of both food and water. Knowing this, Lee strikes a culinary deal. He sends over some fresh food in exchange for good British porter and cheese. But at last the transports are ready and Clinton figuratively slinks back north to besieged New York.

There, on July 12, the British advantage becomes even more overwhelming when Howe's brother, Admiral Richard Howe, appears with 150 transports loaded with more Hessians and convoyed by more warships. The Hessians can't wait to land. They've been crammed into quarters so small that they've had to lie against each other spoon fashion. To shift sides one man had to call "About face!" and the whole lot then turned over in unison.

Admiral Howe — "Black Dick," they call him — is a sharp contrast to his brother. One of the great sailors of his time, extremely serious, he has one thing in common with brother William: as a good Whig, he doesn't want to shed American blood if he can help it, and before he left England, he was given instructions to make peace if he could.

Events have made that all but impossible by this time. Instead, there is one last flare-up of the *rage militaire*. Less than a year ago, Ben Franklin had declared that he'd never heard an American, "drunk or sober," say he wanted separation from Mother England. Aristocrats haven't wanted it because their fortunes depend on trade with England and the West Indies. But a good many of the Sons of Liberty also depend on this cash flow.

Lexington and Concord were major shocks, and Breed's Hill changed some minds too. Then, while Washington was still contemplating Dorchester Heights, Tom Paine's *Common Sense* appeared and this patriotic sermon was read by everybody; officers knew some in their ranks couldn't read, so they read it to the men. In March, a South Carolinian wrote, "It made independents of the majority of the country." Probably nowhere near a majority, in fact, but just the same a great morale booster in the wake of the news from Canada.

As the two armies square off facing each other in Brooklyn and Long Island, Thomas Jefferson is sitting in a rented furnished second-floor Philadelphia apartment, writing the practical realization of what Paine advocates—a Declaration of Independence. On these warm June nights, he bends over his folding writing box and produces a historic document, in which Adams and Franklin, reading the first draft, make only minor changes.

Presented to Congress on July 2, the Declaration is carried by a vote of nine colonies, but further study is ordered before adoption. Not to worry. John Adams writes to Abigail declaring July 2 to be the most memorable day in the rather brief history of America, and predicts that it "will be celebrated by succeeding generations as the great anniversary festival." He's wrong by two days but no one's quibbling. On July 4, all the colonies adopt the Declaration, and when Caesar Rodney hears that his Delaware delegation is divided, he rides all night through a terrible storm, strides into the hall still booted and spurred, and casts the tie-breaking vote.

There's a little less fervor on the part of others. Adams reports that "there were several who signed with regret, and several others, with many doubts and much lukewarmness." Mr. Harrison, the portly delegate from Virginia, and Mr. Gerry, the thin man from Massachusetts, even exchange a little gallows humor. Mr. Harrison says to his fellow Signer, "When the hanging scene comes to be exhibited, I shall have the advantage over you on account of my size. All will be over with me in a moment, but you will be kicking in the air half an hour after I am gone."

New York lies in the shadow of the great British war fleet, but when the Declaration is read to the troops, they give it three cheers and, with a crowd of civilians, descend on Bowling Green, where an equestrian statue of George III dominates the scene, the subject of some ridicule because Wilton of London, who executed the work, forgot to put stirrups on the horse. It's a moot point now because the crowd pulls down the statue and sends its four thousand pounds of lead to Connecticut, to be made into bullets. Ten ounces of gold leaf are also retrieved.

That night the air in New York and in other colonial towns is filled with the sound of joyous celebration, but not everyone is entirely happy about it. The fear of democracy lifts its unlikely head in this supposed struggle for freedom, and Lieutenant Alexander Graydon writes to a friend: "Innovations are always dangerous, particularly here, where the populace have so great an ascendancy, and popular governments I could never approve of. . . .The greatest danger is that subtle, designing knaves, or weak insignificant blockheads may take the lead in public affairs."

The Declaration is a blow to the Howe brothers' hopes of an early settlement, but they're not giving up. Black Dick takes a devious route, sending a letter to Adjutant General Joseph Reed by way of Reed's wife's brother. Reed sends it on to Congress. Then Howe dispatches a naval officer under a flag of truce to meet with Reed, and the officer hands him a letter addressed to George Washington Esq. No such person, Reed replies tartly; everyone knows he's *General* George Washington, and he won't deliver the letter. Rebuffed, the officer returns. The commander thinks he should tell Congress that he would not ordinarily quibble about such a thing, but he's going to insist on respect.

Now it's the other Howe's turn, and he makes the same mistake. Under a flag of truce, he sends a letter asking that his adjutant general hold a meeting with *General* Washington. Unfortunately, the envelope is addressed to "George Washington, Esq., etc., etc." The commander refuses once more, but at least he's given a verbal account of what's in the letter, and it turns out to be mostly a complaint about General Prescott, the commander at Montreal who gave Ethan Allen such a hard time, and who now alleges he has been mistreated as a prisoner. The commander reminds Howe that Allen and other American prisoners are being treated as badly or worse. The adjutant general who brought the letter says it's beyond Howe's power to do anything about it, a plain lie, and remarks that the general hopes a reconciliation is still possible; he repeats that the King has given the Howes special powers as peace commissioners. Washington replies that the only power either Howe possesses, as far as he can see, is to pardon the Americans, but since the prisoners have done nothing wrong, they don't need to be pardoned. In any case, the British should be negotiating with Congress, not him. He asks the adjutant general politely if he would like to stay for lunch, but the messenger declines.

It's clear to both the brothers that the Americans are not about to listen to peace talk, particularly since the Declaration. Very well, then, let's give them a generous sampling of British power and see what they say then. Washington is not shrinking from a test of strength. There have been so many peace rumors floating around that the morale of the troops has been affected, and positive action is needed to hold his twenty thousand men together. What these troops will do when the action starts is a large question mark. Most have never fought in the field, they don't have enough of anything, including clothing, and enlistments for some are nearly running out. He's quite prepared (or so he thinks) to see some of them turn tail and run.

On the other side, spirits are quite different, especially on Staten Island. Captain Francis Rawdon writes to his uncle, the Earl of Huntingdon: "The fair nymphs of this isle are in wonderful tribulation, as the fresh meat our men have got here has made them as riotous as satyrs. A girl cannot step into the bushes to pluck a rose without running the most imminent risk of being ravished, and they are so little accustomed to these vigorous methods that they don't bear them with the proper resignation, and of consequence we have most entertaining courts-martial every day." The "nymphs" are indeed not amused by this brutality. One complains that not only was she forced by seven men, but they took her old prayer book, which she loved. Another tells Lord Percy that his grenadiers have deflowered her, and Percy asks her a macho question: "Since it was dark, how does she know this?" She says, "Oh, good God!, they could be nothing else, and if Your Lordship will examine, I'm sure you will find it so."

So the stage is set for a great battle, first of the war. The British have already flexed their muscles, insolently sailing up the Hudson past the shore batteries, just to prove they can do it, letting go a few broadsides as they pass, which sends New York into a state of panic. The commander worries about this episode: "When the men-of-war passed up the river, the shrieks and cries of these poor creatures [he means women, children, and the infirm] was truly distressing, and I fear will have an unhappy effect on the ears and minds of our young and inexperienced soldiery." He is also aghast at the officers and men who, instead of springing to their posts as the ships came up the river, stood like tourists on the banks to watch them go by. Less than half of the artillerymen ever went to their guns, and of those who did, some were killed and wounded because they were so busy watching the ships that they forgot to sponge their guns. Other soldiers who should have been there were instead, as one of their disgusted comrades writes, "at their cups or whoring."

On the eve of battle, something far more serious occurs. General Nathanael Greene, who is in command on mosquito-infested Long Island, comes down with a raging fever and has to be removed. For reasons never clear, Washington replaces him with John Sullivan—unlucky Sullivan, still sulking from what happened to him in Canada. "He has his wants, and he has his foibles," the commander says philosophically, but is Long Island the place to have them?

On August 20, only a day after Sullivan takes command, an omen from the heavens. One of the worst storms the city has ever seen strikes about sundown. The rolling clouds threaten tornadoes, lightning comes in "masses of sheets and fires," the thunder is a continuous barrage, and a great cloud spins like a wheel over the city. For three hours, British and Americans alike are battered. A soldier is struck in the street and rendered deaf, dumb, and blind. Three officers of Alexander McDougall's regiment are killed by a single bolt, the points of their swords melted off and the coins melted in their pockets. Their bodies are black and crisped. Ten men from Connecticut regiments camped down by the river are killed by a single bolt and are buried in a mass grave. In the calm morning light, numerous houses are seen to have been struck by lightning and their inhabitants injured. Was it a tornado, as the citizens assert? "A most violent gust," Washington says conservatively.

In the aftermath of the storm comes General Howe, landing twenty-five thousand crack troops and forty pieces of artillery on Long Island. They are brought over from the ships by landing craft, a scarlet flood of uniforms, while bands on the fleet spur them forward with military music. Three days later, the Hessians come ashore, and Washington's army is now outnumbered two to one, not including the men-of-war and their broadsides.

Washington himself comes over from New York to take command of the Brooklyn line at Sullivan's rear. An enlisted man remembers: "I saw him walk along the lines and give his orders in person to the colonels of each regiment. I also heard Washington say, 'If I see any man turn his back today, I will shoot him through. I have two pistols loaded, but I will not ask any man to go further than I do. I will fight so long as I have a leg or an arm.'"

Howe's strategy is simple and well conceived: catch the Americans in a trap by an enveloping movement. Clinton takes off from Flat-bush with an advance guard, Percy commands the main body, but Howe is directing the whole operation. Among the other command-ers is a man who truly hates Americans, General Sir James Grant, who has hated them since he fought in the French and Indian War. Washington returns the compliment. He has a bitter memory of how Grant borrowed most of his Virginia militia in the 1758 action against Fort Duquesne and lost them all. Grant, who is a member of Parliament, has boasted that he could march right through North America with no more than 5,000 men. Now he has his 5,000 but finds himself set back on his heels by Stirling, who has only 1,700.

That's a small victory, however. Otherwise, the day is disastrous for the Americans. At the beginning, everyone does his own thing. Some regiments march into battle with bands playing, others fight frontier fashion from behind trees and walls. But the day turns omi-nous when the Hessians, who have been told by British officers that the Americans give no quarter, respond by spitting some of them against trees with their bayonets and killing entire contingents of men who have already laid down their arms.

Poor Sullivan is flanked and surrounded, and his men are the chief victims of the Hessians' bayonet charge. In terror, they break and run. Sullivan himself is taken prisoner. "The last I heard of him," a soldier writes home, "he was in a cornfield close by our lines with a pistol in each hand, and the enemy had formed a line each side of him, and he was directly between them."

A call goes out for reinforcements from New York, and they are promptly sent. Among them is fifteen-year-old Private Joseph Plumb Martin, who tells us what it was like, of the fear that grips raw and untried men who come to reinforce in the midst of a battle. "We soon landed at Brooklyn," Martin writes, "marched up the ascent from the ferry to the plain. We now began to meet the wounded men, another sight I was unacquainted with, some with broken arms, some with broken legs, and some with broken heads. The sight of these a little daunted me, and made me think of home."

Martin soon comes upon something worse. Soldiers fleeing from Sullivan's broken forces collide with Stirling's men and tell them what the Hessians are doing, and that's enough for these regiments too. Stirling, leading Maryland and Delaware troops, fights on for a time with raw courage, but the whole army is in panicky retreat, the enemy harassing them at every step. Martin and his comrades come up to a creek just in time to see another tragedy.

With the tide in, this creek has become a millpond and the British have driven the Americans into it. "Such as could swim," Martin reports later, "got across; those that could not swim and could not procure anything to buoy them up, sunk. The British, having several fieldpieces stationed by a brick house, were pouring the canister and grape upon the Americans like a shower of hail. . . . There was in this action a regiment of Maryland troops (volunteer), all young gentlemen. When they came out of the water and mud to us, looking like water rats, it was a truly pitiful sight. Many of them were killed in the pond and more were drowned."

The battle's over and the result is a total British victory. It's only afternoon and there are hours of daylight left. All Howe has to do is attack the American fortifications in Brooklyn, where Putnam is waiting for him with no prospect of saving himself, and the war will be over, the rebel army shattered. The British are thirsting now to move in for the kill. But here comes the Breed's Hill syndrome to save the Americans once more. Howe orders his forces to retire. Again some of his officers rage about this decision, and he has to threaten them repeatedly to make them obey. In his report, he says blandly that he was only "following the dictates of prudence rather than those of vigor. I would not risk the loss that might have been sustained in the assault."

All this gives Washington time to bring additional men from the mainland to back up Putnam, but on the twenty-ninth another heavy rainstorm soaks the none too plentiful ammunition, and it's also clear that the Americans are in serious danger of being cut off from the mainland by the British fleet. A council of war decides to take the only option available—abandon Long Island.

Easier said than done. It's going to take a master stroke, and a little luck besides. For once, Washington is able to bring it off and accomplishes what will go down as his most brilliant maneuver in the war. Unfortunately, the weather won't cooperate. The rain keeps coming down and it's turning into a nor'easter. The commander's men have no tents and not much clothing, so they stand there ankle-deep in water at some places, and the only consolation is that the storm is preventing Howe from coming up the East River and cutting them off.

On the night of the twenty-ninth, the great retreat from Long Island begins. It's a neat trick if they can do it—get an entire army across a mile-wide river under the noses of an enemy force three times larger, whose ships can destroy them at any moment. As soon as it's dark, the evacuation starts in gusty, squally weather, but then, near midnight, the wind shifts to the south and dies down. Welcome, thick fog begins to move in.

Washington is following an ingenious scheme. The idea is that regiments are to leave from the front line one by one, those remaining filling the gaps, so that the retreat is screened right up to the moment of complete withdrawal. Everything goes slowly but well until about 2:00 A.M., when a foul-up occurs, threatening to blow everything apart. First a cannon goes off accidentally, but for some reason the British aren't alarmed. Then Alexander Scammell, Washington's aide-de-camp, gets his orders mixed up. He says all the regiments are to march on down to the ferry, one by one as he reaches them.

Mifflin, commanding the left, protests that he is following the original plan and won't go, but Scammell insists the new orders are correct and Mifflin obeys. As his men come down toward the ferry, Washington rides up on his gray horse, orders them to halt, and demands to know where they're going. Mifflin rushes up, and Washington says to him, "Good God, Mifflin! I'm afraid you have ruined us by unseasonably withdrawing the troops from the lines."

"I've done so by your order, sir," Mifflin responds. Washington denies he gave any such order.

"By God, I *did* get the order," Mifflin says heatedly. "Did Scammell serve as your aide for the day, or did he not?" The commander admits he did, and Mifflin says triumphantly, "Then I had orders through him."

Washington says there's been a terrible mistake, and Mifflin's men must go back because there's so much confusion at the ferry that, if the British discover they've left, everything will be lost. Mifflin takes the troops back; the British haven't missed them.

Another bit of luck. A Loyalist woman who lives near the ferry sees what's going on and sends her black slave to warn the British, but the first officer he sees turns out to be a Hessian who speaks practically no English and puts him under arrest.

In the dense fog of early morning, John Glover's Marblehead men row the last of the army across, with Washington in one of the boats. As the fog lifts with the rising sun, the British discover what's happened and rush down to the ferry. It's a narrow thing. They compel one boat to turn back, capture a few men who haven't got away, and open fire on the receding craft, with no effect. The battle for Long Island is definitely over. Military historians today think it should never have been fought, that it was a major mistake to deploy Americans on Long Island when the British controlled the water. Howe has lost another opportunity, but so has brother Richard, who lets the Americans thumb their noses at his mighty fleet.

Nothing, however, detracts from Washington's brilliant stroke—getting seven thousand men away safely onto Manhattan Island, with all their baggage, field guns, horses, equipment, stores, and provisions. And they haven't lost a man in this operation. The American army has been saved from utter ruin by a commander who hasn't slept for forty-eight hours.

You'd never recognize what happened on Long Island from the report Howe sends to London. It so pleases the King that William Howe is knighted.

Instead of being properly grateful for Washington's extraordinary feat, the citizens of New York are dismayed. When the troops returned, beaten but more or less intact, Brother Shewkirk, pastor of New York's Moravian congregation, writes: "In the morning, unexpectedly and to the surprise of the city, it was found that all that could come back was come back; and that they had abandoned Long Island, when many had thought to surround the King's troops and make them prisoners with little trouble. The language was not otherwise. It was a surprising change: the merry tunes on drums and fifes had ceased, and they were hardly heard for a couple of days. It seemed a general damp had spread, and the sight of the scattered people up and down the streets was indeed moving, many looked sickly, emaciated, cast down, etc.; the wet clothes, tents—as many as they had brought away—and other things were lying about before the houses and in the streets to dry. In general, everything seemed to be in confusion."

Another fallout from the battle has become part of American legend. Washington doesn't know what Howe may do next, so the need for intelligence is great. Here his inexperience shows. He should have sent out several agents to penetrate the enemy camp, but instead he orders Colonel Thomas Knowlton to find one volunteer. Knowlton first asks Lieutenant James Sprague, but the lieutenant is a veteran who fought in the French and Indian War and he says he's willing to fight the British, "but as far as going among them and being taken and hung up like a dog, I will not do it." In the code of the times, he has a right to refuse. Knowlton's eyes turn toward others in the room but they glance away quickly. Then comes a stir at the door, and Nathan Hale, still looking frail from a recent illness, says, "I will undertake it, sir."

This sacrificial lamb is a Yale athlete, class of '73, a Haddam schoolmaster who looks like the all-American boy, tall and handsome, intensely patriotic. He knows absolutely nothing about spying, has never been given any training in it, is not provided with any cover or contacts, or even any money. No line of communication has been set up for him, and worse, he carries notes that will surely convict him if he's caught. They're simply going to throw him out there and trust to luck.

Hale discusses the situation with a Yale classmate, Captain William Hull, who is horrified and tries to discourage him from carrying out this insane assignment. Hull says Hale is too frank and open to be a spy, deceit is not a part of his character, but "who respects the character of a spy?" Hale gives him a dedicated answer: "Every kind of service necessary to the public good becomes honorable by being necessary."

Hale leaves Harlem Heights accompanied by Sergeant Stephen Hempstead, who is to go with him as far as he safely can, then wait for his return. At Norwalk, he finds the American sloop *Schuyler*, whose captain ferries him across the Sound and drops him off near Huntington. He's wearing a uniform of sorts, the frontier hunting shirt often worn by officers in the field, but now he changes into civilian clothes and assumes the character of a Dutch schoolmaster, pretending to look for a teaching job, and carrying his Yale diploma with him for credentials.

Not much is known about what happens next, except for what Captain John Montresor, chief engineer of the British army, will report when he calls on American officers under a truce flag after Hale has been hanged. Apparently the novice spy has done what he was asked to do, sketching fortifications, noting down numbers and positions of troops. At some point he hears that the British have chased the Americans out of Manhattan, but instead of escaping to his own lines, he goes over to New York for a look at the new positions.

He's been in enemy territory more than a week by this time, and his danger increases every day. On the night of September 21, his luck runs out and he's arrested. There are several theories about how it happened, none of them provable. Taken to Howe's headquarters, in the Beekman house at the corner of First Avenue and Fifty-first Street, he admits his guilt and Howe orders him hanged. No trial.

Howe is touched by Hale's demeanor, but not so much that he doesn't confine him in the Beekman greenhouse overnight, where later mythmakers will say a letter written to his mother was torn up before his eyes, and other cruelties were visited on him. No truth in all this; his mother has been dead for years. They won't give him a Bible or a clergyman, though. Still calm and dignified, he is hanged in an artillery park. Some historians have given him a more flowery farewell, but he actually says, "I only regret that I have but one life to lose for my country." Quite logical, too. As a Yale man and a schoolmaster, he's studied Joseph Addison's *Cato* and knows the familiar lines, "What a pity is it/That we can die but once to serve our country." All educated Americans know this play, and Washington himself frequently quotes from it.

So this exemplary man swings from the gallows, secure in the history books, as it turns out, but also, as so often in war, he dies for nothing. Nothing is gained, everything is lost.

By this time his fellow Americans don't give him a thought. The retreat from Long Island has turned into a rout from Manhattan and much worse is to come.

8

✛   ✛   ✛

How We Lost New York—and Much Else

In the aftermath of Long Island, morale has never been lower. A good many of the militia are beginning to think of the war as a bad thing, and they're getting out of it. The commander reports despairingly to Congress that they're leaving "almost by whole regiments, by half ones and by companies at a time." He has, he says, a "want of confidence in the generality of the troops." That's the understatement of 1776.

Washington is getting conflicting advice. Greene, John Jay, and some others are urging him to get out of New York and burn it down. Congress is horrified at the idea. We'll need it later on, the members say, and forbid him to do it. Even his generals are divided about what to do next, so Washington makes his own decision and splits what's left of his army between Manhattan and Kingsbridge.

Howe, as usual, also seems to be indecisive, and at least one of his brother's commanders, Sir George Collins, sitting in his cabin aboard the *Rainbow*, vents his frustration in a sarcastic letter home. "Far from taking the rash resolution of hastily passing over the East River and crushing at once a frightened, trembling enemy, he [Howe] generously gave them time to recover from their panic—to throw up fresh works—to make new arrangements—and to recover from the torpid state the rebellion was in from its late shock. For many succeeding days our brave veterans, consisting of twenty-two thousand men, stood on the banks of the East River, like Moses on Mount

Pisgah, looking at their promised land, little more than half a mile distant. The rebels' standards waved insolently in the air from many different quarters of New York. The British troops could scarcely contain their indignation at the sight and at their own inactivity; the officers were displeased and amazed."

It's worse for the Americans than Sir George thinks. Tents are too wet to be used, so troops have to be quartered in houses, and the men are more undisciplined than ever, violently abusing their officers. Looting is the order of the day, in spite of being forbidden. A two days' supply of pork and bread is parceled out in case there has to be a sudden move, and that's not very reassuring.

As for the commander, after the ordeal of Long Island, he's too exhausted even to write a letter, and whether he knows it or not, for the first time his leadership is being questioned. Colonel John Haslet writes to Caesar Rodney to complain that Washington is surrounded by "beardless youth and inexperience. We have alarm upon alarm. Orders now issued, and the next moment reversed. Would to heaven General Lee were here, in the language of officers and men."

It seems to many in the army that they haven't completed a strategic retreat, as Washington insists is the case, but they've been routed and might just possibly be destroyed. Young Major Lewis Morris writes to his father, General Morris (of Morrisania, but now sitting with Congress in Philadelphia): "As for the militia of Connecticut, Brigadier Oliver Wolcott and his brigade have got the cannon fever and very prudently skulked home. Such people are only a nuisance and had better be in the chimney corner than in the field of Mars. We have men enough without them who will fight."

A council of war on September 12 decides what to do about New York. Leave it, the officers vote unanimously. Horses and wagons are impressed, and river boats assembled, but when Howe sees this activity going on, he moves quickly—at last. For what happens next, we have the eyewitness account of our friend Private Joseph Martin, last seen learning about war on Long Island.

The British assault begins with a heavy cannonade, and before dark, four warships move up the East River and anchor. Defenses have been prepared, but Private Martin scorns them. These "lines," he says, "are nothing more than a ditch dug along on the bank of the river, with the dirt thrown out towards the water." British lookouts on board the ships can hear the American sentinels call out the password, "All is well," and they return a jeering reply: "We will alter your tune before tomorrow night."

So an uneasy night passes, and at dawn the Americans wake to find the ships no more than a musket shot away, preparing to land troops. Martin reports: "All of a sudden, there came such a peal of thunder from the British shipping that I thought my head would go with the sound." After the barrage come the redcoats, in such formidable numbers that the American forces drawn up to defend this landing at Kip's Bay simply roll back, as though tossed by a wave.

Once again Howe doesn't seem to understand that he's facing a demoralized army that could be crushed easily. Instead, arriving by prearrangement at Murray Hill about 2:00 P.M. with his generals, he decides to wait for the landing craft to bring over the remainder of his forces; for some reason, they've been slow about it.

At this point, another legend enters the scene. Howe and his generals have stopped outside the Murray Hill home of Mrs. Murray herself. The enduring myth pictures her as some kind of patriotic siren who invites the generals inside and entertains them while Washington and his troops make their escape. Unfortunately for myth, Mrs. Murray is a middle-aged Quaker lady, the mother of twelve, who simply looks out the window on this blistering hot day and sees a number of fine-looking officers who seem to be overheated. She invites them into her parlor for a glass of Madeira, which they gratefully accept, having nothing else to do at the moment.

While this is taking place, Washington is going through one of his worst moments of the war. He has been staying up at Roger Morris's house on Harlem Heights, but when he hears the British have landed and his troops are retreating—again—he gallops down to the scene, and not far from Mrs. Murray's finds that indeed his men are fleeing up the Post Road as fast as they can go, leaving everything behind. Private Martin says the ground is "literally covered with arms, knapsacks, staves, coats, hats."

Riding into this confusion, George tries to rally the men. "Take the walls! Take the cornfield!" he yells, and a few of them do. Putnam rides up and they work together for a moment, but it's no use. These men are out of control. The commander's rage is spectacular. Throwing his hat on the ground (some say he did it three times), he cries out, "Are these the men with whom I am to defend America?" Snapping a pistol at them (unloaded), he takes his riding cane and beats about him indiscriminately—soldiers, officers, a colonel, even a brigadier general. Nothing helps. Sixty or seventy Hessians appear and begin to charge. Those Americans who had been persuaded to make a stand fling their muskets away at the sight of them, and follow with knapsacks, coats, and hats, taking to their heels and leaving their commander no more than eighty yards from the oncoming Germans. Filled with rage and despair, Washington seems unaware of his danger and simply sits his horse as the Hessians bear down on him. Only an aide who seizes his bridle and hurries him away saves him from being shot or captured, but it's a near thing.

The British have accomplished this rout with only about four thousand men, less than a third of their total force, while Washington has three or four times that number, who might have won the day if they hadn't fled. The rest of Howe's troops don't get there until about 5:00 P.M., and by that time the Americans have escaped.

Not all is flight and panic. Putnam gallops through the retreating troops and manages to rally some of them, flying about on his foam-flecked horse, encouraging everyone. After the British establish a line from Bloomingdale, at Ninety-seventh Street and Broadway, all across Manhattan to Horne's Hook, at Eighty-sixth Street and the East River, Putnam and his men are caught behind it, but after dark they slip through to Harlem, with the help of a patriotic farm boy who gives wrong directions to British scouts trying to find them.

Next day, September 16, after all this defeat and disgrace, the Americans redeem themselves briefly in what the commander terms "a brisk little skirmish" and history calls the Battle of Harlem Heights. It begins just before dawn, when Lieutenant Colonel Thomas Knowlton, a Breed's Hill veteran, lands a party of 120 rangers to reconnoiter the British lines. Coming down over Claremont Hill, at 126th Street, he flushes out General Alexander Leslie's pickets and there's a half hour of desultory firing.

Since this is getting him nowhere, Knowlton begins to retreat in orderly fashion, and Leslie, thinking he's got the damned rebels on the run again, pursues with three hundred light infantry. Joseph Reed, who's with Knowlton, reports what's happening to Washington, who decides to cut off these pesky redcoats. Washington's resolve is further strengthened when the British, moving along toward a valley called Hollow Way, just below Riverside Drive at 130th Street, find themselves in such high humor that they instruct a bugler to blow the hunting call that means the fox has been run to earth.

As an old Virginia fox hunter himself, Washington is particularly outraged by this piece of insolence, and as Reed says later, "I never felt such a sensation before, it seemed to crown our disgrace." Making sure there are no support troops lurking behind, Washington attacks. Knowlton falls mortally wounded in the first few minutes, but the rangers press on, and in about an hour, the British have had enough and retreat to a buckwheat field about where Barnard College now stands. There they get some reinforcements—two light infantry battalions, the Black Watch Highlanders, some grenadiers, a Hessian grenadier battalion, along with a company of Hessian jägers. Washington also brings up reinforcements and a two-hour battle takes place in which the British find themselves pushed backward over hill and dale to a point near their own main line at 105th Street.

By this time the American troops are so excited by having the British on the run for once that they're all for pursuing them right into the main line, where Cornwallis is hurrying up with heavy reinforcements. With some difficulty, Washington persuades them not to commit suicide, and they slip away, back to their own lines. A very small victory, true, but a wonderful morale builder.

Captain John Chilton, a tobacco planter from Fauquier County, Virginia, writes home: "Our men observed the best order, not quitting their ranks, though exposed to a constant and warm fire. I can't say enough in their praise; they behaved like soldiers who fought from principle alone."

Tench Tilghman, a Philadelphia merchant who is serving without either rank or pay, writes to his father: "These troops, though young, charged with as much bravery as I can conceive! They gave two fires and then rushed right forward." And Joseph Reed reports to his wife: "You can hardly conceive the change it has made in our army. The men have recovered their spirits and feel a confidence which before they had quite lost." It will be some time before they feel this sensation again.

Private Martin witnesses a bizarre yet extremely touching spectacle that night. Just at dusk he's burying a fallen soldier near Roger Morris's house, later known as the Jumel Mansion. Just as the body is laid in the grave, two young women who look like sisters walk down from the house and stand by the graveside; the soldiers respectfully step back a little. One sister asks if they intend to throw the dirt on his face and, assured that they do, she takes a fine white gauze handkerchief from her neck and asks that it be spread over the dead soldier's countenance. This is done while both sisters stand weeping. When the grave is filled, they walk slowly back up to the house. No one knows who this dead man is, but still he has mourners.

Earlier that day, while the "little skirmish" is going on, an incident occurs that throws a rather uncertain light, for the first time, on Washington's friend and aide, Joseph Reed. Ebenezer Leffingwell, a sergeant from the Connecticut Continental regiment, is ordered by his officers to hustle up more ammunition, and while he's about it, he encounters Reed, who accuses him of deserting his post during an enemy action. The sergeant protests that he's only carrying out the orders of his superiors, but Reed draws his sword and says he'll kill him if he doesn't return immediately to the battle. Leffingwell, who knows an injustice when he sees one, cocks his musket and prepares to defend himself, but he's seized, later tried for mutiny, and sentenced to be shot.

His fellows in the Connecticut regiment appear on execution day, form a square, and when the sergeant appears, bound and blindfolded, he kneels on the ground and no one is sure exactly what these troops may do. At the last moment, a messenger rushes up with a reprieve from the commander. Private Martin is there and speculates: "I believe it was well . . . for his blood would not have been the only blood that would have been spilt; the troops were greatly exasperated and they showed what their feelings were by their lively and repeated cheerings after the reprieve, but more so by their secret and open threats before it."

Such incipient small mutinies are not all the commander has to worry about as he proceeds to get the rest of his army off Manhattan Island and onto the mainland again. The deep antagonism between Northern and Southern troops that has since the Cambridge camps been simmering beneath the surface—and breaking out on occasion—has been exacerbated by the disgrace of Kip's Bay. The Southerners blame it on the New Englanders, and show their contempt openly. To his brother Thomas, Caesar Rodney charges: "That the New England men behaved in a most dastardly, cowardly and scandalous manner is most certain."

Naturally, the Yankees don't fancy being called cowards, and tensions grow. And here comes Reed again. Joseph Trumbull,

Connecticut's commissary general, accuses him of doing "more to raise and keep up a jealousy between the New England and other troops than all the men in the army beside. . . . His stinking pride has gone so far that I expect every day to hear he is called to account by some officer or other." A New England brigadier general says of the animosity, "It has already risen to such a height that the Pennsylvania and New England troops would as soon fight each other as the enemy." All this cools down considerably later on as these very different colonists are compelled to march, camp, and fight together, discovering they're more alike than they thought. At the moment they're sharing a common fate. They've been pushed off Manhattan Island and no one is sure what's going to happen next.

As for the British, they've taken over New York and it's going to be their principal base until the end of the war. They have an immediate task of bringing it under some kind of military and political control. In the last hours of the American occupation, it's become a lawless city. With no guards to stop it, looting is endemic. Ferry boats crisscross to Paulus Hook, carrying the Committee of Safety and all the Whigs able to make their escape. That leaves only a few Loyalists to welcome the conquering British, but they do it joyfully. A woman enters the fort at the Battery, pulls down the American flag, stamps on it, and raises the British emblem. Officers from the fleet coming ashore are raised on welcoming shoulders and carried triumphantly through the streets. It's the hour of deliverance for Loyalists, and New York is going to be theirs for a long time.

But not intact. After little more than a week of British possession, on September 21, in the early-morning hours, fire breaks out in a small wooden house, near a Whitehall Slip wharf. It's a clear night with a brisk wind, which carries the sparks in every direction. Church bells don't give the usual alarm because the Americans have taken them all down, to be converted into cannon. It's too soon to have adequate, trained fire companies, and many engines and pumps don't work.

The result is a night of horror as a large part of the town burns down, the flames leaping from wooden house to wooden house, feeding on their cedar shingles. This fire is no respecter of anyone or anything. Black Dick sends in seamen and soldiers to fight the inferno, and they pull down many of the buildings in order to save the city.

Naturally, everyone believes the Americans set it, and angry mobs kill anyone who looks like a Whig or who doesn't seem to be doing his part to stop the fire. Thus an unfortunate drunken carpenter, Wright White, known as a "violent Loyalist," is suspected of impeding the firefighters and is summarily hanged from a tavern signpost. Another innocent who happens to have a box of matches on his person is tossed into the flames. Still another suspect is first bayoneted, then hung up by his feet.

About two in the morning, the wind changes from southwest to southeast and that saves the main part of town, concentrating the fire between Broadway and the North River. St. Paul's Chapel is saved, but nearly everything else in this area is gone. Howe has not permitted all his troops to fight the fire because he thinks it's a sinister plot by the rebels to set the city ablaze and then attack. After daybreak, he relents, but by then the disaster is complete.

In his diary, Lieutenant Frederick Mackenzie writes: "It is almost impossible to conceive a scene of more horror and distress. The sick, the aged, women, and children, half-naked, were seen going they knew not where, and taking refuge in houses which were at a distance from the fire, but from whence in several instances were driven a second and even a third time by the devouring element, and at last, in a state of despair, laying themselves down on the Common. The terror was increased by the horrid noise of the burning and falling houses, the pulling down of such wooden buildings as served to conduct the fire, the rattling of above one hundred wagons sent in from the army, constantly employed in conveying to the Common such goods and effects as could be saved; the confused voices of so many men; the shrieks and cries of the women and children.

"The appearance of the Trinity Church, when completely in flames, was a very grand sight, for the spire being entirely framed of wood and covered with shingles, a lofty pyramid of fire appeared, and as soon as the shingles were burnt away, the frame appeared with every piece of timber burning until the principal timbers were burnt through, when the whole fell with a great noise."

Nathan Hale was executed the morning after the fire, and some historians have speculated that it was British fury over the blaze that led them to a quick and summary judgment in his case.

They get over their anger, though, as the two armies face each other in the vicinity of Fort Washington, looking across the river at Fort Lee, while the commander and the remaining forces establish headquarters at White Plains.

There, in the brisk October weather, Washington gets a small favorable breeze from Canada. Good news, of a sort, for a change. After the American withdrawal, Sir Guy Carleton had intended to penetrate the Hudson Valley and join the British troops below, but to do so he had to stop and build a fleet of boats at St. John to carry his attack down Lake Champlain. He knew that Schuyler and Gates, left to hold the line in the Northern Department, had about nine thousand men available to oppose him, but his spies told him they were badly equipped and clothed, and many were still suffering from the smallpox that broke out during the retreat from Canada. They should be no obstacle, Carleton believed.

Matters were even worse with the Americans than he thought. John Adams called smallpox "ten times more terrible than Britons, Canadians and Indians together," and when we read the journal of Dr. Lewis Beebe, who was trying to take care of the troops, it's clear Adams wasn't exaggerating. Beebe wasn't really qualified to be a doctor; at one point in his life he was a preacher, and in the end, he wound up keeping a liquor shop in New York. But, suffering from dysentery himself, he did what he could. When a man died, he reported, it wasn't easy to find eight or so others well enough to carry the corpse about fifteen rods to be buried.

On June 7, Beebe wrote in his journal: "Here in the hospital is to be seen at the same time some dead, some dying, others at the point of death, some whistling, some singing and many cursing and swearing. This is a strange composition and its chief intention has not as yet been discovered; however it appears very plain that it is wonderfully calculated for a campaign. Visited many of the sick in the hospital—was moved with a compassionate feeling for poor distressed soldiers who, when they are taken sick, are thrown into this dirty, stinking place and left to take care of themselves. No attendance, no provision made, but what must be loathed and abhorred by all both well and sick." And three days later: "Nothing to be heard from morning to night but 'Doctor! Doctor! Doctor!' from every side till one is deaf, dumb and blind, and almost dead; add to all this, we have nothing to eat. . . ." On June 17: "The most shocking of all spectacles was to see a large barn crowded full of men with this disorder, many of which could not see, speak, or walk. One—nay, two—had large maggots, an inch long, crawl out of their ears, were on almost every part of the body."

In August, Dr. Jonathan Pitts wrote from Fort George that more than one thousand sick men were crowded into sheds, ill with dysentery, "bilious putrid fevers," and smallpox. There were five doctors and four assistants to care for the entire lot, but in any case, they had no medicine to treat the patients—"in this dilemma our inventions are exhausted for substitutes." In September, Samuel Wigglesworth wrote to the New Hampshire Committee of Safety: "It would make a heart of stone melt to hear the moans and see the distresses of the sick and dying. I scarce pass a tent but I hear men solemnly declaring that they will never engage in another campaign without being assured of a better supply of medicines."

Who volunteered to jump into this hellhole and save the day against Sir Guy Carleton? None other than that determined hero from New Haven, Benedict Arnold. With his customary persistence, he got himself sent to join Gates and in the waning days of summer he immediately organized those able to work into a task force for building ships. If Carleton was to be stopped, he reasoned, it would have to be on the water; for now, the Americans were simply inadequate on land. He recruited two hundred able-bodied shipwrights and carpenters, ordered sailcloth and naval supplies, and while these were arriving from coastal towns in Connecticut, Massachusetts, and Maine, the sound of axes rang in the forest around the lake.

What emerged was a rather odd fleet: two small schooners, two sloops, four galleys, eight gondolas. There wasn't much to recommend it. They would be slow, overgunned, and worst of all, most of the freshwater sailors manning them had never seen the deck of a ship. Arnold couldn't even test the guns because, as always, there wasn't enough powder.

Arnold was nothing if not absolutely intrepid. When the fleet was ready, he ventured out boldly on the lake and formed a battle line between Valcour Island and the western shore. The British took notice, and on October 11, they moved their own squadron—a ship, two schooners, a floating battery, a large gondola, twenty gunboats, four armed longboats—into position. The British enjoyed every advantage. Their ships were larger and better built, their guns superior, and they were manned by officers and men of the Royal Navy. They were also getting help from Indian allies who sat in treetops along the shore and took potshots at the Americans.

In spite of all the inequalities, Arnold's flotilla fought desperately for seven hours, and as the sun set, the British withdrew to regroup. The Americans suffered numerous casualties, but they lost only one schooner and a gondola. Still, Carleton considered them beaten and he was only waiting until morning to finish the job.

During the foggy night, however, Arnold slipped away and two days later resumed the battle at Split Rock. This time British superiority prevailed. Arnold's galley was shattered; he ordered his ship and what remained of the fleet to be run up on shore, where he set fire to the lot. Then he and his part-time sailors escaped to Crown Point, ten miles away. Carleton took this post too, but by that time Arnold and his men had reached more heavily defended Ticonderoga.

How could Arnold's optimistic dispatches make a victory out of this one? Well, he's delayed Carleton so long that the season is running out, just as it did for the Americans when they invaded Canada. No danger that Carleton will continue his march southward now. Instead, convinced that Ticonderoga is too well defended to be taken by anything but a long siege, he retreats into Canada. True, Arnold has given Burgoyne a base for next year's campaign, but Schuyler is now able to release some badly needed troops for Washington's main army. In later years, Admiral Mahan, no lover of land power, will say that a soldier, Benedict Arnold, saved the Revolution by his naval delaying action. As for Arnold, he's disappointed. He intended to win.

At White Plains, meanwhile, Howe is pursuing his usual leisurely course, and the idle troops on both sides are getting to know each other. In this weeks-long lull, until mid-October, the Americans are well fed for once, although there isn't much variety in their diet, which is mostly beef, pork, peas, rum, and brandy. The two forces are so close to each other that the initial firing between pickets seems irrelevant and the officers on both sides stop it, coming to an unspoken understanding. Are they really enemies? they begin to ask. Fraternization is in the air. General Heath writes: "They were so civil to each other, on their posts, that one day at a part of the creek where it was practicable, the British sentinel asked the American, who was nearly opposite to him, if he could give him a chaw of tobacco; the latter, having in his pocket a piece of a thick twisted roll, sent it across the creek to the British sentinel, who after taking off his bite, sent the remainder back again."

Lee arrives in camp, bringing division with him, and there is an immediate argument between him and Washington as to which of two heights to occupy. Other officers join in. The commander suggests reasonably that they go look at the sites, but while they're doing so, a light horseman gallops up on his winded horse and reports, "The British are in the camp, sir."

"Gentlemen, we have now other business than reconnoitering," Washington says, and plunges off with the others at full gallop. It turns out to be a momentary false alarm, only a feint. What's happened is that Howe has decided to do what he should have done long before, that is, move onto the mainland himself so that he can cut the Americans' communications and threaten their rear. He comes by way of Hell Gate and Throg's Neck, and on October 25 he is on the Bronx River with 13,000 men, only four miles from White Plains. Three days later, he attacks.

Washington has taken advantage of the time Howe has generously given him. He's deployed 2,000 men at Fort Washington, over 4,000 more at Fort Lee, and he has the rest at White Plains, anchored in a swamp at the left and on the right by the river. The battle begins at a place called Chatterton's Hill, where Colonel Haslet's Delaware regiment, about 1,500 men, supported by two guns from Alexander Hamilton's battery, are about to confront 4,000 redcoats.

It's Breed's Hill all over again, even the weather. A witness writes: "A bright autumnal sun shed its full luster on the polished arms and the rich array of dress and military equipage gave an imposing grandeur to the scene." There's considerably less grandeur on the hill. Twice the British climb it, and twice they're forced back by deadly fire, but there are just too many of them, and the third time they succeed, leaving more than three hundred killed and wounded on the hillside—a high price to pay. The militia do much better than they did at Breed's, wavering at last but retreating in good order with their guns and men, losing less than two hundred.

But what's going on here? The attack at Chatterton's Hill was supposed to have been a diversion, to be synchronized with Howe's assault on the main American position. It never happens, and the general even refuses later to give Parliament a believable excuse. He did it "for political reasons," he says, although to this day we don't know what they were. However, he can't simply sit there, so three days later, heavily reinforced, he prepares another attack, and this time a torrential rainstorm saves him from action.

Seeing himself outnumbered, Washington removes his men under cover of darkness on November 1 to a much stronger defensive position five miles away at North Castle, beyond the Croton River. Howe doesn't pursue. Instead, he takes up a position at Dobbs Ferry, so that his army lies between the commander and Fort Washington, where he's also in a position to threaten Fort Lee.

Now Washington is really alarmed. He wants to abandon both forts, but Congress and all his generals oppose losing Fort Washington, so he does the best he can, leaving five thousand men at North Castle and sending three thousand more up to Peekskill. Then he crosses the river to Fort Lee with Greene and Putnam, and he's scarcely out of the boat before he's a horrified witness to the worst American defeat in the war thus far.

This time Howe makes no mistake. He understands the importance of Fort Washington and he attacks it with more skill than he's displayed until now. In less than two hours, it's over. At first the militia stand firm but they can't resist the pressure, or the sight of the Hessians' cold steel, already being used on prisoners. It costs the British and Hessians 458 killed and wounded, the Americans only 39 killed, 96 wounded, but the worst statistic is the captured—2,818 men. Howe's officers urge him to kill the whole garrison, which he has the right to do under eighteenth-century rules of warfare, but he can't stomach such wholesale brutality. If he had done so, the war might possibly have been over because Congress would have been unable to raise another army at that juncture.

The British aren't impressed with the part of the army they've captured. Lieutenant Mackenzie writes in his diary: "The rebel prisoners were in general but very indifferently clothed. Few of them appeared to have a second shirt, nor did they appear to have washed themselves during the campaign. A great many of them were lads under fifteen and old men, and few had the appearance of soldiers. Their odd figures frequently excited the laughter of our soldiers."

Taking advantage of this American disaster, Howe presses forward. On a cold, rainy November night, he dispatches his ablest general, Cornwallis, with four thousand men to cross the river and threaten Greene, who is holding Fort Lee with about three thousand men while Washington is in Hackensack, trying frantically to rouse up the New Jersey militia. Cornwallis means to surprise Greene, but an officer on patrol five or six miles north of the fort sights the advance column and gallops back to rout Greene from his bed. The Americans flee so rapidly that they leave the kettles boiling for their breakfast, their tents standing, their supplies intact, taking only what they can carry.

If Washington thinks he was considered a fox run to earth on Harlem Heights, there's no doubt that the pack is in full cry behind him now, so close that some of his men are picked off and 105 are captured. He has only about 3,000 left, "much broken and dispirited," and he's losing some of them along the way as he flees south through New Jersey. At Fort Lee, the British have captured many cannon, besides three hundred tents, hundreds of muskets, and enough shot, shell, and cartridges to fight a battle, not to mention more than a thousand barrels of flour. A redcoat writes that these rebels fled "like scared rabbits. They have left some poor pork, a few greasy proclamations, and of that scoundrel *Common Sense* man's letters."

As the wild flight continues, the clear weather turns to freezing rain. Along the way, Washington sends frantic appeals to the Jersey militia to turn out and join him, and he also sends a series of letters to Lee, who's been left with the troops at New Castle, urging him to come with all possible speed. But Lee gives him a series of equivocal answers. The loss of the two forts has sent him into a state of shock, so it's said, but it has also convinced him that if he'd been in command, it would never have happened, and that notion is reinforced by a letter from Washington's good friend and aide, Joseph Reed, who at last discloses where his heart is.

"I do not mean to flatter," says the commander's most trusted friend and officer, "nor praise you at the expense of any other, but I confess I do think that it is entirely owing to you that this army and the liberties of America so far as they are depending on it are not totally cut off. You have decision, a quality often missing in minds otherwise valuable." Reed is quite willing to include Greene in his condemnation, by implication: "They hold us very cheap in consequence of the late affair at Mount Washington, where both the plan of defense and execution were contemptible. . . . Oh! General—an indecisive mind is one of the greatest misfortunes that can befall an army. How often have I lamented it in this campaign."

Lee believes what Reed wants him to believe, that the trusted aide speaks for the whole army, and from that moment he feels he's no longer a subordinate but the man who ought to be in command.

That's why he gives equivocal answers to Washington's urgent orders to join him with his men. Of course he does have one good excuse. Most of his soldiers aren't fit to march anywhere, half-sick and some half-naked as they are. Just the same, there's no point and some danger in staying where he is, so on December 5 he crosses the Hudson and arrives in Morristown on the eighth, his army's progress marked by bloody tracks in the snow. Three times along the way Washington has sent messengers to find him, and now, from Morristown, Lee sends some more evasive replies and ignores the commander's direct orders to make haste. On the night of December 12, he finds himself staying at an inn in Basking Ridge, where he writes to his friend Horatio Gates: "Entre nous, a certain great man is most damnably deficient—he has thrown me into a situation where I have my choice of difficulties—if I stay in this province I risk myself and army and if I do not stay the province is lost forever."

He goes to bed that night, probably not alone, and next morning, as Captain James Wilkinson recalls in his memoirs, he spends most of the early hours "in altercation with certain military corps who were of his command, particularly the Connecticut light horse, several of whom appeared in large full-bottomed perukes, and were treated very irreverently; the call of the adjutant general for orders also occupied some of his time, and we did not sit down to breakfast before ten o'clock. General Lee was engaged in answering General Gates's letter [the one quoted above] and I had risen from the table and was looking out of an end window down a lane about one hundred yards in length, which led to the house from the main road, when I discovered a party of British dragoons turn a corner of the avenue at a full charge. Startled at this unexpected spectacle, I exclaimed, 'Here, sir, are the British cavalry!'"

What Wilkinson sees is another of the war's most colorful characters, Banastre Tarleton, the dashing cavalryman who will be remembered forever, and not with love, in the South, and who now enters the stage with a capture that does his reputation no harm.

Tarleton comes from a rich Liverpool family (his father was mayor) and after his Oxford education was headed for the law until his father bought him a commission in the King's Dragoon Guards at the very moment in 1775 when George III's other soldiers were having unforeseen difficulties at Lexington, Concord, and Breed's Hill. Tarleton was eager to jump into the fight and volunteered as soon as his training was finished. He was sent first to help Clinton's operation against Charleston, early in 1776, but when the 16th Light Dragoons arrived in New York, he was transferred to this unit, and that's how it happens he's hunting enemy generals in New Jersey. No one who meets him in the field doubts his extraordinary ability to maneuver cavalry with rapidity and daring; those who encounter him person- ally find him a cold, vindictive man, a ruthless commander who leaves a trail of blood across the land.

But now, while Lee is taking his time, Tarleton, scouting in the vicinity with a small force, captures some Americans whom he threatens with his saber until they tell him where Lee is. He pushes ahead with only five men, deliberately making so much noise that the sentries think an army is coming and flee in panic. Tarleton tells his mother in a letter home: "I ordered my men to fire into the house thro' every window and door, and cut up as many of the guard as they could. An old woman upon her knees begged for life and told me General Lee was in the house. This assurance gave me pleasure."

Inside, Lee is alarmed but collected, according to Captain Wilkinson's account, and shouts, "'Damn the guard, why don't they fire?' The women of the house at this moment entered the room and proposed to him to conceal himself in a bed, which he rejected with evident disgust. I caught up my pistols which lay on the table, thrust the letter he had been writing into my pocket, and passed into a room at the opposite end of the house, where I had seen the guard in the morning. Here I discovered their arms but the men were absent. I stepped out the door and perceived the dragoons chasing them in different directions, and receiving a very uncivil salutation, I returned into the house."

Wilkinson takes up a position with a pistol in each hand and pre- pares to defend himself. There's a brief exchange of fire between Tarleton's men and two French colonels in Lee's entourage, as well as from a few remaining members of the guard. But then, as Tarleton tells his mother, "I fired twice through the door of the house and then addressed myself to this effect: I knew General Lee was in the house, that if he would surrender himself, he and his attendants should be safe, but if my summons was not complied with immediately, the house should be burnt and every person without exception should be put to the sword."

At that moment, one of his men tells him Lee is trying to escape by the back door, a maneuver Wilkinson loyally overlooks in his account. Tarleton gallops to that spot, seizes one of the French colonels with Lee, shoots the other and a few of the guard who are assisting the escape. Lee himself surrenders to a mere sentry. And what a disgraceful surrender it is. Wilkinson grits his teeth and tells the worst of it: "A general shout ensued, the trumpet sounded the assembly, and the unfortunate Lee, mounted on my horse, which stood ready at the door, was hurried off in triumph, bareheaded, in his slippers and blanket coat, his collar open, and his shirt very much soiled from several days' use."

We won't be seeing him again until he's exchanged near the end of the terrible winter at Valley Forge. In the meantime, he'll be busy advising the British how to defeat the Americans.

When the news that Lee has been captured reaches Washington, he doesn't understand that the British have done him a favor and regards it as simply another piece of bad news, of the kind which fills all his waking hours. The flight through New Jersey has been a continuous nightmare. Greene has hurried to join him, collecting a few recruits at Hackensack, but the commander sees his little army slowly vanishing before his eyes from the daily desertions. Cornwallis is following rapidly on his heels, marching as much as twenty miles in a day, but when he gets to the Raritan, the Americans are saved once more by Howe, who orders his general to stop until he can catch up with him at New Brunswick. Even so, Cornwallis's advance elements come into Princeton no more than an hour after the Americans' rear guard has left it. Lord Stirling has joined the retreat at New Brunswick with a thousand men, but they're not much help, "broken down and fatigued—some without shoes, some have no shirts," and in the bargain many of them are suffering from "barrel fever," that is, drinking and fighting.

Why don't the British jump on this ragtag remnant of an army and end the war, as they could so easily do? We know about Howe's psychological problems, but why is the extremely able Cornwallis now going about the pursuit in such a leisurely way? His spies report that, a day after Washington passed through New Brunswick, the Maryland and New Jersey militia brigades deserted, with the British only ten miles away. But instead of moving in for the kill, Cornwallis pauses in New Brunswick, for no discernible reason, giving Washington time to get the troops he has left, including the sick and all his baggage, across the Delaware into Pennsylvania. He discourages further pursuit by sinking every boat he can find on the river for a distance of seventy miles above Philadelphia. Cornwallis arrives in Trenton just in time to see the last of the American boats safely on the river en route to the opposite shore.

In Philadelphia, there is near panic. The war is no longer safely in Boston or New York, but right on the doorstep, and what's to stop the British from coming inside? Congress immediately begins its own retreat—to Baltimore. Washington sends Putnam and a small force down to fortify the city and place it under martial law. Mifflin comes along to see what can be done about acquiring food and other supplies, as well as stirring up the militia.

Howe may have failed to end the war in New Jersey, but he's now so confident the end is near that he divides his forces. On December 8, Clinton descends on Rhode Island and Newport with six thousand men, and for the next three years the British will continue to control that part of the coast. Howe believes he has the Americans beaten in every sense except actual surrender. With Lee's capture, he is sure the rebels have lost their best general, and apparently Lee's captors think so too because they report that when they reached New Brunswick with their prisoner, a scene of wild celebration occurred, in which everyone got drunk, including Lee's horse, and a band played all night.

With things under control, or so he believes, Howe decides to spend a comfortable winter in New York, in the arms of his mistress, Mrs. Joshua Loring. He has spun a web, or at least an encirclement, around the Americans, with fourteen thousand men in posts stretching from Staten Island to Princeton, with southern anchors at Trenton and Bordentown, where three thousand Hessians and Highlanders are stationed. They (and the British troops as well) have been ordered to behave decently toward the local inhabitants, especially the Loyalists, but these confident and bored occupiers disregard the orders and embark on a reign of terror that spares no one. They take whatever they fancy, without payment, whether it's hay, oats, Indian corn, cattle, horses, or women. They take beds and furniture right out from under the noses of distraught families, insulting them while they're doing so, and if the civilians make any trouble, they take their clothes too. Once it becomes clear to the Loyalists that their loyalty will get them nowhere, a number switch sides. American occupiers may take things, but usually they pay for what they take.

However, they don't take any nonsense, either. Sergeant Joseph White, an artilleryman in the Continental Army, relates that after he has crossed the Delaware, his unit is lodged in the back room of a tavern, whose owner refuses to take what he calls "rebel money." The sergeant goes to his commander, who happens to be Putnam, and reports this impasse. The general says bluntly, "You go and tell him, for me, that if he refuses to take our money, take what you want without any pay."

White conveys this information, but the tavern owner says, "Your Yankee general dare not give such orders." The sergeant then takes matters into his own hands. Placing two men at the cellar door as sentries, he lights a candle and takes two others down the stairs. "We found it full of good things," he reports later, "a large pile of cheeses, hams of bacon, a large tub of honey, barrels of cider, and one barrel marked cider-royal, which was very strong; also all kinds of spirits."

Meanwhile, the owner takes his complaint directly to Putnam. "I don't like your rebel money," he says. As White tells it, "The general flew around like a top. He called for a file of men. A corporal and four men came. 'Take this Tory rascal to the main guardhouse.'" White thinks it only fair to send over a ham of bacon, one large cheese, and a bucket full of cider royal to the general, who wants to know who sent them, and sends back his thanks.

Such bright moments are rare on the Pennsylvania side of the Delaware as the winter closes in and Washington tries to decide what to do. Fortunately a morale booster appears in the form of a pamphlet titled "The American Crisis," by Tom Paine, who marched down New Jersey as a volunteer with the retreating Americans, and is said to have written this inspirational essay on the top of a drumhead. Future generations unto our own time will quote its most memorable phrase, "these are the times that try men's souls," and it's possible some unenthusiastic militiamen will squirm to hear themselves referred to by inference as "sunshine patriots." It's the civilians, however, who seize upon Paine's call to their better natures. His essay is the talk of the Philadelphia streets, and soon everyone is quoting from it.

Nevertheless, the fortunes of this war have reached their lowest point yet as far as Washington is concerned, and it's at this critical moment that he is about to justify the word some future historians will apply to him—"indispensable."

First he establishes an intelligence network that will give him a steady flow of information he's been needing badly. He spreads out a screen of secret agents across lower New Jersey. Some of these spies ride about the country dressed as simple farm folk (which is usually what they are), selling a commodity the Germans especially are eager to buy, tobacco. These are not soldiers, but farmers who have volunteered for this dangerous work; only one is ever caught and hanged.

A different kind of spy is John Honeyman, a New Jersey weaver and butcher from Griggstown. At least one historian (British at that) thinks John saved the Americans from eclipse by the information he supplied. Washington is looking for someone to send across the river and find out what the British are doing, whether they're building boats in anticipation of an attack, or whether they're as quiet as they appear to be. Honeyman volunteers for the mission. He passes himself off first as a captured Tory who has escaped and is to be brought alive to the commander if he turns up again.

His neighbors, who of course are not in on the plot, think he's a turncoat and an eighteen-year-old patriot named Abraham Baird comes around to his home with a mob, intending to destroy it. Honeyman's wife is forced to show them a protective order signed by Washington in order to save the property, although that leaks the secret to several people.

This spy, now posing as a butcher and horse trader, is a cool customer. He was in General Wolfe's bodyguard at Quebec in the French and Indian War, and had helped carry the mortally wounded commander off the field, "walking most of the way in blood," as he likes to say in telling the story. Since he's a veteran of the British army, with a commendable record, he's ideally cast as a spy. The master plan is to have him be captured by the Americans and taken to Washington.

Before that occurs, he's successful in gaining the confidence of Colonel Johann Rall, commander of Howe's southern anchor across the river. This Hessian veteran, who fought in the European theater of the Seven Years' War, and also joined the Russians against the Turks, at fifty-five is still vigorous, as well as pigheaded and arrogant. A British officer calls him "noisy, but not sullen, unacquainted with the language, and a drunkard." Rall's contempt for the colonials is complete. He calls them "country clowns" and refuses to take them seriously.

Howe had ordered him to build redoubts at his Trenton base, but he sees no reason to give the "clowns" that much credibility. Instead, he takes two of his six fieldpieces and mounts them on each side of his headquarters entrance as ornaments. He likes to have the Hessian band march around on snowy mornings to entertain him, and at all hours he is more or less immersed in good liquor.

All this information is conveyed to Washington by Honeyman, who is then permitted to escape and return to the British lines, where he tells Rall that he has nothing to fear from the Americans. They are far too weak for an attack, he assures his Hessian friend.

Something of that fear, however, is in Washington's mind. Benjamin Rush, a Philadelphia doctor and a signer of the Declaration of Independence, visits him on December 23 and finds him "much depressed and lamented the ragged and dissolving state of his army. While I was talking to him, I observed him to play with his pen and ink upon several small pieces of paper. One of them by accident fell upon the floor near my feet. I was struck with the inscription upon it. It was, 'Victory or Death.'"

It will be the countersign for the incredible stroke Washington is about ready to launch, a do-or-die attack that will either be considered a masterful leap from near ruin or else an obituary for a stillborn republic.

What he plans is nothing less than to recross the river and strike at Rall while he and his men are lost in Christmas cheer. In his diary, Colonel John Fitzgerald, Washington's Irish aide, observes that the "Hessians make a great deal of Christmas in Germany [in contrast to America], and no doubt the Hessians will drink a great deal of beer and have a dance tonight. They will be sleepy tomorrow morning."

The assault is prepared carefully. The men are given three days' cooked rations, along with new flints and ammunition. Boats are to be manned by the same crews who got the army off Long Island, Colonel John Glover's Marblehead fishermen. In his diary at 6:00 P.M. on Christmas Day, John Fitzgerald writes: "It is fearfully cold and raw and a snowstorm is setting in. The wind northeast and beats in the face of the men. It will be a terrible night for the soldiers who have no shoes. Some of them have tied only rags around their feet; others are barefoot, but I have not heard a man complain." No doubt some of these soldiers are thinking that in just eight days their enlistments will run out. If the attack is unsuccessful, they will never be seen again.

And almost immediately things begin to go wrong. The attack force is intended to work its way in before dawn, but it's delayed for three hours. Blocking and diversionary forces never get to the other side at all, their commanders deciding at the last minute that the river, with its floating ice, is too dangerous. Washington, however, leads the attacking force across successfully—not standing up heroically as he appears in the familiar picture; the Marblehead men would never have permitted such lunacy—and arrives just before daylight.

Sitting in the ferry house at 3:00 A.M., waiting for the other troops to arrive, Fitzgerald seizes a moment and writes in his diary: "I have never seen Washington so determined as he is now. He stands on the bank of the river, wrapped in his cloak, superintending the landing of his troops. He is calm and collected, but very determined. The storm is changing to sleet and cuts like a knife. The last cannon is being landed, and we are ready to mount our horses."

They start out, nearly three hours behind schedule. At the Bear Tavern, the army splits into two divisions, one of them under the ever-ready Sullivan, who reports a little later that his men's muskets are so wet from the storm that they can't be used. Washington instructs the messenger: "Tell General Sullivan to use the bayonet. I'm resolved to take Trenton."

As so often happens, historic events begin with mundane scenes. Washington's men come upon a house where a man is chopping wood outside, and the commander asks politely, "Can you tell me where the Hessian picket is?" The chopper seems stricken dumb by this request, but Fitzgerald intervenes quickly: "You needn't be frightened. It's General Washington who asks the question." Apparently that's a familiar name. The man brightens up and points toward a nearby house. It's now just 8:00 A.M.

"Looking down the road," Fitzgerald writes later, "I saw a Hessian running out from the house. He yelled in Dutch and swung his arms. Three or four others came out with their guns. Two of them fired at us, but the bullets whistled over our heads. Some of General [Adam] Stephen's men rushed forward and captured two. The others took to their heels, running toward Mr. Calhoun's house, where the picket guard was stationed, about twenty men under Captain Altenbockum. They came running out of the house. The captain flourished his sword and tried to form his men. Some of them fired at us, others ran toward the village. The next moment we heard drums beat and a bugle sound, and then from the west came the boom of a cannon. General Washington's face lighted up instantly, for he knew that it was one of Sullivan's guns.

"We could see a great commotion down toward the meeting house, men running here and there, officers swinging their swords, artillerymen harnessing their horses. Captain [Thomas] Forrest limbered his guns. Washington gave the order to advance, and we rushed on to the junction of King and Queen streets. Forrest wheeled six of his cannon into position to sweep both streets. The riflemen under Colonel [Edward] Hand and [Charles] Scott's and Lawrence's battalions were upon the run through the fields on the left to gain possession of the Princeton road. The Hessians were just ready to open fire with two of their cannon when Captain [William] Washington and Lieutenant [James] Monroe with their men rushed forward and captured them.

"We saw Rall come riding up the street from his headquarters, which were at Stacy Potts' house. We could hear him shouting in Dutch, 'My brave soldiers, advance!' But the soldiers were frightened and confused, rebels firing on them from fences and houses, were falling fast."

It doesn't take long. The Hessians try to find shelter in an apple orchard, where their officers attempt to rally them, but the oncoming Americans keep picking off these officers, and at last they get the colonel himself. Rall falls from his horse, mortally wounded, and with that his soldiers throw down their guns.

Meanwhile, Colonel John Stark, New Hampshire's pride, has been coming up the river road with his men, driving another detachment of Hessians pell-mell ahead of him. Sullivan's men have taken the bridge on the Bordentown road and sealed off retreat. It's reported that Greene's men have charged into town, shouting, "These are the times that try men's souls!" while Knox's cannon pours volleys down Trenton's two main streets, sending shrieking women and hysterical children flying in every direction. The Battle of Trenton, if we can call this skirmish a battle, is over quickly and Washington has pulled it off. The country clowns, supposedly on the point of vanishing, have struck a serious blow at Howe's southern anchor and given themselves a badly needed shot of confidence. One reason for their success is the note from a Loyalist farmer discovered in Rall's pocket, still neatly folded and unread, a message warning him, in plenty of time, that the Americans were coming.

A third of Rall's Hessians have escaped, however, because Washington's blocking force never got across the river. Still, it's an impressive haul: 948 prisoners, 1,000 muskets and rifles, 6 cannon, a quantity of instruments for military bands. The commander's first victory in the field has cost him only two men, and they were frozen on the march to Trenton.

Talking to Rall's adjutant, Lieutenant Piel, that afternoon, Fitzgerald hears some interesting details about the Hessians' collapse. As predicted, Rall and his officers sat down to a grand dinner at the Trenton Tavern on Christmas Day. They drank a great deal of wine and then sat up most of the night playing cards. Rall had been in bed, sound asleep, only a short time when the battle erupted. Piel had tried to shake his drink-sodden commander awake and, thinking he had succeeded, went outside to help rally the men. When Rall failed to appear, he went back and found the colonel in his nightshirt, muttering, "What's the matter? What's the matter?" As soon as he had absorbed the information that a battle was taking place, he dressed and rushed out, just in time to get himself shot a few minutes later. Forty of his comrades were killed or wounded. Besides the frozen men, the Americans have lost just two wounded, William Washington and James Monroe.

While Rall lies dying, the commander and Greene go to see him. With his last breath, the colonel asks that his men be kindly treated, and Washington promises they will be, a promise he keeps, although they hardly deserve it. The officers have nothing to fear. By the conventions of eighteenth-century warfare, the upper classes spare each other, generally speaking, and so, on the twenty-eighth, here is Washington sitting down to dinner with all the remaining Hessian officers, the wine is passed, and there are no visible signs of malice on either side.

Just the same, the war must go on. The Americans recross the Delaware, get their clothes washed and something to eat, and on December 30 they're ready to make a second crossing and pick up where they left off. "Ready" may not be quite the word. A sergeant writes: "At this time our troops were in a destitute and deplorable condition. The horses attached to our cannon were without shoes, and when passing over the ice, they would slide in every direction and could advance only with the assistance of the soldiers. Our men, too, were without shoes or other comfortable clothing; and as traces of our march towards Princeton, the ground was literally marked with the blood of the soldiers' feet."

On New Year's Eve, another crisis. Enlistments will run out with the year, leaving only 1,500 regulars available, plus what remains of the always doubtful militia. Washington has only one option. The men eligible for release are lined up and he makes a powerful plea for them to stay just one more month. Drums beat for volunteers. Not a man steps forward. One observant sergeant writes: "The general wheeled his horse about, rode in front of the regiment, and addressing us again, said, 'My brave fellows, you have done all I asked you to do and more than could reasonably be expected. But your country is at stake, your wives, your houses, and all that you hold dear. You have worn yourselves out with fatigues and hardships, but we know not how to spare you. If you will consent to stay only one month longer, you will render that service to the cause of liberty and to your country which you probably never can do under any other circumstances. The present is emphatically the crisis which is to decide our destiny.' "

Once more the drums roll, while a murmuring rises in the ranks. "I'll stay if you will," "We can't go home now." A few step forward, others follow, until there are about two hundred volunteers, all of them Continentals, no militia. It's only a drop in the personnel bucket, but it will have to do.

As the New Year begins, Howe is safe in the arms of New York and Mrs. Loring, but he's sufficiently disturbed by what happened to Rall that he decides to send Cornwallis, who had been about to depart for London to see his sick wife, to stabilize the situation. The march is not easy. So much rain has fallen that the men are sometimes up to their thighs in mud. In Maidenhead, at 10:00 A.M. on January 2, they encounter the Americans, firing from a dense wood and intending to delay the British advance as long as possible. They're so successful that it's 4:00 P.M. before Cornwallis gets to Trenton. However, there he is with nearly 6,000 men, while the best the Americans have been able to muster is 5,200. Since his troops have been marching and fighting since dawn, Cornwallis decides to let them rest for the night; he can "bag the fox," as he puts it, tomorrow morning.

Washington holds a council of war that evening and a piece of strategy straight out of the Old Testament is decided upon. They will steal away silently in the night, leaving campfires blazing, and march to Princeton, where they will not only be able to threaten the British rear but may even be able to seize their war chest, containing £70,000, in New Brunswick.

All goes according to plan. Heavy cloth muffles the artillery wheels, the men march swiftly and silently, the campfires burn deceptively. The men are weary and the roads bad but they make eleven miles that night. In the frosty dawn, they're two miles from Princeton, but it turns out they're not intact. Fugitives from Hugh Mercer's brigade appear and relate how they ran into two regiments of a British brigade under Colonel Charles Mawhood, who mistook them for Hessians at first (how could he?) and then decided they were Americans fleeing from Cornwallis. In the brief fight that followed, Mercer and several officers were killed.

Washington himself re-forms the fugitives, brings up some veteran New Englanders to support them, and they charge Mawhood's men, who break and run. No doubt remembering Harlem Heights, the commander joins in the pursuit, allegedly shouting, "It's a fine fox chase, my boys." The British are demoralized. Some escape to Cornwallis, others keep running until they reach New Brunswick. Still others hole up in Princeton College, thinking they will be safe, but the Americans plant cannon before the door and they surrender — "a haughty, crabbed set of men," one observer writes, "as they fully exhibited while prisoners on their march to the country."

The Battle of Princeton is over in no more than an hour, but while it lasts, it's savage. Washington is a central figure, sitting his white horse at one point only thirty yards from the British, while Fitzgerald hides his face, expecting to see him fall any minute. Luck and the smoke of battle save him. A young Pennsylvania naval officer writes home to his wife Susan: "I shall never forget what I felt at Princeton on his account, when I saw him brave all the dangers of the field and his important life hanging as it were by a single hair with a thousand deaths flying around him. Believe me, I thought not of myself." No doubt about it. Rising out of the despair of December to defeat Rall, and then to stop Cornwallis at Princeton, all in ten brilliant days — this is Washington's finest hour in the war, not to be duplicated.

There are real losses from the battle, however. There's poor Hugh

Mercer, the victim of a bayonet, and Colonel John Haslet, of Delaware, a handsome, athletic man who gets a bullet in the brain. Like Rall, he had a note in his pocket too, but he'd read it—an order detaching him for recruiting service, about which he had said nothing so he wouldn't miss the battle.

But the loss that haunts Washington is his inability to follow up the victory at Princeton. He firmly believes that he would win the war if he could only muster 800 or so fresh troops able to march just seventeen more miles to New Brunswick, where the British treasure lies. His exhausted troops can go no farther, however—shivering, hungry, and half-naked as they are, he halts them just short of being able to destroy the British stores and magazines and steal their war chest.

The Americans stagger into Pluckemin on January 6, a village resting on a high triangular plateau with Thimble Mountain rising behind it—an ideal defensive position. While the men camp in the snow-covered woods, Washington establishes his headquarters at Arnold's Tavern, on the village green. Looking at his ragged army of four thousand men, about to settle down in winter quarters, it's hard to believe these are the same troops who, according to one of Howe's officers, "boxed us about in New Jersey as if we had no feelings." For the first time, there is something of patriotic fervor in the song that drifts from the tents that night: "We'll drink our own liquor, our brandy from peaches/A fig for the English, they may kiss all our breeches/ These bloodsucking, beer-drinking puppies retreat/But our peach-brandy fellows can never be beat. Derry down, down, down, etc."

In Cornwallis's camp, there's no singing at all. These are frustrated, cursing men, aware that Washington has not only beaten them for once but has got away with it by retreating for the winter into virtually impregnable hills and woods where it would be madness to follow. Howe isn't much inclined to follow anyway. We'll get them another time, he seems to be saying; winter's not a good time to fight, and he doesn't think much of summer either. Meanwhile, there's New York. Orders emerge from it. All of New Jersey is to be evacuated, except for a line along the river from New Brunswick to Perth Amboy. For Howe, a pleasant winter lies ahead, the pleasure of his blond beauty and the celebration of his new knighthood as Companion of the Bath, awarded him for his great victories in New York and environs. Everyone seems to have forgotten that these were supposed to end the Revolution.

1777

9

✛   ✛   ✛

The Fall of Johnny Burgoyne

Sitting comfortably in New York, Howe had thought in September that these Americans were, after all, either English by birth or the descendants of Englishmen, for the most part. Why should brothers be trying to kill one another? he asked himself once more, and decided that he would make one more attempt at some kind of settlement so he and the others could get out of this damned climate where it's either too hot or too cold.

The instrument of negotiation was readily at hand—General John Sullivan, last seen in a Long Island cornfield at the moment of his capture, would be useful as an exchange emissary to Congress. Howe shipped him off to Philadelphia with a proposal that this body send him a delegation to talk about peace. Sullivan happily carried the message, and Congress appointed a truly distinguished committee—Franklin, Adams, and Edward Rutledge—to meet with Howe. On September 11, these gentlemen proceeded to Perth Amboy, where a barge took them to Staten Island; Howe was waiting to meet them there in the nondescript Billopp house at Tottenville, known to later generations as the Conference House.

At his most gracious and hospitable, Howe served his guests good claret, equally good bread, cold ham, tongue, and mutton, after which they began to exchange views on reconciliation. The British host declared expansively that it had long been his belief that differences between the mother country and the colonies could be ironed out with the application of reason and common sense.

After that, the meeting quickly deteriorated. Howe concluded his opening remarks by saying that he had been both surprised and displeased by passage of the Declaration of Independence. "That act, gentlemen," he said, "if it cannot be got over, precludes all treaty making." Just to make it worse, he added that in any case he could only negotiate with them in their roles as private citizens, not as members of Congress, a body the King didn't recognize.

"Your Lordship may consider me in what light you please," Adams replied with acerbity, "except that of a British subject."

Howe tried again. "It is desirable to put a stop to these ruinous extremities," he said, "as well for the sake of our country as yours. The question is: is there no way of turning back this step of independence, and thus opening the door to a full discussion?"

Franklin reminded him that the situation had changed a great deal since Congress first petitioned the King for redress of grievances: "Forces have been sent out, and towns have been burnt. We cannot expect happiness under the domination of Great Britain. All former attachments are obliterated."

Adams tried to point out something that Howe was going to find difficult to understand. When it declared independence, he explained, Congress acted on instructions from each colony, and so "it is not in our power, therefore, my lord, to treat otherwise than as independent states."

"I can answer for South Carolina," Rutledge interrupted. "With regard to the people consenting to come again under the English government, it is impossible. They would not, even if Congress should desire it."

Strained silence for a moment. Howe leaned back, his face reflecting his disappointment. He didn't bear these Americans any ill will, but he would never understand them. Sighing, he closed the meeting: "If such are your sentiments, gentlemen, I only lament that it is not in my power to bring about the accommodation I wish. . . . I'm sorry, gentlemen, that you have had the trouble of coming so far to so little purpose."

Still the gracious host, he accompanied his guests to the shore and saw them off. The last chance for peace went with them, but it was never a serious possibility anyway. Howe and those who thought like him were willing to make all kinds of concessions to restore the status quo—except independence. The alternative was now clear: victory or ruin, for one side or the other.

A good many Americans would have voted for ruin if asked in the spring of 1777. Recruiting is extremely slow, and even though the army is larger this year than it will ever be again, it's still far below the number authorized by Congress. Three years is the term of service in the Continental Army, with a twenty-dollar bounty. Those who enlist for the duration are promised a hundred acres of land after the war. All these incentives are offset by the stories returning soldiers bring home from the front; nothing will induce some of them to return.

Recruiting itself is an unsavory scandal. The officers doing it are becoming accomplished grafters, keeping the bounty money and reporting the men who were to get it as deserters, which in fact is often the case. These officers also spend recruiting money on themselves and turn in false reports. Even worse is the conduct of towns and individual citizens who cheat on quotas and conscription. There is no end to the ingenuity of these accomplished grafters. Bounty jumpers, prisoners of war, and British deserters all appear on their rolls. One man's name may be listed on the quota for several towns, which might also claim men already in the army. Recruits are bought and sold like soft goods, by entrepreneurs collecting not only bounty money but the sums paid for substitutes.

So lunatic is this operation that the army finds itself with Loyalists in its ranks. The *Connecticut Courant* reports: "The officers on the recruiting service enlisted soldiers at assemblies and balls, and the inhabitants were busily employed in recruiting the children and servants of their neighbors, and forbidding their own to engage." All over the colonies, swamps and woodlands shelter deserters and draft evaders who are trying to stay as near home as possible. Some become criminals in order to live. Entire counties in Virginia are terrorized by runaway slaves, deserters, and men evading service.

There are also some citizens who are trying to live as though the war doesn't exist, making money and spending it. In the army are those who still can't shake off the bigotries they never left behind. While Washington's forces were preparing to brave the Delaware on Christmas night, the old North-South hatreds persisted in far-off Ticonderoga.

Colonel Asa Whitcomb, commander of the 6th Continental Regiment, from Massachusetts, had made a servant of his soldier son and set him up as a cobbler in the commanding officer's own room, an action which brought down on the colonel the contemptuous sneers of his fellow officers from Pennsylvania. One of them, Lieutenant Colonel Thomas Craig, of the 2nd Pennsylvania Regiment, got drunk and decided he would demolish the cobbler's bench, which he did, and for good measure, beat up the colonel as well.

Hearing the commotion, other Pennsylvania officers and soldiers came running, with their muskets, to "dare the Yankees." In fact, they launched an armed attack on the barracks of the Massachusetts men, getting off thirty or forty rounds of precious ammunition. Several of the Massachusetts men were wounded severely. Sober again, Craig tried to make it up by sending a detachment into the woods to shoot a bear, which was shared by both regiments. This, however, was not much more than a bandage on a problem that won't go away. Soldiers and civilians alike are sure that their counterparts from some other part of the country are letting down the side.

One thing both sides agree on is the pillaging and atrocities committed by the British in their progress through New York and New Jersey. In April, a congressional committee issues a devastating report. It complains about the "wanton destruction of property" and the inhuman treatment of prisoners, a subject that's going to become a sore point later on. The report notes that common British soldiers sometimes express sympathy for the terrible condition of the prisoners, "but never the officers."

Another paragraph discloses that, the day before the Battle of Princeton, the British decided to give no quarter, although this was never set forth in general orders. "Officers wounded and disabled, some of the first rank," the report says, "were barbarously mangled or put to death. A minister of the gospel, who neither was nor had been in arms, was massacred in cold blood at Trenton, though humbly supplicating for mercy." Women civilians fared no better. There were many instances, says the report, "of most indecent treatment and actual ravishment of married and single women."

What has happened here is that the Americans have just discovered war. To the British regulars and Hessians who have fought on the Continent, this is the kind of brutality that's taken for granted in wartime. Most Americans were not touched by the French and Indian War, the only other one they've known; it was a bush war, fought largely on frontiers.

Some Americans are learning how it's done. The Reverend Dr. John

Peter Gabriel Muhlenberg describes in his diary for September 17, 1777, what he saw when he went to his church to officiate at a funeral service. A regiment of Pennsylvanians had taken over the church and a nearby schoolhouse, spreading dirty straw over the church floor and eating on the altar. When the soldiers saw Muhlenberg, they began to mock him and one officer asked another sitting at the organ to play a Hessian march. When Muhlenberg asked the colonel in command if this was how civil and religious freedom was protected, the colonel replied airily that it was difficult to discipline militia.

Going outside, Muhlenberg encountered the schoolmaster, who was in tears. The soldiers had destroyed his buckwheat patch, and plundered and trodden down his garden vegetables, as they had in the pastor's garden, where three acres of buckwheat intended to tide him over the winter were destroyed. The militia had turned twenty horses and oxen into this stand of buckwheat, ruining it. When he protested, says Muhlenberg, they called him a Tory and threatened to burn down his house and stable. Ironically, the British called the reverend doctor a rebel.

As the winter drags on, Washington, holed up in Morristown, is playing a perilous game. Inexplicably, Howe doesn't seem to know that the Americans have only about a thousand men remaining, and if he finds out, the war could end suddenly. So George keeps his troops busy attacking British foraging parties, to give the impression of power. His militiamen also help by lurking behind trees or other cover and picking off any of the enemy they can find.

This shadow boxing is having a bad effect on British morale. A disillusioned Tory in New York, Justice Thomas Jones, complains in a letter that Howe is "diverting himself in feasting, gunning, banqueting, and in the arms of Mrs. Loring. Not a stick of wood, a spear of grass, or a kernel of corn could the troops in New Jersey procure without fighting for it, unless sent from New York." Every foraging party is attacked, he says, and hundreds of small skirmishes are occurring.

The real enemy at Morristown is smallpox. Washington orders the whole army inoculated, but the men fear the inoculation almost as much as the disease. The soldiers are near to open revolt at one point, declaring the commander is taking liberties with their lives and health. Why doesn't Howe learn about the Americans' desperate situation from his spies and close in for the kill? We're still wondering, after all these years.

But he doesn't, and the warm spring sunlight, after a bitterly cold and snowy winter, does wonders for everybody's morale, aided considerably by the addition of eight thousand Continentals. Martha arrives to join George, and the wives of other officers turn up, reviving social life. An acute observer of this scene is Martha Hungerfield Bland, only twenty-five but already twice married, her current husband a tall, handsome Virginian. Mrs. Bland was ill for four weeks after her smallpox vaccination in Philadelphia and her face is left pocked but, as she says, in Morristown there are "few smooth faces and no beauties." She examines the village girls and finds them wanting. Some are "exceedingly pretty," she says, "but they appear to have souls formed for the distaff rather than the tender passions. Desperate and dreadful are their favorite words."

An intimacy springs up between the Blands and the Washingtons. They have dinner or otherwise socialize together two or three times a week. Mrs. Bland reports that the other Martha refers to her husband as her "old man." She sees a side of Washington that isn't often observed. When they have parties on horseback, she says, he "throws off the hero and takes on the chatty agreeable companion. He can be downright impudent sometimes," and adds slyly to her correspondent, "such impudence, Fanny, as you and I like." Really!

Martha Bland has a sharp eye for the men around the commander. Fitzgerald she dismisses as "an agreeable broad-shouldered Irishman," but Colonel George Johnson, "who is exceedingly witty at everybody else's expense, can't allow other people to be so on his own, though they often take the liberty." She finds Alexander Hamilton a "sensible, genteel, polite young fellow," and Tench Tilghman "a modest, worthy man." All, she concludes, "are polite, social gentlemen who make the day pass with a great deal of satisfaction to the visitors."

News of Lee filters back from New York, where it appears that this oddball prisoner is not only advising on the best way for the British to win the war (organizing the Tories is the key), but is proving to be more congenial and talkative than when he was on the other side. He simply can't help telling people what to do, or what they should have done. After dining with him, Colonel John Maxwell writes to a friend: "Lee being rather gay with liquor, said that when our army went to West Chester, if we had either landed at first in the right place where we should have met with no considerable obstructions, or if afterwards at White Plains one of our brigades (which were the Hessians) had pushed up briskly and turned their left flank, we had cut off their retreat and finished the whole business of the controversy at once."

When he isn't carrying on his active social life, Lee is busy devising a master plan for the war, which he means to present to the Howe brothers. It calls for taking Philadelphia by sea, occupying Annapolis and Alexandria, and so dividing the colonies on a north-south axis. The plan has its merits but the Howe brothers will never see it. Lee is such an eccentric that his captors find it hard to take him seriously, and in fact they would like to get rid of him if they could, but at the moment the Americans aren't holding any officer of equivalent rank to make an exchange possible.

This deficiency is suddenly remedied in July when the unfortunate Major General Richard Prescott, Ethan Allen's persecutor in Montreal, is captured for the second time in the war under circumstances that raise whoops of delight on both sides of the Atlantic. Now the commander of British forces in Rhode Island, he left his headquarters one night for the house of a Mr. Overing, near Newport, where he planned, as the later account goes, "to lodge there that night with some of his whores."

Apprised by spies of this clandestine maneuver, Colonel William Barton organized a party of thirty-eight men and seven volunteers, piled them into five boats at Warwick Neck, and set sail for the Overing house. For what follows we have the eyewitness account of Abel Porter, one of the volunteers, who was there with his brother James. These two quietly took out three sentinels and then entered the house. Overing (or Mrs. Overing in some accounts) looked up and cried out, "Captain Porter, what is the matter?" James knew the family and he said, "You needn't be scared. We're not going to hurt you. Where is the general?" As expected, he was upstairs.

The Porter brothers and Colonel Barton hurried up and burst into a bedroom. Here accounts differ. Some say an aide who was there jumped through a window wearing only his shirt and was seized a few rods away. No one says anything about the "whores" who were supposed to be the purpose of the general's visit.

Years later, Abel Porter remembered that Prescott, not his aide, rose up in bed when his visitors broke in, and with remarkable calm, said: "Gentlemen, your business requires haste, but do, for God's sake, let me get my clothes," to which Colonel Barton answered, "By God, it's no time for clothes." So they took him barelegged through a field of barley, prickling his legs, and the party reembarked. On the way back, a British post on shore saw them and fired but the shots struck the water harmlessly. (A fortunes-of-war footnote: one of the three captured sentries will teach school in Pownal, Vermont, after the Revolution is over, and Abel Porter will send one of his children to class there.)

When the circumstances of his capture get out, Prescott is relentlessly lampooned in the American and London papers, but as far as Lee is concerned, this is his passport back to the American side, since the British don't seem to be listening to him. It takes the best part of a year, but the exchange is finally made.

Other diversions are taking place in New England as spring makes war possible again. In late April, two thousand British soldiers land at Compo Point, near Norwalk, Connecticut, and march to Danbury, much of which they burn down. The colony is threatened, and who springs to its defense? Who else but Benedict Arnold, the ever-ready fireman, who has been going through one of his depressed periods again. After his exploits on Lake Champlain, he expected to be promoted to major general, but instead, Congress elevated five juniors over his head. This is the worst betrayal yet, and indeed it's a mean enough rejection by politicians of a brave officer who just wants to fight for his country, and it creates a considerable stir. Washington tries to smooth things over, but it's no good. Arnold says he'll never again trust a politician and sulks moodily in Providence until he hears the news from Norwalk.

Emergencies bring out the best in Arnold. Getting into his uniform, he rounds up all the militia he can find, and sets out to pursue the invading British, placing himself under the tolerant command of old General Wooster, whose overweight frame is sagging in the saddle, and whose mind is none too clear either.

Just before the British reach Ridgefield on their way back to their boats, Arnold catches them. There's a bloody skirmish during which Arnold has his horse shot from under him, throwing him down in the muck. He looks up to see a British soldier leaning over him with a bayonet. "You're my prisoner!" the soldier announces. "Not yet," Arnold says and, pulling out his pistol, kills the soldier, barely avoiding his falling body.

The air is full of musket shot and grape, but Arnold makes his way toward the safety of a nearby swamp. On the way, he discovers that Wooster had been mortally wounded. At last! He's in command! Gathering his militia together, he forces the British to retreat toward Norwalk, and attacks them on the banks of the Saugatuck. In the end, it's a clear victory for Arnold, and Congress has to give in, confronted by such a conspicuous display of bravery and enterprise. They make him a major general, but they won't restore his seniority. It's sulking time again. Arnold resigns once more.

Other enterprising leaders spring up in this coastal warfare. In mid-May, Elnathan Jennings is a temporary resident of Connecticut, having been pushed out of his house in Southampton township the year before when the British took over Long Island and New York. Jennings has served in the Connecticut line at White Plains, and now he's a Continental sergeant. He has a plan, which he unfolds to his superior, Colonel Return J. Meigs—a bold attack on Sag Harbor. Meigs consults Washington and gets his approval.

The expedition is organized on the green at New Haven. Meigs asks for 110 men who are good oarsmen as volunteers, and 300 men instantly step forward. Those selected get into whaleboats at Long Wharf in Guilford and row over to Long Island, carrying their boats across the beach into Southold Bay. Crossing, they land at dawn on Joseph's Island, where they hide the boats in a thicket of red cedars. Next night, Jennings launches them again and they row quietly to within two and a half miles of Sag Harbor, near the guardhouse, which happens to be the schoolhouse where Jennings got his education.

Leaving a detachment to keep the boats afloat, the party sneaks through thick brush and across fields until they sight the guardhouse and are no more than fifty yards from two sentries. A quick flurry and the sentries and guards are seized except for one who escapes. Jennings leaves some men to guard the prisoners and takes the others about two hundred yards to his uncle's house, where he seizes another prisoner, an American defector. The raiders march another hundred yards to the barracks and grab everyone there, then they hurry on to Sag Harbor's Long Wharf, where they take more prisoners and burn twelve brigs and schooners, besides a quantity of hay and corn. By this time the British are aware of what's going on, and they bombard the invaders with grapeshot, so Jennings hurries back to the boats with ninety prisoners, whom he puts on two small vessels and guards them across to Black Rock, where he marches them on to New Haven. Jennings has pulled off one of the most daring and successful raids of the war, and without losing a man.

All such expeditions, of course, are sideshows to the main theaters of action. In New Jersey, the army is recovering a little, although the desertion rate is so high that, according to the British, three thousand Americans have joined them in the first five months of 1777. In spite of these defections, Washington has managed to get together nearly nine thousand men by the middle of May, enough to break up winter quarters and take a position at Middlebrook, twenty miles south, on the left bank of the Raritan.

Howe has twice as many men, and he marches them from Amboy to Brunswick, where he splits his force with the idea of cutting off Sullivan, who's in Princeton, and persuading Washington to come out on the plains where he can be annihilated. The commander sees through this elementary strategy, brings in Sullivan, and doesn't move. Now Howe turns around and pretends to retreat toward Brunswick, hoping *that* will draw Washington out. This time he has a little more success. Washington sends Greene to attack the British rear, while he comes down nearer with the rest of the army. On the morning of June 26, Howe springs his trap. Suddenly turning his forces around, he tries to encircle the Americans and cut them off from the heights. But Washington hears the preliminary firing, guesses what's occurring, and quickly pulls back into safety.

Howe gives up the whole expedition as a bad job and removes his entire army back to Amboy and then to Staten Island. A witness to all this is Howe's fellow countryman, Nicholas Cresswell, one of those confirmed British travelers, who once visited Washington at Mount Vernon before the war. He can't understand what Howe thinks he's doing, and why he's taking so long to end this uprising of people Cresswell frankly despises. "That a Negro-driver [he means Washington] should with a ragged banditti of undisciplined people," he fumes, "the scum and refuse of all nations on earth, so long keep a British general at bay, nay, even oblige him, with as fine an army of veteran soldiers as ever England had on the American continent, to retreat, is astonishing. General Howe, a man brought up to war from his youth, to be puzzled and plagued for two years together with a Virginia tobacco-planter! O! Britain, how thy laurels tarnish in the hands of such a lubber! Washington, my enemy as he is, I should be sorry if he should be brought to an ignominious death."

If Cresswell thought the luster of the British army and its generals had been tarnished at this juncture, he must have been apoplectic at what now takes place in the Northern Department, where Gentleman Johnny Burgoyne is at last about to carry out the much-delayed grand plan by which British forces moving out of Canada would strike down the Hudson and effectively trap the Americans in a giant vise.

Burgoyne had arrived at Quebec on May 6 to carry out this plan, after spending a good deal of time in London selling it to the authorities. What he wanted, of course, was an independent command, and now he has it, after several morning rides in Hyde Park with the King, who makes the final decision. It's now the British Plan of the Year, and Burgoyne prepares carefully for it during six weeks in Quebec. Carleton provides him with 8,300 men, 600 artillerymen, with 138 guns, 650 Canadian and Tory auxiliary troops, 400 Indians drawn from the Six Nations—all these to be added to 3,700 British regulars and 3,000 Germans, commanded by Baron Friedrich Adolph von Riedesel, a legendary disciplinarian and at thirty-nine one of the ablest generals Burgoyne could ask for. The baron has brought his family with him, his lively baroness, their three small daughters, and two maids, all of whom travel in a large calash made for the expedition. The baroness, an observant and accomplished diarist, is going to provide us with some revealing snapshots of what's about to happen.

A formidable force indeed. When it's all assembled, the expedition stretches out for three miles, and to anyone but Burgoyne, it's clear there's too much of everything. Why does he need all that artillery, for instance? It's cumbersome, difficult to move, and not much use for the kind of fighting that lies ahead. Worse than that, from the standpoint of military maneuvering, the line of wagons is so long because Burgoyne has brought all the comforts of home with him—a splendid collection of good French wines, his adoring mistress, who was the wife of a commissary official; the ladies of several officers; and a large assortment of camp followers of various kinds. At the head of this incredible caravansary, Gentleman Johnny himself, of whom the Baroness von Riedesel cannot forbear to write, a little cattily: "It is very true that General Burgoyne likes to make himself easy and that he spent his nights in singing and drinking and diverting himself with his mistress, who was as fond of champagne as himself."

Still, with all their numerous handicaps, the British are in better shape than the Americans gathering to oppose them. The first obstacle is Fort Ticonderoga, lightly guarded and further weakened by quarreling between officers and men, and by the running feud of the two generals who are supposed to be coordinating the resistance, Generals Schuyler and Gates. Schuyler, as we've observed, is both aristocratic and autocratic, which makes him unpopular with the men and not a favorite in Congress either. Writing home to his wife, a Connecticut chaplain explains: "The general is somewhat haughty and overbearing. He has never been accustomed to seeing men that are reasonably well taught and able to give a clear opinion and to state their grounds for it, who were not also persons of some wealth and rank." This, of course, is anathema to New Englanders.

Gates, on the other hand, is the beau ideal of the Yankees. Not that he looks like one. His thick-lensed spectacles keep sliding down his large hooked nose, and as the historian George Scheer notes, he looks "like a friendly old granny." Burgoyne puts it another way. He calls Gates "that old midwife." The general doesn't care what anyone calls him as long as he's numero uno, and he'll do anything necessary to achieve that status.

Burgoyne approaches Ticonderoga with unjustified caution. It should be like shooting ducks in a barrel. The 2,300 barefoot, ragged survivors of a desperate winter who man the fort are under the immediate command of Colonel Anthony Wayne, who calls it "the last place in the world that God made . . . finished in the dark . . . the ancient Golgotha or place of skulls." Nonetheless, Burgoyne orders an enveloping movement, as though a real army were inside. On July 2, they establish an artillery position on Mount Defiance, and when General Arthur St. Clair, Wayne's superior, sees that, he orders an immediate withdrawal, an action the commander will not find it easy to forgive. The Americans evacuate by night to Skenesboro, crossing over into Vermont.

They nearly get away with it, but in the midst of this hasty withdrawal, the residence of the French commander at Mount Independence, General Roche de Fermoy, inconveniently catches fire and the resulting huge blaze wakes up the British. They pursue the Americans, who panic until the retreat becomes a rout. The chief pursuer is General Simon Fraser, that much-admired Scotsman from Balmain, who is helped in the early going because four American artillerymen left to defend a bridge of boats are too drunk to fire their cannon. At dawn, Baron Riedesel takes Independence and goes on to support Fraser. Burgoyne's naval elements destroy several American galleys and bateaux trying to escape on the lake. By midafternoon, the British are at Skenesboro, but the Americans burn the defenses and continue retreating to Fort Anne, where they make a brief counterattack before they fire this fort too and fall back on Fort Edward.

The Americans manage to add a little more to this debacle. At Hubbardton, Vermont, Fraser encounters two New Englanders, Seth Warner, a Vermonter, and Colonel Turbott Francis, of Massachusetts, in charge of the army's rear guard. Fraser attacks them at 5:00 A.M., with 850 men, and for a while it's a fierce battle, but then Riedesel arrives, with only 80 men but he's brought his band along. They play the Fatherland's battle hymn to give the impression of a host, and the Americans retreat again in disorder, leaving 200 dead behind them. Francis is killed, but Warner survives to hear himself roundly criticized for his tactics.

So Burgoyne is off to an excellent start. Ticonderoga is in his hands, along with several other smaller forts, more than two hundred boats and at least a hundred cannon have been seized. It's such a decisive setback that the news ripples through the colonies like a cold chill, and in London, the King is said to have rushed into his wife's boudoir to announce that he has beaten the Americans.

But the Americans seem intent on beating themselves. There's a great deal of finger pointing. Schuyler is not only blamed for losing Ticonderoga, but it's charged that the British paid him off. Gates has already made it clear that he isn't going to put up with this divided command any longer, and if Washington won't choose between him and Schuyler (Washington seems curiously indecisive about it), Gates intends to go directly to Congress, which he does. John Adams writes gloomily to Abigail: "I think we shall never defend a post until we shoot a general."

Gates storms into Philadelphia, and takes a seat before the delegates, as one of them puts it, "in a very easy, cavalier posture in an elbow chair and began to open his budget." William Duer, the delegate from New York, writes of the occasion: "It is impossible to give an idea of the unhappy figure which General Gates made. His manner ungraciously and totally void of all dignity, his delivery incoherent and interrupted with frequent chasms in which he was peering over his tattered notes, and the tenor of his discourse a compound of vanity, folly, and rudeness."

Apparently most of Duer's fellow delegates think otherwise. They not only give Gates sole command of the Northern Department but invest him with powers almost as great as those of the commander.

Another warrior is returning in glory too. Arnold has been morosely sitting in Philadelphia quarters, resigned again because Congress wouldn't restore his seniority when it made him a major general, and he's trying to imagine without much luck what it would be like to be a civilian for the rest of the war when news of Burgoyne's initial success reaches the city. Urgent help is required. So Congress pretends it never got Arnold's resignation letter and orders him north. He's needed! That's what he wants at the moment, more than anything. On the way, he stops off to see Washington, who understands it won't be easy for Arnold to serve under Arthur St. Clair, one of the men who was promoted over his head, and a man Washington now regards as incompetent because he gave up Ticonderoga so easily.

Arriving on the scene, Arnold gets a different kind of assignment than he's ever had before—to fight the war in the wilderness, the interior. Back in June, while Burgoyne was getting his invasion force ready, he had sent Colonel Barry St. Leger, another Britisher who had fought with Wolfe in the French and Indian War, to raid the Mohawk Valley. With a force of seven hundred regulars and Loyalists, St. Leger had the help of a thousand Indians under that charismatic Mohawk leader, Joseph Brant, who got his education in Connecticut from the Reverend Eleazer Wheelock, later president of Dartmouth. Brant moves easily in both the native and white worlds. He has been presented at court to George III, and has had his picture painted by Romney.

St. Leger arrived in Oswego about the middle of July, where two more battalions of Indians from all the Iroquois tribes (except the Oneidas) joined him, under Sir John Johnson, the Loyalist son of Sir William Johnson, dead these seven years, who did his best in life to keep the Six Nations at peace.

Arriving at Oswego, St. Leger laid siege to it at once. Colonel Peter

Gansevoort, who commanded, had only 750 men to defend it, but he hoped that General Nicholas Herkimer was going to arrive with 800 of the Tryon County militia. What the colonel didn't know was that Molly Brant, Sir William Johnson's widow and Joseph's sister, had also heard about Herkimer's relief force and relayed the information to St. Leger, who sent Brant to ambush Herkimer in a wooded ravine near Oriskany. Herkimer's men walked into the trap, but they didn't panic. Emulating the Indians, they took to trees and whatever shelter they could find and fought back. It was a bloody struggle, hand to hand, knives and hatchets slashing, no quarter. Stricken with a wound that would be mortal, Herkimer had his men place him in his saddle on the ground, with his back against a tree, and from there, pipe clenched firmly in his teeth, he directed the defense. Meanwhile, a sortie from the fort at Oswego fell on the British camp and destroyed it. When this news reached the Oriskany battle scene, Loyalists and Indians fled and Herkimer was able to retreat with two-thirds of his force intact.

But St. Leger was not a man to give up easily. With a still menacing force, he once more laid siege to Oswego, which was now in a desperate condition. Two messengers slipped through the besiegers during a storm at night and brought the news to Schuyler, who called a council of war. Schuyler was ready and willing to help, but some officers argued that he would only weaken the main army, a charge that so angered Schuyler that he broke off his pipe stem in his mouth. He would take the responsibility himself, he said, and called for a volunteer leader to command the rescue party. No one stepped forward—no one except freshly minted Major General Benedict Arnold.

At last, a command! Not much of one, to be sure, but Arnold optimistically believes the country militia along the way will rise to help him. It's a case of overoptimism. Everybody is too terrified of St. Leger's army.

Arnold is an impulsive man, but he knows better than to throw his thousand militia against an overwhelmingly superior force, so he resorts to an ingenious deception that occurs to him when his men bring in as captive one Hon-Yost Schuyler (no relation), a mentally defective nephew of Herkimer. The Indians know him well, and respect him too, believing he has been touched by the Great Spirit. At first, Arnold threatens to hang him but when the young man's mother pleads for his life, a plan occurs to the general. He tells Hon-Yost that he will be spared if he goes to St. Leger and tells him the Americans are coming in great numbers, enough to overwhelm him. Hon-Yost is not so disturbed that he doesn't see this as a bargain, especially when he is told that his brother will be held as hostage. He agrees.

This unique messenger of doom for the British has his coat riddled with bullet holes, to indicate a narrow escape, and sets off with a friendly Oneida who will back up his story. Even before he reaches St. Leger's camp, spies have reported Arnold's approach, and that has made the Indians uneasy. Then, when Hon-Yost makes his dramatic appearance and tells them of his hair-raising escape from the great American army, the Indians show a particular interest in his story and want to know how many men Arnold has. Silently, Hon-Yost indicates the leaves on the trees, and that's enough. The Indians take all the British clothing and liquor they can lay their hands on, and disappear. That so alarms the Loyalists that they throw away their equipment and flee too. With what he has left, St. Leger retreats, so hastily he leaves his tents standing. Arnold arrives on August 24 and the siege is over.

This proves to be only the beginning of real trouble for Burgoyne. After his first triumphant thrust, he pauses in Skenesboro to regroup, which for him means living pleasantly in Philip Skene's yellow fieldstone house, eating extremely well, and complaining about the scarcity of first-class Madeira and port. He has no complaints about his mistress.

While Johnny is living with an abundance of everything, Schuyler is carrying out a scorched-earth policy, trying to persuade the locals to scatter their herds, burn their crops, and not leave anything around that might be useful to the enemy.

Burgoyne is in no hurry. He waits for his miles of supply train to catch up with him; it takes thirty carts just to carry his own baggage. His Indian allies pass the time in their own way, and one afternoon a party of them come into camp waving triumphantly a fresh scalp of long, blond female hair. A woman prisoner recognizes it at once; it belonged to her twenty-three-year-old neighbor, Jane McCrea.

Thus another legend is born, and it will be a long time before the real story emerges. It seems that Jane had been living with her patriot brother but had been spending as much time as possible near Fort Edward with a cousin of General Fraser's, a Mrs. McNeil, a woman noted for her obesity. Jane was there because that's where her Loyalist lover, David Jones, was on duty, and she hoped to marry him before the war swallowed him up. But on July 27, Indians invaded the McNeil cabin, seized both women, and put them on horses, to be taken to the British.

Since all those involved are Loyalists, they weren't exactly prisoners. Mrs. McNeil is so fat the Indians have a hard time getting her on a horse. Her escorts are the last to leave, but the first to arrive at the British camp. Mrs. McNeil chews out Cousin Fraser for sending Indians to get her (she's wearing only a chemise), and while she's doing it, the other Indians appear, waving Jane's scalp. Apparently they don't know or care about political affiliations. All they can say is that they quarreled over this beautiful white girl along the way, everything got out of control, and they wound up shooting, scalping, stripping, and mutilating poor Jane, after which they crushed her skull with a tomahawk for good measure.

Besides the grief of Mrs. McNeil and David Jones, Fraser is outraged, but when Burgoyne hears about it, he's wild. From the beginning he's enforced a policy of forbidding scalping and indiscriminate killing by the Indian allies, so strictly that some disgruntled tribesmen have deserted. Now he's so shocked that he would hang the Indians responsible for Jane's death, until other officers point out that this could well cost the services of the remaining Indians.

Burgoyne has another worry. When this story gets out in the countryside, it's going to profoundly irritate a good many people who don't know, or care, whether Jane was a Loyalist or not. He's exactly right. Hundreds of householders see in Jane McCrea's fate something that might well happen to their own families, and there's a rush to join Schuyler, even though they still call him "that damned Dutchman." They conveniently forget, too, that the Americans have been using whatever Indian allies they could persuade ever since the days of Breed's Hill.

Consequently, that blond scalp haunts the minds of many a Vermont and New Hampshire militiaman as they prepare to resist Burgoyne's next move. His spies have told him that there are large supplies of food and ammunition, as well as plenty of horses and oxen, at Bennington, all of which he needs.

Believing incorrectly that this seizure will require no great effort, Burgoyne sends Lieutenant Colonel Friedrich Baum with a mixed bag of troops—Germans, British, provincials, Indians—to capture the Bennington goodies. He hopes the Americans will think this force means the entire British army is on its way, and that Colonel Baum, an experienced Hessian officer who speaks no English, will have little trouble. But his intelligence has been faulty. The general believes the only force opposing him is Seth Warner's Manchester militia, and doesn't know that General John Stark, an old (in his forties) farmer who has fought with Rogers' Rangers and in this war from Breed's Hill to Trenton, has a large body of troops waiting for him.

Stark shares something with Arnold. When he was passed over for promotion, he resigned and went home, but when the New Hampshire legislature made him a brigadier general, it took him only a week to recruit 1,500 men. He insists that his little army be independent of both Congress and the Continental Army, and the New Hampshire legislators don't quibble about it. There's one small problem. When he joins the slowly assembling force to resist Burgoyne, he finds himself nominally under the command of Benjamin Lincoln, one of Washington's fattest generals (of whom there does seem to be an oversupply), who has been named to head all the militia in this theater. Stark waves his New Hampshire commission under Lincoln's nose, and no issue is made of it, although Lincoln does send a report to Congress noting the insubordination.

While Lincoln is off conferring with Schuyler, Stark marches his men toward Bennington, twenty miles away, and on the morning of the fourteenth, one of his detachments encounters Baum, coming the other way. There's a brief, indecisive skirmish, after which Baum, realizing that this isn't going to be a walkover, sends a note back to Burgoyne telling him that prisoners say there may be as many as 1,800 men at Bennington, and he will fall on them tomorrow. "People are flocking to us hourly but want to be armed," he reports. "The savages cannot be controlled; they ruin and take everything they please."

Baum doesn't fall on anyone next day because heavy rain and high winds prevent any fighting. He spends the time fortifying his position, and after a rather nervous night, he's on the march, joined from time to time by men who say they're Loyalists and want muskets. They fill Baum so full of stories about Bennington being occupied by people as loyal as they are that Baum actually believes Stark's army is really a body of Loyalists ready to help him seize the Bennington stores;

consequently he instructs his advance guard not to fire on them.

What a disillusionment! The loyal helpers turn out to be Americans after all, and they surround Baum's small force on every side. The Indian allies flee; they want no part of this one. For nearly two hours, Baum holds out, expecting reinforcements from Burgoyne at any moment. Then a dismaying incident occurs. A tumbril containing all his spare ammunition blows up with a tremendous roar, momentarily stopping the battle, but the Americans realize what's happened and storm the parapet in the resulting confusion.

A lieutenant aptly named Glich writes of what follows: "For a few seconds, the scene which ensued defies all power of language to describe. The bayonet, the butt of the rifle, the saber, the pike were in full play; and men fell, as they rarely fall in modern war, under the direct blows of their enemies." Baum's outnumbered Hessians are being cut down or else surrendering to a collection of New England farmers fighting in their shirtsleeves.

Burgoyne finally gets around to dispatching a relief force, 550 Brunswick grenadiers complete with fieldpieces, looking extremely military in their blue coats and leather breeches. Their commander, Lieutenant Colonel Heinrich von Braymann, moves as slowly as Burgoyne, so by the time he gets there the battle is over as far as Baum's concerned. The rescuers immediately encounter Stark's troops, now reinforced by Seth Warner's men, fresh and eager to fight. Baum, mortally wounded, is not there to see the result, and just as well. Only 9 of his 374 Germans remain, and his camp is looted.

Braymann puts up a good fight but it's no use. These Hessians have never seen anything like the combatants the Americans are capable of producing. David Holbrook, a Sturbridge boy in the Massachusetts militia, gives us some idea. As Colonel Warner moved in, he recalled later, "an old man, with an old Queen Anne's iron sword and mounted upon an old black mare, with about ninety robust men following," appeared and filed in front of the company commander. "Just as the old man had got his mare to the spot and halted, his mare fell, and he jumped upon a large white oak stump and gave the command. Captain Parker, seeing the old man's company between him and the enemy, ordered his men to file in between their files, which were then some distance apart, and the battle then became desperate." At its height, Holbrook heard "a tremendous crash up in the woods at the right wing of the American troops, which was seconded by a yell," the most terrible Holbrook had ever heard. Then he heard Warner's voice: "Fix bayonets! Charge!"

The old man on the stump cried out, "Charge, boys!" jumped down, and ran toward the enemy. His men followed, some with and some without bayonets. The Hessians were completely disconcerted. They broke and ran. An American seized one of their cannon, swung it around, and fired it at the retreating enemy, mowing down a large number of them. Those Americans who weren't too tired pursued and killed a few more, taking a number of prisoners.

It's the most convincing American victory yet. They don't even know how many they've killed, and three or four of the wounded are dying every day in the Bennington Meeting House, "which smells so it is enough to kill anyone in it." Stark is an overnight hero, and in October, a grateful Congress will make him a brigadier general in the Continental Army. At the moment, however, he's irate. In the heat of battle, someone has stolen his little brown mare, with her doeskin saddle.

A deep sense of apprehension runs through Burgoyne's camp, and none is more chilled by it than the general himself. Was it only two months ago that he considered himself in the vanguard of a triumphal march through the hapless Americans, to unite with Clinton? Now, in only sixty days, St. Leger has been soundly defeated on his left, and the Bennington farmers have decimated his right. On August 3, he gets a letter from Howe telling him not to expect any help from that quarter, he's on his own. If that's the case, the way things look now, the party's over.

Or is it? After all, these previous affairs have only been large-scale skirmishes, he tells himself, and he has yet to engage the main American army. It's waiting for him. Gates now has Daniel Morgan's celebrated riflemen with him, and he has his good and brave friend (for now, anyway) Arnold at hand. Gates is also in full command, by courtesy of Congress.

On September 8, he marches six thousand men to a high plateau near Saratoga known as Bemis Heights, looking over the Hudson, and orders his talented Polish engineer, Colonel Thaddeus Kosciuszko, to lay out the lines. Burgoyne, on the other hand, is in a bad way. He may be outnumbered, and he's losing troops every day. The Loyalists haven't turned out, the Indians have given him up as a bad job, and even the Germans are deserting. His overgrown supply line is now so strung out that it's becoming difficult to feed the troops, and they're muttering. He's also in danger of having his communications cut.

Nevertheless, in spite of all his faults, Burgoyne is not a man to run away. Resolutely, he marches on toward Bemis Heights but, without proper scouts, doesn't know he's there until one morning he hears drums tapping far ahead. He stops about four miles short of the American lines, but only when one of his foraging parties is surprised and cut to pieces does he realize just how close he is.

Clearly, it's time to attack, and at once he makes a serious mistake by dividing his forces, sending a German column under Riedesel along the river road to attack the left. It is arranged that three signal guns will warn Riedesel that Burgoyne is in position and the battle can begin. Unfortunately for this plan, American observers high up in the trees have been watching the movements of the columns, and they know exactly what's taking place on this bright September morning, the nineteenth.

What will soon be a historic dispute is about to erupt at American headquarters. Gates is content to let the British come to him, but Arnold insists it's better to meet them in a wooded area known as Freeman's Farm. They argue about it for a half hour or so, while the British signal guns boom that the attack is on, and then Gates suddenly gives in, sending Arnold with Morgan's riflemen and a New Hampshire regiment to meet the enemy at Freeman's Farm.

Nothing could have made Arnold happier. He and his men simply roll back the van of Fraser's main force, but it's like him that he carries on this charge so enthusiastically that he loses formation, and when Fraser brings up his main column, the Americans suffer for it. But Arnold holds his ground, and when he finds a weak spot in the British line, he sends three regiments plunging into it. For one glorious moment, he is on the verge of a great victory. Morgan's men are dispersed, but their leader rallies them with his famous turkey call, and they do well until Burgoyne's main force emerges from the woods.

A clearing quickly becomes a bloody killing ground as the British and Americans surge back and forth across it. So furiously do Arnold and his men fight that a British officer concludes later they must have been drunk. Incredibly, the battle goes on for four hours. Lieutenant William Digby, another British officer, remembered that the "explosion of fire, the heavy artillery, joining in concert like great peals of thunder, assisted by the echoes of the woods, almost deafened us with the noise. This crash of cannon and musketry never ceased till darkness parted us."

In the freezing cold of the night, the cries of the dying sound through the woods. In the fog at dawn, both sides gather in the wounded who are still alive. A burial detail inters the dead, as many as twenty in a single grave, but even in death the officers have their own private hole in the ground. The shrieks and curses of the severely wounded fill the air as they're carried to hospitals a mile away.

Arnold wants to go on next day, but Gates reins him in. The British can claim a technical victory, although American losses are only three hundred, while the British have lost nearly six thousand. Burgoyne still has plenty of manpower and, if he chooses to attack, he's in a good position to destroy the American army, which is nearly out of ammunition and their leaders confused. But Burgoyne has Howe's disease: he decides to sit tight and wait until he hears from Clinton, thus losing his last opportunity to save himself and deal the American cause a staggering blow.

The anticipated letter from Clinton finally arrives on Sunday morning, the twenty-first, and Burgoyne welcomes it as a reprieve. Clinton says that, in ten days or so, he plans to bring Burgoyne about two thousand men. The general replies at once. For God's sake, hurry, is its substance; I can hold out until sometime in October, but no longer. Sickness and desertions are weakening his army every day, and his supplies are melting. After the war, Burgoyne remembered: "The armies were so near that not a night passed without firing and sometimes concerted attacks on our advanced pickets. I do not believe either officer or soldier ever slept during that interval without his clothes, or that any general officer or commander of a regiment passed a single night without being upon his legs occasionally at different hours and constantly an hour before daylight." And a German soldier wrote: "At no time did the Jews await the coming of the Messiah with greater expectancy than we awaited the coming of General Clinton."

But where is Clinton? He's taking his time, knocking off the Americans' Hudson River forts in the vicinity of Peekskill and West Point. With three thousand men, he lands at Verplanck's Point and a messenger hands him Burgoyne's anguished message: should he go on to Albany, Johnny asks (what an optimist!), or should he retreat to Canada while he still can? Clinton doesn't answer right away. He wants to deal with the forts first, and he does—Fort Montgomery, falling easily; then Fort Clinton, after a hard fight; and finally, Fort Constitution, across from West Point.

Now Clinton has time to answer Burgoyne's message, and it's a deathblow to the general. "Nothing now between us but Gates," Clinton begins. "I sincerely hope this little success of ours may facilitate your operations." Then the crusher. He will not presume to order, or even advise, Burgoyne what to do, and he says nothing at all about moving against the Americans' rear at Saratoga, as he had promised earlier. Burgoyne never gets to read this dismissal of his hopes. The messenger carrying it is captured by the Americans, and when they learn it's carried in a silver bullet he's just swallowed, they make him vomit it up. A second urgent message from Burgoyne reaches Clinton, but he's already on his way back to New York to assemble more troops when an order comes from Howe to bring his entire force down to Pennsylvania, where they're more urgently needed. Thus goes the last hope of catching Gates in a pincers, still another lost opportunity to win the war.

For Burgoyne, it's going to come down to a final desperate battle. Gates is facing him with about eleven thousand men, all well fed and feeling confident, while the British are on half rations, the salt pork and flour are about gone, horses are starving to death, and this once resplendent army is in tatters, much like the conditions in which they're accustomed to seeing the Americans.

It's desperation time. Burgoyne's officers are almost frantically urging him to retreat, but he won't hear of it. He's going to fall on Gates's left flank and try to encircle him from the rear. On the morning of October 7, his advance guard beats the call to arms, a summons heard by Gates's aide, James Wilkinson, who's out reconnoitering. He reports, mistakenly, that it's not an attack, just a foraging party. At the time, several officers, including Arnold, are dining with Gates at his headquarters, on ox's heart and other field delicacies, when the firing from advanced pickets increases. Everybody rises from the table, and Arnold asks, "Shall I go out and see what's the matter?" "I'm afraid to trust you, Arnold." What a betrayal, from a man he thought was his friend and advocate. No doubt Gates is remembering Lake Champlain, or Arnold's overexuberance at Freeman's Farm, or simply the entire history of his young general. In any case, it leads him to exert unusual caution. Swallowing the rebuff, Arnold pleads, "Pray let me go. I'll be careful, and if our advance doesn't need support, I'll promise not to commit you."

At this point, modern historians differ. Most say that Gates permitted Arnold to lead forces at this second Battle of Freeman's Farm, but one of Arnold's most noted biographers, James Thomas Flexner, says the overwhelming evidence tells a different story, although many of the details are the same. At first, in this version, Gates keeps Arnold with him and they work out orders together, although the partnership is now not amicable. In fact, Arnold is still seething because Gates did not mention either him or his division in his report on the September 19 battle. After a hot exchange between the two over this slight, Arnold had asked for a pass to Washington, where he hoped to plead his case, and Gates would have loved to get him out of camp, but his officers, many of them Schuyler's admirers, begged Arnold to stay and he did.

Now, as Burgoyne advances tentatively, the response on the American side is also tentative because Gates doesn't want to give the British a chance for a pitched battle. When a messenger brings the news that nothing much is happening, Arnold loses his patience. "By God, I'll soon put an end to it," he shouts and, jumping on his horse, gallops off at full speed. Gates sends Wilkinson after him to bring him back, which he does, and the apron strings are retied.

That night, Lieutenant Colonel Richard E. Varick, Arnold's good friend, is dining with Gates when the commander says something disparaging about his impulsive general. Varick leaps to his feet, resigns on the spot as Muster Master, and says he would rather see Gates "drawn and quartered" than serve under him. After this outburst, he hurries to Arnold, who's brooding as usual, and Arnold appoints him to his general staff, a public insult to Gates.

Next morning, the British are attacking the American left in earnest, and Arnold demands permission to lead a response. He's refused. To rub it in, Gates removes Arnold's riflemen and attaches them to his own troops.

As the battle develops and the sound of it fills the morning air, Arnold is in a state of mounting excitement. Gates won't even talk to him. Arnold jumps on his big black stallion and wheels around nervously, getting himself more worked up until finally the inevitable explosion occurs. Shouting "Victory or death!" he gallops off toward the battle, right under Gates's horrified gaze. Again, Gates sends Wilkinson after his insubordinate general, but the aide will never catch him this time. A cheer goes up from the troops when they sight Arnold, and Samuel Woodruff, of Windsor, Connecticut, at his side, testifies that from this moment on "he behaved, as I then thought, more like a madman than a cool and discreet officer." Gathering up men as he goes along, and shouting, "Come on, my brave boys, come on!" he leads them up an exposed slope toward the Hessians, who break his charge, but Arnold rallies the men, and this time it's the Hessians who break and run.

Arnold has the field to himself. Wilkinson, trying to follow, remembered: "In a square space of ten or fifteen yards lay eighteen grenadiers in the agonies of death, and three officers propped up against the stumps of trees, two of them mortally wounded, bleeding and almost speechless. I found the courageous Colonel Gilley astraddle on a brass twelve-pounder and exulting in the capture, while a surgeon, a man of great worth, who was dressing one of the [British] officers, raising his blood-smeared hands in a frenzy of patriotism, exclaimed, 'Wilkinson, I have dipped my hands in British blood!'"

The Americans are indulging in a premature celebration when Fraser appears on the scene, halts the fleeing British, turns them around, and a new phase of the battle suddenly opens. In a way, as Flexner has pointed out, it's a struggle between individual champions, like medieval warfare. Here, on the one hand, is the highborn Fraser, who learned the art of war on European battlefields, galloping about on his iron-gray horse, exhorting the troops, leading the charge, exposing himself to enemy fire recklessly. And on the other side, Arnold, a nobody from New Haven who until two years ago had done nothing but march with the town militia. He's charging about on his own stallion, waving his sword, rallying *his* troops, commanding everybody.

Fraser falls, and once more the British break and run. At this point, Major John Armstrong, Jr., catches up to Arnold and relays Gates's order to return to headquarters. Arnold simply ignores him and, leading the men who follow him as though he were some kind of military Pied Piper, dashes through the woods into an open space called Freeman's Field. Some of the British have fortified themselves inside a hollow square of logs, an impregnable position. Undaunted, Arnold decides to attack others who are occupying two log cabins.

Still on his emotional high, he recklessly spurs his horse into the open space between the armies, thereby exposing himself to fire from both sides. He leads a wild assault on the cabins and overpowers them, leaving the British exposed on left and right, behind a redoubt. Shouting to the troops, "Follow me, my boys!" he gallops toward this rampart of logs, and a wave of his troops pours in after him. In a few minutes of furious combat, the British are overwhelmed, and Burgoyne's entire position is thrown into serious danger. He has no other option but retreat, and the second Battle of Freeman's Farm is over, a clear victory not only for the Americans but for Arnold. "It was his doing," Burgoyne writes later to Clinton.

Arnold doesn't see the battle's end. In the charge on the redoubt, his horse leaps into the air and falls dead, throwing him clear—and coming down hard on the bad leg that is his souvenir from Quebec. He tries to rise, can't make it, and has to be carried from the field as darkness ends hostilities for the day. At headquarters, the doctors want to amputate his leg, but just before he loses consciousness, Arnold forbids them to do it. In time, he'll partially recover, but his days as a field general for the Americans are over.

Gates can hardly reprimand him for gross insubordination—indeed, graciously mentions "the gallant General Arnold" in his dispatches. After all, this loose cannon of an officer has just struck a major blow for the cause, one that will have vital consequences. Gates certainly can't claim much glory for himself. While the battle was going on, he sat in his headquarters, arguing about the Revolution with Sir Francis Clark, Burgoyne's aide-de-camp, now a prisoner and mortally wounded, a fact that arouses no pity in Gates. When Clark won't admit he's right, Gates stomps out of the room and says angrily to an aide, "Did you ever hear so impudent a son of a bitch?"

Meanwhile, the other hero of the day, Fraser, is also approaching the end. Baroness Riedesel has been expecting him for dinner that night—in this strange world of eighteenth-century warfare, the amenities are preserved—but about three o'clock, her guest is brought in on a litter. She writes in her diary: "Our dining table which was already spread was taken away and in its place they fixed up a bed for the general. The general said to the surgeon, 'Do not conceal anything from me. Must I die?' The ball had gone through his bowels. Unfortunately, however, the general had eaten a hearty breakfast, by reason of which the intestines were distended and the ball, as the surgeon said, had not gone between the intestines but through them. I heard him often amidst his groans exclaim, 'Oh, fatal ambition! Poor General Burgoyne! My poor wife!' Prayers were read to him. He then sent a message to General Burgoyne begging that he would have him buried the following day at six o'clock in the evening on the top of a hill which was a sort of redoubt."

As he wished, so it is. He dies at eight the next morning, and at sundown on a calm October evening, he's buried. The service is interrupted by American cannoneers, who don't know it's a funeral and keep up an intermittent fire.

After dark, Burgoyne begins a full retreat, refusing to discard either his useless cannon, which slow his progress to a crawl, or the long train of baggage carts, which won't help him now. After a night and a day of travel, he's gone no more than seven miles and stops for the night in Schuyler's splendid house, which he burns next morning, for no apparent reason, and tries to resume progress.

It isn't easy. Baroness Riedesel writes: "The greatest misery and the utmost disorder prevailed in the army. The commissaries had forgotten to distribute provisions. . . . There were cattle enough but not one had been killed. More than thirty officers came to me who could endure hunger no longer. I had coffee and tea made and divided among them all the provisions with which my carriage was constantly filled, for we had a cook who, although an arrant knave, was fruitful in all expedients, and often in the night crossed small rivers to steal from the country people sheep, poultry, and pigs. He would then charge us a high price for them, a circumstance, however, that we only learned a long time afterward. . . . The whole army clamored for a retreat, and my husband promised to make it possible, provided only that no time was lost. But General Burgoyne, to whom an order had been promised if he brought about a junction with the army of General Howe, could not determine upon this course and lost everything by his loitering. About two o'clock in the afternoon [October 10] the firing of cannon and small arms was again heard, and all was alarm and confusion."

What the baroness heard was the sound of a net the Americans are drawing around Burgoyne's army. Stark has captured Fort Edward and so blocked retreat from there to Fort George. Brigadier General John Fellows, leading 1,300 Massachusetts militia, has taken up a blocking position near Saratoga. When the morning fog lifts next day, Gates begins to draw the net tight.

What it means to draw the net if you happen to be inside it is related by the indefatigable baroness, who gives us a harrowing picture: "On the following morning the cannonade again began, but from a different side. I advised all to go out of the cellar for a little while, during which time I would have it cleaned as otherwise we would all be sick. They followed my suggestion, and I at once set many hands to work, which was in the highest degree necessary, for the women and children being afraid to venture forth had soiled the whole cellar. I had just given the cellar a good sweeping and had fumigated them by sprinkling vinegar on burning coals and each one had found his place prepared for him, when a fresh and terrible cannonade threw us all once more into alarm. Many persons, who had no right to come in, threw themselves against the door. My children were already under the cellar steps and we would all have been crushed if God had not given me strength enough to place myself before the door and with extended arms prevent all from coming in. Eleven cannon balls went through the house and we could plainly hear them rolling over our heads."

For six days, the baroness, her children, and the wives and children of other officers made the cellar their home, hanging up curtains to provide a little privacy, nursing the wounded, comforting the dying, keeping up one another's spirits, and taking care of the children,

Then, at last, after four councils of war, Burgoyne makes the only decision he can make: surrender. There is a final cat-and-mouse game to be played, because Burgoyne, although he hasn't heard from Clinton, still hopes the general is marching northward after his Hudson Valley successes. Gates, who had been greatly alarmed when he heard about the fall of these forts, is afraid that might indeed be the case and he's in a hurry. Consequently, when Major Kingston, Burgoyne's adjutant general, gives him a letter from his commander requesting a cease-fire until he can formulate his terms (according to custom, the defeated general has the right to propose terms of honor), Gates startles the major by taking a paper from his pocket with the terms written out, asserting Burgoyne must accept them, custom or no custom.

Still hoping against hope for Clinton's arrival, and if not, at least a decent compromise, Burgoyne offers counterterms, and to the astonishment of everyone on both sides, Gates accepts them. They're simple enough. Burgoyne's remaining five thousand effectives will lay down their arms on October 17, march to Boston, and be shipped out to England after swearing never to serve again in the war. This is the famous Saratoga Convention, and Burgoyne, even though he's made a good deal, still vainly hoping for Clinton's last-minute arrival, tries to drag out the negotiations, and at one point even considers breaking the Convention.

At last Gentleman Johnny has to accept the inevitable. On the seventeenth, as scheduled, he suffers the humiliation of seeing his army marching to its end between two lines of Americans, whose flags are snapping in the October breeze while the fifes and drums play "Yankee Doodle." The air is rank with the stench of still unburied horses. A young British lieutenant writes: "I never shall forget the appearance of their troops on our marching past them; a dead silence universally reigned through their numerous columns, and even then, they seemed struck with our situation and dared scarce lift their eyes to view British troops in such a situation. I must say their decent behavior during the time (to us so greatly fallen) merited the utmost appreciation and praise."

Wilkinson, Gates's aide, has gone to escort Burgoyne, and the fallen general asks to be introduced to Gates, who meets him at the head of his camp. Burgoyne is wearing a rich, royal uniform, Gates has on what Wilkinson calls "a plain blue frock." The two men approach each other on horseback and halt within a sword's length of each other.

"The fortunes of war, General Gates," Burgoyne says, raising his hat gracefully, "has made me your prisoner."

"I shall always be ready to bear testimony," Gates says, "that it has not been through any fault of Your Excellency." These generals hang together; both of them know the fault can't be laid anywhere else than at Burgoyne's door.

Gates greets and shakes hands with the other British officers and Baron Riedesel, who has just had the first night's sleep he's enjoyed in six days. As the British troops pass by to lay down their arms, the two generals stand side by side, Burgoyne looking resplendent, Gates a plain man in a plain blue coat, peering through his thick spectacles. Then they face each other, and without a word, Burgoyne hands over his sword. Gates takes it with a bow and hands it back.

With all these formalities out of the way, we can get down to the serious business of eating and drinking. The principal officers of both sides sit at a makeshift table created by laying two planks across empty beer barrels. It isn't the kind of dining Burgoyne is accustomed to. No tablecloth, only four plates available, but plenty of good food—ham, a goose, beef, and boiled mutton, washed down with New England rum mixed with water. The two generals get the only two glasses available; everybody else makes do with basins. When dinner is over, Gates embarrasses his new friend by calling on him for a toast, and Burgoyne, perhaps gulping a little, proposes, "General Washington," and Gates, politically crossing himself, gives, "The King," who would no doubt not appreciate it.

The ceremonies are over and Burgoyne's army begins its last march. In Cambridge, Hannah Winthrop describes its arrival there in a November letter to Mercy Warren: "Last Thursday, which was a very stormy day, a large number of British troops came softly through the town via Watertown to Prospect Hill. On Friday we heard the Hessians were to make a procession in the same route. We thought we should have nothing to do with them, but view them as they passed.

"To be sure, the sight was truly astonishing. I never had the least idea that the Creation produced such a sordid set of creatures in human figure—poor, dirty, emaciated men, great numbers of women, who seemed to be the beasts of burden, having a bushel basket on their back, by which they were bent double; the contents seemed to be pots and kettles, various sorts of furniture, children peeping through gridirons and other utensils, some very young infants who were born on the road, the women's bare feet, clothed in dirty rags; such effluvia filled the air while they were passing, had not they been smoking all the time, I should have been apprehensive of being contaminated by them."

Hannah notes that Burgoyne rode at the head of this pitiful procession, followed by other officers in blue cloaks. At the end of it were the baggage wagons, "drawn by poor, half-starved horses." Then, in a patriotic burst, Hannah says she saw bringing up the rear a guard of "fine, noble-looking" Americans, "brawny, victorious yeomanry, who assisted in bringing these sons of slavery to terms; some of our wagons drawn by fat oxen, driven by joyous-looking Yankees closed the cavalcade."

Hannah and other Bostonians thought the prisoners would be quartered out of sight, but next morning, she writes, "we beheld an inundation of these disagreeable objects filling our streets! How mortifying it is! They demanded houses and even Harvard College for quarters. Did the brave General Gates ever mean this? Did our legislature ever intend the military should prevail above the civil? Is there not a degree of unkindness in loading poor Cambridge, almost ruined before this great army seemed to be let loose upon us, and what will be the consequences time will discover. . . ." In short, not in our backyard.

For Burgoyne, it's social life as usual. He dines in Boston with General Heath, and rides through the town, returning on foot to Charlestown Ferry, followed, as Hannah says disdainfully, "by a great number of spectators as ever attended a pope and generally observed to an officer with him the decent and modest behavior of the inhabitants as he passed, saying if he had been conducting prisoners through the city of London, not all the guards of Majesty could have prevented insults. He likewise acknowledges Lincoln and Arnold to be great generals. It is said we shall have not less than seven thousand persons to feed in Cambridge and its environs, more than its inhabitants."

It depends, of course, on who you are. The British and Hessian troops, without arms and in the hands of the enemy, are undergoing further privations on the streets of Cambridge. If you're the Baroness Riedesel, however, you have an entirely different view of the conquerors. After the surrender, her husband sent for her to come with her children to Gates's headquarters, where she was welcomed warmly. The generals were dining together, and an American officer who thought it might be embarrassing for her to sit down with them invited her to his tent for a "frugal meal," which turned out to be "excellent smoked tongue, beefsteaks, potatoes, good butter and bread. Never have I eaten a better meal."

Her host, it appeared, was General Schuyler, who treated her as one aristocrat to another, inviting her to take up residence temporarily in his Albany house, where he also expected Burygoyne. Her husband consented, and she traveled to Albany, escorted by a French officer, where Schuyler's wife and daughters received her cordially, as they did Burgoyne. They didn't seem to mind that he had recently burned down their great country house. Moved by such magnanimity, Burgoyne said to Schuyler, "Is it to me, who have done you so much injury, that you show so much kindness?" And Schuyler responded, "That is the fate of war. Let us say no more about it."

But, for others, the fate of war is madness. After the second Battle of Freeman's Farm, Captain John Henry, Patrick Henry's son, who distinguished himself that day, walked among the American dead, pausing to look down on the faces of men he had known well, perhaps lived with in Virginia, and an uncontrollable anger welled up in him. Something snapped. Drawing out his sword, he broke it, threw it on the ground, and returned to camp, raving like the demented man he had suddenly become. Nine months later, when it's plain that he'll never fight again, he will go home. "Give me liberty or give me death," his father's celebrated words, have helped to bring about this war. For Captain Henry, liberty isn't worth it. He sinks into an obscurity so complete that few historians of our time even mention his defection.

An unsung hero of Burgoyne's fall is Alexander Bryan, an amateur secret agent who lives near Bemis Heights. In September, Gates asked him to "go into Burgoyne's army" and find out the "heft" of his artillery. Leaving a pregnant wife and sick child at home, on Gates's promise to send an army doctor to care for them, he bought a piece of cloth, and under pretense of trying to find a tailor, examined Burgoyne's positions. Suspected and pursued, he had to spend a night in the chill waters of a creek to avoid capture, but eventually brought word that the British meant to attack Bemis Heights, and on his information, so it is said, Gates made his successful counterplans. Bryan goes home and finds that the general never sent the promised doctor. His son is dead, and his wife has given birth prematurely and nearly died. His neighbors think he's joined the enemy. So much for patriotism, and little enough reward for information on which this entire decisive engagement may have turned.

In the aftermath of the surrender, controversy breaks out over the Convention. Congress doesn't trust the British. It believes the source of all evil in London will either break the Convention and send the troops back, or else station them in England to free an equivalent number for service overseas. So they renege on the terms and send the hapless prisoners from one place to another in the colonies, most of them winding up in Virginia, until the end of the war.

The British accuse Congress of perfidy, and even Americans join in.

It isn't until our own time that evidence turns up proving that, far from doing the British an injustice, Congress wasn't suspicious enough. A letter from Howe to Burgoyne discloses that Sir William intended to have the transports carrying the Convention troops home diverted to New York, where they would be exchanged for American prisoners.

Most Americans aren't much concerned about what happens to Burgoyne's army in the days after its collapse at Saratoga. It has been the colonials' only major victory, and they won't have another until Yorktown. Suddenly people aren't talking gloomily about a long war. Things are looking up, and if we're not out of the trenches by Christmas, it won't be much longer. In France, Burgoyne's defeat finally tips the scales and the reluctant French ministers decide it's safe now to come to the aid of the Americans and deal their old enemies the British a serious blow in their continuing worldwide conflict. In the end it's French intervention that proves to be decisive.

But such good news is a long way off. As 1777 dwindles away, some of the war's worst hours lie just ahead. Euphoria vanishes and it won't be long before survival seems like a more probable outcome than final victory.

10

✛   ✛   ✛

Two Roads to Philadelphia

W hat *is* the matter with Howe? Whatever became of the grand plan for early victory that he sold earlier in the year to Lord Germain, who's been trying to run the war virtually singlehanded from London? Give me an army of ten thousand men, he had demanded, to operate in the direction of Boston, and another ten thousand to move up the Hudson to Albany, while a small force remains behind to protect New Jersey. In short, contain Washington.

Splendid idea, Germain agreed, but then Howe has another of those inexplicable changes of mind. It isn't the capture of Boston and Albany, then in conjunction with Burgoyne's army to destroy Gates's Northern Army that will win the war, although it surely would have. Philadelphia! That's where Howe wants to go, and if that means leaving Johnny Burgoyne to fend for himself, that's not *his* problem. As we've seen, Burgoyne found this incomprehensible and the failure of Howe to support him meant the end for him at Saratoga and environs. Germain thinks it's incomprehensible too, but by the time communications can be sent across the Atlantic, Howe is already planning the best way to seize Philadelphia.

It's the familiar British confusion at the top, and as the historian Willard Wallace observes, Germain is even more responsible than Howe for Burgoyne's disaster because he has insisted on trying to do the impossible and coordinate American operations from London. That gives complicated characters like Howe altogether too much freedom. Blandly, he assures Germain that everything's going to be all right because he will conduct a quick and effective campaign in

Pennsylvania in plenty of time to turn northward and help Burgoyne. However this may play in London, to Clinton in New York it's madness. Besides, he doesn't fancy being left in command of a garrison in which more than half the men are Loyalist militia.

If Howe has one supporter, it's his distinguished prisoner, General Charles Lee, who is still afraid he might be hanged as a deserter from the British army unless he displays his loyalty in some way. Knowing Howe's virtual obsession with seizing Philadelphia, he offers a plan to accomplish it by way of the Chesapeake, and curiously enough, that's the way Howe wants to do it.

In the American camp, meanwhile, Washington has spent the earlier months of 1777 trying to raise an army and figuring out what Howe is going to do next. One is as difficult as the other. Congress, appearing to have lost its grasp of reality, grandly authorizes seventy-five thousand troops for him, but by the middle of March, the commander has only three thousand of them in New Jersey, and more than two-thirds of these are militia. Two months later, the number is still not much more than eight thousand. Twice Howe tries to lure him into open space, where the regulars can finish him off, but it doesn't work and Sir William finally gives up and begins his preparations to assault Philadelphia by water.

He starts by embarking fifteen thousand troops in New York on the first hot days of early July and keeps them cursing and melting away aboard ship until the twenty-third, before the fleet sails past Sandy Hook lighthouse, disdainfully referred to by his secretary as "a stinking edifice, by means of the oil and the provincials stationed at it."

When news of Howe's departure reaches Washington, he can scarcely believe the general would desert Burgoyne in what the commander fervently hopes will soon be his hour of need. It would be flattering to think that Howe believes the best way to help Johnny is to lure Washington southward into Pennsylvania, but that's exactly what he does believe.

Now it's Washington's turn to make some highly questionable decisions. By moving his army northward to join Gates, he would have been in a position to overwhelm Burgoyne weeks before the Saratoga victory, with plenty of time left to move south quickly and confront Howe. As it is, he weakened his own meager forces by sending three thousand of them to reinforce Gates, and does what

Howe wants him to do: he follows the British into Pennsylvania.

Before he starts off, however, a most unexpected recruit shows up. Shortly after Howe's troops set sail, Washington is drowsing through a soporific luncheon given in his honor by Pennsylvania officials when he suddenly notices a guest who surely doesn't belong in this dreary cast of characters. Who is that handsome young man, and why is he here?

After the luncheon is over, as Washington stands chatting with these respectable citizens and his officers, the odd guest walks straight up to him and introduces himself—the Marquis de Lafayette, no doubt omitting his full name, which is Marie Paul Yves Roch Gilbert du Motier. Lafayette will do nicely, thank you. That he's of patrician background is obvious to Washington; in appearance and manners he's obviously not in the same class with these Philadelphia merchants, what with his rosy, dimpled cheeks.

It's love at first sight, Damon and Pythias. They respond to each other with spontaneous warmth. Lafayette has found the father he's been deprived of ever since his own was killed by an English bullet at the Battle of Hastenbeck. Washington has found the son he never had, or so many of his later biographers believe.

The young Frenchman's passage to this historic moment has not been easy. He's never been taken seriously at home, where he's thought of himself as one destined to become a great leader, an idea laughed at by Marie Antoinette and received by others with reactions ranging from tolerance to irritation. Worst of all, from the standpoint of those in a position to advance him, he's incredibly persistent. As the French historian Claude Manceron describes him, he's a "tall, gawky lad who dances badly and married too young, a clown of an army captain." But when he heard about the Revolution in America, in August 1775, Lafayette suddenly discovered something to live for.

He called it "the final struggle for freedom, and defeat would have left it homeless and without hope." In March 1777, he burst into the bedroom of his friend, Louis Philippe de Ségur, just before daybreak and announced that he was leaving for America—secretly—and wanted to take Ségur and another friend with him, adding a few other adventurers with American plans of their own.

With the help of his more influential friends, he visited Silas Deane, the American representative in Paris, who was simply astounded by the presumption of this nineteen-year-old who wanted to be commissioned in the American army, but after some high-powered persuasion, Deane gave in to him and commissioned the upstart a major general, "acting," he said, "on behalf of the supreme Congress," which of course had given him no such authority.

Lafayette had a stormy voyage to America, dumped off finally with his friends in Charleston. He got no hero's welcome. He and his companions were directed to apply to Congress, more than seven hundred miles away in Philadelphia. They set out on June 2, and it was a long and arduous trip, with much suffering along the way. It took them until July 27 to reach their destination. The city was chaotic, with Howe reported to be on the way. Lafayette and his friends tried to meet with the president of Congress, most of whose members had already fled to Baltimore, but an underling shunted them off and, even worse, called them a band of adventurers. True, the army needed officers, but it would be better if they were engineers and spoke English. Already a veritable swarm of émigrés had been besieging the authorities, trying to get into the army, most of them French, but also Germans, Poles (Count Casimir Pulaski and Kosciuszko among them), and Spaniards, among others. Washington complained, "I am plagued and wearied by the importunities of some, the discontent of others."

But Lafayette, having come so far, was not about to give up. He composed a letter to Congress, describing himself and his progress, including Silas Deane, and at the end set down a magic sentence: "For the sacrifice I have made, it is my right to demand two favors: one is to serve at my own expense, the other, to begin my service as a volunteer."

Open, sesame! Here is a Frenchman who wants to serve for free— and who knows, maybe he has ability. So they accept this young man who has not held more than a reserve captain's commission at home and has never heard a shot fired in anger. Now he's an instant major general, as Congress puts it, "in consideration of his zeal, his illustrious family and connections . . . given the fact that he has left his home and country at his own expense . . . that he asks no salary or maintenance and simply desires to risk his life for our cause." Almost at once, Lafayette is translated into the presence of the Great Man, his new father. He's reached his goal at last, although there's an agonizing wait until the middle of August before his commission, the real one, comes through.

Meanwhile, the American army is on its way to Philadelphia. There's a delightful pause (for the officers, at least) in Germantown. While the troops swelter in the hot, humid weather of early August, Lieutenant James McMichael writes in his diary: "The largest collection of young ladies I almost ever beheld came to camp. They marched in three columns. The field officers paraded the rest of the officers and detached scouting parties to prevent being surrounded by them. For my part, being sent on scout, I at last sighted the ladies and gave them to know that they must repair to hq., upon which they accompanied me as prisoners. But on parading them at the colonel's marquee, they were dismissed, after we had treated them with a double bowl of Sangaree." Following such innocent merriment, it's on to Philadelphia and the serious business of killing Brits.

On August 20, Lafayette catches up with the army at last, fully equipped with his commission, and like all those foreigners who view the Americans for the first time, he finds the sight incredible. "About eleven thousand men," he writes home, "poorly armed and miserably clad, offered an amazing display; among the motley assortment of dress and occasional undress, the best garments were hunting blouses; loose-fitting gray sailcloth jackets common in the Carolinas." Washington makes him welcome, introduces him around, and treats him as though he's the commander's personal discovery. Heady stuff, indeed.

At 3:00 A.M., on a Sunday morning, August 24, the army assembles and General Orders are issued. Drums and fifes are ordered to play a quickstep, "but with such moderation that the men may step to it with ease and without dancing along, or totally disregarding the music." To pacify the fears of tense and divided Philadelphia, especially its women, the commander urges his officers to "use every reasonable method in their power to get rid of all such as are not absolutely necessary" of "the multitude of women in particular, especially those who are pregnant and have children." If there's going to be any stone throwing or other disturbances from Tories, he doesn't want anyone hurt, even Tory women.

About 7:00 A.M., the army marches into Philadelphia under gray, rainy skies that soon clear while the troops are taking three hours to march through. In spite of orders to the drum-and-fife corps, it doesn't quite work out that way. John Adams writes apologetically to Abigail: "Our soldiers have not yet quite the air of soldiers. They don't stay exactly in time. They don't hold up their heads quite erect, nor turn their toes so exactly as they might. They don't all of them cock their hats; and such as do, don't all wear them the same way."

There's a pause near Wilmington, after the march-through, and then in early September the Americans approach Howe along the Brandywine River, at Chadd's Ford, on the road to Philadelphia. Washington establishes his headquarters at Benjamin King's Tavern, about three-quarters of a mile east of the ford. Learning from spies that the British main body is at Birmingham Meeting House, he wants to get there by the shortest, fastest route possible and, in search of a guide, appropriates an elderly resident named Joseph Brown, who is not inclined to be of any help; he's full of excuses. One of the officers dismounts, takes Brown by the arm, and tells him that if he doesn't guide them there by the nearest and best route he will be run through on the spot.

This is a convincing argument, and Brown sets off on his horse, with Washington and his staff close behind. William Darlington, who was there, recalled years later that Brown's horse "leapt all the fences without difficulty, and was followed in like manner by the others. The head of Washington's horse . . . was constantly at the flank of the one on which he was mounted, and the general was continually repeating to him, 'Push along, old man—push along, old man.' When they reached the road, about half a mile west of Dilworthstown, Brown said the bullets were flying so thick that he felt very uncomfortable; and as Washington no longer required nor paid attention to his guide, the latter embraced the first opportunity to dismount and make his escape."

Washington has arrived just in time to avert a calamity. Cornwallis, following the plan Howe devised for the Battle of Long Island, has hurled his regulars at three regiments commanded by Sullivan, with such force that they break and start to run, throwing down their muskets so they can move faster. The commander sees a sight that's becoming all too familiar—panic-stricken Americans running away from the battlefield. He and other officers rally them, and Greene's division comes up to help, but a rout becomes a retreat, largely because Greene has moved his two brigades nearly four miles in forty-five minutes. Sullivan's men pass through their lines and regroup. A British officer wrote later of the battle: "There was a most infernal fire of cannon and musketry. Most incessant shouting, 'Incline to the right! Incline to the left! Halt! Charge!' etc. The balls plowing up the ground. The trees cracking over one's head. The branches riven by the artillery. The leaves falling as in autumn to the grapeshot."

Lafayette has plunged into the Brandywine battle with the enthusiasm of a man who's waited all his life to do just that. At first, he's with Washington as an aide, sending and receiving dispatches through the long, hot day, until about half past four, when the events at Birmingham Court House take place. He begs Father George to send him there. The commander has already observed him in the midst of things, trying to stem the retreat apparently without even noticing the bullets going by him, and so he lets him go. Lafayette joins the other officers who are trying to rally Greene's fleeing force and turn them back into battle.

Language is no problem. He jumps from his horse, just like Washington, and wades into the panic-stricken men, and with Lord Stirling manages a brief stand, but it's no use. This regiment breaks too, and the retreat that's nearly a rout continues. It isn't until Lafayette climbs on his horse again that he realizes he's wounded, a musket ball in his left thigh. Glorious pain! Just what he's always wanted, and in his first battle! He won't let anyone do anything about it until the battle quiets down at nightfall.

A surgeon cuts through his boot and finds he damaged some tendons and lost a great deal of blood. "A scratch," he calls it when he writes to his wife next day, but it's more than that. No matter. Lafayette is a happy man at last. After a month in the tender care of the Moravian Brothers (about whom he makes tasteless fun later), he's as good as new again. Even better, because Washington has written a highly commendatory letter about his conduct at Brandywine.

After watching the battle from behind the British lines, a young Quaker ventures out on the field when it's over and reports: "Awful was the scene to behold—such a number of fellow beings lying together severely wounded and some mortally—a few dead but a small proportion of them, considering the immense quantity of powder and ball that had been discharged. It was now time for the surgeons to exert themselves. . . .

"Some of the doors of the meetinghouse were torn off and the wounded carried thereon into the house to be occupied for a hospital. The wounded officers were first attended to. After assisting in carrying two of them into the house, I was disposed to see an operation performed by one of the surgeons, who was preparing to amputate a limb by having a brass clamp or screw fitting thereon a little above the knee joint. He had a knife in his hand, the blade of which was . . . circular . . . and was about to make the incision, when he recollected that it might be necessary for the wounded man to take something to support him during the operation. He mentioned to some of the attendants to give him a little water or brandy . . . to which he (the patient) replied, 'No, Doctor, it is not necessary, my spirits are up enough without it.' He then observed, 'that he had heard some of them say there was some water in the house, and if there was he would like a little to wet his mouth.' "

It's been a brutal affair there at Brandywine, much of it hand to hand with bayonets, but the Americans have had to retreat under the sheer weight of enemy numbers, Greene finally accomplishing this in more or less good order as darkness sets in. When Howe makes up his report, he lists 90 killed, 480 wounded, and 6 missing. The Americans can't provide an accurate count because they've had to leave the dead where they fell, but it's estimated that 300 were killed and twice that number wounded. Washington might not admit it, but he's simply been outgeneraled by Howe this time, and if Howe once again doesn't follow up his advantage, that can be excused because it's getting dark and his troops, only two weeks away from their arduous sea voyage, are exhausted.

Some of the Americans aren't ready to break off so easily. Captain Enoch Anderson, of Delaware, displaying more bravery than good sense, decides as the elder captain in command that he will take 150 men, mostly from the Maryland Line, and pursue the redcoats, who are now moving off in good order. What happens if he catches them? Apparently the captain hasn't thought about that. In a letter to his nephew, he describes the pursuit: "After dark we began our march and by daybreak we reached Darby Creek and a little after sunrise came to old Chester . . . .We were certainly in a dangerous situation—on the bank of the Delaware, the enemy close by, and we were in the land of the Tories. The British were on the march, bearing northwardly. We marched all this day, keeping near the British army. When they marched, we marched, when they stopped, we stopped. Our guide was the beating of the drums.

"Night came on, there was no house we dare go into, we had no tents. I had no blanket even and must make no fire. Some had blankets, however. The night was very cold. I kept myself tolerably comfortable by walking about, but was very sleepy and could not sleep for the cold."

At daybreak they're off again, and after a long day of shadowing the redcoats, they finally sight them near sundown, marching through a meadow just ahead. That night the captain and his men move off a little for safety's sake, but at sunrise they're once more within sight of the enemy. Heavy rain falls, wetting everyone to the skin, but as the captain says, "we marched ourselves dry."

This strange pursuit goes on for several days longer, the Americans near the British through the daylight hours, finding cold comfort on the leaves and grass at night. Seven days after the pursuit began, Anderson hears that the main American army has crossed over the Schuylkill, and he means to do likewise. The water's high after the rains, and the men enter it in platoons, with the opposite shore two hundred yards away. Anderson orders his men to link arms and keep close to each other, and after a tense trip through waist-deep water, they crawl up on the opposite shore at nightfall. Now they feel safe in making a fire and putting their feet up to it, sleeping comfortably and drying out their clothes by morning. Next afternoon they reach Washington's headquarters after nine days on the road, during which, as Anderson reports, "We never had our clothes off, lodged in no house, in a manner on half allowance of provisions and had to beg on the road." All this accomplishes nothing whatever, but Washington thinks it demonstrates good morale.

The commander's own morale could use some boosting. After the defeat at Brandywine (for which neither he nor anyone else is blamed; Congress even votes to send thirty hogsheads of rum to the army "for their gallant behavior"), he takes the offensive again only three days later at Warren's Tavern, just twenty miles west of Philadelphia, where he surprises the British, who have no idea he's so near, but he takes so much time preparing the attack that Howe has an opportunity to get ready for it, and then two days of hard rain end the hope of contact. That's when Washington makes his crossing of the Schuylkill, with Anthony Wayne left behind as a rear guard, instructed also to nibble away at Howe's left flank if possible.

It's not possible. A savage calamity befalls poor Wayne, and it happens, ironically, in the neighborhood where he grew up as a boy. He's made his camp two miles from Paoli Tavern, thinking to attack

Howe's baggage train, if nothing more. But a British spy locates him, and Howe sends Major General Charles Grey, with the 2nd Light Infantry Battalion and the 42nd ("Black Watch") and 44th regiments to rout him out. After that night's business, the general will be known as "No Flint" Grey. What he does will be burned into the American consciousness as the Paoli Massacre.

"No Flint" means simply cold steel, a deadly bayonet assault on Wayne's unsuspecting camp. More British brutality? Not at all. As Major André points out reasonably in his memoirs, if Grey's men came in firing, Wayne would know where they were and have time either to organize resistance or to escape. By not returning fire when they're discovered, the British will know where the Americans are and where to charge.

It works out with appalling efficiency. Grey, a master of the surprise attack, falls on the camp shortly after midnight, four sentries fire and run. Wayne's men turn out but much too late. Washington's biographer, Douglas Southall Freeman, wrote: "Those Continentals who thoughtlessly ran in front of the campfire were shot down; many who sought the shadows were bayoneted. Wayne succeeded, somewhat surprisingly, in getting his cannon beyond the reach of the enemy and he collected his survivors after daylight, but he had lost at least 150 killed, captured or wounded." Another historian, Willard Wallace, estimated three hundred Americans killed and wounded, with nearly a hundred more captured. The British lost only eight men.

By any measurement, it's a slaughter, and as the news of it sends a shock of revulsion through the colonies, this affair is labeled "the Paoli Massacre." Something of the sheer horror of it is in the letter Major Samuel Hay writes to his friend Colonel William Irvine a few days later: "I went to the ground to see the wounded. The scene was shocking—the poor men groaning under their wounds, which were all by stabs of bayonets and cuts of Light Horsemen's swords. Col. Grier is wounded in the side by a bayonet, superficially slanting to the breastbone. Captain Wilson's stabbed in the side, but not dangerous, and it did not take the guts or belly. He got also a bad stroke on the head with the cock nail of the locks of a musket. Andrew Irvine was run through the fleshy part of the thigh with a bayonet. They are all lying near David Jones' tavern. . . ."

This is an opportunity not to be missed by American propagandists. As their story of the affair spreads, it's charged that the British gave no quarter, which is belied by the fact that they took seventy-one prisoners when they withdrew, leaving those badly wounded at houses along the way. It's said by the propagandists that the British massacred defenseless patriots who tried to surrender, but the military view of it comes from General Heath, who observes simply that "the bayonet was chiefly made use of, and it proved but too efficacious." Wayne is charged with failing to heed timely warning of the attack; however, a court-martial dismisses this notion and acquits him "with the highest honors."

However wrong, even mysterious, Howe's actions may be at critical moments, in the days after Brandywine, he demonstrates that, when he isn't distracted by Mrs. Loring or his disturbed psyche, he's a skillful general. He makes a serious feint at Washington's right wing, and the commander prudently moves his troops farther up the Schuylkill. Then Howe backtracks, crosses the river himself at Swede's Ford, and drives a neat wedge between the Americans and Philadelphia.

The city is in a panic, especially when Alexander Hamilton assures Congress that neither Washington nor anyone else can defend it. Prudently, Congress makes a quick exit to York, saying, in effect, "Let George do it," by giving Washington virtual dictatorial powers. It isn't more power Washington needs, but more soldiers.

After that, the result is a literal walk-in. On September 26, Howe leads his troops into Philadelphia. The redcoats march between lines of thousands of inhabitants crowding the streets, while others hang out upper-story windows or even the tops of their houses. The Whigs say it's now a nest of Tories and go into hiding. In Paris, Franklin is told, "Howe has captured Philadelphia." The old man knows better. Shaking his head, he replies, "No, Philadelphia has captured Howe!" An astute observation.

The general, of course, doesn't see it that way. After throwing Burgoyne to the wolves, and successfully routing the rebels, he means to relax in this city he finds is increasingly to his extravagant tastes. He doesn't even authorize entrenchments for the nine thousand men he's positioned at Germantown, and he doesn't seem much concerned about the two thousand others in New Jersey.

Has this annoying general made another mistake? Washington

wonders. Maybe he's spread out his forces too widely and left the main part of it, in Germantown, relatively unprotected. No doubt with memories of the success at Trenton in mind, he decides to stage a surprise attack on Germantown on the morning of October 4, with the ultimate objective of annihilating Howe's divided forces. Splendid idea, but the reality is that he's sending raw, poorly trained and equipped Continentals against Howe's main force, and while this questionable army, the best he can summon up, is carrying out its assignment, he expects his militia, in even worse shape, to crush the British flanks. Surely it's sheer necessity to *do* something that drives him to this decision. Congress has given him extraordinary power, and he's expected to use it.

His battle plan is too complicated to succeed, but everyone's more than willing, especially Wayne, who's going to lead the charge with the memory of Paoli still fresh. In the early-morning hours of October darkness, Washington deploys four columns for the coming assault. The mist is rising and visibility is so poor that the men pin pieces of white paper to their hats so that those behind them can follow. They start off down the road from their camp at Chester with no means of communication between them, and they're expected to travel over different roads and arrive simultaneously at daybreak. The distance between the right and left wings of this force is as much as seven miles. All that's required for probable failure is for one column to arrive late. Greene, for example, with nearly half the army under his command, takes the wrong road, but somehow all four manage to reach Germantown at about the agreed-upon hour.

Howe's spies have told him they're coming, but he isn't alarmed. Moreover, he's quite unaware that his own movements are being reported by Washington's spy network, several of its operatives women, who have made the Rising Sun Tavern, near Frankford Mills, a rendezvous point. In fact, Major Benjamin Tallmadge has rescued one of them, a young girl who had gone into Philadelphia posing as a seller of eggs. On patrol, Tallmadge saw her leave the British lines and walk toward the Rising Sun. He picked her up and took her there, got her detailed report, and then, looking out the door, he saw the British approaching. Jumping on his horse, he looked down and there was the girl, begging for protection. Gallantly, he swooped her up and they rode for three miles with "considerable firing of pistols, and not a little wheeling and charging." The girl got off near Germantown, and then disappeared.

With such daring espionage, attacks are seldom a surprise and that's the case as the two armies come together at Germantown. Wayne's column, as planned, leads the charge but the British beat him to it and charge first, although they have only about three hundred men at this particular point on the line. Twice the British charge, and twice they're thrown back, the second time regulars have retreated in battle from Americans since Breed's Hill. Their losses are so great that it's only sensible to retreat, but the officers have trouble getting them to obey; retreating from Americans is simply unacceptable.

At this point, Howe arrives and can't believe what he sees. He falls into a fit of rage equaling (and resembling) Washington's outburst on Murray Hill. "For shame, light infantry!" he yells at them. "I never saw you retreat before! Form! Form! It's only a scouting party."

Plainly, it's much more than that. Through the fog, a mass of American infantry can be seen moving forward, and their cannon open up on Howe and his officers, who are sitting their horses under a large chestnut tree. The general has been having a conversation with a man he doesn't realize is one of Washington's spies. "He rode off immediately, full speed," writes one of the light infantry officers who's just been shamed, and he adds, with relish, "I never saw people enjoy a discharge of grape before, but all felt pleased to hear the grape rattle about the commander-in-chief's ears after he accused the battalion of having run away from a scouting party."

As Washington's battle plan unravels, however, the outcome is still in doubt. Lieutenant Colonel Thomas Musgrave, of the British 40th Regiment, and twenty men are barricaded inside the house belonging to Pennsylvania's chief justice, William Chew. They bar the doors and secure the shutters as Lieutenant Colonel Matthew Smith, of Virginia, arrives with an overwhelming force and voluntarily carries a flag of truce toward the house, intending to demand surrender. A shot fells him, and he dies a little later. Other officers order up the three-pounders and they aim at the doors while the men lay down a barrage of round and grape at the upper windows. A pause, and the Americans try to force their way in, but Musgrave won't give up. After a half hour of futile effort, the Americans are forced to bypass Chew's house.

The noise of this skirmish has reached other ears, among them those of General Adam Stephen, who's been drunk since sunup and thinks nothing of abandoning the American plan of attack and bringing his division to help out. Wayne hears the sounds of battle too, but he thinks it's Sullivan in trouble, as usual, and also hurries toward the action. The two divisions meet, but in the fog, smoke, and general confusion, each thinks the other is the enemy, and fires away with such good effect that both break and run. Their panic spreads, and once more it's the old familiar story—Washington trying desperately to rally them while they run by, some holding up empty cartridge boxes by way of explanation, others never slowing down and averting their eyes from the commander.

With all its defects, the attack on Germantown should have been an American victory, but instead it turns into a defeat. Trying to figure it out, General George Weedon writes: "Our men behaved with the greatest intrepidity for three hours, driving them from their camps, fieldpieces, stone walls, houses, etc. Trophies lay at our feet, but so certain were we of making a general defeat of it that we passed them by in the pursuit and by that means lost the chief part of them again, for when the unlucky idea struck our men to fall back, the utmost exertions to rally them again was in vain, and a few minutes evinced the absolute necessity of drawing them off in the best manner we could."

Blame is parceled out freely. Washington and others think too much time was spent assaulting the Chew house. Others blame Wayne and Stephen for their case of mistaken identity. Still others believe it was the fog and smoke that caused the confusion, and there are many soldiers who remember how they called out for ammunition when theirs was spent and the enemy, overhearing, took advantage of this perennial and vital shortage. Certainly it's the lack of ammunition and reinforcements that everyone agrees is a major cause of this defeat.

Tom Paine has his own view of the event. As secretary to the Foreign Committee of Congress, he's been with the army as an observer, and at 5:00 A.M. on the day of battle he was riding toward Germantown to see the action. When he was five or six miles away, he met the wounded already making their way toward the rear in wagons, on horseback, and walking if they could. He wrote to Franklin: "I passed General [Francis] Nash on a litter made of poles but did not know him. . . . About two miles after, I passed a promiscuous crowd of wounded and otherwise, who were halted at a house. Colonel [Clement] Biddle was among them, who called after me that if I went further on that road I would be taken. . . . I never could, and cannot now [six months later] learn, and I believe no man can inform truly the cause of that day's miscarriage. The retreat was extraordinary. Nobody hurried themselves. Everyone marched at his own pace."

And no wonder. Each of these retreating men Paine saw had marched at least fourteen miles the previous night, they were already fatigued when they fought, and now they're near exhaustion. When they finally come to rest at Pennypacker's Mill, twenty-four miles from the scene of their defeat, most of them have been without food for twenty-four hours, and they've been desperate for water since that morning. They owe their escape to the fact that the British themselves have been too exhausted to pursue.

"We ran from victory," Wayne says disgustedly, echoing Washington's puzzled summary: "In the midst of the most promising appearances, when everything gave the most flattering hopes of victory, the troops began suddenly to retreat; and entirely left the field, in spite of every effort that could be made to rally them." Not all, though. Greene, isolated, coolly saved not only most of his division but his guns as well, in spite of everything Cornwallis could do to stop him, vainly pursuing him for five miles—by any measurement, a remarkable feat.

Germantown took only two hours and a half, but the Americans lost 152 killed, 521 wounded, and 400 captured. The British lost a total of 534 men.

In the aftermath, Howe mops up after victory. Withdrawing the main army to Philadelphia, he quickly captures American forts on the Delaware so that the first British ships can sail safely up the river. Early in December, he also threatens the American positions at Whitemarsh, but it's no more than a skirmish and Howe doesn't bother to pursue it. As Washington describes this action, with some sarcasm: "General Howe, after making great preparations, and threatening to drive us beyond the mountains, came out with his whole force last Thursday evening, and after maneuvering around us till the Monday following, decamped very hastily and marched back to Philadelphia."

Years later, applying for his pension, a Pennsylvanian named William Hutchinson provided a final summary of Germantown. After the battle, he was in a house being used as a hospital, where, as he recalled, "the floor was covered with human blood; amputated arms and legs lay in different places in appalling array, the mournful memorials of an unfortunate and fatal battle, which indeed it truly was."

Now, as the December gloom deepens, the American army nearly falls apart. Whatever energy exists is spent in the never-ending search for food and firewood, and if a soldier is lucky he might even liberate some shoes and blankets from an unwilling farmer. Some desert, some drown themselves in rum, discipline falls to a dangerously low point as many officers are charged with cowardice at Germantown and before. Non-commissioned officers are reduced to the ranks by the dozen. Daily floggings are common.

As the demoralized army moves toward winter quarters, it stops at a place called "The Gulf," on Gulf Creek, now West Conshohocken, Pennsylvania, where the men are told that Congress has ordered a Continental Thanksgiving to be observed.

Our old friend, Private Joseph Martin, is there to tell us about it with a broad sarcasm that reflects the state of mind in camp. "The army had all the cause in the world to be particularly thankful," Joe says, "if not for being well off, at least that it was no worse. . . ." Willing or not, the troops are ordered to participate, and Martin says: "We had nothing to eat for two or three days previous, except for what the trees of the fields and forests afforded us," but Congress has decreed "a sumptuous Thanksgiving to close the year of high living. . . . To add something extraordinary to our present stock of provisions, our country, ever mindful of its suffering army, opened her sympathizing heart so wide, upon this occasion, as to give us something to make the world stare. . . . It gave each and every man half a gill of rice and a tablespoonful of vinegar."

Then they had to hear a sermon delivered. The text was, "And the soldiers said unto Him, And what shall we do? And He said unto them, Do violence to no man, nor accuse anyone falsely." To which, Martin adds bitterly, He should have added, "And be content with your wages." The sermon was greeted with "shouting from a hundred tongues," an understandable response from men who, as Martin reports, were now "not only starved but naked. The greatest part were not only shirtless and barefoot, but destitute of all over-clothing, especially blankets. I procured a small piece of raw cowhide and made myself a pair of moccasins, which kept my feet (while they lasted) from the frozen ground, although, as I well remember, the hard edges so galled my ankles, while on a march, that it was with much difficulty and pain that I could wear them afterwards; but the only alternative I had was to endure this inconvenience or to go barefoot, as hundreds of my companions had to, till they might be tracked by their blood upon the rough frozen ground."

In this sorry state, the army, on December 20, entered that American Gethsemane we still recall with pain—Valley Forge.

1778

11

✛   ✛   ✛

Times That Try Men's Souls

Private Joseph Martin remembered his first sight of Valley Forge. It was dark, there was no water, "and I was perishing with thirst. I searched for water till I was weary, and came to my tent without finding any. Fatigue and thirst, joined with hunger, almost made me desperate. I felt at that instant as if I would have taken victuals or drink from the best friend I had on earth by force."

Two soldiers passed by him with full canteens, but they wouldn't give him any and it was so dark they couldn't tell him where they got it. He begged for a swallow, offered them a threepence, all he had in the world, and got his grudging drink. "I lay there two nights and one day," he wrote later, "and had not a morsel of anything to eat all the time, save half of a small pumpkin, which I cooked by placing it upon a rock, the skin side uppermost and making a fire upon it. By the time it was heated through I devoured it with as keen an appetite as I should a pie made of it at some other time."

Martin was one of the more fortunate who didn't spend the whole winter at Valley Forge. His regiment went on to Milltown, now Downingtown, halfway between Philadelphia and Lancaster, where he became a part of a more or less permanent foraging party.

In our national memory, perpetuated by artists, Valley Forge is an image of snow and bitter cold, and we think of Washington, kneeling in what looks like a snowdrift, asking God to ease the burden, something he would never have thought of doing. In fact, it's one of the mildest winters on record there, no more than two inches of snow. The enemies are rain and mud, and the chill that goes with them—

these and, of course, the lack of almost everything that human beings need to live. The other enemies include hunger, disease, and the constant choking smoke of greenwood fires that make the soldiers' huts habitable. Many of these men haven't been paid for a year. Many others have not much more than a torn blanket with which to protect themselves. And there will be three periods during the winter when there's no food of any kind.

How can this be, in the heart of an agricultural country which has just produced one of its best fall harvests, war or no war? There's an abundance of beef in Connecticut, and plenty of pork in New Jersey. Boston warehouses are filled with cloth. New York reports surpluses of wheat, barley, and rye. So why are we starving and aching with misery in Valley Forge?

Greed and profiteering, also plain old human meanness. Even if these didn't exist, however, it's a country with such appalling roads and too few wheeled vehicles to travel them that moving supplies from one place to another is a logistical nightmare. General Mifflin, who's been serving as quartermaster, resigns the job in November 1777, and for three months Congress doesn't appoint a successor. These, of course, are the worst months in winter quarters.

The nearest sources of supply for Valley Forge are the abundant Pennsylvania farms, but the farmers won't sell to their fellow Americans if they can get higher prices from the British in Philadelphia. William Ellery, who signed the Declaration for Rhode Island, looks about him in the Continental Congress and at the burgeoning states and writes, with disgust: "The love of country and public virtues are annihilated. If Diogenes were alive and were to search America with candles, would he find an honest man?"

A colonel from New York writes to his governor, George Clinton, pleading for supplies from the stores of his home state: "I have upwards of seventy men unfit for duty only for the want of clothing, twenty of which have no breeches at all, so that they are obliged to take their blankets to cover their nakedness and as many without a single shirt, stocking, or shoe, about thirty fit for duty, the rest sick or lame, and, God knows, it won't be long before they will all be laid up, as the poor fellows are obliged to fetch wood and water on their backs half a mile with bare legs in snow or mud."

The men live in a city of log huts, twelve to a hut. Officers of the company share a hut. They're claustrophobic, these quarters, only fourteen by sixteen feet, reeking with smoke from round-the-clock fires. Before real deprivation sets in, flour or some other kind of ground grain is the primary—and sometimes the only—food. Soldiers mix water with it and bake it in pans over the coals. Fire cakes, they're called. One officer has a cherished recipe for cooking spoiled pork and hog fodder when it's available. Company-grade officers share the general misery, but the field-grade and general officers are much better supplied.

It's not a place where men sit huddled up and miserable, although they do that too. The camp is always bustling, with civilians coming and going on visits, and soldiers leaving and departing on furloughs. Nor are the food shortages common to all; some units fare better than others. Shortage of clothing is more prevalent and there are even some officers who wear blankets instead of overcoats, and apparently think nothing of standing next to men in rags. It isn't that no clothing is available, but civilians are competing for it and frequently get there first. Soldiers desperate for money are willing to break all the laws and sell what clothing they do have, even their muskets, for money to buy food and liquor. They have their own priorities. So have the civilians. Connecticut's beef supply disappears because the state puts a ceiling on the exorbitant prices farmers are getting for it, so they refuse to sell. Boston merchants have plenty of clothing on their shelves but they won't sell it, even at outrageous prices, for anything but cash. Private contractors are getting rich. They load up Pennsylvania wagons with flour and iron and send them north, while New Jersey pork rots for lack of transport. It's graft, speculation, selfishness, and incredible mismanagement everywhere, then and throughout the war.

But it's the day-to-day misery that's so awful. Lafayette, getting over his Brandywine wounds, writes home: "The unfortunate soldiers were in want of everything; they had neither coats, nor hats, nor shirts, nor shoes; their feet and legs froze till they grew black, and it was often necessary to amputate them."

A surgeon named Albigence Waldo gives us the best picture of what it's like at Valley Forge in the diary he keeps. Waldo is a remarkable man. A Pomfret, Connecticut, boy, he's grown up to be one of the best surgeons of his day and has already been a huge help in inoculating the army against smallpox. He may be best known for his charities, which are so numerous he often doesn't have enough for his family. Waldo loves music, painting, and drawing, and on proper occasions he appears as an accomplished orator.

Waldo came to Valley Forge optimistic that maybe it wouldn't be such a bad place after all, but soon enough he's writing: "Poor food—hard lodging—cold weather—fatigue—nasty clothes—nasty cookery—vomit half my time—smoked out of my senses—the Devil's in't—I can't endure it—why are we sent here to starve and freeze—what sweet felicities have I left at home! A charming wife—pretty children—good beds—good food—good cookery—all agreeable—all harmonious. Here all confusion—smoke and cold, hunger and filthiness—a pox on my bad luck."

Waldo writes of a young soldier who comes to him nearly naked, crying out in wretchedness and despair: "I am sick, my feet lame, my legs are sore, my body covered with this tormenting itch—my clothes are worn out, my constitution is broken, my former activity is exhausted by fatigue, hunger, and cold. I fail fast. I shall soon be no more! And all the reward I shall get will be, 'poor Will is dead!'"

For himself, Waldo is bitter about the people back home who "are willing we should suffer everything for their benefit and advantage, and yet are the first to condemn us for not doing more!"

If anyone's worse off, Waldo says, it's the poor Americans in Philadelphia and New York prisons, where one prisoner is so desperate from hunger that he eats his own fingers up to the first joint. Others eat clay, lime, stone chips from walls, and some who fall dead in the yard have pieces of bark, wood, or stone still in their mouths, unable to swallow them.

The cry of "No meat! No meat!" sounds dismally in the camp streets at Valley Forge, and once when a butcher does bring in a quarter of very poor beef, displaying white buttons on the knees of his breeches, a soldier cries out, "There, there, Tom, is some more of your fat beef, by my soul I can see butcher's breeches' buttons through it."

Paradoxically, Waldo believes that in some ways the officers are worse off than the soldiers. A soldier's family is provided for by public expense "if the articles they want are above the common price," but an officer's family is not so protected and has to beg for necessities, and then pay exorbitant prices for them. Officers constantly get letters of complaint from their families at home; Richard Montgomery's Janet wasn't the first. Usually the men read these when they're wet, cold, ill, or exhausted, which is much of the time.

As Waldo puts it, these missives are "filled with the most heart-breaking tender complaints a woman is capable of writing; acquainting him with the incredible difficulty with which she procures a little bread for herself and children—and finally concluding with expressions bordering on despair, of procuring a sufficiency of food to keep soul and body together through the winter—that her money is of very little consequence to her—that she begs of him to consider that charity begins at home, and not suffer his family to perish with want in the midst of plenty."

No wonder more than fifty officers of General Greene's division resign their commissions in a single day, and six or seven more the next day. Washington remarks grimly that in the end he may be left alone with the soldiers. Waldo himself, in ill health and the recipient of the same kind of letters from home that he's been writing about in his diary, resigns in October 1779.

As for the other ranks, they write home too and exchange miseries, but somehow the public doesn't really understand what's happening at Valley Forge, because Washington makes every effort to keep the desperate condition of the army a secret from the general public, which wants to hear only good news, as though he had any to give them. Consequently it's a big surprise to most people when they find out about it later. There's plenty of finger-pointing, as usual. Governors want to know why Congress is being so negligent (Washington would like to know that, too); at home, at least some citizens are outraged when they learn of the army's condition, although that's hard to understand, considering the correspondence that's been going on. The revelation is enough to produce a little more in the way of beef and grain.

But the gulf continues to grow between public and army. The soldiers think civilians are living good lives at their expense, and that all they know or care about the war is who wins or loses the battles. As for the civilians, they assume that the army can take care of itself, and want as little to do with it as possible unless their own welfare is threatened. They're also indignant about bounty money. All this is producing a kind of stubborn pride at Valley Forge. "We're going to survive in spite of Congress and the home front," they seem to be saying. "If those people back home think the war is already won, we know better. We know that we'll all be up the creek if we don't survive and persist."

With such an army, in such circumstances, is discipline a problem? Washington thinks it is, and he's stern about it. He's afraid the army will simply disintegrate if discipline is not imposed. And he's strict about class lines. A Virginia lieutenant is charged with buying a pair of shoes from a Continental soldier, thus making him unable to serve. It's also charged that this officer eats with the soldiers sometimes, takes their bread, and doesn't return it. He's accused of other things, too, but a court-martial acquits him of everything except fraternizing and buying shoes. That's too much; he's discharged.

Another court-martial board convicts an officer of being AWOL, of associating with a soldier, and stealing. That's enough to have his sword broken over his head on the parade ground, and for him to be discharged. The board adds "that it be esteemed a crime of the blackest dye in an officer or even a soldier to associate with him after the execution of this just, though mild punishment."

The general himself lived briefly among his men, in his marquee, when he first arrived at Valley Forge, but that was only until a suitable house could be found for headquarters, a two-story stone affair belonging to Isaac Potts. It's much too small to accommodate Washington and his staff in the style they're accustomed to, particularly at this moment when there are nine aides at the beginning and another before the winter ends.

When Martha arrives on February 10, she thinks the house is inadequate for the inevitable entertaining, and insists on the building of a log cabin for dining, which, as she writes to Mercy Warren, "has made our quarters much more tolerable than they were at first."

The entertaining begins at once. Lady Stirling and her daughters are there, along with the wives of other generals, and life in the officer class goes on much as usual. Knox and his Lucy gossip in their letters about whether Greene and his vivacious wife Kitty are getting on. They are. A few local young ladies enjoy the company of the aides. There are dinners and teas and frequent evening affairs. But the house is finally so crowded that Hamilton has to sleep in a hall bedroom and the Potts family is removed entirely to an attic over the kitchen, to which the log cabin for dining is attached.

In the little room he uses as an office, the general engages in endless correspondence, trying to wake up Congress to the seriousness of his situation, and answering with some irony and indignation a complaint from the Pennsylvania Assembly, which wants to know what he's doing in winter quarters when he should be out campaigning.

"I can assure these gentlemen," Washington replies, "that it is a much easier and less distressing thing to draw remonstrances in a comfortable room by a good fireside, than to occupy a cold, bleak hill, and sleep under frost and snow, without clothes or blankets. However, although they seem to have little feeling for the naked and distressed soldiers, I feel superabundantly for them, and from my soul I pity those miseries which it is neither in my power to relieve or prevent."

Washington spends time, too, in drawing up a detailed fifty-page plan for a new system of administering the army. Congress sends up a six-man commission (further complicating the housing problem) to stay in camp and work on the plan with him. By the time they sort it all out, and Congress has approved it, the crisis at Valley Forge will be over.

Late in February, what proves to be the most important event of the terrible winter occurs when Frederick William Augustus Henry Ferdinand, the Baron von Steuben, arrives at headquarters with a small retinue. Washington greets with interest this stout, balding man who has a big nose, and whose blue uniform, conspicuous because it's new, displays a jeweled Star of the Order of Fidelity of Baden. What in the world is *that*? It takes awhile to find out, because the baron speaks no English, but he's brought along a translator, his seventeen-year-old secretary, Pierre Duponceau, as well as two aides and a German servant, not to mention a spectacular Italian greyhound trotting at his heels. Not another Lee, we hope.

Steuben has a letter of introduction from Franklin and another from Silas Deane, informing Washington that the new arrival is already a lieutenant general in the Prussian King's service who wants to enlist, like Lafayette, so that he may render his services and "deserve the title of a citizen of America by fighting for the cause of your liberty."

Well, now, we may have something here. Washington is understandably cautious (one Lafayette is enough), but as his own interpreter, Laurens, helps him carry on a conversation, he thaws considerably. Of course he has no way of knowing that in some respects he's talking to a complete fraud. Steuben is no more a lieutenant general in anybody's army (as he claims) than he is a baron, and he's telling a barefaced lie when he says he served twenty-two years under the King of Prussia. Franklin must have been astute enough to know this, and perhaps he even knew that Steuben was actually an unemployed penniless captain who was kicked out of the King's army fourteen years earlier, and that since then he's been a chamberlain in some minor European court. In other words, he's a jovial, lying adventurer.

This isn't to say, however, that the baron doesn't have his good points. He's well educated and well read, and has had excellent army training. His father was a respected Prussian officer, and because of that, young Steuben was one of thirteen officers who had the benefit of Frederick the Great's personal instruction in general-staff duties. Further conversation discloses that he does, in fact, possess exceptional abilities. Accompanied by Laurens and Hamilton, he makes a rather discouraging tour of the camp, and in a few days Washington appoints him acting inspector general, without rank, with a mission to drill and train the army, which must seem like the most impossible job in the world. Steuben doesn't even have a set of regulations; he has to write his own—in French.

While he's gearing up, Duponceau is finding life at Valley Forge not as bad as it might be, and he's quite frank about it. "We who lived in good quarters," he wrote much later in his memoirs, "did not feel the misery of the times so much as the common soldiers and the subaltern officers, yet we had more than once to share our rations with the sentry at our door. We put the best face we could upon the matter.

"Once, with the baron's permission, his aides invited a number of young officers to dine at our quarters, on condition that none should be admitted that had on a whole pair of breeches. This was understood of course as *pars pro toto*, but torn clothes were an indispensable requisite for admission and in this the guests were very sure not to fail. The dinner took place. The guests clubbed their rations, and we feasted sumptuously on tough beefsteaks and potatoes with hickory nuts for our dessert. In lieu of wine, we had some kind of spirits with which we made salamanders, that is to say, after filling our glasses, we set the liquor on fire and drank it up flame and all. Such a set of ragged and at the same time merry fellows were never before brought together. The baron loved to speak of that dinner of his *sans culottes*, as he called us. Thus the denomination was first invented in

America and applied to the brave officers and soldiers of our Revolution-army. . . . In the midst of all our distresses, there were some bright sides to the picture. . . ."

Duponceau is also a fascinated guest at the table and hearth of General Greene and Kitty, who are living in Isaac Walker's house. Foreign officers like to come there because Kitty speaks French and has read French literature. Other lively guests are likely to be Lady Stirling; her daughter, Lady Kitty Alexander; and her companion, Miss Nancy Brown, described as "a distinguished belle." Then there's Mrs. Biddle, the wife of Colonel Clement Biddle, and an assortment of other ladies.

"They often met at each other's quarters," Duponceau recalls, "and sometimes at General Washington's, where the evening was spent in conversation over a dish of tea or coffee. There were no levees, or formal soirees; no dancing, cardplaying, or amusements of any kind, except singing. Every gentleman or lady who could sing was called upon in turn for a song."

These relatively spartan entertainments are still much better than what's happening in the huts below, where the women are likely to be the wives of enlisted men who, for reasons of devotion or economy, can't be separated from them, along with the washerwomen who eke out a hard existence over the tubs for little pay, and of course large numbers of whores who seem to appear magically wherever the army stops, much to Washington's disgust.

There are also some other little ironies. Surgeon Waldo tells of visiting a dying soldier, an Indian, "an obedient, good-natured fellow" who "has fought for those very people who disinherited his forefathers," and his own generation as well. Others like him are serving on every field of battle, but none more unusual than another native Duponceau encounters one morning before breakfast, while he's walking in the woods.

From a long way off he hears a "most powerful voice. . . yet melodious." Someone's singing an aria from a fashionable French opera, here in the wilds of America. Duponceau can't believe it. "I thought myself for a moment at the Comédie Italienne and was lost in astonishment," he recalls, "when suddenly I saw . . . before me a tall Indian . . . in American regimentals and two large epaulets on his shoulders." The singer introduces himself. He's an Abenaki from Canada, a Catholic convert, who's been with the Americans since he joined Montgomery on the way to Montreal. Since then, he's been commissioned a Continental colonel, but where he learned to sing French opera Duponceau doesn't tell us.

Hardships and social life aside, the winter produces an unremitting stream of unexpected problems. When General Mifflin resigned as quartermaster, he left behind him an Augean stable of incredible mismanagement. A congressional committee coming to inspect finds abandoned wagons scattered over the countryside. Spades, shovels, and tomahawks, more than three thousand of them, are found here and there, simply thrown away. Investigating congressmen entering a farmer's barn find quantities of badly needed tents and tent-cloth, and their recovery saves a few poor fellows from sleeping on the frozen ground. There's plenty of straw around, too, for sleeping on, but no wagons to bring it in. Soldiers have to construct small carriages and yoke themselves to them like oxen when they want to move wood or provisions that are too heavy to carry on their backs. General Greene, with great reluctance, takes over the quartermaster's job temporarily.

Some bad pennies turn up. General Richard Prescott, whom we last saw being taken from a questionable house in Rhode Island without his breeches, is exchanged for Lee, who arrives at Valley Forge. It's hard to understand Washington. What is it with him and Lee? He sends out a party of horse under Colonel Richard Kidder Meade, who's foremost among the Lee haters, to escort this plainly disloyal fellow into camp, as though he's making a triumphal entry. The commander dismounts and receives him "as if he had been his brother," says a disgusted eyewitness. Not only is he given high military honors, but he's "entertained with an elegant dinner, and the music playing the whole time." They even find a room for him in this crowded house, just behind Martha's sitting room.

Next morning Lee emerges very late, and they've waited breakfast for him. He looks dirty, Meade records in his journal, "as if he had been in the street all night. Soon after I discovered that he had brought a miserable dirty hussy with him from Philadelphia (a British sergeant's wife) and had actually taken her into his room by a back door, and who had slept with him that night."

This is quite enough for Martha when she hears about it. Washington may do what he likes, but Lee is no longer on her A list. Of course he doesn't care. Because he's on parole and therefore can't

resume active military duty, he leaves at once for his home in Virginia, stopping off to give Congress the benefit of his advice. He also encounters Commissary of Prisoners Elias Boudinot and tells him he's found the army in a worse situation than he expected, and that General Washington is "not fit to command a sergeant's guard." Good old Charlie, he hasn't changed a bit!

There's another bad apple on the American side. His name is Thomas Conway, a former colonel in the French army, an Irishman with a sharp tongue and outsized ambitions. He has his virtues. As a brigadier general since 1777, he's commanded a brigade whose training is exemplary. During the previous September, however, he asked Congress to make him a major general, as it had just done for another foreigner, the Baron de Kalb. Congress was perfectly willing, but Washington balked at promoting Conway over the heads of men he thought more deserving, and rubbed it in by observing that this applicant's merits existed "more in his own imagination than in reality." That's how to make an enemy. An embarrassed Congress tried to appoint Conway inspector general, but before that could happen, the legislators decided to reconstitute the Board of War, naming Gates as its president. This made Gates the technical superior of Washington, and cast a new light on the Conway matter.

The Irish troublemaker seized the moment. He wrote an audacious letter to Congress in which he implied that his present commanding officer, Lord Stirling, was habitually drunk after dinner, and went on to denigrate the military ability of other officers—all charges in which there was at least some truth. Then, two weeks later, Conway made a mistake by writing a second letter, this one to Gates, laying on the blarney with a thick brush, and asserting his passionate wish to serve under Horatio. In passing, he expanded on the first letter and told Gates he didn't think much of either Washington's army or the men leading it, including the commander.

This letter was read not only by Gates but by his young adjutant, James Wilkinson, then at the beginning of what will later be referred to as his "long, checkered, and on the whole dishonorable career." Gates sent his adjutant south with the official report of Burgoyne's surrender, and on the way, Wilkinson took the opportunity to stop and visit his girl and see old friends, all of whom wanted to help him celebrate the surrender. Maybe it was the celebratory wine, but Wil-

kinson carelessly mentioned Conway's letter to Major William Mc-Williams, Stirling's adjutant, who immediately told his chief about it, and the story was then repeated to Washington.

On November 9, the commander takes notice of this correspondence, which some would call traitorous, by sending Conway a brief note that he takes as a slap in the face and is alarmed enough to reply with a flat denial that he ever attacked Washington. Now Gates gets into it. Learning about what's going on, he's also alarmed, as well as angry, and sends off a letter to Washington denying that he's had anything to do with this affair, about which he professes to know nothing. He sends a copy of this letter to Congress, where it arrives a week after they've given Conway his appointment as inspector general, which makes him independent of Washington.

The commander isn't willing to let this matter drop. He tells Gates that Wilkinson has been his informant, however unwittingly, and that leads to a shouting match between Gates and Wilkinson, ending when the latter challenges his general to a duel. Gates avoids suicide by backing down, after which Conway has the gall to report at Valley Forge, where the social temperature is so much colder than the climate that he hurries away again.

Is there some kind of conspiracy going on here, something deserving of what will later be called the Conway Cabal? Congress decides to find out and, in the customary way, appoints a committee of investigation, on which Gates and two other generals, Mifflin and Pickering, decline to serve. The affair gets into the public domain and civilians who want to throw out Washington and replace him with Gates step up their criticism of one and praise for the other.

Gates chooses this moment to propose his idea of invading Canada again, with Lafayette in command and Conway under him. The young Frenchman may be inexperienced, but he sees through this maneuver; after all, Washington is his hero. He tells the president of Congress, Henry Laurens, that he won't take the command if Conway is his second; he'll go back to France first. (Fat chance!) He adds, loyally, that he thinks Washington has been grossly insulted and he won't accept any command that doesn't permit the general to appoint his second. Congress and the Board of War agree, but they're not happy about it. Taking the cue, Washington appoints Baron de Kalb.

Arriving at Albany in the middle of February to carry out Gates's harebrained plan, Lafayette finds Conway already there and appar-

ently under the impression that he's to organize the expedition, but even *he* has sense enough to see that the whole idea is a prescription for another disaster in the North. When he sees Conway, Lafayette goes up like a balloon and accuses Congress directly of deceiving him, whereupon they recall both him and De Kalb and, to get Conway out of the way, send him to the Peekskill camp.

Conway doesn't know when he's beaten. He tells Congress how wrong they are about the whole matter, and demands that Washington give him a division to command. Getting nowhere with this approach, he threatens to hand in his resignation, which Congress gratefully accepts, much to Conway's astonishment. Gates is shoved upstairs to command the Hudson River forts, and the Board of War over which he's supposed to preside is now just a name on the door.

Was it really a conspiracy, a cabal? We're still debating it, but at the time, Washington's officers at Valley Forge think there's plenty of fire beneath all this smoke and they're outraged. Oddly enough, it's Conway who eventually apologizes for the whole messy business, after he's wounded in the summer of 1778 during a duel with General John Cadwalader. Lying there at what he thinks is death's door, he dictates a letter to Washington in which he expresses grief "for having done, written, or said anything disagreeable," the understatement of that year. Recovering unexpectedly, Conway decides he's had enough of the Americans and returns to France.

If there's anyone else who's been at risk in this affair, it's Lafayette. When he first got to Valley Forge, he wrote home: "I read, I study, I examine, I listen, I reflect, and upon the result of all this I make an effort to form my opinion and to put into it as much common sense as I can. I am cautious not to talk much, lest I should say some foolish thing." That was pre-Conway, and it may be he was too brash in advancing himself while he was defending his adopted Father George. It was also naive of him to let himself be drawn into the Conway affair. But he couldn't resist that title Gates dangled in front of him: "Commander of the Northern Army."

There's no end to the problems that Washington is called upon to deal with, and not all of them involve the conditions at Valley Forge or ambitious Irishmen. One of the most exasperating, because it involves the home front, is the treatment of American prisoners, especially in New York, from which atrocity stories emerge almost daily in letters home and elsewhere.

To find out what's actually occurring, Washington sends his own commissary general of prisoners, Elias Boudinot, to investigate conditions in New York. Surprisingly, Clinton has agreed to show him anything he wants to see, and he arrives early in February. He finds the city in worse condition than usual. Even the Loyalists don't like living under a harsh military dictatorship. They had petitioned earlier "to be restored to the King's peace," by which they meant civilian authority, but the Howe brothers had no intention of relinquishing power to anybody, and didn't even answer the petition.

So the city has been ruled by a succession of generals. New York is crowded to the walls with refugees, with soldiers everywhere, including foreigners who don't speak English. Food and fuel are constantly in short supply, and everyone is fearful of attack by the Americans or the French. The city is stricken periodically by epidemics of disease. Not a place you'd want to be even if you weren't in prison. Loyalists find they've been deprived of that great English right, trial by jury. The soldiers can do whatever they like with them and get away with it, but God help them if *they* attack or offend the military.

As for Clinton, he enjoys being a military dictator. No mercy from that quarter even if you're British. As for American prisoners, the worst that can happen to them if they're brought to New York is to be confined on the prison ship *Jersey*, anchored in Wallabout Bay, Brooklyn, along with three hospital ships, the *Scorpion*, the *Stromboli*, and the *Hunter*, to take up the overflow.

The *Jersey* is already infamous. More than ten thousand Americans will die in this hellhole before the war is over, and the very mention of its name is enough to terrify a soldier. Thomas Dring, a Rhode Islander from Newport, finds himself aboard for nearly five months and tells us it was there that he was "taught the utmost extent of human misery."

Dring remembers being struck first by the loathsome smell of the ship. Then he's thrust down in the hold, hot and dark, filled with vermin. Some of the prisoners have smallpox, so Dring inoculates himself with a common pin, taking the necessary matter from a dying victim. He survives, others do not. Prisoners get two-thirds of what the crew gets to eat, but it's mostly inedible—a "sweet oil" in place of butter, so putrid it can't be used. Dring gives his portion to half-starved Frenchmen who take it eagerly.

These haggard, emaciated men are confined to the main decks below, and the lowest is the worst. Seeing its human content, Dring recalls later: "The faces of many of them were covered with dirt and filthy; their long hair and beards matted and foul; clothed in rags, and with scarcely a sufficient supply of these to cover their disgusting bodies." The night is full of frightful noises, groans of the sick and dying, curses poured out on the subhumans who act as keepers, and restless murmurs from men confined in suffocating heat, breathing in poisoned air, all these mingling with the cries of those in delirium.

Yet the human spirit is indomitable. A work party of prisoners taken up on deck on the Fourth of July somehow manages to fix a row of tiny American flags on the boom; where they came from, no one knows. The prisoners refuse to take them down, so the keepers do it and trample them. These guards happen to be Scots, "the objects of our greatest hatred," Dring says. The prisoners give them a July 4 serenade of patriotic songs, punctuated by an occasional huzzah, leading the guards to drive them below at the points of their bayonets. The men go on singing just the same, and when they're ordered to stop that night and refuse to do so, the guards come down with drawn swords and cut everyone they can reach. That night no one gets any water in the dreadful heat, and the cries for it are horrible to hear.

During any given period of twenty-four hours, an average number of five men will die on the *Jersey*, but the morning after the July 4 serenade, twice that many are found. Some of them have been mortally wounded by the guards' cold steel, but it's so dark their comrades can't even discover where they are.

There are prisoners all over the place. Besides the prison ships in America, equally loathsome jails exist in England; churches are used as jails in New York. Only officers can hope for parole, and get it. Henry Laurens will be captured at sea on his way to become ambassador to Holland, but gets special treatment in the Tower of London, and eventually is exchanged for Cornwallis after Yorktown.

But the problem of British mistreatment of prisoners is something that deeply disturbs Washington, and that's why he's sending Boudinot to New York, even though he knows that Lord Germain has decreed that these rebels have no right to be treated as prisoners of war, and he won't change his mind until a year after Yorktown, when it doesn't make much difference.

After he returns to Valley Forge, Boudinot files a report that tells of an elaborate deception by the British, although he doesn't seem to realize it. For example, he found the hospitals "in tolerable good order, neat and clean and the sick much better taken care of than I expected," although there's abundant evidence by eyewitnesses that the opposite is true. He found the notorious Sugar House prison "comfortable and warm," and astonishingly placed some blame for its condition not on the captors but on the captives. Some of the privates, he says, "appear to be a set of sad villains, who rob each other of their clothes and blankets, and many of them sell their own shoes, blankets, and even shirts for rum. . . ."

The British didn't succeed in creating an entire Potemkin village, however. Boudinot visited some prisons where nothing much was concealed, and he was "greatly distressed with the wretched situation of so many of the human species." So the British put on a little show for him. They brought a collection of prisoners into a large room, along with their chief keeper, Mrs. Loring's brutal husband, and the captives were invited to complain at will.

"They repeated to me," says Boudinot's report to Washington, "instances of the most shocking barbarity in the presence of the keeper of the provost, whom they charged as the author of the beating and knocking down officers of rank on the most trifling occasion, locking them up in dark, damp dungeons, for asking more water than usual in warm weather, or for not going to bed immediately on order of the sergeant. Officers have been locked up in the dungeons for examinations, and left there without further inquiry or any charge brought against them for many months. That besides prisoners of war, there are many inhabitants here, as committeemen, commissioners, oppressors of the Friends of Government, etc. etc. who are wretched beyond description." Still, it was the treatment of officers that really disturbed Boudinot. Privates can't expect much.

Taking notes, Boudinot compiled a few of the worst cases and laid them before General James Robertson, the British military commander at the time, who said he'd discharge all the officers except for seven on parole. He also said he'd curb the excesses of the sergeants. But Robertson had been pulling the wool over Boudinot's eyes from the beginning. Meeting the American emissary at breakfast after his arrival, he displayed "the greatest civility and good humor," and after they'd eaten, he asked for news from the front and talked about topics of the day as though it was a social call. Robertson said smoothly that he knew a good many stories were circulating about the prisoners and assured Boudinot he'd find them "a parcel of damned lies." The American could go anywhere he liked and see anything he wanted to see; they'd had plenty of time to prepare for this visit. Boudinot, of course, didn't see much. When he investigated some of the charges made by captive officers, he found, astonishingly, that "most of the cases examined into turned out wholly false or too trifling to be regarded. . . ."

There was only one exception to this elaborate piece of deceit and cover-up, and that was Loring himself. When Boudinot confronted him with a collection of horror stories and asked him if they were true, this accomplished sadist answered "with great insolence" that every word was true. A British officer present took him to task, and asked him how he dared to treat gentlemen—he meant the officers, of course—with such cruelty. Loring put his hands on his hips and told the officer that he was as much an absolute ruler of the prisons as Howe was of the army. When Boudinot told Robertson this story, confirmed by the accompanying British officer, the general assured him with a straight face that the authors of all the atrocities would be punished. If Boudinot believed that, he'd believe anything—but he did.

One of the prisoners Boudinot spoke to was our old friend Ethan Allen, last seen being led away in chains in Montreal. As usual, he had a story to tell, and he'd soon tell it in a memoir. How much of it is true and how much the product of Allen's creative mind is hard to tell, but most of it has the ring of authenticity.

After his capture he was sent with other prisoners aboard the *Gaspée*, another hellhole, where he was chained up in the lowest, worst part of the vessel, unable to lie down any way except on his back. The captain of the guard wouldn't loosen his leg irons so he could lie on his side. He spent much of the time trading invective with his captors, although one officer sent him food from his own table and a drink of grog every day. He was aboard this ship six weeks, before he was put aboard the *Adamant*, with other prisoners, en route to England.

The captain of this vessel was no sailor but a London merchant named Brook Watson, whom Allen described as "a man of malicious and cruel disposition." Among the other passengers was Colonel Guy

Johnson, Sir William's son, who'd been helping the British with their frontier war in the Mohawk Valley. The ship's crew were a hard-bitten lot who treated the prisoners with bitter cruelty. They put thirty-four men into an enclosure measuring twenty by twenty-two feet, with two tubs for excrement. It was a miracle that no one died during the passage.

Allen was absolutely incorrigible. When a lieutenant told him he should have been executed and spit in his face, he sprang on the lieutenant, handcuffs and all, knocked him down, and even chased him into a cabin, after which he challenged him to fight. They had to drive Allen with bayonets into the place where the other prisoners were. For all of them, it was utter misery on this voyage—diarrhea, fever, terrible thirst, unremitting darkness, body lice. Forty-six days of rolling hell.

Once in England, a new confinement, in Pendennis Castle, a mile outside Falmouth, while Parliament debated whether or not to execute Allen. His reputation had preceded him, and people came from all over just to stare at him, some from as much as fifty miles away. Allen loved it. He wrote in his memoir: "It was a common thing for me to be taken out of close confinement into a spacious green in the castle, or rather parade, where numbers of gentlemen and ladies were ready to see and hear me. I often entertained such audiences with harangues on the impracticability of Great Britain's conquering the then colonies of America. I expatiated on American freedom." At least he was being treated well.

It was a short confinement. On January 8, 1778, Allen and other prisoners were put on a frigate for America, which arrived in May. He was taken to New York and put on parole in November. He lived there until jailed again for violating parole. The British think he's mad, and Allen doesn't disabuse them. In May 1778, he's put on a sloop and taken over to Staten Island, where General John Campbell greets him in his own quarters and they have dinner and a few drinks with a covey of field officers. Three days later, another Campbell, Colonel Archibald, arrives to be exchanged for Allen, and all these gentlemen have a glass of wine together, as though none of the horrors Allen has gone through existed. He can't resist giving them a parting lecture on the treatment of American prisoners. Back behind the American lines, he goes directly to Valley Forge, where Washington greets him and he tells his story all over again.

Boudinot's report and Allen's tale anger and disturb the general but there's not much he can do about it. Wrangles between the two sides over prison conditions last through the entire war, kept alive by the stories of those who escape or are paroled.

Trouble is that not all the British are monsters. Some prison commissaries and ships' captains treat their prisoners kindly, and in England, citizens dip into their own pockets to alleviate the suffering of Americans. There's also the fact that the Americans, too, have their prison ships, at Boston and New London, which are not shining examples of humane treatment, and they also have an equivalent of the *Jersey* on land, in the copper mines of Simsbury, Connecticut, where British men and women prisoners live in conditions people don't want to know about. The women there, and the American women in Wallabout Bay, exhibit exemplary bravery in the face of their captors' sadism. Nevertheless, as one historian puts it, "Some of the most brutal and heroic moments of the war occurred inside these prisons and along escape routes."

On the whole, the Convention prisoners, those remains of Burgoyne's army whom Congress changed its mind about sending back to England, fare better than the others, although before they're marched south in January and February of 1778, they have to endure an American equivalent of Loring, a Colonel Hanley, who commits an atrocity related by Lieutenant Colonel Thomas Amburey, whose memoir, *Travels Through the Interior Part of America*, will become a classic.

On December 19, as Amburey tells it, Hanley goes to the barracks to release some British soldiers. He calls off a few names until he gets to Corporal Reeves, of the 9th Regiment, who's in jail for "insulting a provincial officer." Reeves says he's sorry; he was drunk and didn't know what he was doing.

"By God, sir," Hanley says, "had you served me so, I would have run you through the body, and I believe you to be a great rascal."

"I'm no rascal," Reeves replies, "but a good soldier, and my officers know it."

Hanley tells him to shut up, but Reeves repeats what he said, and goes on to say that he hopes for the opportunity to fight under Howe for King and country.

"Damn your King and country," shouts Hanley, irate. "When you had arms, you were willing enough to lay them down." And again he admonishes Reeves to be silent. But Reeves again repeats what he just said, whereupon Hanley orders the guard to run him through. Not a man steps forward to do it, so Hanley dismounts, grabs a firelock with fixed bayonet from one of them, and stabs Reeves in the left breast. Holding the steel there, Hanley tells him that if he says another word he'll get it through his body.

"I care not," Reeves answers resolutely. "I'll stand by my King and country until I die."

At that, Hanley, who had withdrawn the bayonet, moves as though to run him through, but two prisoners standing next to Reeves deflect the steel just in time so it goes over his shoulder. One of these men then tells Hanley that if he takes Reeves's life, he'll have to kill all of them, because they feel the same way. Hanley loses his nerve, returns the gun, and sends Reeves to the guardhouse, dismissing the others.

This isn't the first time Hanley's been in trouble. Three days earlier, he was in the American adjutant general's office when British sergeants were there, applying for passes. One of them, named Fleming, who didn't know Hanley, thought he was Colonel Keith, the deputy adjutant general, and with a respectful salute and cap in hand, started to address him. Hanley threw a clenched fist in his face and yelled, "You rascals, I'll make damnation fly out of ye, for I will myself, one of these nights, go the rounds, and if I hear the least word or noise in your barracks, I'll put shot amongst you and make flames of hell jump out of ye, and turn your barracks inside out." If he was a sentinel, he adds, and any British soldiers looked at him sulkily, he'd blow their brains out.

In the early months of 1778, the Covenant troops leave Hanley behind and start marching toward Virginia for internment. Baroness Riedesel is right on hand to tell us about the trip. The country is so wild, she says, it "inspired me with terror." They were in constant danger from the "breakneck roads," and they all suffered from cold and lack of food. By the time they got to Virginia, only a day away from the march's end, they were down to nothing but tea.

A farmer gives her a handful of acrid fruit, but as soon as the caravan reaches a house, she stops and begs for something to eat. "They refused me with hard words," she says, "saying there was nothing for dogs of Royalists." Seeing some Indian meal, she persists, begging for a couple of handfuls so she can mix it with water and make bread. The lady of the house answers, "No, that's for our Negroes, who work for us, but you have wished to kill us."

Captain Edmonston, who's with her, offers the woman two guineas for the meal, knowing how hungry the baroness's children are, but she says, "Not for a hundred would I give you any; and should you all die of hunger, it will be so much the better." The captain is so enraged by this that he starts to take the meal by force, but the baroness restrains him. Maybe there will be "better disposed people ahead," she says.

They travel on, however, without seeing even a hut. The horses are exhausted, and so are her three children, and for the first time, the baroness begins to lose her spirit. Edmonston is so touched by her plight that he goes from man to man in the caravan, begging for something to eat, until at last the driver of a baggage wagon gives him a hunk of old bread which, the baroness reports, "had been considerably gnawed at, since, on account of its hardness, no one could bite off the smallest piece." Nevertheless, its appearance brings joy to the eyes of her children.

Such well-bred kids! She gives the first piece to the youngest, Caroline, who simply says, "My sisters are more hungry than I." But the others insist she have it first, so the baroness divides it and gives it to all three, while the tears run down her cheeks, and Edmonston can't even stand to watch the scene. He gives a guinea to the driver, who tells him it was his last piece of bread.

At last they arrive in a Virginia town called Colle, where the baron, who has gone on ahead with the troops, is waiting for her. The caravan stops at last, having traveled 678 miles in twelve weeks, through Connecticut, New York, New Jersey, Pennsylvania, and Maryland.

Life then becomes much better. They live in a house owned by an Italian, who is soon to leave it for a time. He rations out the scarce food, but at least it's an improvement. He gives them the head, neck, and giblets of a ram, telling them it will make good soup, and "half of a putrid ham." The troops are at Charlottesville, two hours away, and they endure privation at first, living in houses without plaster, doors, or windows, but they industriously build themselves a little village, with gardens behind the houses and a place for poultry. Later, they get fresh meat and meal in fairly good supply. The baron spends a hundred guineas to build a large house for his family, and it's "exceedingly pretty," the baroness says. Blacks bring them everything they need in poultry and vegetables. Soon their only problems are the heat, the rattlesnakes, and violent storms that last five or six days and tear up trees by the roots.

By 1780, the baron will be exchanged; he will serve for a time in Canada, then as commander of Long Island, and at last, in August 1783, sail for home from Quebec, with the last of Johnny Burgoyne's ill-fated army. The only missing pieces will be most of the Hessians, who find Pennsylvania much to their liking on the way to Virginia and will slip away daily until few are left.

On the whole, the British suffer less than American prisoners but, as Henry Commager tells us, that's not necessarily because the Americans are more humane, but because they have so few facilities they can use as prisons, and little experience in doing such things. Nor are they anxious to waste precious food and fuel on prisoners. Consequently, they make little effort to round up the Hessians, believing correctly that they will melt productively into the farming landscape. Loyalists, it seems, fare the worst. Many more are killed than captured.

There's one foreigner, however, who's more than welcome in America, and that's the fake baron, Steuben, who in the warm spring of 1778 is accomplishing a miracle at Valley Forge, something that takes Washington's mind momentarily off Boudinot's prison report and his other problems as well.

At the beginning, Steuben has his doubts about whether he can make real soldiers out of these provincial troops. He writes to an old comrade-in-arms: "In the first place, the genius of this nation is not in the least to be compared with that of the Prussians, Austrians, or French. You say to your soldier, 'Do this,' and he does it, but I am obliged to say, 'This is the way you ought to do that,' and then he does it." The British belief that commissioned officers are too good to stoop to drill instruction has taken root in America; consequently there's no corps of trained sergeants. Steuben has not only to be drillmaster but to train other drillmasters at the same time.

Steuben, indeed, has to do everything from scratch. As we've seen, no regulations exist so he has to write them out, lesson by lesson, after which they have to be translated and copies made to be passed out. While the men practice the first lesson, he's writing the second, and so on. He spends hours on the drill ground. Colonel Alexander

Scammell writes admiringly: "To see a gentleman dignified with a lieutenant colonel's commission from the great Prussian monarch condescend with a grace peculiar to himself to take under his direction a squad of ten or twelve men in the capacity of a drill sergeant, commands the admiration of both officers and men."

On muddy fields, from six in the morning until six at night, he's drilling the troops, tirelessly. He still finds time to instruct the adjutants in the art of maneuvering. Since he doesn't speak much English, he can't properly convey a drill sergeant's vocabulary, so he swears in German, French, and a mixture of both. Once he pleads, "My dear Walker and my dear Duponceau, come and swear for me in English. These fellows won't do what I bid them."

By March 24, he has the whole army drilling, and he's galloping from place to place to oversee the brigade inspectors he's created. Those who aren't drilling at the moment watch the others. Steuben waves his arms, turns purple, swears, and at one point turns to Walker and cries, "*Viens, Walker, mon ami, mon bon ami, sacré! Doddam de gaucheries of dese badnuts. Je ne puis plus.* I can curse dem no more." For their part, the soldiers learn to love him and enjoy his goddamns, and since Steuben is also a showman, he uses his language problem to endear himself further.

As the summer approaches, the baron has wrought a miracle. For the first time, the army has a Table of Organization, and an American light infantry to be proud of. He even installs a system of accountability to protect public property. Washington is so relieved and relaxed by what he sees that on warm spring days he's out there playing ball with his officers, or (King George forbid!) playing cricket.

Steuben's victory is complete. No drillmaster in military history has ever succeeded in so capturing the love and admiration of his men. After the war, officers of the 2nd Jersey Line write to him: "The esteem you have ever borne for our army—the unremitted labor which you have exercised for the establishment of our honor and good character, as well as your affectionate anxiety and participation in our sufferings, have endeared you to us in a superlative degree. . . .We conceive it to be our duty, and we feel unusual pleasure in doing it, to give you these individual assurances of gratitude and love." It's enough to make a real drill sergeant cry!

All the soldiers remember that Steuben has been the first one on the parade ground, before sunrise, that he'll bawl you out for negligence, but apologize publicly if he makes a mistake. Steuben also hates to eat alone, so he doesn't ignore the company-grade officers, as the senior officers do, but invites them to dinner. New Englanders love this "leveling" general. The dinners are occasionally memorable (Steuben has a passion for good food), and when the war is over, the baron will still enjoy entertaining veterans in New York.

Of course it's not a complete miracle. That would have been beyond even Steuben's genius. These soldiers are never going to be models of discipline, and it isn't until 1782 that those who are still fighting in the South show that they've fully mastered what he's taught them. Even then some of the old problems persist, but just the same, Steuben has given Washington exactly what he needed—trained troops. On a bright morning in May, they parade for him, with dogwood wreaths in their hats, fifes and drums filling the air with music, marching past a regimental Maypole.

Two days later, they've really got something to celebrate. News arrives that the French signed a treaty with the Americans on February 6. They're coming to help! That calls for a huge celebration. Washington officially presents Steuben as inspector general of the United States, and when the ceremonies are over, it's like what a West Point or Annapolis graduation will one day be—thousands of hats sailing into the warm spring air.

No one, certainly not Washington, gives a thought to the fact that the Americans have just made an alliance with a monarch who's more absolute than George III, who is capable of even worse arbitrary behavior, and who doesn't give a sou for freedom, in America or anywhere else. No matter. The nightmare of the winter is over. Howe has had it much too easy in Philadelphia, and now, thanks to Steuben, Washington is going to confront him with a new American army.

12

✛   ✛   ✛

The British in Philadelphia

When Ben Franklin remarks that Philadelphia has taken Howe instead of the other way around, he knows what he's talking about. Ben understands his city from high to low and he believes correctly that it will envelop the British general and his men in a soft cocoon. For Howe, that's no threat. He's had about enough of this war, and looks forward to a pleasant winter while the Americans are hanging on by their fingernails in Valley Forge.

The chief attraction in Philadelphia is girls. As Philip Young, a literary historian who has examined this period, describes them, they are "all provincial American girls, all beautiful, well-born, well-bred, well-to-do, Loyalist, and Anglican." None of them who enjoy both social stature and hints of public scandal is a patriot.

Contributing to their happiness are the British officers, upper-class fellows whose ideas of morality are a culture shock to the colonials. Fathers and brothers can only wring their hands. These "wanton wives and wicked daughters," one of them says disgustedly, are taken by these relocated officers "almost without a trial—damn them!" A disapproving Hessian thinks there isn't much difference between Philadelphia and Sodom and Gomorrah.

For the other ranks, there are great sprawls of whores, some brought down from New York, where whoring is a growth industry. In both New York and Philadelphia, there is some competition from soldiers desperate for money who sell their wives to their officers. Single men openly advertise for mistresses in the newspapers, the beginnings of the "Personals" column.

Outside the cities, where whores are scarcer, British troops turn easily to rape. In one little New Jersey town, sixteen girls are raped, and six men assault a thirteen-year-old. Both sides pretend to deplore "the lust and brutality" of the other side, but they don't do much about it. Howe publicly condemns the carnal behavior of his troops, calling it "a disgrace to the country they belong to," but considering the source, no one regards this statement as any assurance that discipline will be imposed. Some Southern women prove to be highly resistant. Near Charleston, when British dragoons assail the virtue of several ladies, they fight back even when officers threaten to cut them with their swords—and do.

Washington frequently issues orders to "prevent an inundation of bad women," but it's a losing battle. He partially succeeds in preventing these women from riding with the men in the baggage trains, but American girls thwarted in this pursuit simply switch over to the British, who are already well supplied with more than three thousand camp followers, many of them wives. The British take a much more realistic view of what's going on than the Americans. When it looked as though Loyalist wives in New York would be threatened with massive assaults on their citadels, the War Office in London sent in a small army of 3,500 women to be the army's "intimate property," as they delicately put it, transporting them to New York in twenty ships.

As Young observes, the "good women" aren't even remembered except as appendages of husbands, or women doing men's jobs like the legendary Molly Pitcher. Large numbers of lower-class women are completely displaced by the war and have no homes. Inevitably, a few heroines emerge. There's Deborah Sampson, who disguises herself as a man, enlists in the American army, and survives for a long time until a "malignant fever" strikes her and a doctor, reaching for her heart, discovers the deception. The doctor doesn't tell, but his niece falls in love with Debbie (as a male) and she finally has to send this lovesick girl a letter signed "your Own Sex," disclosing the truth. Eventually she's honorably discharged, gets a pension authorized by Washington himself, marries, and raises a family.

"Molly Pitcher" is actually Mary Ludwig Hayes, who will soon become a part of popular history at the Battle of Monmouth, when she services a gun after her husband is wounded. She's not the only one to do this job; another wife who helps out in the same way suffers a "shredded breast." Stories are told of a woman who shed her dress so she could run faster to get powder for a besieged fort. Still another formidable woman shot or hanged the Tories who invaded her cabin. Molly Pitcher, though, is the one who will become the legend. A soldier who saw her in action at Monmouth remembers that, just as she reached for a cartridge, "a cannon ball from the enemy passed directly between her legs without doing any other damage than carrying away all the lower part of her petticoat." Molly jokes that it's lucky the ball wasn't a little higher or she'd have lost "something else." Unfortunately, this vulgar, illiterate heroine takes to drink, remarries, is widely known as "Dirty Kate," and eventually leads one of Washington's aides to wonder how it is that, married to an old and decrepit second husband, she has contrived to become pregnant.

Some society belles are quite apolitical, like the Van Horne girls, eight in all including cousins, but principally Hannah, Betsey, and Sukey, who "bestowed their favors on friend and foe alike." Sukey becomes the mistress of a Flatbush Tory, one of her cousins marries James Rivington, the famous Tory printer and editor, but Mary becomes the bride of Stephen Moylan, one of Washington's aides. Hannah, who traces her ancestry to original Dutch settlers, and whose money comes from enterprising New York merchants, has a father who's the master of Phil's Hall, the great house Hannah's grandfather built on the banks of the Raritan, near New Brunswick.

Phil's Hall is a splendid example of Revolutionary ambivalence. As Young observes, "Its politics, like the girls', were adjustable." That makes it possible for Cornwallis to have breakfast there, and a Continental general to sit down for dinner on the same day. Father Van Horne is the host; he's been paroled on his own property. Hannah made a British marriage in 1771 to Edward Foy, then secretary to John Murray, the Earl of Dunmore, who was royal governor of New York. Later, they went to England, where Foy joined the British army and traveled to America with the Baron von Riedesel, becoming his commissary. Hannah came over with the baroness and may or may not have become Burgoyne's mistress, but in any case Foy left her at this point.

In 1783, Hannah will marry Colonel Thomas Carleton, Sir Guy's brother, who will be made governor of New Brunswick the following year. In the end, Hannah will survive scandal and two marriages. She will sail away on a visit to England and never return to America, dying there, still respectable, at eighty-three.

It's ladies from the same social background as the Van Horne girls who make life so pleasant in Philadelphia for Howe and his officers. A few unfortunate Whigs who stayed on might as well be in prison, and some of them are. Captured American soldiers pull up grass in the prison yard to eat the roots, while elsewhere in the city many of their female compatriots are joining with the Loyalist women in taking advantage of a social season never before seen in this sedate city.

The dark, statuesque Rebecca Franks writes to her exiled friend, Mrs. William Pace, a congressman's wife, and discloses what life has become for a girl like herself who is both beautiful and a Loyalist. "You can have no idea of the life of continued amusement I live in. I can scarce have a moment to myself . . . and most elegantly am I dressed for a ball this evening at Smith's, where we have one every Thursday. No loss for partners, even I am engaged to seven different gentlemen, for you must know, 'tis a fixed rule never to dance but two dances at a time with the same person. . . ."

Not all the rebel girls are content to join in this excitement. There's Polly Redman, for instance, who greatly annoys British officers by singing patriotic songs like "War and Washington" and "Burgoyne's Defeat" when she's in their presence. But some otherwise patriotic American girls just can't let the opportunity go by. One of them writes defensively to a friend that she must make allowance for "young people in the bloom of life and spirits, after being so long deprived of the gaieties and amusements of life which ages and spirits called for. . . . The known Whig ladies were treated with equal politeness and attention with the Tory ladies."

For some girls, the new social freedom is also a tragedy. They've grown up with the same crowd, gone to the same schools, and now the war divides them, but it's a measure of their political convictions that they keep on writing to each other when they're separated. Sally Wister, for example, went to Anthony Benezet's fashionable Quaker school, and after being exiled by the British occupation to a farmhouse on the Wissahickon River, fifteen miles from Philadelphia, she carried on a correspondence with Deborah Morris, one of her Tory school friends. Exile turns out to be not all that bad.

In Philadelphia, Sally had been a lively but cloistered young woman. Suddenly she's thrust into the society of gallant officers who come and go through the farmhouse of Hannah Foulkes, where she's staying. For a while, it's exciting but in the end it doesn't work. Much attached to her mother and deeply religious, Sally will not succumb to any of them and will die a spinster.

In her letters and diaries, however, Sally gives us a sense of what the war meant to such a woman: "How new is our situation! I feel in good spirits, though surrounded by an army, the house full of soldiers, the yard alive with soldier—very peaceable sort of men, though. They eat like other folks, talk like them, and behave themselves with elegance, so will not be afraid of them, that I won't."

Carrying on a mild flirtation with one Captain Fernival, she says he "has the handsomest face I ever saw, a very fine person." But there's also Major Stoddard, "so bashful, so famous, etc. He is almost nineteen, nephew to the general, and acts as major of brigade to him. . . . He is large in his person, manly, and an engaging countenance and address." Fernival "chats at every opportunity," but he's married. Sally has also heard "strange things" about the major, although all she reports is that he's rich and so bashful he can scarcely look at the ladies. Sally hopes she has charms "sufficient to pierce the heart of a soldier. . . . Who knows what mischief I yet may do?" Unfortunately, she never gets around to do it.

Of all the Philadelphia girls, Whig or Tory, who charmed the British, only one is unforgotten—seventeen-year-old Peggy Shippen, who will ultimately marry Benedict Arnold. When Howe's sixty-three ships discharged the British troops into Philadelphia, it changed her life forever. The city itself was momentarily transformed. As James Flexner tells us: "Fine gentlemen in laces, naval officers in cocked hats, pigtailed sailors trained to be respectful to young ladies carrying parasols. Stores which had only homespun now began to show goods and fashions from George III's court." And, for Peggy, a flood of elegant young men in her parlor, more than she had ever thought could be there.

Peggy is a complicated girl, and will be even more complicated as a woman. She looks like a colonial Barbie doll, blond, finely cut features, lovely figure, gray-blue eyes. Peggy may look like a toy, but she has some of the business acumen of her doting father, Edward Shippen, who is not only judge of the Vice-Admiralty Court, but also town clerk and a member of the Common Council, as well as protonotary of the Supreme Court. Obviously an accomplished man, but one who seems to be in a more or less constant state of apprehension.

One cause of his apprehension is his daughter. He doesn't know why she suddenly goes off into hysterical fits on slight provocation. For another thing, he's never quite sure just where he stands politically. He thinks the colonies may have been unjustly treated, but was that any reason to destroy the entire system, of which he was a successful part? For a while he tried to work both sides of the street. During the First Continental Congress, he invited the delegates to a series of dinners, and Peggy met them all, including Washington, when she was only fourteen. After the war began, he tried to stay neutral. Peggy was fifteen when she first heard about Arnold, as her father reported his exploits at Saratoga.

Although she is a dutiful daughter, Peggy can't wait to grow up; consequently, when British ships sail up the Delaware, she's as excited as her father is fearful. He isn't at all sure how the newcomers are going to regard his ambivalence, so he moves his family to a farm he owns in Amwell, New Jersey, where he starts an entirely new career as a rural storekeeper. This lasts until New Jersey passes an act to deal severely with traitors. Do they mean him?

Unable to make up his mind, Edward tries to keep both his farm and his town house, and he's at the latter when Howe arrives, although he's been spending some recent time at the farm, where Peggy has seen American officers for the first time. It's like Peggy to admire these officers and to ignore the ragged troops when they wave to her. Edward entertains the officers at the farm, but events force him to make up his mind at last, and he takes the family back to live in British-occupied Philadelphia, although the Pennsylvania Assembly has passed a law similar to New Jersey's.

Now Peggy is in her glory. Her father's parlor swarms with young, aristocratic officers who want to flirt with her and God knows what else. Peggy is queen of the Philadelphia ball. "We were all in love with her," confesses Captain A. S. Hammond, master of the *Roebuck*. Her father, meanwhile, is desperately trying to stay neutral, and refuses to hold any public office while the British are there, which means the family has no money and has to live on a store of gold.

There's a good deal of sexual ambivalence among the officers. They may boast that they'll father a bastard for every rebel they kill, but if they get a socially well-connected American girl in trouble, it's a different matter. Howe, the consummate hypocrite, is quite strict about it; he'll make them marry such girls.

One of the new friends Peggy acquires is a handsome young officer, John André, whom we first saw struggling through the snows of Canada. He's come a long way since then. Now he's a favorite of Howe's, and perhaps even more so of Clinton. As Flexner points out, we don't know now (and probably never will) exactly what Peggy's relations with young André are. She will keep a lock of his hair until the day she dies, so Arnold can't have been the first man in her heart.

André, it seems certain, doesn't take her seriously. He's too ambitious to think of marrying her and, like most of his friends, he regards the American girls as charming playthings, but not much more than that. André thinks of Peggy and her friends as, so he says, "the little society of Third and Fourth streets," where he plays the flute for their delight, dances with them, spins long tales of life in Europe, talks knowledgeably of art, and quotes poetry to them, his own and others. André has numerous talents. He's also a modestly talented artist and fascinates the girls by sketching them. If Peggy is enchanted with him, she certainly isn't the only one, but André's sins are military, not amatory. He wants to be a general.

The scene in this "little society" is summarized neatly by Flexner: "Edward trembled, his daughters floated down in new dresses not yet paid for, disappeared with officers, military bands played with frenzy all night, the girls danced faster, came home at dawn." Meanwhile, beyond the city's suburbs, Washington's pickets are coming ever closer.

In the midst of all this gaiety, Howe is preparing to leave the city and America. He's resigned his command, and is only waiting to be called home. The call comes in the spring, just as Baron Steuben is getting the American army in shape at Valley Forge. André and twenty other officers club together and raise £3,312 to give Howe the greatest sendoff a general ever got from his loyal officers. They plan an elaborate pageant which they call a Meshianza (there are various spellings), which means a medley, or mixture, of entertainments. André appoints himself "a complete milliner," as he puts it, to decorate the ladies' heads personally. He wants to put them all in Turkish costumes, but some fathers put their paternal feet down on that.

The Meshianza, or however you want to spell it, goes on for twelve hours. The guests embark in barges, boats, and galleys from Knight's Wharf and cruise to a confiscated Whig residence, about a half mile upriver. It sits on a gentle rise three hundred yards from the water, and the gallants and their ladies walk up to it through lines of grenadiers and guards, the girls (or at least the lucky ones) in their Turkish costumes, splendid in the fantastic hairdos André has created for them. All but one. Peggy's missing, lying alone sobbing in her darkened bedroom. A delegation of Quakers had called on her father, and when they left, he summoned his daughters to tell them that he wasn't about to let them go in their Turkish costumes, and if they refused to change, they wouldn't go.

The extravaganza whirls on into the night, with splendid fireworks, an elaborate midnight banquet at which the guests sit in a dining place more than two hundred feet long and are served by slaves in costume. At one point during the evening, the officers fancy themselves as medieval knights, and divide into jousting teams called "The Knights of the Burning Mountain" and "the Knights of the Blended Rose."

While everyone's making a little more than merry, reality intrudes. The British fortifications in Germantown go up in flames, after some of Washington's light-horse troops creep up and pour kettles of whale oil on them, setting them afire with their flints. Drums roll, cannon sound, Howe does his best to reassure the revelers that it isn't anything, really, but many of the officers leave abruptly. Having successfully disrupted the party, the Americans disappear, and when the British try to pursue, they encounter a volley from the Kentucky riflemen and think better of it.

The Meshianza gets decidedly mixed reviews. Many of the Loyalists in Philadelphia think it's an outrageous waste of money and time. When news of it reaches London, the newspapers echo this opinion. Howe isn't exactly popular at home right now, and people can't swallow the idea of giving such a triumphal sendoff to a general who's almost lost the war, or at least seems far from winning it. André, of course, has an entirely different view. These aristocratic officers, he contends, have set a fine example for the barbarous Americans to follow. And of course the Philadelphia ladies have never had a better time in their lives.

Mrs. Henry Drinker, whose husband has fared badly at the hands of the British, writes bitterly: "This may be remembered by many for the scenes of folly and vanity. . . . How insensible do these people appear, while our land is so greatly desolated, and death and sore destruction has overtaken and impends over so many." She's echoed by Ambrose Serle, whose employer was Howe's brother. Ambrose is "appalled by the folly and extravagance of it." And an old artillery major has the last word: "The Knights of the Burning Mountain are tomfools and the Knights of the Blended Rose are damned fools. I know of no other distinction between them."

Just two days before the Meshianza, Arnold turned up at Valley Forge, still not well after three and a half months in the hospital, but he couldn't stay away. He recovered fairly rapidly in the Albany hospital, after forbidding the doctors to amputate his beleaguered leg, but Congress has done nothing to improve his state of mind. It had a gold medal struck off for Gates, making him the hero of Saratoga instead of Arnold, and then it failed to restore his rank. That blow sent him into a physical and mental tailspin, quite ill again and spending his waking hours denouncing Gates. But quiet pressure from Washington and others has persuaded Congress to give the commander power to restore his rank.

The interval of indecision proved to be too long for Arnold. He had all that time in the hospital to go over, again and again, the injustices done him from the beginning, and he came out bitter. Not even the hero's welcome New Haven gave him on the way to Valley Forge cheered him up more than momentarily. At least the commander is glad to see him, moved by observing him still unable to stand on his bad leg, and promises to make him military governor of Philadelphia when the British leave, as they seem about to do. That's a more fateful decision than anyone imagines at the time.

There's much else to decide in early May at Valley Forge, now that Steuben's given us a reasonable facsimile of an army and the British show signs of evacuation. But what are they doing? On the eighteenth, Washington sends Lafayette to make a reconnaissance and find out. The British might be forgiven for thinking it's more than a reconnaissance because the young Frenchman is at the head of three thousand men, including a hundred Indians who joined them at Barren Hill, about twelve miles from the city. The Indians are Iroquois, just arrived at Valley Forge, the vanguard of three hundred others authorized by Congress, but when the commander sees them, he changes his mind and stops the recruiting. He's never trusted Indians before and can't bring himself to do it now.

Lafayette doesn't find out much and nearly loses his army. He gets close enough to see that the British are indeed evacuating Philadelphia, but he's too close and they pursue him back across the Schuylkill. The men escape only because they ford the river with just their heads showing. As for the Iroquois, they encounter British cavalry for the first time and scatter to the winds, although the British dragoons have been quite as terrorized by their war whoops. Lafayette is lucky to get his little army back to camp, where a sad letter from home awaits him: his first daughter has died six months earlier.

It's a critical point in the war for the British. More than ever, they'd like to have peace and get out of America, now that they have to face France and maybe Spain as well. They put out peace feelers, making what they think are handsome concessions, but neither side will budge on the one sticking point—independence.

Well, if that's the way it has to be, Clinton, who has taken over from Howe, must devise a new overall strategy. He decides not to fight on land for a while if he can help it and instead to use the army to guard his naval bases. Maybe he'll send part of the fleet to attack the French base in St. Lucia. Meanwhile, he'll send three thousand troops to Florida to protect his flank, and get out of Philadelphia so that this part of the army can be deployed to hold New York, which he's always morbidly afraid of losing. If things go badly, he has a fallback plan—evacuate New York, hold Rhode Island if possible, establish a base in Halifax, and make his headquarters in Quebec. If that emergency plan proves to be unnecessary, and if the French concentrate on their West Indies bases, as he hopes, he can open up a fresh area of hostilities in the South, which is swarming with belligerent Tories. He's always believed the South is the key to victory.

Meanwhile, there's a little problem in evacuating Philadelphia. The nearest place Clinton can embark his troops for New York is New Castle, forty miles from the city. If the weather turns bad, he's afraid Washington will attack New York before he can get there. Another problem is a thousand or so Loyalists he really can't leave behind in Philadelphia, and they've made it clear they intend to come, along with their household goods, and go into exile somewhere. There's no help for it. On June 18, the British depart from the city—eleven thousand troops, a baggage train twelve miles long, and the Loyalists, destroying bridges behind them. Another opportunity for the Americans.

They're no sooner on their way than Arnold rides triumphantly into the city, galloping at the head of the light horse, "with drawn swords in their hands," frightening the nervous citizens. Civilians follow them, coming home and finding Philadelphia much changed. As one writes: "The face of the suburbs on the north side is so much altered that people who were born here and have lived here all their lives are much at a loss to find out the situation of particular houses. The houses themselves are destroyed and redoubts built in the neighborhood of the spots where some of them formerly stood. Trees have been all cut down, and fertile fields laid waste. In short, the whole is one promiscuous scene of ruin."

Once in the city, however, this returnee is surprised to find that it has "suffered so little but the morale of the inhabitants has suffered vastly. The enemy introduced new fashions and made old vices more common, the former are the most absurd, ridiculous, and preposterous you can conceive. . . . So far as they concern the gentlemen, they appear to be principally confined to the *hat*, which is now amazingly broad-brimmed and cocked very sharp. The females who stayed in the city while it was in possession of the enemy cut a curious figure. Their hats, which are of the flat, round kind, are of the size of a large, japanned tea-waiter. Their caps exceed any of the sarcastic prints you have seen, and their hair is dressed with the assistance of wool, etc., in such a manner as to appear too heavy to be supported by their necks. If the caps would not blow off, a northwester would certainly throw these belles off their center as Yorick did the milliner—by accident. . . .

"You will probably be surprised by this, but you may rely on it as a fact: indeed many people do not hesitate in supposing that most of the young ladies who were in the city with the enemy and wear the present fashionable dresses have purchased them at the expense of their virtue. It is agreed on all hands the British officers played the devil with the girls. The privates, I suppose, were satisfied with the common prostitutes. Last Saturday an imitation of the Mischanza . . . was humbly attempted. A noted strumpet was paraded through the streets with her head dressed in the modern British taste, to the no small amusement of a vast crowd. . . ."

Congress comes back too, but it has to meet in the College Hall because the British have left the State House "in a most filthy and sordid situation, as were many of the public and private buildings in the city." As always, some houses have been used for stables, with holes cut in the parlor floor so they can be cleaned.

But at least the redcoats are gone, and now Washington is after them, in weather that vacillates between hot and muggy, and tropical downpours. Both armies have trouble traveling, as the soaked roads crumble beneath wheels and feet. Many of the Americans are used to this weather, but most of the British army, especially the Hessians, never seem to become accustomed to this damned American climate, and they struggle along with their heavy clothing, packs, and equipment, nearly a hundred pounds of it per man. Sunstroke fells entire squads of men when the rains stop, and heat prostration takes down more. All the while, the Americans are snapping at them, just as the British did to Washington when he was tumbling down New Jersey after losing New York. In this situation, the American revenge is more effective because they're able to destroy bridges, fell trees across the road, and pour dirt into wells. In a week, Clinton has inched forward less than forty miles, although his forces have been a little reduced by the daily desertion of Hessians.

The Americans haven't been moving much more rapidly. Leaving Valley Forge on June 18, they crossed the Delaware at Coryell's Ferry north of Trenton, and made their first contact with Clinton on the twenty-fourth. Then the British general changed his mind and, instead of making for South Amboy, decided Sandy Hook would be better. At Hopewell, Washington calls a council of war. With opportunity practically waving in their faces, most of the officers vote not to attack. Hamilton's in a rage about this decision, which he says "would have done honor to the most honorable society of midwives, and to them only." Lee takes exactly the opposite view. He's not really committed to the American cause in any case, and he isn't even willing to acknowledge what Steuben has accomplished. He simply thinks it would be madness to attack Clinton's regulars.

In the end, the commander decides on a compromise. He sends 1,500 men under Scott to harass the British left rear and flank, with Maxwell's brigade and Morgan's regiment supporting the New Jersey militia, who may need it. Everyone agrees to this plan except Lee. First he asserts the command should be his, by reason of seniority, but then he says he'll defer to Lafayette. But after talking it over with his friends (he still has some), he reasserts himself, then changes his mind once more, and finally becomes so importunate that Washington, as Hamilton reports, "got tired of such fickle behavior and ordered the marquis to proceed."

Anticipating the action, Clinton sends his best troops to defend the rear, and once more placing more confidence in Lee than he deserves, Washington gives him command of the entire advance corps of about five thousand picked troops. So now, with Clinton and his strong rear guard on both sides of the Monmouth Court House, Lee is coming at him one way, Lafayette is advancing from another, and Washington is backing them up with the rest of the army. Lee and Lafayette come together, and Lee arbitrarily takes command of the entire advance corps.

A mile or two beyond Monmouth Court House, Lee catches up with the British rear guard. According to Hamilton, that amounts to no more than a thousand men, but Lee doesn't fall on them. Why not? Washington is not far away, with eight thousand more troops. Hamilton's wrong about the strength of the opposition, though; the British have about the same number of men as the Americans.

They face each other on this hot and sultry Sunday morning, June 28, and the Americans are at last in a position to deal the British a mortal blow from which they're not likely to recover. It's Lee, the incredible Lee, who throws it all away. He sends out orders to Lafayette, Scott, and Wayne—orders so contradictory that all coordination is lost. Confusion sets in and Clinton takes advantage of it, pressing an attack. Instead of falling on their enemy, the Americans are now retreating in more disorder, and it even looks as though the familiar rout might be impending.

Washington can't understand what's going on up ahead; Lee hasn't sent him any messages. He dispatches an aide to find out, and the messenger brings back a typical Lee answer: "Tell the general I'm doing well enough." Washington scents trouble and starts toward the action to find out for himself. In a few minutes he sees something he's viewed too often before—American soldiers retreating. They tell him the whole army is falling back. Washington can scarcely believe what he's hearing. He spurs on to a wooded ridge, from which he can see men jammed on a road and moving toward him. Again, he sends two aides on ahead to find out what's happening, and one of them comes back to say he can't see any reason for a retreat.

Now Washington is really agitated. Spurring ahead, he comes upon more fleeing soldiers and asks them, "By whose order are the troops retreating?" They say, "By General Lee's." That's enough. "Damn him!" the commander mutters, and takes over the action himself. He's near enough now to see the advancing British, so he sends two Connecticut units to make a stand behind a fence and at least secure the retreat. Then he forms a line of artillery on a hill to support them and gallops off to find Lee.

Tench Tilghman tells us what happened when the two men met. Washington "rode up to him with some degree of astonishment and asked him what was the meaning of this? General Lee answered, 'Sir, sir?' I took it that General Lee did not hear the question distinctly." Washington repeats himself, and Lee plunges into a torrent of self-justification—intelligence has been contradictory, people aren't obeying his orders, so how can he attack the British, and in any case, he thinks the entire action is a mistake.

That does it. In a towering rage, Washington tells him that, no matter what Lee's opinions may be, he expects to be obeyed. He's abrupt and harsh, and that sets off Lee, who thinks the commander is casting aspersions on both his bravery and his ability. Another listener to this conversation, Lieutenant Thomas Washington, reports that Lee says, "Sir, these troops are not able to meet British grenadiers," to which Washington replies, "Sir, they *are* able, and by God, they shall do it." Then he gives the order to counterattack.

Some say later that Washington's language was even more colorful. Years afterward, someone asked General Charles Scott if the commander swore. "Yes, sir," Scott replied, "he swore on that day till the leaves shook on the trees. Charming! Delightful! Never have I enjoyed such swearing before or since. . . . He swore like an angel from heaven." An old man's memory? Or did loyal Tilghman clean up his story a little for later consumption? No matter, whatever Washington said, he was more than justified in saying it.

The commander has arrived just in time. He turns the retreat around and, as Lafayette writes admiringly, rides "all along the line amid the shouts of the soldiers, cheering them by his voice and example and restoring to our standard the fortunes of the fight. . . ."

Now we'll see if Steuben's training will pay off. It does. The British attack the New England troops head on, and they hold amazingly well until they have to fall back, outnumbered, but it's no rout. British artillery gets the range of the American batteries on the hill, and they duel until Clinton's big guns are mostly disabled. Then Washington sends his men through an orchard against the British right wing, so they can use trees and bushes for protection, and these redcoats have to fall back to the main body, pursued by three or four platoons, among them our old Massachusetts friend, Private Joseph Martin.

"We overtook the enemy just as they were entering the meadow," Joe writes, "which was rather bushy. They were retreating in line, though in some disorder. I singled out a man and took my aim directly between his shoulders (they were divested of their packs); he was a good mark, being a broad-shouldered fellow, but what became of him I know not; the fire and smoke hid him from my sight. One thing I know, I took as deliberate aim at him as ever I did at any game in my life."

In the end, it's Washington who saves the day. "By his presence, exertions, and superior conduct," James McHenry wrote later, "[he] regained the glory of the day, at all times he appeared in as much danger as any soldier in the field."

That night Washington sleeps on the ground, wrapped in his cloak. It's been a long day and an incredible one. He's had the satisfaction of seeing the grenadiers come charging up the hill, the sun flashing on their bayonets, against Wayne's detachment, which held its fire until the last minute and it was Breed's Hill all over again, after which they counterattacked with their bayonets, just as Steuben taught them, and after a fierce struggle, in which British Colonel Henry Monckton was killed, they had to retreat. Wayne got them away before the British support troops came up.

As darkness began to creep in, Clinton withdrew, because, as he said reasonably, "Our men were so overpowered with fatigue that I could press the affair no further." The fighting had begun soon after noon and ended at six—the longest battle of the war, and the last pitched battle to be fought in the North. The British lost 358 dead, wounded, and missing, but almost half of these were victims of fatigue and heat. American losses were about the same. Washington says it's a victory, and so does Congress, but actually it's a draw.

In the morning, Clinton and all his men are gone. They've stolen away, just as Washington did earlier in the war, not very far from there. He lets them go. No point in pressing his luck. Clinton has escaped with arms and baggage intact (losing six hundred more Hessian deserters on the way to Sandy Hook), but since the general's object was the safety of New York, not a triumph in the field, Washington believes he can claim a legitimate victory.

Wayne writes to his friend Richard Peters in Philadelphia: "Tell the Philadelphia ladies that the heavenly, sweet, pretty redcoats, the accomplished gentlemen of the guards and grenadiers, have humbled themselves on the plains of Monmouth. The 'Knights of the Blended Rose' and 'Burning Mount' have resigned their laurels to rebel officers who will lay them at the feet of those virtuous daughters of America who cheerfully gave up ease and affluence in a city for liberty and peace of mind in a cottage. . . ."

That's a comforting thought to hold on to as the Americans, on July 5, make what Washington calls an "inconceivably discouraging march," twenty miles to Brunswick, suffering through terrible heat and dust, with almost no water before they can lie down to rest.

In the aftermath, Lee just can't let it go. His monumental ego lies in ruins. He writes to Washington claiming that "misinformation of some very stupid" person must have led the general to think he was disobeying orders, not to mention bad conduct and want of courage. He wants to know what grounds Washington has to believe these things, so he can defend himself, and then he brazenly claims that, in any case, neither the commander nor any of his generals was on the spot to judge the merit of his maneuvers, and adds, unbelievably, that "the success of the day was entirely owing to them. . . ." Lee tries to put the blame on Washington, who he says is "guilty of an act of cruel injustice towards a man who certainly has some pretentions to the regard of every servant of this country," and he adds, "I have a right to demand some reparation." If there's one thing Lee doesn't lack, it's gall.

Both Wayne and Scott feel compelled to tell Washington what really happened. The retreat, they say, was not for "want of numbers, position, or the wishes of both officers and men to maintain that post," but because Lee completely failed them.

Lee's letter only stirs up Washington's anger all over again. He replies, saying Lee's communication was "highly improper," and as soon as possible, he intends to give Lee the opportunity either to justify himself to the army, Congress, America, and the world, or to disclose that he was "guilty of a breach of orders and of misbehavior before the enemy and making an unnecessary, disorderly, and shameful retreat." In other words, let a court-martial decide.

Lee tosses off an irate reply, really losing control now, referring to "the temporary power of office and the tinsel dignity attending it," and announcing that he's retiring from the army. He follows this up with a third letter, making a formal demand for a court-martial. Washington has had it. He has Lee placed under arrest, charged with disobeying orders, not attacking the enemy, misbehaving before the enemy, and showing disrespect by the letters he's written.

So the court-martial is convened. Staff officers like Hamilton and Laurens are particularly angry about Lee, whose own aides testify for him, along with a few artillerymen, including, surprisingly, Henry Knox. The court convicts him on three counts and sentences him to be suspended from any command for a year. Trailed by his dogs and cursing his enemies to the end, Lee departs and that is the end of his military career.

Lee's last years are squalid. For a while he carries on his feud in the papers and through his friends in Congress. He appeals the court's verdict, but it's confirmed by a close vote. Retiring to his Virginia farm, he never gets over what's happened to him. He writes a disrespectful letter to Congress and finds himself discharged from the army for his pains. His continuing attacks on Washington provoke a duel with Henry Laurens's son John, but no one is killed. To Lee, it's all Hamilton's fault, that "son of a bitch" who meant to ruin him all along and lied at the trial.

In his last days, he lives in a house that looks more like a barn, without glass in the windows, and the interior rooms designated by chalk lines on the floor. Until his death in 1782, he still has grandiose plans for a Western military colony. John Shy argues that Lee's services to the Revolution were substantial. He thought the Revolution was "a fight by free men for their natural rights, a popular war of mass resistance, based on military service as an obligation of citizenship." But Lee never understood that he'd gotten it all wrong, and he was far too egocentric to believe in any other point of view. As far as the commander and his officers and men are concerned, they're delighted to get on with the war after Monmouth, minus Lee.

With Clinton safely in New York—Howe's transports were waiting for him at Sandy Hook—there's nothing to keep Washington in New Jersey. He turns his army northward toward the Hudson, marching there by way of New Brunswick and Paramus. Crossing the river, he camps once again at White Plains. *Déjà vu.* He was there only two years ago, he writes to a friend, and now both armies are just about where they were then. He likes to think it's the hand of Providence that has brought him this far (it's always "Providence," never "God"), but there's a great deal of luck in it too. The same can be said for the British. At Monmouth, they could have lost the war, but the weather and Lee, despite himself, saved them. Is it possible that all this can go on for nearly five more years before a peace treaty is officially signed at last?

13

+   +   +

Other Fronts, Other Battles

Howe is the star of the show in 1778, but he walks off the stage before the year's over, leaving Washington with no immediate rival except Clinton. The commander has considerable claim to stardom himself after holding the army together at Valley Forge and emerging with new force to drive Clinton back into New York.

The contest between major players overshadows everything else that's happening in the country, but people involved in these other events don't think they're in sideshows. It feels more like a main event if you're about to be killed. This year the Revolution spreads out. New England has another taste of the war, New York State is the scene of savage frontier fighting, and the British are opening up the South.

The fact is that the Revolution itself is now becoming a sideshow as far as the British are concerned. They're caught up in a global war, since Spain and Holland have aligned themselves with France. The mighty British fleet has to divide itself among such widely separate theaters as the American coast, the West Indies, the Mediterranean off Gibraltar, even the Indian Ocean. It's no wonder London finds it hard to concentrate on the rebellious Americans; Britain has its back to the wall.

France now looms larger on the American scene. Admiral Charles Hector Théodat, Comte d'Estaing, arrives with a respectable fleet off the Delaware Capes on July 8, and on August 4, Lafayette is rowed out in a longboat to the admiral's flagship, the *Languedoc*, to give him an official welcome. While the Provençal sailors raise a cry strange in America, "*Vive le Roi*!" Lafayette climbs aboard and is at once gathered up in a smothering bear hug by the admiral, who happens to be his cousin. "You have won the opinion of the public to your side," D'Estaing exclaims. "You will spur us into action." Well, maybe, but certainly not right away.

Talking to his rather frail twenty-year-old cousin—a *general*?—about the people back home, D'Estaing loses something of his grim, bad-tempered approach to everything, a surprise to any of his sullen officers who may be present. They hate him. Not many of the fleet's crew are still alive after a stormy crossing, and that makes it impossible to do what Washington desires—make a frontal attack on New York. In any case, the admiral says, they can't get over the bar into the harbor. What other mischief can we do, then? Lafayette offers Washington's alternative plan, an attack on Newport and the six thousand British who are holding down that Rhode Island base.

Not a good idea, the French officers say. Now that they're here, their main object for the moment is to stay alive. After two days of arguing over the proposal, word comes that an English fleet of thirty-six ships, under "Black Dick" Howe, is on the way, and that solves the problem instantly. D'Estaing puts his cousin ashore, hoists his battle flags, and his seventeen ships prepare to take on the English. The weather is clear, visibility to the horizon, and the armies on shore can see the French parade past them. But when the British fleet sights D'Estaing, Admiral Howe feels symptoms of panic and withdraws, although he outnumbers the French two to one.

Next day the forces of nature check in and end the argument temporarily. A tremendous storm blows up, sweeps away tents on land, and at sea scatters both fleets. With her mast and rudder gone, the *Languedoc* has to be ignominiously towed, but she's luckier than the *César*, which goes down with all hands. Howe takes his own cripples back to New York. D'Estaing manages to get what remains of his fleet into Boston Harbor, where he declares, in his usual style, that he can't do anything for the Americans, and if they're angry about it, he doesn't particularly care.

This is a blow to Lafayette, who's playing the role of negotiator between the two countries, and now sees the possible becoming the improbable. He shuttles back and forth between the two sides, who are beginning to hate each other. What bothers the Americans most is that D'Estaing refuses to disembark the army reinforcements he has on board. Sullivan writes angrily: "No possible reason can be assigned for the Count d'Estaing's taking with him the land forces which he has on board. We therefore do, in the most solemn manner, protest against the measure, as derogatory to the honor of France."

Caught in the middle, poor Lafayette begins to feel he's becoming the enemy of the people he's supposed to be helping—he, "the friend of America, the friend of General Washington." He protests, "I am more upon a warlike footing in the American lines than when I come near the British lines at Newport." He makes one last, desperate attempt to convince his cousin, riding up to Boston and pleading earnestly, but the admiral is adamant. He wants to go home. The first French expedition to America is off the tracks before it ever starts to roll, leaving Lafayette nowhere. "One half of the Americans say that I am passionately attached to my country," he complains, "and the others say that since the arrival of the French fleet, I have gone mad, and I neither eat, drink, nor sleep but according to the direction of the wind." He wants out too by this time.

The two brigades Washington has sent to Providence for the support of the planned assault on Newport march away again. So do the seven thousand New England militia, under John Hancock, who've turned out for the occasion, much to the disappointment of John; it's his first campaign as an army officer. Disappointing, too, for ever-ready John Sullivan, who had not waited for D'Estaing when the admiral initially put out to sea after his arrival, and sent ten thousand men so close to the British at Newport that siege lines were drawn and artillery duels took place. All in vain. In his militia is an old friend, Paul Revere, there with his son, Captain Paul, Jr. The father writes to his "Dear One" at home: "It seems as if half Boston was here." They don't stay long, though. When it's clear that D'Estaing isn't going to help them, five thousand of the militia desert in just a few days.

At least one unit distinguishes itself before the party's over. When the British move out of Newport to attack after Sullivan begins a retreat, it's an all-black Rhode Island regiment that stands firm against both artillery and the Hessians, saving Sullivan from another disaster. John Glover's Marblehead men complete the job that night by getting Sullivan's men back to the mainland, with all their stores and baggage.

Sullivan is so angry that he continues to carry on a personal and public feud against D'Estaing, despite admonitions from Washington to pipe down. D'Estaing's replies, as usual, are polite and noncommittal.

This miniature war between the Americans and their new allies continues to heat up and leads to an ugly incident in Boston on September 5, when the French set up a bakery on shore to supply the fleet, at a time when the city is almost without bread of its own and no one can even get flour. As the delicious smell of baking bread fills the Boston air from the French ovens, a small crowd of Bostonians gathers, seeking to buy it. The bakers say no. A fight breaks out, and it's aggravated because neither side speaks the other's language. French officers move in to prevent mayhem, only to see one of their lieutenants killed. That cools things down, but only a display of common sense by American officials and the tactfulness of their French counterparts prevents something worse.

Boston does its best to smooth things over. The dead officer is buried under King's Chapel, in its historic vaults, and the Assembly appropriates money for a statue to commemorate him. Everybody unbends enough so that, a few days later, Hancock invites D'Estaing and his officers to dinner.

More damage control sets in. The Americans put out the story that the whole thing was instigated by parolees from Burgoyne's army, who haven't started South yet, and some British sailors from a privateer. Greene reports to Washington: "The admiral and all the French officers are now upon an exceedingly good footing with the gentlemen of the town." Hancock's house is a continuing hospitality center from morning till night. John even proposes giving D'Estaing a present, a picture of Washington, and the admiral says he'll receive it on board with a salute from his ship's guns. But there are lukewarm sentiments about the commander in Boston; some fear a personality cult is developing, and they quietly derail the presentation ceremony so that "the danger of characters becoming too important" will be averted, as they delicately put it.

Underneath it all, however, the French and the Americans don't really like each other, and the new allies share the British impression of the American army. When Lafayette's aide, the Chevalier de Pontgibaut, first gets a look at Hancock's militia, he writes home: "I have never seen a more laughable spectacle. All the tailors and apothecaries in the country must have been called out. . . . One would recognize them in their round wigs. They were mounted on bad nags and looked like a flock of ducks in cross-belts. The infantry was no better than the cavalry and appeared to be cut after the same pattern. I guessed that these warriors were more anxious to eat up our supplies than to make a close acquaintance with the enemy, and I was not mistaken; they soon disappeared." Once an aristocrat, always an aristocrat.

So the arrival of the French saviors and the fiasco at Newport ends with D'Estaing sailing off toward Martinique, where the British are threatening the French colonies. There's a lull in everybody's life in the Northern Department. Clinton is sitting in New York. Washington has his army spread out from White Plains to Connecticut, with a few remaining in New Jersey, and it's soon time to go into winter quarters at Middlebrook.

As for Lafayette, he's plunged into gloom once more. Near the end of November, he suffers a severe "diarrhea of the gut," meaning dysentery. He thinks he's going to die. He manages to visit Father George at Fishkill and spends twenty days in bed under the care of the commander's personal physician. He seems to improve, and in December he goes up to Boston, where he credits the rest of his recovery to good Madeira. He's had enough of the Revolution for now, however; it could be a big career mistake for him to stay with it, and he's going home to think it over. Before he sails for France, on January 10, 1779, he writes to Washington: "Farewell, my dear General, I hope your French friend will ever be dear to you; I hope I shall soon see you again, and tell you myself with what emotion I now leave the coast you inhabit." But as the French historian, Claude Manceron, notes: "What he mostly hopes is that he'll get home in time for that descent upon England everyone's talking about." Lafayette wouldn't miss that long-anticipated invasion for anything. "If they went without me," he admits, "I should hang myself."

Lafayette's departure is as ambiguous as the new alliance. Many in America think he's been a dilettante all along and is simply tired of the game. At home, where he has numerous enemies, he's erroneously quoted as saying he made a mistake by coming in the first place. At least he has the profound written thanks of Congress, who send him home on the navy's best frigate, which has been renamed the *Alliance* in his honor. Maybe he can't forget the "bruised and bleeding country" he rode four hundred miles through to board his ship in Boston, but for now he's overcome with fatigue and disappointment. He's still not well, and he's not sure he wants to fight another day. We'll see.

With the war practically shut down in the North for the time being, the British seem frustrated too. Clinton gets a set of instructions from London that tell him the government still hasn't grasped what kind of war it's fighting in America. Bring Washington into a general engagement, Lord Germain instructs him, or else drive him out of harm's way into the far reaches of New Jersey, then keep him penned up there while the British fleet sweeps up and down the Atlantic coast. His Lordship recommends that the Indians and British troops attack strategic points on the frontier meanwhile. Clinton tries to explain tactfully that he's been trying to get Washington into a general engagement ever since the war began, but since Howe hadn't been able to do it with a larger force than what Clinton has now, he doesn't see how he can accomplish it.

Obviously, however, he has to do *something*; sitting in New York isn't going to satisfy them back home. The best course to take, if he can do it, is to invade the South, bring it firmly under British control, and thereby cut off supplies to the other colonies. To do that, he has to capture either Charleston or Savannah, or both. He decides it will be Georgia first, which will make it easier to get into South Carolina.

In November, Clinton gathers up 3,500 British, Hessians, and Tories from New York and New Jersey, places them under the command of Lieutenant Colonel Archibald Campbell, and ships them off in a convoy under Commodore Hyde Parker. They travel a little farther than Clinton intended, and land two miles below Savannah on December 29. Campbell hopes he'll soon be reinforced from the British outpost at St. Augustine. Thus the stage is set for a new theater of war in the South.

All that stands between Campbell and Savannah is an American Howe, Major General Robert Howe, who commands a thousand Georgia and South Carolina militia. He's holding the city, with his forces anchored on the right by a swamp and on the left by rice paddies. But Campbell takes a few stray prisoners and learns from them that Howe has only a mini-army, so he feints to the left, then sends a force through the swamp, simply brushing aside the Georgia militia as they emerge, and plunges straight into the American right.

It doesn't take long. Howe's militia flee after putting up a minimal resistance, leaving more than five hundred dead, wounded, or captured, besides most of their matériel. The British loss is insignificant, and Campbell takes Savannah.

Far from there, war is blazing on another front. Somehow this conflict gets lost in the wilderness where it's taking place, and few except those caught up in it are aware of what's going on. It's not like the other fronts. A major difference is the manipulation of the Indians by both sides as allies. In citing its list of grievances against George III, the Declaration lists the way the British have stirred up the Indians against the colonists, as indeed they've been doing since at least 1774. But the Americans have done the same thing—that is, secured Indian allies—beginning with the Stockbridge tribe's participation in the siege of Boston. Since then, some Indians have joined the army, others have appeared at particular battles.

The British make no bones about it, however. It's official policy to urge the tribes to raise their hatchets against "His Majesty's rebellious subjects." As an inducement, they promise the usual—large shipments of goods to be doled out as rewards, since it's assumed that Indians won't fight unless they're bribed. As usual, too, not all these promises will ever be fulfilled. The British have no compunction about turning Indians loose on the civilian population. They're realists. It's war, isn't it?

American policy is to give Washington leave to employ tribesmen as he feels necessary, and to offer a reward for any British officer or soldier taken prisoner either on the frontier or in the Indian country.

The Tories take full advantage of the situation. They persuade the Six Nations to join forces with them and set the entire frontier ablaze from New York State and Pennsylvania to Virginia and beyond in the South, where the back settlements are constantly harassed.

"Virginia" means something else in these days—a rather vaguely defined part of the continent extending as far west as the Ohio Valley and Illinois country, threatened respectively by British forts at Detroit and Niagara, and posing a similar threat to New York and Pennsylvania.

Leaders in the wilderness war tend to be colorful personalities. At Detroit, the commander is Colonel Henry Hamilton, nicknamed "the Hair Buyer" because he's said to reward Indians for every American scalp they bring in. He also rewards Loyalists who serve with him (not that they need much inducement) with bounties of two hundred acres of land, in addition to their regular army pay. On the Virginia frontier, there's George Rogers Clark, who's on his way to becoming a legend, a man who sometimes can't decide who it is he hates more, Henry Hamilton or George III. Like Washington, he began his career as a surveyor, but now this tall redhead with the "black, penetrating eyes" is a moving figure on the frontier, only twenty-four full of ideas, like conquering the British-held villages north of the Ohio, then moving on to take Detroit. The Virginia Assembly made him a lieutenant colonel of Virginia militia, Washington's old outfit, in January 1778, and told him to go ahead with his plan.

He's given minimal help, £1,200 and the authority to draw supplies at Fort Pitt. With these, he's expected to overpower Vincennes, a French town that's a strong British post, and then Detroit if he thinks he can do it. Clark needs men, of course, and that's a sticking point. He has to have recruits beyond the Virginia militia, but the few hundred settlers who live in the campaign's territory aren't about to leave their homes and hearths undefended. Nevertheless, Clark gathers up about 175 frontiersmen, piles them into flatboats, and sends them out on the broad Monongahela. These men know the territory like the backs of their hands, and they travel fast. By the Fourth of July, they're only a mile from Kaskaskia, but in the meantime they've exhausted their provisions and haven't eaten for two days.

That doesn't discourage the hardy band. They find some boats and cross the Kaskaskia River at night, guided by sounds of what they think is "Negroes at a dance" emanating from this little town of 250 homes nestled under the protection of its fort. The subsequent attack on it is a piece of cake. Clark surrounds the place and captures it without a shot. He then gives the French inhabitants some news they haven't heard: France and America are now glorious allies, which sends them into "transports of joy." They make no difficulty about taking an oath of allegiance to Virginia.

Clark moves on to other French outposts left over from the French and Indian War, capturing Vincennes with the same ease. By this time, however, he has a major problem. On the one hand, he has militia clamoring to go home, and on the other he's acquired several thousand Indian allies in whom he places very little trust. He spends the summer in this delicate position, and in the fall, he hears that

Hamilton is coming after him from Detroit with a small force of five hundred men, including three hundred Indians.

Hamilton moves slowly and it's December before he retakes Vincennes in a snowstorm and captures the entire American garrison Clark has left there—a captain and three soldiers. One of the prisoners is a former soldier, now a fur trader and merchant, who says he's Francis Vigo, an Italian from St. Louis. He seems harmless enough and Hamilton lets him go. Actually, he's volunteered himself and what money he has to further Clark's campaign. When he turns up at Kaskaskia, Clark sends him back to spy on Vincennes, and Vigo returns from this mission to report that Hamilton has only about eighty men in the fort and that they possess only three cannon. He adds that Hamilton plans to attack Clark just as soon as the winter is over.

Clark doesn't want to wait. He conceives a plan that anyone else might have thought was harebrained. He knows there are some people who think he's mad, but he's sure Hamilton doesn't think he'd be crazy enough to "attempt to march eighty leagues through a drowned country in the dead of winter." That means he won't be expecting an attack, and this is exactly what Clark plans to do.

In January 1779, he has his men build a large row galley, armed with six light guns, and sends it off with 46 soldiers the following month. His belief is that the Wabash River, the highway Hamilton has to use, is going to be so overflowing that he can't get guns and supplies. Mustering a force of 120 men, half of them French volunteers, Clark sets off overland across the "drowned country" in the direction of Vincennes. He has to cross prairies flooded by the water from four rivers. When it isn't water, it's mud, often ankle-deep. Vincennes, he hears, is surrounded by water for five miles.

Clark wrote later in his memoirs: "My object now was to keep the men in spirits. I suffered them to shoot guns on all occasions and feast on them, like the Indians' war dances, each company by turns inviting the other to their feasts, which was the case every night. . . . Myself and principal officers hailing on the woodsmen, shouting now and then, and running as much through the mud and water as any of them. Thus insensibly without a murmur were these men led on to the banks of the Little Wabash, which we reached on the thirteenth, through incredible difficulties far surpassing anything any of us had ever experienced."

By the time they're twenty miles from Vincennes, they're facing a solid body of water, where two tributaries have flowed together, shattered trees thrusting up from the water. But nothing daunts Clark. He floats men and supplies across in a large canoe and a "platform," as he calls it, swims the horses across, and leads his men through three feet of water until they can find ground to camp on. A drummer boy floats along with the others on his drum.

This spectacular feat cheers up the men to no end. After pitching camp, Clark writes: "They really began to think themselves superior to other men, and that neither the rivers or seasons could stop their progress. . . . They wound themselves up to such a pitch that they took Vincennes, divided the spoils, and before bedtime, were far advanced on their route to Detroit." In their imaginations, of course.

By any measurement, the campaign is one of the war's most remarkable exhibitions of sheer courage, especially considering that these men's provisions have been spoiled by this time and they can't find game to shoot in the drowned lands. Those who falter are helped through waist-deep water by those who are stronger, and always before them is the spectacle of their leader, who fearlessly plunges into freezing water up to his shoulders, signaling his men to follow him, which they do willingly. For two days and two nights they plunge on, now without any food, and at daybreak on the third day they hear the morning gun sounding from Vincennes.

First they have to cross the Wabash, and when they do that, they're rewarded by finding a deer to stay their hunger and enable them to navigate the eight miles or so of water that lies between them and the fort. "I unfortunately spoke serious to one of the officers," Clark wrote later. "The whole was alarmed without knowing what I said. They ran from one to another, bewailing their situation. I viewed their situation for about one minute, whispered to those near me to [do] as I did, immediately took some water in my hand, poured on powder, blacked my face, gave the war whoop, and marched into the water without saying a word. The party gasped and fell in, one after another, without saying a word, like a flock of sheep. I ordered those that was near me to begin a favorite song of theirs. It soon passed through the line and the whole went on cheerfully."

In the early afternoon of February 22, this intrepid expedition emerges from the water and stops on a knoll. They can see Vincennes.

Clark sends a messenger to tell the inhabitants he means to attack the fort that night, so they should stay indoors. In the evening, before dark, and knowing the garrison is watching, he parades his little force in and around the hillocks to make it look as though he has at least a thousand men. Then, about eight o'clock, it's into the deep water again before they can reach the town's high ground. They enter it "with colors flying and drums brassed," welcomed by the French inhabitants, and spend the rest of the night exchanging fire with Hamilton and his garrison in the fort.

Next morning, shortly after 8:00 A.M., Clark sends a flag to Hamilton, demanding unconditional surrender, which is refused. That afternoon Hamilton thinks better of it and wants to negotiate, but this parley bogs down on the surrender terms. Soon after, a party of Indians appears and Clark's men attack them, killing two outright and executing the others later in the day in spite of an existing truce. These frontiersmen, Clark included, hate Indians and the execution is particularly gruesome. One victim is lucky enough to be tomahawked immediately. The others are bound and forced to sit in a circle. One by one they sing their death song, and when it's finished, they're tomahawked too. One escapes. An American officer remembers that this man once saved his father's life.

A bizarre fate overtakes the chief of these Indians. When they sink a hatchet in his head, he takes it out and hands it back. They try again, with the same result, and a third time. Frustrated, his executioners put a rope around his neck, drag him down to the river, and throw him in to drown. Clark has taken part in all this himself, and he's still washing the blood from his hands when he meets Hamilton face-to-face. He makes no apologies. Later, he says he was only trying to show the other Indians that they were making a mistake if they thought the English would protect them.

As for Hamilton, he exhibits some humanity by agreeing to surrender himself rather than risk his men's lives. Clark responds with some human feelings of his own. He paroles the soldiers and sends the officers, including Hamilton, away to Virginia, where Governor Thomas Jefferson establishes that the colonel was indeed a "hair buyer" and so refuses to exchange him.

At Vincennes, Clark grandly claims the entire territory, which is more than half the size of all the other colonies combined. By executing the Indians, he has persuaded many of the others that they should join the American side, and his only failure is getting Virginia to give him enough men and supplies to go on and take Detroit.

While Clark is establishing himself firmly in American history, John Sullivan comes in for a piece of the action too. His entry is a response to what the historians will call "the Wyoming Valley Massacre." This valley, in northwestern Pennsylvania, remote from the war, becomes a theater of terror in the spring of 1778 as Loyalists and Indians together launch a campaign against the Americans who live there. These patriots have forced their Tory neighbors to flee, and have then taken over their land. In spite of outposts intended to be a defense, about eight hundred Loyalists and Indians overrun the territory and dominate several hundred militia who have made the mistake of leaving a fort's safety to fight in open country, an error not many survive. Then the Indians lay waste to the valley, taking 277 scalps as they burn down more than a thousand houses, together with mills, forges, and granaries. Some citizens escape only to die of starvation in the swamps where they've sought refuge. Women are taken as slaves.

Obviously, Washington can't let this terrorism go unavenged. While Clark's Vincennes prisoners are on their way to Virginia, he orders another expedition commanded by two generals, Sullivan and James Clinton, of New York. Much to its leader's satisfaction, this becomes known as Sullivan's Expedition, just the kind of recognition he's always hoped for. Washington's instructions are explicit. He's shocked by what happened in the Wyoming Valley and tells Sullivan to invade the country of the Six Nations and destroy it.

These aren't collections of tepees he's talking about, but log cabins and houses built of framed timber and stone. Along with the Cherokees, these Indians of the Mohawk Valley have the most advanced society of the Eastern tribes. Washington also instructs Sullivan to take as many prisoners as possible, of every age and both sexes. They'll be useful as hostages against future good behavior.

Sullivan is given nearly four thousand men for the job. He separates them into two columns. One means to head up the Susquehanna Valley from Wyoming, the other under Clinton taking a northern route through the Mohawk Valley to Canajoharie, where they expect to meet and move into the territory they're to devastate.

For a revenge party, it's more than formidable, especially Sullivan's column, which requires 1,200 pack horses for the baggage. Artillery and stores are loaded on 120 boats and launched up the Susquehanna. More than 700 head of cattle trail the soldiers to provide food. Sullivan, who's never inclined to stint himself, reserves 20 horses to carry his personal effects. With the beating of drums and occasional bursts of music from a regimental band, Sullivan's army strikes off through the wilderness and surprisingly, without much hindrance, unites with Clinton's column on August 22, 1779.

Now we have a real army. Put together, the combined trains of these columns string out to a length that would make a seasoned strategist faint at the sight. Lucky that Sullivan isn't marching against British regulars. There are those in the force who don't think all that equipment is necessary for wilderness fighting. "The sight of carriages in this part of the world is very odd," Major John Burrows reports tactfully, "as there is nothing but a footpath." Sergeant Moses Fallows complains: "We marched much impeded by the artillery and ammunition wagons through thick woods and difficult defiles. Such cursing, cutting, and digging, oversetting wagons, cannon, and pack horses into the river, etc., is not to be seen every day. The army was obliged to take seven hours at one place."

An advance scout who's climbed a tree is first to spot the Indians they've come to destroy. At Newtown, they're lying in ambush, but the advance warning gives them away, and they flee from the white man's cannon, which blast them from their defense works. Only a dozen Indians are killed, and two prisoners are taken. One of them is a black man, the other a white man painted black. The latter is discovered lying facedown, pretending to be dead, but when they roll him over and wash his face, he's ready to talk.

His commanders, he discloses, have been Captain Walter Butler, the notorious Tory leader, and two battalions of his rangers, plus a few British regulars, and a Tory band under Guy Johnson. This band is known as the Royal Greens. Joseph Brant is the chief commander of about four hundred Indians.

In this skirmish, the Americans suffer a few losses—three dead, thirty-six wounded. A party is sent out to scoop up any dead Indians who may be lying around, and a few are discovered. Lieutenant William Barton, of the 1st New Jersey regiment, tells us what happened to them: "Towards noon they found them, and skinned two of them from their hips down for boot legs, one pair for the major, the other for myself."

Sullivan resumes his progress, as relentless as Sherman's march to the sea nearly a century later. Newtown is burned to the ground, and so are Catherine's Town, Appletown, Kanadaseages, and Kanagha. All told, more than forty towns are leveled and their surrounding fields and orchards destroyed.

On both sides, atrocities. A small detachment of Morgan's riflemen, led by Lieutenant Thomas Boyd, kill an Indian while they're scouting a town and fall into a dispute about his scalp. While they're arguing, a party of Indians attacks them and kills twenty-two men.

Next day, when the main body enters the town Boyd's men were scouting, they find the body of the lieutenant and a rifleman, stripped naked and their heads cut off. The skin of Boyd's head has been taken off entirely, and his eyes punched out, but the other man's head is not found. Both bodies have been stabbed with spears at least forty times in forty different places, while knives have cut great gashes in their flesh. Boyd's penis and testicles have been almost severed and left hanging, while his fingers and toenails have been torn off. Dogs have eaten away part of the men's shoulders. The remainder of Boyd's scouting party is found three days later, "tomahawked, scalped, and butchered."

For their part, some of Sullivan's men find a house where an old squaw and a sick Indian have found refuge. They're locked inside and the house is burned.

By the end of the month, Sullivan's expedition is back in Wyoming, mission accomplished. In the devastated Indian country, the tribes have to depend on whatever food the British will give them, and hundreds die of starvation and disease during the winter. The power of the Six Nations, the most formidable in the East, is broken for good.

Sullivan fails to bring back any hostages, and there's some complaint about that. "The nests are destroyed, but the birds are still on the wing," Major Jeremiah Fogg complains in his journal. Some people are never satisfied.

When the horror of Sullivan's Expedition seeps back into the seaboard cities, there are those who view it with disgust. But many more merely recite the details of Wyoming Valley, and of the Cherry Valley Massacre, which had occurred earlier, on November 11, 1778. That's when Major John Butler, Walter's son, operating out of Fort Niagara, embarked on an ambitious plan to "break up the back settlements" in Pennsylvania, New York, and New Jersey.

With the help of an Indian contingent, young Butler led his rangers through November cold and rain on a 150-mile march that was all heavy going, past Otsego Lake to the isolated Cherry Valley, where Americans had settled since 1740, and whose fort was defended by Colonel Ichabod Alden and the 7th Massachusetts, about 250 men.

Getting wind of Butler's advance, Alden sent out a scouting party, which was captured in its sleep by Butler's men, who reported that the rebels were camped outside the fort. Several inches of snow fell that night. It turned to thick haze and rain in the morning, which helped conceal Butler's approach. It wasn't a complete surprise, though. As the rangers and their Indian allies approached, a passing civilian on his way to the fort was encountered and shot, but he was only wounded and escaped to give the alarm.

Butler ordered a halt to check out the arms, and while he was doing this, a party of Senecas hurried on ahead and attacked a house about four hundred yards from the fort, where Alden had his headquarters, with his officers and nearly forty men. The Senecas overran the house and killed Alden as he was running to the fort. Another officer was captured, and several were killed. But the fort itself held out, and in the middle of the afternoon the raiders withdrew and turned their attention to the town.

What followed were hours of horror and confusion. Forty houses were burned and more than thirty civilians killed, thirteen of them in a single house. A sortie from the fort saved some of the settlers, who escaped to the woods. Butler took seventy-one prisoners, but he released most of them next day, after which he returned to Niagara, taking along two women and their seven children as hostages, with a few black servants who had nowhere else to go.

After these events, the history of frontier warfare is scanty. In the spring of 1779, Colonel Daniel Brodhead, a quarrelsome man, succeeds the even more quarrelsome General Lachlan McIntosh as head of the Western Department, with headquarters at Pittsburgh. In August he sets out with six hundred men, and after struggling through country "almost impossible by reason of the stupendous heights and frightful declivities," he enters New York State, stifles a halfhearted Indian resistance, and in a march of four hundred miles in thirty-three days, round trip, he burns any number of Indian villages and fields of standing grain, returning without losing a man.

In November 1781, a footnote. Colonel Marinus Willett will pursue a force of British and Indians who have been holding out in Fort Herkimer, in the Mohawk Valley, cross the river, march twenty miles through a snowstorm, and catch up with them at a difficult ford over Canada Creek, virtually annihilating them. One of the slain will be Walter Butler, the commander at Cherry Valley, who always called himself a major. But there's a final irony. In his pocket, they will find a commission disclosing that he's only a captain. He will be alive when they find him, and an Indian ally of Willett's will end Butler's life with no more mercy than he's shown. Brant will be more fortunate. He will escape.

In this border warfare, fought over great distances, there are no pitched battles, and in the end, it appears that the Americans have won, but on the other hand, the war will end with the major forts at Detroit and Niagara still in British hands, and they're going to be a prickly handful in the War of 1812. They're places the Indians know well. They come to these forts from as far south as Virginia and Kentucky, bringing prisoners and scalps. The Shawnees will capture Daniel Boone in the Blue Licks and take him to Detroit. Ties between British and Tories and their Indian allies are sometimes strained but mostly they remain unbroken, and these alliances will survive almost intact into Mr. Madison's War.

Meanwhile, back in the main theaters of action, the dramatic and eventful year of 1778 has begun to wind down everywhere, as though a curtain is descending, separating the Revolution into two acts. Washington has problems, and they're not all on the battlefield by any means. One is the ease with which the British spy network continues to get information from the American side. Not only is this network well organized, operating mostly out of New York, but it numbers such extraordinary artists as Ann Bates, whom John Bakeless, a historian of Revolutionary espionage, calls the most successful female spy in history. She's worth remembering.

Ann (whose last name is sometimes spelled Beats) is well trained and absolutely fearless. She slips in and out of the American lines as though she owned them, and while she's inside makes notes that are precise and accurate, not to say valuable. Once, unbelievably, she walks right into Washington's headquarters and listens in on a conversation about official matters. Twice she's captured but talks her way out. In fact, she repeatedly escapes capture by narrow margins.

Before the war, Ann was a Philadelphia schoolteacher, earning £30 a year, not enough to hold body and soul together, so she kept bees on the side and sold the honey, besides raising a few sheep and running a small store. She was recruited by another British spy, a civilian named John Craigie, who recognized her talents. She was already married to Joseph Bates, an ordnance repairman in the British artillery, and after the evacuation of Philadelphia, she naturally wanted to leave too.

When Ann got to New York, in May 1778, Craigie asked her to join the spy ring, and after that meeting, she became one of this accomplished company of spooks. Her first exploit is spectacular. Returning to Philadelphia, she persuades Arnold, now the military commander there, to give her a pass to Washington's headquarters. Her mission is to find out what the commander is doing and what he intends to do. In her pocket is a secret token that will identify her as a spy to an American officer in the 6th Pennsylvania Line who happens to be a British secret agent. She also carries five guineas for expenses.

Ann decides to disguise herself in a somewhat threadbare outfit, posing as a peddler carrying medicinal rhubarb, thread, needles, combs, and knives. On her way, she has to wade across the Crosswicke River in water up to her armpits because the bridge is down. On July 2, she finally arrives at Washington's camp in White Plains, only to find out that the traitorous American officer she's supposed to seek out has resigned. Very well, she'll do it herself. As Bakeless tells us, she peddles her way through the entire army, making notes along the way. She knows about artillery because her husband was in charge of repairing Clinton's field guns, so she's able to gather valuable intelligence.

On her way back to New York, only four miles from White Plains, she's stopped and arrested as a suspicious person. Stripped and searched (by a woman), nothing is found but her peddler's stock and three dollars. The secret token has disappeared. Arriving safely in New York with the information that's stored in her head, she gets one day of rest and debriefing before Clinton sends her out again, once more as a peddler, and she spends another week in the American camp. She wanders around, completely fearless, and no one disturbs her. She even penetrates Washington's headquarters again but hears nothing of value.

It's back to New York for a few days' rest, and then once more—White Plains. This time the security is tighter, but still no one seems to notice that she's hanging around headquarters, listening to the officers talk. One of these conversations is particularly fruitful. An officer just arrived asks to be brought up to date with information and gets it. So does Ann. She even walks through the artillery park with no trouble. This time the information she brings back saves the British garrison in Rhode Island.

On the prowl again in September, she follows Washington's army as it moves toward Danbury and attaches herself to the general's own column, traveling with it as far as North Castle, near the Connecticut border. After a brief detour to New Jersey, she rejoins the Americans, but a British deserter spots her and she barely escapes. At last she's captured by General Charles Scott, who's been in charge of American intelligence for a time and can't find out where the information leak is. Incredibly, Ann lies herself to freedom again. Scott even gives her a pass.

Clinton decides it's no longer safe for her to follow Washington, so she spends the next months operating around Philadelphia and New York, using a chain of Tory safe houses the British have set up across the mid-Atlantic states. Once, sent by André to bring in another woman spy from the cold, she gets as far as the New Jersey shore of the Hudson with her comrade, and while she's waiting for three days until it's safe to cross, hiding from American scouting parties and trying to shelter from bad weather, she manages to compile a report on Philadelphia shipping. (After Yorktown, she and her husband will sail for England, and her remarkable career will be ended.)

Ann Bates and a host of others complicate Washington's life, but his worst non-military complication is the Continental Congress, with which he always seems to be in conflict, never more so than in this critical year of 1778. He's far from being alone in complaining about these gentlemen. John Adams, who's one of them, declares that its business "is tedious beyond description. This assembly is like no other that ever existed. Every man in it is a great man, an orator, a critic, a statesman, and therefore every man upon every question must show his oratory, his criticism, and his political abilities." Nothing much is going to change in that quarter.

It's not surprising, however, that Congress is such a mess, considering its varied composition. City lawyers rub shoulders with country squires.

Self-made men find themselves in the company of those who have inherited great wealth. Radicals and conservatives are hopelessly intermixed. The hotheads are constantly at odds with the more sophisticated. Most of these delegates are well educated and articulate, but that seems to have given them the conviction that they are invariably right.

Adams isn't the only member who abhors his colleagues. Gouverneur Morris, for instance, can't take serving in this body more than a year. "What a lot of damned scoundrels we had in the Second Congress," he recalls later. The public's getting tired of them too. The First Congress didn't open its sessions to the public, and consequently got away with a great deal. Now the daily wranglings are a discouragement to everyone.

After spending a few days with this body in 1778, Washington writes: "Party disputes and personal quarrels are the great business of the day while the momentous concerns of an empire, a great and accumulated debt, ruined finances, depreciated money, and want of credit . . . are but second considerations and postponed from day to day, from week to week."

All true, but in spite of themselves, these first fruits of democracy don't dissolve, they don't give up, and the country escapes what has occurred in other revolutionary countries. No strong man with supreme power on his mind emerges to fill the political vacuum created by a weak governing body at a time of high emotions and violent dissent.

Slowly, slowly, the American Revolution is beginning to tilt the other way in spite of all the reasons it has to collapse, and after the end of this critical year, a denouement begins to approach, at tortoise speed.

14

✛   ✛   ✛

The Year of Indecision

I n the early winter months of 1779, there's good news and bad
news. The good news is that this fourth winter of the war finds
the Americans far better off than they were only a year ago at
Valley Forge. Clustered in and around Middlebrook (Bound Brook
today), the army has more and better provisions than it's had for a
long time. During the previous October, shipments of coats, breeches,
and shoes from France enabled the soldiers to look a little more
uniform in appearance than as though it was every man for himself.
Whole divisions have new coats, breeches, and shoes.

The bad news, however, more than outweighs the good. From its
peak strength in the summer of 1778, the army now appears to be
shrinking again at an alarming rate. After four years, civilians also
are beginning to tire of the war, although they don't have much to
complain about by comparison with the army's plight. In Salem,
Massachusetts, a merchant named John White makes a gloomy note
on his almanac: "We shall forever have reason (I fear) to lament our
gloried Revolution, because I have only changed taskmasters, the
later the worse, because they are poor creatures. [He means Congress.] Our country is too poor to be a separate nation. . . . The high
sheriff of this country is a tanner; two magistrates, one a tanner, the
other a joiner, neither of them could speak or read English. . . . It is
impossible such men should be equal to the business. . . ."

At least the winter is mild, for once. After the first of the year,
there's not much snow, or even frost. Among the officers at headquarters, in striking contrast to the year before, the weeks go by pleas-

antly, almost like peacetime in some respects. The men, too, living in decent huts, are healthier than they've been since the war began.

Washington lives four miles from town in the John Wallace house, which is comfortable but crowded. After spending two months in Philadelphia, he returns in February, bringing Martha with him. She entertains, as she loves to do, but the wives of the other generals quartered nearby are her social rivals and it's a busy scene after dark.

The Knoxes, for instance, are living in Jacob Van de Veer's house, later known as the Ludlow farm, in Pluckamin, and there, on February 18, Lucy gives an entertainment to honor the new alliance with France, although precious little has come of it so far. The guests include all the other generals and all the local notables within reach. Sixteen cannon are discharged at 4:00 P.M. as a salute to the un-forthcoming French, and afterward everyone sits down to dinner in a large public building. Evening fireworks are a prelude to a ball, which is opened by Washington and Lucy Knox. Her husband reports afterward that the guests danced all night. "We had about seventy ladies, all of the first *ton* in the state and between three and four hundred gentlemen. . . . The illuminating, fireworks, etc., were more than pretty. . . ."

The most memorable parties, however, are those Kitty Greene gives in the two-story Holland-brick farmhouse belonging to old Derrick van Veghten, perched on the banks of the Raritan, where she and Nathanael are quartered. It's Kitty herself who makes it so special. Everyone is in love with this soft, dark-eyed beauty, who at only twenty-five is intelligent, poised, and more worldly than most of the other ladies. On March 19, she throws a splendid party at which, as Greene writes to his friend, Colonel Jeremiah Wadsworth: "His Excellency and Mrs. Greene danced upwards of three hours without sitting down. . . . Upon the whole, we had a pretty little frisk."

Washington's lengthy whirl with Kitty is just the kind of thing that stirs up gossip in their small circle. There's no word of truth in any of it, of course. Nathanael's bad leg prevents him from enjoying the pleasures of the dance, and he's proud of his Kitty, who always seems to be the belle of the ball. He's honored that the commander danced with her for three hours, and his report of the occasion certainly gives no intimation of jealousy. Anyway, Kitty's hair isn't the right color. Even as President, at other social occasions, George is always looking for (and often noting down) the dark-haired ladies who remind him of Sally Fairfax, his lost love. Besides, he adores dancing.

All this innocent merriment is making the winter at Middlebrook more than bearable, at least for the officers. One of them writes home: "We spend our time very socially here; are never disturbed by the enemy, have plenty of provisions, and no want of whiskey or grog. We sometimes get good spirits, punch, etc., and have Madeira sometimes. We have a variety of amusements. Last evening the tragedy of Cato was performed at Brunswick by officers of the army." Just as the British did in besieged Boston.

The good times don't last. Rations begin to run short once more, and the number of officers who want to go home begins to rise again. One of them writes to his folks: "We have been without bread or rice more than five days out of seven for these three weeks past. . . .This whole part of the country are starving for want of bread. They have been drove to the necessity of grinding flaxseed and oats together for bread. . . ."

In the ranks, the situation is worse and discipline becomes a serious problem again. Major Henry Lee advocates killing all the deserters as soon as they're caught, but Washington tells his fellow Virginian he's being too harsh. Lee remains unconvinced. One of his scouting parties scoops up three deserters, and the major decides he'll kill all of them as an example, but finally settles on disposing of just one.

Who's going to be the unlucky man? Lots are drawn (it's only fair) and the short straw falls to a corporal, who apparently doesn't have devoted friends because the two who are spared bring his head back to camp on a pole and stick it up on a gallows as a warning to others. Washington is not amused and reprimands Lee, but he knows a potential image problem when he sees one and tells the major: "You will send to have the body buried lest it fall into the enemy's hands."

Discipline and good spirits improve markedly by late spring, but the reports from the home front continue to be worse every day. When he was in Philadelphia at the beginning of the year, Washington was appalled by what he saw there—"a carnival of idleness, dissipation, and extravagance, including speculation, peculation, and an insatiable search for riches." The American dream already in operation. Personal quarrels and political party disputes were the order of the day, he found, regardless of the war, and he sets down a laundry list of other ills—the country's growing debt, financial ruin on every hand, depreciating money, and the scarcity of credit.

"I can't help asking," he inquired plaintively, "where is Mason, Wythe, Jefferson, Nicholas, Pendleton, Nelson, and another I could name. . . ." He couldn't believe Philadelphia's extravagance—dinners and similar entertainments that cost as much as £400. And all this while officers are quitting his and the country's service because they can't afford to stay in the army, while others, as he says, "are sinking by sure degrees into beggary and want."

Want has driven some officers into what can only be called treason. Governor William Livingston, of New Jersey, writes to Sullivan from Morristown on August 19 that he has enough evidence to convince him that there's a considerable traffic between people in his state and the enemy, using flags of truce and passports obtained from army officers in Elizabeth Town, Newark, and other places.

Livingston lists a few of the consequences of this traffic: "Persons of dubious political character, as I am informed, have been sent over; provisions for the aid and comfort of the British troops furnished; a pernicious and unlawful traffic carried on; the little specie left among us collected with the greatest avidity to maintain this execrable trade; and the Continental currency by that means further depreciated, opportunities afforded the enemy for circulating their counterfeit bills, and the disaffected of conveying to them intelligence of every movement and designed operation of our troops, the confidence of the people in the integrity of our officers diminished, and a universal murmuring excited among the friends of the common cause."

Quite a list. And Livingston is far from the only one who has the feeling that the home front is collapsing in greed and indifference. Lieutenant Samuel Shaw writes to his parents: "I wish seriously that the ensuing campaign may terminate the war. The people of America seem to have lost sight entirely of the whole principle which animated them at the commencement of it. That patriotic ardor which then inspired each breast; that glorious, I had almost said godlike, enthusiasm—has given place to avarice, and every rascally practice which tends to the gratification of that sordid and most disgraceful passion. I don't know as it would be too bold an assertion to say that its depreciation is equal to that of the currency—thirty for one. You may perhaps charitably think that I strain the matter, but I do not. I speak feelingly. By the arts of monopolizers and extortioners, and the little, the very little, attention by authority to counteract them, our currency is reduced to a mere name."

One of the most articulate complainers on the higher levels is Alexander Hamilton, who is rapidly losing whatever faith in democracy he may have had. Writing to John Holt, a Poughkeepsie printer, on October 19, he rages: "While every method is taken to bring to justice those men whose principles and practices have been hostile to the present Revolution, it is to be lamented that the conduct of another class, equally criminal, and, if possible, more mischievous, has hitherto passed with impunity, and almost without notice. I mean that tribe who, taking advantage of the times, have carried the spirit of monopoly and extortion to an excess which scarcely admits of a parallel. Emboldened by the success of progressive impositions, it has extended to all the necessities of life. The exorbitant price of every article, and the depreciation upon our currency, are evils derived essentially from this source. When avarice takes the lead in a state, it is commonly the forerunner of its fall. How shocking is it to discover among ourselves, at this early period, the strongest symptom of this fatal disease."

Not everybody is sitting on his hands deploring the situation. Plenty of ordinary people are suffering from the misdeeds of others, and they're mad as hell and don't intend to put up with it if they can help it. In Pennsylvania, the Radical Party tries vainly to get Congress to cut waste, impose more taxes, and try to get new loans, but Congress dithers, and meanwhile the soaring cost of living and renewed scarcities are creating waves of discontent everywhere in the colonies. People want price controls, and the punishment of merchants and financiers who won't cooperate for the general good.

The popular feeling against speculators reaches a high tide during the summer and fall. A mob attacks the Philadelphia residence of James Wilson. His sin appears to be that he's the lawyer who was counsel for the powerful Penn family, who have brought suit against the state, and he's also defended merchants who have been brought before committees trying to enforce price controls.

There's more to it than that, however. Wilson, it appears, is a truly bad apple. His notorious speculations continue even when he's appointed a justice of the Supreme Court. He's over his ears in land speculation, and he has to hide from his creditors. When some of his friends—merchants, war speculators, and conservatives—find themselves confronting an enraged mob, they take refuge in Wilson's house, along with the owner's friend, General Mifflin, who left his job as army quartermaster under a cloud so black it hasn't stopped raining yet. The lawyer's house is labeled at once "Fort Wilson."

One of the observers of this drama is Captain Allen McLane, among the army's most notable officers, who writes in his journal: "I was standing on the front steps of my house in Walnut Street and observed Colonel Grayson beckoning to me from the door of the War Office. I went to him, and he told me he was glad I had not left the city, for that he had great apprehensions that several of our most respectable citizens, then assembled at Mr. Wilson's house, would be massacred, as they were determined to defend themselves against the armed mob that had assembled on the Commons this morning and were moving down Second Street, expecting to find Mr. Wilson and his friends at the City Tavern, but they were within pistol shot of the War Office."

McLane can hear the mob coming, moving but not marching to an impromptu fife and drum corps. In a few minutes, he sees the vanguard entering Walnut Street. Grayson asks him if he can identify any of the leaders and McLane tells him he thinks the man fronting the mob is a militia officer named Captain Faulkner. Grayson suggests that maybe the mob can be persuaded to turn up Dock Street to Third Street, and they make the attempt. It's all very civil at first. McLane introduces Grayson to Faulkner as a member of the Board of War, and the colonel expresses his fear that the consequences of attacking Mr. Wilson in his house could be serious. Faulkner replies, civilly enough, that they have no designs on either Wilson or his house, that their only intention is to support the laws and the Committee of Trade. This is another way of saying that these demonstrators represent the city's laboring people who are desperate over the high price of life's necessities.

While this conversation is taking place, others who can't hear it are pressing forward from the rear. Two men, armed with muskets and fixed bayonets, run up to find out why the march has halted, and Faulkner's explanation doesn't please them. They order him to resume the march up Walnut Street. Grayson then tries to reason with one of the men, while McLane takes on the other, a man named Pickering, who answers by threatening the captain with his bayonet, even "sometimes bringing himself in the attitude of a charge from trailed arms."

Faulkner and another less belligerent member of the mob try to pacify the armed men, but the word is given to continue the march up Walnut Street. By this time the mob, with pressure from the rear, has pressed in so closely that Grayson and McLane find it almost impossible to remain on their feet, so they link arms and determine they'll squeeze out of this mess as soon as it reaches the War Office. They find themselves in the company of some marchers who aren't protesters but citizens who've been taken prisoner along the way on suspicion of being sympathetic to the speculators and the rich.

As the mob flows past McLane's house, he sees his wife and a friend at a second-story window. Mrs. McLane, seeing her husband pass by, a virtual prisoner, screams and faints. Grayson and McLane are, in fact, prisoners since they can't get out of the mob, as they'd hoped.

Within a pistol shot of Wilson's house, Captain Campbell, an officer in the Continental Army, appears at an upper window and orders the mob to pass on. He's answered by a volley of musketry, which in turn is answered by those inside the house. This is something the protesters hadn't expected, and they scatter in all directions, leaving Grayson and McLane under the eaves of a house and exposed to fire from the mob, which has passed and tries to gather itself again. The two run into Wilson's garden, but that's worse because now they're between two fires, from the mob and the house, since the protesters have now spread out into the yards of neighbors.

A few minutes later, Mifflin recognizes them and orders a back door opened, and they go inside. At the same moment, some faint hearts in Fort Wilson become seriously alarmed and jump out second-story windows. Mifflin conducts McLane and Grayson upstairs to where Wilson and his friends have taken refuge on the third floor. Looking out the window, McLane can see that the mob has set up a fieldpiece on Dock Street, and on Third Street he sees a number of desperate-looking men in their shirt sleeves moving toward the house. They're carrying iron bars and large hammers. Forcing the doors and windows, they rush inside. They're met by a volley from the defenders, firing from staircases and cellar windows, which drops several of the intruders and causes the others to flee, leaving their wounded behind. Some of Wilson's friends run downstairs, shut the doors again, and barricade them.

At this point, the cavalry comes riding over the hill, so to speak, as President of the Supreme Executive Council of Pennsylvania James

Reed, with a detachment of the 1st Troop of City Horse, appears. The mob is now completely disorganized. Reed asks McLane to round up all the rioters he can, and says justice will be done. Of course it's a question of exactly whose side justice is on. We can't have citizens besieged in their homes, can we, but on the other hand, if these same citizens happen to be enemies of the less fortunate and are mercilessly exploiting them, what should be done?

Politically, the answer is the same as always: nothing. Tensions continue to exist in Philadelphia and elsewhere as the strains of the war tear at the seams of this embryonic democratic society. Things aren't going to get better right away.

At least some matters can be decided on the battlefield, and Clinton makes an effort to get military affairs moving again. If it's at all possible, he intends to get Washington into a position where he can be annihilated. The commander hasn't been idle during the winter and spring, however. He built defenses on the Hudson, particularly at West Point, where he established headquarters during the summer. He also built a fort at Verplanck's Point on the east side of the river, and started another on the opposite side at Stony Point. Observing this, Clinton sees an opportunity to get at the exasperating general.

Late in May, he moves up the river with 6,000 men and takes both these forts, hoping it will lure Washington out into the open. Clinton thinks that threatening the Americans' supply depots at Trenton and Easton will be enough to bring him rushing to their defense and so get himself involved in a major engagement. Washington doesn't bite. He simply retreats to safer ground in the Highlands after the river forts are seized.

Clinton then launches some diversionary actions. He dispatches Colonel William Tryon, the colonial governor of New York, with his 70th Foot, on another destructive pillage of Connecticut towns, something he's enjoyed doing since he savaged Danbury in 1777. Tryon is a vindictive man who can't bear the loss of the perquisites he enjoyed before the war, and he's in a more or less constant rage against the damned rebels, so he accepts the assignment with pleasure. Ill health doesn't impede him, although by next year he'll have to go back to England because of it. He raids New Haven, East Haven, Fairfield, Greene's Farms, and Norwalk, going far beyond his orders from Clinton in destroying these towns.

Clinton is baffled, however, by the absence of a main event. Why doesn't Washington come out and fight? It's because the general has a countermove in mind; he means to take back the forts at Stony Point and Verplanck's Point. Stony Point comes first, and this time it's one of the American army's real successes, even though it's a small one and short-lived. General Wayne takes 1,200 men, with 300 in reserve, to do the job. Secrecy is essential, so Wayne simply removes the nearby inhabitants, including their barking dogs, from the territory near the fort. Even so, he doesn't trust the dogs not to bark and has them killed.

Shortly after 11:00 A.M. on the morning of July 15, Wayne's troops march out. They're handpicked veterans, young and strong, well equipped. Before dark, they're only a mile and a half from the fort. Wayne halts them and outlines what they have to do, which is formidable. First they must wade through two feet of water for twenty minutes before they can reach the solid ground below this promontory, which juts out into the Hudson for a half mile. On the river side are sheer rock walls, while inland the land slopes down to a marsh they'll have to get through. Fortunately it isn't high tide, because then the Point becomes virtually an island.

As they pause before the assault, Wayne has a premonition he may be killed and writes a letter to his closest friend, Dr. Sharp Delaney. One thing that's on his mind is his bitter, longstanding quarrel with Arthur St. Clair, and fearing this old enemy might try to blacken his name after he dies, he asks Delaney to do what he can to prevent it. He also asks the doctor to see that his small son and daughter have an education because, as he says, he fears their mother "will not survive this strike."

Wayne and his men then have something to eat, after which he gives the signal to advance. As they slosh through the marsh, it's clear that you can kill barking dogs but you can't suppress the sound of hundreds of men splashing through the water, so the British hear them coming. By this time it's midnight and a full moon is up, destroying any further secrecy.

In its pages soon after, the New York *Journal* gives a somewhat overblown but generally accurate account of the assault. "With fixed bayonets and uncharged pieces," the *Journal* reports, the men "advanced with quick but silent motion through a heavy fire of cannon and musketry till, getting over the abatis and scrambling up the prec-

ipice, the enemy called out, 'Come on, ye damn'd rebels! Come on!'"
The paper credits Wayne's men with a fitting but unlikely answer:
"'Don't be in such a hurry, my lads. We will be with you presently.'"

Back to reality. "In a little more than twenty minutes from the time
the enemy first began to fire, our troops, overcoming all obstructions
and resistance, entered the fort. Spurred on by their resentment of the
former cruel bayoneting which many of them and others of our people had experienced [the *Journal* is thinking here of the Paoli Massa-
cre] and of the more recent and savage barbarity of plundering and
burning of unguarded towns, murdering old and unarmed men,
abusing and forcing defenseless women, and reducing multitudes of
innocent people from comfortable livings to the most distressful want
of the means of subsistence—deeply affected by these cruel injuries,
our people entered the fort with the resolution of putting every man
to the sword. But the cry of 'Mercy, mercy! Dear Americans, mercy!
Quarter! Brave Americans, quarter! Quarter!' disarmed their resentment in an instant, insomuch that even Colonel [Henry] Johnson, the
commandant, freely and candidly acknowledges that not a drop of
blood was spilled unnecessarily. . . ."

Well, that shows how much you can believe of what you read in
the colonial papers, which are no more than loyal propaganda or-
gans. If the British ever uttered such poetic cries for mercy, they must
not have been heard, because the Americans *do* use their bayonets to
good effect, killing 63 of the British offenders with them. Steuben,
who taught them all they know about this art, would be proud.
Moreover, besides 70 of the wounded defenders, 543 men are captured, as are 15 guns. The Americans lose only 15 dead, and only 84
are wounded.

One of the wounded is Wayne himself. Felled with a bloody scalp
wound, he shouts, "Carry me up to the fort, boys," and when they
do, he calls out again, "Let's go forward!" Wayne stumbles into the
fort, his head crimson, held up by two soldiers. The place is quickly
secured, and then the fort's guns are turned on the British sloop-of-
war lying in the river below, compelling it to scurry away downriver.
The battle's over. It isn't a great strategic victory, but it's a tremendous
morale booster for the Americans, and it has a chilling effect on the
British. Clinton is so discouraged, he considers resigning and going
back to England, but Germain isn't about to let him off the hook so
easily.

Washington arrives on the scene, looks over the situation, and decides that he isn't going to be able to defend this fort any more successfully than the British did, so he orders it abandoned. Verplanck's Point is next on his list, but preparation for the assault takes so long that Clinton has time to summon Tryon's troops, who are about to sail for New London, and prepares to give it a blow. Reinforced with these men, he moves up the river, repossesses the fort, and makes it a little stronger.

Meanwhile various other sideshows are going on in the North during this year when it seems everyone is holding his breath. In July, Massachusetts launches its own private war by sending nearly a thousand militia under Generals Solomon Lovell and Peleg Wadsworth to attack the British force at Castine, Maine, ferrying them there in armed vessels commanded by Commodore Dudley Saltonstall. Marines are aboard to supplement the militia, and when they all land on July 25, quarreling breaks out between the regulars and the others, and the expedition breaks down. In fact, it's threatened.

Inside the fort, a young ensign, John Moore, who will later become Sir John and win fame for his exploits in the Peninsular War, organizes a brisk defense that completely frustrates the attackers. While the Americans are trying to get their act together, Sir George Collier appears at the head of a powerful small squadron. Collier is not exactly a happy camper in the Maine woods. Irritable from a bout of fever, he considers Maine so dreary that only wild beasts could live in it. That doesn't prevent him from summarily breaking up the Americans' siege, sending them scurrying up the Penobscot River in their ships, which their crews run ashore to be burned or destroyed. This panic is worth £2,000,000 worth of lost ships. The Marines and their disdained allies the militia are left to make their way back home through the wilderness as best they can.

When they get back, somebody has to be blamed for this fiasco, and the General Court of Massachusetts holds an inquiry which censures Saltonstall. But Washington simply shrugs when he hears of the affair and dismisses it as "an unfortunate expedition," which, as he points out, he didn't authorize anyway. One more example of the lack of coordination that continues to haunt the Americans.

The soldiers themselves sometimes find a grim humor in this helter-skelter warfare. In August, Colonel Henry Jackson takes four hundred men of what is called the Additional Continental Regiment on a forced march from Rhode Island to Boston, covering forty miles in twenty-four hours. They march all night through a hard rain and are "broken down with fatigue" when they finally get to Boston Neck just as the sun comes up. A tavern looms in the dawn light. Its traditional sign depicts a man's head and shoulders sticking out of a globe representing the earth. His arms reach out, but the rest of his body is inside the globe. A cartoon balloon emanating from his mouth says, "Oh! how shall I get through this world?" Regarding it, one of the soldiers says, "Enlist, damn you, enlist, and you will soon get through this world! Our regiment will all be through it in an hour or two, if we don't halt by the way."

Legendary figures emerge from time to time in this haphazard year. One of them is a perennial favorite with the boys: Israel Putnam, known to everyone affectionately as "Old Put." Joseph Rundel, who enlisted from Fairfield, Connecticut, in February 1778, when he was not quite sixteen, and became the general's "waiter," realized years afterward that his general played the role of folk hero to the hilt.

Rundel gives us a revisionist view of one of the war's most cherished legends at the time. Tryon, in one of his early sorties, came up against Putnam near the meeting house at a place called Horseneck, an outpost about three miles from Reading (now Redding), Connecticut. In spite of defensive cannon fire, Putnam had to retreat in face of a superior force, and the retreat became a rout. Putnam advised his soldiers to save themselves as best they could. He led the parade by jumping on his horse and galloping away at full speed, with the British in close pursuit. About sixty rods from the meeting house, he came to a steep flight of stone steps and, according to the legend that quickly sprang up, he guided his horse down the entire flight and escaped.

Rundel, who was close behind, tells us what really happened: "He rode down a flight of stone steps, the top of which were about sixty rods from the meeting house. He did not ride down more than fifteen or twenty of them (there being, I think, about one hundred of them in the whole). He then dismounted and led down the horse as fast as possible. I was at the bottom of the steps as soon as he was. He then mounted his horse, told me to make my escape in a swamp not far off, and he rode off."

What if he *didn't* ride the whole way? Putnam was a memorable character in the war and unquestionably a brave one. A modern historian, John Dann, characterizes him accurately as a man with "a ready wit, the appearance of hoary wisdom, and a remarkable presence." As for the incident of the stone steps, says Dann, "If it appeared more spectacular than that to those who watched him descend from the top, the general would have been the last person in the world to contradict the impression."

Rundel escaped that adventure but was later captured and suffered the horrors of the Sugar House Prison in New York before a second escape that would have been remarkable for anyone, let alone a teenage boy. He returned and served with Putnam until the general retired.

While all these minor alarms and excursions are going on in the North, Clinton doggedly pursues the strategy in the South that he began near the end of 1778. To counter it, Congress sends another of Washington's fat generals, Benjamin Lincoln, to take command. Lincoln may be overweight, but he's not lacking in determination or courage. Arriving in Charleston on December 19, 1778, he finds only 1,500 men able and willing to fight, so he has to round up more militia, and when he has a force of 3,500, he pushes toward Savannah, which he takes on January 3. Hearing that Colonel Archibald Campbell is marching toward Brier Creek, he sends General John Ashe after him with 1,500 troops.

It's a proper move, but it turns out to be a mistake because Colonel Mark Prevost, the younger brother of General Augustine Prevost, who had commanded at St. Augustine before he came up with his troops to help Campbell, is an astute strategist despite his youth. He circles Ashe's army and attacks it from the rear, while a smaller division assails the front. Before it's over, Ashe has lost nearly four hundred men killed, wounded, or captured, while the British loss is a negligible sixteen. Six hundred American militia escape and set off for home; another four hundred resist temptation and finally get back to Lincoln's main army.

Lincoln is discouraged by this setback, but he's not ready to give up. Prevost now moves against Charleston and on May 12, calls on it to surrender. These South Carolinians in the city have been through this before, and remembering how valiantly they resisted in 1776,

Lincoln feels certain they'll hold firm. Instead, they suggest to Prevost that the city remain neutral until the war is over, which the British commander rejects with scorn. Just the same, he thinks it wouldn't be a good idea to attack the city, believing erroneously that its defenses are much too strong for his three thousand troops to assault. His spies also tell him that Count Pulaski, the Polish volunteer (they're coming from all over Europe these days), has arrived in Charleston with cavalry and infantry in unknown numbers, while Lincoln and a larger force may be arriving from Savannah any day. So Prevost prudently withdraws and contents himself with constructing a strong bridgehead at Stono Ferry, on the mainland.

That's where Lincoln finds him, and in the battle that follows, the Americans lose three hundred more men, against the enemy's 130. This southern campaign is beginning to look dismal from the American point of view. Reinforced and much more optimistic now, Prevost goes back to Savannah but summer gets there before he does and both sides tacitly agree not to do anything drastic until fall, because the temperature is now a hundred degrees, with humidity to match, and no one wants to fight in this kind of weather.

At the moment, everything appears to be stalled. On the American side, North and South, the question is, "Are we going to get any more help—or, more accurately, any help at all—from the French?" Since D'Estaing gave the back of his hand to the Americans at Newport, refitted his ships in Boston, and sailed off for the West Indies before Franco-American relations fell apart again, he's been the principal figure in the capture of Grenada and St. Vincent by the French. But in September he reappears in American waters, off the Georgia coast, threatening the British with a large fleet and more than four thousand men.

D'Estaing pounces on whatever British vessels are in the vicinity and takes some happy surprises—a frigate, the *Experiment*, with a cask full of pay for the British troops aboard; besides another frigate, the *Ariel*, and two storeships. One brig eludes him and hastens up the coast to warn Clinton and his new admiral, Marriot Arbuthnot, who is rapidly proving himself to be a real clinker. As one historian describes him, Arbuthnot "appears in contemporary stories as a coarse, blustering bully, and in history as an example of the extremity to which the maladministration of Lord Sandwich had reduced the Navy."

While Clinton is deciding what to do about D'Estaing, the French admiral lays siege to Savannah, where Prevost sits with about three thousand defenders. D'Estaing calls on him to surrender, Prevost refuses. The admiral is not a man celebrated for his patience and he doesn't intend to sit out a siege. Instead, on October 9, he makes the wrong decision and orders an assault. At dawn, in a heavy mist that cuts the visibility close to zero, he coordinates his attack with the American troops on shore, but the whole operation quickly ends in another disaster.

One reason is that an American column loses its way in the swamp and, when it emerges, is cut down by heavy fire. A deserter has informed the British of D'Estaing's plan, enabling them to knock off the swamp-bound invaders; they then pour grapeshot and musket fire into the other column, led by D'Estaing himself. A few brave soldiers manage to get as far as the redoubt and plant the colors there before they're beaten back. The casualty figures are dismal: 837 on the allied side, 155 for the British. From D'Estaing's point of view, the outcome is even worse. He's been wounded twice himself, and the losses among the French troops he put ashore are three times higher than the Americans'. Count Pulaski is one of the casualties; he dies of his wounds.

That's quite enough for D'Estaing—again. Fighting in America isn't like fighting in the West Indies, apparently. He sails off for France, leaving Lincoln without support and compelling him to withdraw. When he hears about this affair, D'Estaing's fellow admiral, the Comte de Grasse, exclaims in a letter: "Great God! It would have been necessary to have seen it to believe it, and, in not saying the half, we would be thought to exaggerate and be partial." In other words, D'Estaing ought to have his military head examined.

This isn't the only fighting going on in the South, however, and although most Americans who aren't involved in it don't know what's occurring around them, today's historians have disclosed that guerrilla warfare in the back country of North and South Carolina was characterized by, as one of them puts it, "a vicious brutality matched in no other part of the country."

Special factors make this possible. For one thing, ethnic differences divide people. The British occupiers are brutal enough in their conduct toward civilians of both sides, but there's also a large and particularly vindictive Tory population in these places who carry on a deadly private war with their former neighbors.

One man's experience gives us at least the flavor of this violent sideshow. When he applied for his pension long after the war, William Gipson, of Monck's Corner, South Carolina, recalled his service in one of these small guerrilla bands, this one a company of patriots intent on sitting as judge, jury, and hangman in the case of any Loyalists they encountered.

Sometime during the winter of 1778–79, "having suffered much from the Tories," Gipson believed it was time to avenge the destruction of his home and property. He joined a small party of Whigs who had suffered similarly from what he called "the disaffected." This band rampaged through Guilford, Randolph, and Surrey counties during the spring, and on a summer day found itself in a house in Guilford County.

"Suddenly two armed men stood at the door," Gipson recalled. "They, seeing the party within, immediately wheeled, and Col. Moore [the leader of Gipson's band] knocked down one of the men, who proved to be the notorious Hugh McPherson, a Tory." The other man was soon captured and both were taken about fifteen miles away, where a summary court-martial was held.

Naturally, both men were condemned. McPherson was shot on the spot. The other man was sentenced to an ingenious kind of torture. He was placed with one foot on a sharp pin driven into a block of wood, then turned around until the pin ran through his foot. This grim device was occasionally used as a disciplinary practice in both the British and American armies, but the spike was ordinarily meant only to produce a mild torture, not to be driven through, as it was in this case, after which the man was turned loose. Gipson wasted no sympathy on him. He believed the prisoner to be a member of a Tory band that once gave his helpless mother a beating.

With so much happening on land, it's easy to overlook the continuous war that's been taking place on the water from the beginning, entirely aside from the major movements we've already seen. New Englanders are a maritime people and they've been resisting British sea power since the start of the war, as the enemy navy pursues its campaign of depredation up and down the coast, but mostly in Maine, Massachusetts, and Connecticut.

What really worries the British, however, is the privateering that these Yankee sailors carry on, for fun and profit. Nobody is safe from these fast, enterprising wolves of the ocean. They strike wherever they can, and the British are constantly losing supply ships and even vessels of war to them. It's guerrilla warfare on the water.

Life on one of these privateers is described by a Boston boy, Joshua Davis, who has shipped aboard the privateer *Jason*, twenty guns, commanded by Commodore John Manley. The *Jason* is surprised near the coast one late June day in 1779 by two British ships, which chase it toward the safety of Portsmouth. While he's escaping, the commodore observes a vicious squall coming up and immediately orders all hands to stand by to take in sail, but before they can do so, the wind strikes the ship a mighty blow that puts her on her beam-ends, meanwhile carrying away its three masts and bowsprit. The pursuing British ships, believing the weather gods have solved their problem, sail away.

The crew tries to repair the damage, finding a man drowned under a foretop sail as they work, and with the help of jury masts they limp into safe waters between the Isle of Shoals and Portsmouth. Manley intends to get his masts replaced, and goes ashore to obtain what he needs. This move produces a small mutiny involving Patrick Cruickshanks, the boatswain; Michael Wall, his mate; and John Graves, captain of the forecastle. They assert that this roadstead where they're anchored is so wild, they don't intend to endanger their lives to step any masts. They'll do it with pleasure, however, if Manley takes the ship into the harbor.

Coming aboard after a visit to Portsmouth, where he's arranged to get necessary supplies, the commodore sees no one working and wants to know why. The situation is explained to him, and Manley goes up in flames. "I'll harbor them!" he shouts, taking a cutlass out of a sentry's hand and running forward with it.

"Boatswain, why do you not go to work?" he shouts.

Patrick begins to explain, but Manley doesn't wait to hear him, striking him on the head with the cutlass so hard that, as Joshua Davis tells us, "his teeth were to be seen from the upper part of his jaw to the lower part of the chin." Manley then turns to Graves with the same question, gets the same answer, and strikes the forecastle captain on the head too, so severely that he has to be taken to the ship's hospital. Then it's Wall's turn, but the bosun's mate dodges the blow, and while Manley is lifting his cutlass for another, Wall pushes him against the stump of the foremast and runs aft, the commodore at his heels, forcing him to jump down the main hatchway between decks, "hurting himself very much."

Manley then tells the other crew members they'll get the same treatment if they don't go to work, and they fall to without further argument. The work on the masts is done in thirty-six hours and the *Jason* puts to sea again. It soon captures two British privateer brigs of sixteen and eighteen guns respectively, and brings them into Boston Harbor.

Manley's early career comes to an abrupt end, however, a little later, off Newfoundland, when a frigate overhauls the *Jason* and nearly destroys her, so that Manley has to call for quarter. He's sent to Mill Prison, near Plymouth, England, and will stay there for two years—the third time he's been captured and imprisoned. By the time he gets out, the war will be over.

Hostilities at sea go on by their own momentum year after year, involving major actions of all kinds, none of them decisive, and numerous small engagements, not to mention individual raids up and down the coast. Congress authorized its own Continental Navy early in the conflict, and eleven of the thirteen states floated their own little navies. Privateers could be licensed either by the states or by Congress, although not all of them bothered to apply. Freebooters operate for their own profit.

What the American effort at sea lacks is any kind of coordination. It's every captain for himself, and it isn't often that they combine to strike a single objective. They even compete in recruiting seamen. The vast theater of war includes not only the Atlantic, but Lake Champlain and the Mississippi, the Caribbean islands, and occasionally the British Isles.

This wild mixture of a navy has one major problem: it is hopelessly outgunned by the British. The privateers do quite well, though. Manned by 20,000 Americans, they take 2,000 prizes and 16,000 British prisoners during the war, besides the West Indian sugar and rum, English woolens and Irish linens, and supplies from England intended for British troops. These successes have a price, however, and sometimes it seems as though the Americans are shooting themselves in the foot, because privateering is so profitable that farmers, laborers, and even soldiers are drawn into it, consequently hurting both the army and the home front, not to mention the Continental Navy. What they accomplish may often be valuable, but it's unfortunately true that greed, not patriotism, makes the privateering business grow. Some captains are carried away by their greed, taking ships of our glorious French ally, and seizing a few belonging to American merchants. There's no other word for all this but profiteering, and it contributes to the inflation and speculation that are crippling the war effort. It will not end until after Yorktown, when the French withdraw and the privateers face a blockade by regular ships of the line. By then it won't matter.

At its peak, however, privateering is fun and games, and even produces its own heroes. One of them is Nathaniel Fanning, of Stonington, Connecticut. Born of sturdy Irish stock, Nathaniel and his seven younger brothers all go to sea. Two are captured and confined in the notorious *Jersey*, where one of them dies, but Nathaniel soon has his own command and raids out of French ports, preying on British convoys. The French offer him a commission and he becomes a naval hero.

Fanning has one piece of spectacular bad luck, however, aboard the brig *Angelica*, out of Boston in May 1778. He runs down what he mistakenly thinks is a merchantman, but it turns out to be a 28-gun frigate, the *Andromeda*, carrying a precious cargo—Howe, on his way home from Philadelphia via New York. The *Angelica* is no match for the frigate and is easily captured.

When the crew and its officers, including Fanning, are brought on board the *Andromeda*, Howe asks them a few questions and then puts the big one: will they join His Majesty's service? There's an emphatic "No!" and Howe loses his temper. Will he never be rid of these bloody stubborn Americans? "You're a set of rebels," he tells them, "and it's more than probable that you'll all be hanged when we get to Portsmouth." Meanwhile, they're stripped of their clothing and thrust down into the darkness of the hold, where they get no food for the next twenty hours, and after that only barely enough to stay alive. As for the *Angelica*, she's already on fire and blows up.

In the darkness of the hold, stark naked and almost suffocating in the heat, the captives plot to seize the ship; their leader is the *Angelica*'s surgeon. He's an enterprising fellow who has discovered that some of the *Andromeda*'s crew are unhappy enough with their lot to smuggle him some arms and cutlasses. Full of optimism, the plotters are about ready to pounce on the evening of June 3, when the hatches are suddenly closed down on them and shut tight. They don't know it, but a captain's clerk has learned of the plot at the last moment and warned Howe.

Now it's a question of survival. Will they die of the heat, or will it be starvation? Howe gives them just enough provisions to keep them alive, and only a half pint of water per man per day. It won't be death from thirst, though. They manage to tap the water casks on which they're lodged, and then find a loose board that enables them to tap a case of Madeira as well and get "decently drunk," as Fanning recalls later. They even find some casks holding food and tap them too, and by carefully concealing these leaks in the dike, they dine on dried fruit, washed down with wine, until they get to Portsmouth.

Brought up on deck and offered a little food, they seize it as though they're half-starved, but Howe and his officers look at them and can't believe what they see. "What, are none of them damned Yankees sick?" Howe wants to know. Someone answers, "Not one," and Howe fires a parting shot: "Damn them! There's nothing but thunder and lightning will kill them."

Or guns in enemy hands, as Fanning rediscovers after a short time in Forton Prison, near Portsmouth, when he's exchanged and hurries off to France to sign up with John Paul Jones as a midshipman on the *Bon Homme Richard*, which sails out of L'Orient on August 14, 1779, straight into the pages of the history books, and also into the territory of myth and legend.

John Paul Jones, born simply John Paul, who is about to become a hero, is a Scot who began his career at twelve as apprentice to a Whitehaven shipowner. He worked his way up through the ranks aboard slave ships, and became a first mate when he was only nineteen. He quickly became a captain when he brought a slave ship home safely after both the captain and first mate died of fever.

As a master, Jones exhibited a tyrannical streak almost at once, flogging a ship's carpenter for neglect of duty until he died. Charged with murder by the victim's father, he went to prison for a time but was subsequently cleared, although the facts remained the same. In the West Indies in 1773, he killed another man, the ringleader of a mutinous crew, and although it's said this unfortunate chap carelessly impaled himself on Jones's sword, the incident added to his reputation. Looking to avoid further trouble, Jones slipped away from Tobago, where the affair occurred, and sailed to America.

When the Revolution began, he was stony broke, living on the charity of friends. The war was a godsend; it offered steady employment. By this time he'd added Jones to his real name and was ready to start over, having taken up residence in Virginia and come to know the delegates to Congress from that state. Consequently, when the American navy was organized, he was commissioned on December 7, 1775, as senior first lieutenant on the *Alfred*, commanded by Dudley Saltonstall.

Given his own command, the *Providence*, in 1776, Jones began to score successes and acquire a better reputation in a country where nothing was known about his past. When Congress created the rank of navy captain later that year, he was eighteenth on the list to be one. That was because the Yankee captains ahead of him weren't overwhelmed by Jones's difficult personality. In a phrase, they didn't like him.

You can't hold back talent for long, however, and in 1777, Congress felt compelled to give him command of the sloop *Ranger*. Ordered to France, he sailed with this ship in April 1778, and with it he raided his old hometown, Whitehaven, tried (unsuccessfully) to kidnap the Earl of Selkirk as a hostage to get better treatment for American prisoners, captured a British sloop in a brilliant action off the Irish coast, and came back to Brest with several prizes and many prisoners. All this in twenty-eight days.

Now Jones has a reputation he can be happy with; he's a hero in France, and the government even consults him on the best way to fight the British navy. Late in the summer of 1779, they give him a small fleet of five naval vessels and two privateers. The flagship is the *Duras*, an old, refurbished East Indiaman, but since Ben Franklin's *Poor Richard's Almanac* is currently enjoying a vogue in Paris, Jones whimsically renames her the *Bon Homme Richard*.

With this fleet, he returns to his earlier hunting grounds off the coast of England, sailing first for Scarborough, a seaport town in Yorkshire. Nothing there. He's about to leave when he sights two sloops-of-war, convoying a fleet. He gives chase, and two of the fleet strike their colors. But then an embarrassment of riches occurs when another fleet of thirty-seven vessels appears, heading for Scarborough. Surveying them through his glass, Jones exclaims to his officers, "That's the very fleet I've been so long cruising for."

In the subsequent battle, Jones's ships scatter away in pursuit of fleeing enemy ships, leaving him alone in the ocean with his forty-gun *Bon Homme Richard* facing the British ship *Serapis*, fifty guns. That isn't the only disadvantage. The *Richard*'s crew is very young, some no older than seventeen, and although the ship carries 380 men, about 300 of whom are Americans, the rest are an untested salmagundi of English, French, Scots, Irish, Portuguese, and Maltese seamen. The *Serapis* crew numbers 305, all British except for 15 East Indians, all under Captain Pearson, an experienced commander.

At 8:15 P.M., the historic battle between these two ships begins, in clear weather and under a rising moon. The sea is calm. Drawing first blood, the *Serapis* knocks out three of the *Richard*'s starboard lower-deck guns, killing most of the men manning them. Because it's a two-decker, the *Serapis* has an advantage, enabling it to rake the *Richard* fore and aft with broadsides, while its crew pours in musket fire. Several of its eighteen-pounders sail right through the American ship, raising terrible havoc. "Our men fell in all parts of the ship by scores," one observer recalls. "At this point, if it had lasted a half hour longer, all the officers and men would have died."

Since it's clearly suicidal, and now impossible, to trade broadsides with the *Serapis*, Jones calls for the grappling hooks. There's no other hope but to board her and duke it out hand to hand. This proves to be more difficult than it sounds. Time after time, the sailing master, whose name is Stacy, tries and fails to get the hooks in. It's part of Jones's eccentric character that in the midst of this desperate effort, he chews out Stacy for swearing. "Mr. Stacy," he says, "it's no time for swearing now, you may by the next moment be in eternity, but let us do our duty." The hooks are finally secured.

The battle has now gone on for forty minutes, during which the *Richard* has been doing its share of damage, trying not only to kill the enemy but to disable the ship by firing at its tops with everything at hand—muskets, blunderbusses, cowhorns, swivels, even pistols.

While the *Richard*'s crew is boarding the *Serapis*, the British try to return the compliment but they're driven back, with losses, followed by the Americans, who also suffer casualties. So it goes for a while, each side trying to board and not really succeeding. Having silenced the sailors stationed in the tops of the *Serapis*, Jones's men now turn their fire on the enemy's decks and sweep them absolutely clean of humanity in twenty-five minutes, also setting the light sails on fire.

Three hours have gone by and there's such confusion on both sides that rumors spread easily. Some of the crew hear that Jones and all his officers have been killed, and that the ship's sinking with four or five feet of water in the hold. A delegation consisting of a gunner, a carpenter, and the master-at-arms is sent up to the quarterdeck, shouting as they come, "Quarters! Quarters! For God's sake, quarters! Our ship is sinking!" They even begin to haul down the flag.

This is news to Jones and Fanning. They know nothing of the kind is happening. Fanning, stationed in the top, even thinks it's the men of the *Serapis* who are crying for quarter. But Jones, on the forecastle, shouts: "What damned rascals are these? Shoot them—kill them!" The carpenter and the master hear him and escape below, but Jones catches the gunner, throwing both his pistols at the man. One strikes him on the head, fracturing his skull, and felling him at the foot of the gangway ladder.

The *Richard* may not be sinking, but both ships are now on fire, and the crews have to leave off fighting and combat the flames with tubs of water. They shed coats and jackets and try to smother the blaze. Momentarily, firing stops. In the comparative silence, the British, having heard the calls for quarter but not Jones's reply, want to know whether the *Richard* has struck, and if so, why don't they pull down their colors?

Jones himself answers them: "Ay, ay, we'll do that when we can fight no longer but we shall see yours come down first, for you must know that Yankees don't haul down their colors until they're fairly beaten."

After that defiance, fighting breaks out all over again, more furiously than ever. The fires keep burning, and the crews have to stop once more and fight the flames. When combat resumes, there isn't much left to fight with—only a few cannon, hand grenades, stinkpots, and ultimately lances and boarding pikes. When the guns are gone, they shoot at each other through the postholes with small arms.

It seems impossible that this confusion could be any worse, but just before midnight it does when the *Richard*'s sister ship, the *Alliance* (the same one that brought Lafayette home), appears and joins in. The moon is now covered by a dark cloud, visibility is virtually zero, and the *Alliance* seems to be blazing away indiscriminately at both ships. Some of the officers on the *Richard* take her for an English man-of-war. Others recognize her, however, and try to hail her, signaling that she's firing at the wrong ship, but her officers neither see nor hear. The *Serapis* is ready to strike at this point, but when they see the Americans being killed by their own comrades, they delay giving up. Somehow the *Richard's* crew manages to hoist three lanterns in a horizontal line, the recognition signal, after which the friendly fire stops, and the end is near.

Actually, the end comes a little after midnight, at twelve thirty-five, in an unexpected way when one of the *Richard's* men, having boarded the *Serapis* and climbed up to her maintop, throws down a hand grenade on the crew huddled between her gun decks. It strikes a hatchway, bounds off, and falls between decks into a pile of loose powder, the remains of a defunct cannon emplacement. An explosion rocks the ship, killing twenty men, and now there's no more doubt. The *Serapis* has to call for quarter.

Jones is willing enough, but nothing happens. What's going on? It's just another strange twist in a strange battle. The captain gives the order to strike colors but the sailors fear they'll be picked off by the American riflemen while they're trying to do it, under the mistaken impression that all these fellows are sharpshooters. Disgusted, Captain Pearson himself climbs up to the quarterdeck and hauls down the flag—the same one he nailed there before the battle, swearing that the infamous pirate Jones would never compel him to strike it.

The infamous pirate now sends over a party of men to take possession of the British ship, but several of its crew don't know the colors have been struck and—blunder upon blunder—kill several of the boarding party. After more than four hours of fighting, it's no wonder they don't know friend from foe.

Pearson comes on board the *Richard* to give up his sword, saying he's reluctant to give it to "a man who may be said to fight with a halter around his neck." Jones, however, is in a mood to be magnanimous, now that hostilities are over and he's won, if you can call it that.

"Sir," he says to Pearson, "you have fought like a hero, and I make no doubt your sovereign will reward you in a most ample manner for it."

Pearson wants to know what country his crew comes from, and Jones says they're Americans. Now it's Pearson's turn to be magnanimous. "Very well," he says, "it's been 'diamond cut diamond' with us," and adds that he considers the Americans actually as brave as his own men. With that, they shake hands and the infamous pirate takes the British scum down to his cabin and opens a bottle of Madeira for a fraternal drink between captains, while both ships continue to burn in places, and the cries of the wounded and dying fill the air.

You could say that Jones won the battle, but the fact is that both ships are wrecks. All three of the *Serapis*'s masts have fallen overboard. On the *Richard*, the pumps are trying to keep her from sinking, and the fires aren't out yet. There are holes in the ship so far under the waterline that they can't be fixed here. Moreover, the combination of rotten wood, pitch, tar, and oakum makes the stubborn fire an increasing menace, since throwing water on it only makes it worse, so it isn't long before the *Richard* has to hang out a distress signal, since it's clear that the ship is going to burn down to the water and sink if it hasn't sunk before then.

The *Alliance*, which has contributed to part of this damage, and two other vessels send over their boats, and the ship's powder is hustled into them before it explodes. During this tense transfer, no one is permitted to leave the ship. Captain's order. The English officers are near panic when the fire on the *Serapis* moves toward its powder room, so Jones invites them to help move the powder, assuring them he won't abandon ship until it's gone.

Eventually everything gets sorted out. Jones and the English officers go aboard the *Serapis*, now free of the *Richard* but in imminent danger of sinking. Wounded men and prisoners are moved to other ships in the squadron, whose crews come aboard the *Serapis* and man the pumps until carpenters can patch up the holes, a job that takes four hours.

But wait—the battle isn't over yet, apparently. One more incredible turn of events. The English prisoners aboard the *Richard*, about fifty of them, have been let go when the battle seemed to be over, but no one has paid much attention to them and they suddenly decide to seize the now evacuated ship, intending to run her ashore. They manage to start her toward land, staggering like the proverbial drunken sailor, but a few Americans come back on board before the prisoners can get away, and although they're badly outnumbered, they overpower the prisoners, killing a couple, wounding others, and driving about thirteen overboard. These men take one of the small boats beside the ship and escape.

Fanning stands on the deck of the *Richard* and later describes what's left of it. Between decks, he writes, "the bloody scene was enough to appall the stoutest heart. Dead lying in heaps, wounded groaning and dying . . . entrails of the dead scattered around, blood everywhere. The *Serapis* and its squadron had been convoying a fleet from the Baltic to Scarborough, about thirty ships, but our squadron took none of them, although they were in sight during the battle, and were seen the morning after near land. No orders to take them. Everyone was trying to save the *Serapis*. If the captain of the *Alliance* had not disobeyed orders before, we could have taken them all."

Fanning takes a party down into the gunroom to remove the officers' trunks, but there's not a piece of them left any larger than a dollar. All the clothing is ruined. Large holes gape in the side. "I think this battle," Fanning concludes, "may be ranked with propriety the most bloody, the hardest fought, and the greatest scene of carnage on both sides ever fought between two ships of war of any nation under heaven." Amen.

Now that the battle's over, Fanning is ready to part company with Jones as soon as possible. Along with other officers and men, he's fed up with the captain's high-handed and arrogant conduct. Back in France, Fanning sails as second in command on a French privateer and becomes a kind of junior grade John Paul Jones, raiding here and there until he's captured yet again by the British and exchanged once more. He keeps on sallying out of French ports until the war is over, after which he will write his memoirs and have some extremely candid things to say about Jones and his tyrannies, which make no impression on the public's regard for the captain as a popular idol, about to take his place in the American mythology.

15

✝   ✝   ✝

Two Roads to Yorktown: The Road from the North

After all the backing and filling of 1779, it's a relief to go into quarters for the winter of 1779–80. After inspecting the site himself, Washington takes his army into a place called Jockey Hollow, three miles south of Morristown. His headquarters is the house of Mrs. Theodosia Ford, recently widowed, where he arrives on a stormy day that forecasts what will be a hard winter. The troops arrive during the first week of December, just in time to fortify themselves against the raging storms that follow one after another, howling through the forest.

As is their custom, many of the men are half-naked but they're out there chopping down oak, walnut, and chestnut trees to make their huts, suffering "much without shoes and stockings, and working half-leg deep in snow." They persevere and in less than two months they create a little community of log houses.

No one can believe this winter. The Hudson is solid ice from New York to Powles Hook, sleighs carry supplies across New York Harbor to Staten Island, and even a cavalry troop takes that passage.

In January, Sullivan leads what's intended to be a surprise party against the British outpost on Staten Island, but someone tips off the redcoats and it's Sullivan who's surprised. His troops have to fall back and spend the night on a bleak hill, swept by a bitter northwest wind, with no shelter and no fuel except rotten fence rails dug up from nearly three feet of snow. Joe Martin is there and he swears the weather "was cold enough to cut a man in two." Sullivan tries to retreat next morning, but the British pursue him and take several prisoners. When he finally gets to safety, some of his men have frozen toes, fingers, ears, and they're also half-starved.

Before the participants in this expedition can recover, heavy snow begins to fall and comes down for nearly four days, immobilizing everything. Martin's report of this ordeal sounds a lot like Arnold's march to Quebec: "We were absolutely, literally starved. I do solemnly declare that I did not put a single morsel of victuals into my mouth for four days and as many nights, except a little black birch bark which I gnawed off a stick of wood, if that can be called victuals. I saw several of the men roast their old shoes and eat them, and I was afterwards informed by one of the officers' waiters that some of the officers killed and ate a favorite little dog that belonged to one of them. The fourth day, just at dark, we obtained a full pound of lean fresh beef and a gill of wheat for each man. . . . All the bread we had was Indian meal."

Snowed in, Washington has plenty of time to brood and plan. He gets the belated news of the Massachusetts militia's fiasco at Penobscot, which he never ordered, and is distressed to hear that Paul Revere has been accused of cowardice and disobedience in the affair, and has lost his commission. The charges turn out to be false, but it will be three years before Paul can get the court-martial convened that will exonerate him.

The same January snowstorm that nearly devastated Sullivan's expedition causes plenty of damage at Morristown. As Dr. James Thatcher records it: "No man could endure its violence many minutes without danger of his life. Several marquees were torn asunder and blown down over the officers' heads in the night, and some of the soldiers were actually covered while in their tents and buried like sheep under the snow. We are greatly favored having a supply of straw for bedding. Over this we spread our blankets and with our clothes and large fires at our feet, while four or five are crowded together, preserve ourselves from freezing. But the sufferings of the poor soldiers can scarcely be described. . . . At night they have a bed of straw on the ground and a single blanket to each man. They are badly clad and some are destitute of shoes."

Before long the snow is six feet deep, and it's nearly impossible to haul fresh supplies into camp. The men get two pounds of meat per man for ten days, but then there begin to be periods of six to eight days without meat or bread. With hunger and the bitter cold, the men can scarcely carry out what duties are required. In these extreme conditions, Washington nevertheless insists on discipline—no fighting, stealing, plundering, or deserting without severe consequences. Some deserters are shot, and one has to run his own brigade's gauntlet, after which he's sentenced to prison for a month on bread and water, which is more than his comrades outside are getting. Sentences of a hundred lashes on the bare back are common, particularly hard to endure when the whipping is done in a freezing wind.

Since the whips are made out of several small, knotted cords, they cut right through the skin at every stroke. Some victims never make an outcry, others chew on a lead bullet between their teeth to prevent doing so. The worst cases get their lashes spread out over several days, just as it was back there in Cambridge, so that the skin becomes inflamed and makes the punishment even more terrible, but as it's been from the beginning, nothing seems to deter the most desperate from stealing, even from each other, and plundering the country people when they get a chance. A few robbers are hanged.

Washington imposes all this with a heavy heart because he understands that men living in such desperate conditions, eating "every kind of horse food but hay," he says, can hardly be blamed for their actions. Just the same, the alternative is anarchy. He does everything he can to get supplies from civilians and the New Jersey civil authorities, and for once they respond generously, so generously, it can be seen later, that without their help the army would have melted away and the war would have been lost.

The storms continue for two months, and then there's a hint of spring in the air. It's possible for the officers to visit friends and kinfolks nearby, even to dance again. They try to do something for the other ranks, especially on days of public celebration, when there's nothing to celebrate. One officer manages to get, somehow, a hogshead of rum for his men on St. Patrick's Day. All told, however, the sufferings of both men and officers at Morristown are worse than they were at Valley Forge. And it seems as though this winter will never end. Early in March, there are still eight inches of snow on the ground.

One victim of the winter is a foreigner, a Spanish official who comes for a visit with Washington, catches pneumonia, and dies.

They bury him in full dress, replete with quantities of diamonds—on his shoe and knee buckles, on his rings. Washington has to have his grave guarded so the soldiers won't "dig for hidden treasure," as he remarks wryly.

What Washington is waiting for these dreary months is not so much the end of winter as some word from Lafayette, preferably his reappearance with definite news of what the French are going to do for the cause, if anything. He knows it will have to be substantial enough to bring an early victory before his tatterdemalion army falls apart.

So what has our young hero been doing since he left Boston in seeming disillusionment at the end of 1778? Well, for a dilettante who's supposed to have had his fill of America, he's been doing yeoman work for the cause in Paris. He argues the case for America with anyone he can get to listen. The men he has to convince are Vergennes, the Foreign Minister, and Maurepas, the Finance Minister. Both men are utterly distracted during 1779 while Lafayette is working on them. Vergennes, who may be the least anti-British Foreign Minister the country has ever had, is dithering about whether it would be advisable, or even safe, to launch a campaign against Britain. Until he decides that, he isn't going to do anything about America. As for Maurepas, he's going out of his mind trying to hold the French economy together in the face of Louis XVI's monumental extravagance. Both these gentlemen are aware they're sitting on a powder keg of popular discontent.

By midsummer of 1779, Vergennes, at least, has begun to see the light. He's convinced now that England is invulnerable because of her naval shield, so the English invasion is off—the one Lafayette had vowed he wouldn't miss for anything. Having lost a foothold in India and getting not much more than a draw with England for control of the West Indies, Vergennes has come around to believing that, if the French can get any leverage at all against the English, it will have to be in America, where large elements of the British army and navy are tied up.

Lafayette, who has worked assiduously on Vergennes to convince him that this is indeed the case, strikes while the political iron is hot. In July, he presents Vergennes with a plan to help America. It's going to make Maurepas faint when he sees how much it will cost, but in twenty-six pages of closely argued prose, Lafayette lays out a plan of campaign that can't help but give France a big strategic and political boost—if it works. He holds out a carrot to Maurepas. Success also means that France will be first in line for some lucrative commerce.

Vergennes isn't a man to do things in a hurry. Even with Lafayette constantly nudging him until he's a nuisance, the minister doesn't make up his mind until February 1780, and that's about the time he succeeds in convincing Maurepas. When he lays the plan before Louis for final approval, Vergennes and the King decide that it will be best to cover the royal posterior in case of disaster, so the orders are that, if things go wrong in America after the French get there, and it looks as though the expeditionary force might be caught up in one of those famous American retreats, the instructions are to get everybody out of the country as quickly as possible and regroup in the safety of Santo Domingo.

There's still a long way to go before this relief expedition can get under way. A commander has to be appointed, the job Lafayette would give his eyeteeth or a whole set of molars to have. Vergennes, however, isn't going to trust the honor of France to a twenty-two-year-old boy who may be a major general in America but is still a reserve captain in France. Instead, he gives the nod to Jean-Baptiste Donatien de Vimeur, the Comte de Rochambeau, an experienced general of fifty-five, who until now has believed his next command would be the campaign against England.

Rochambeau is a strange man, quiet, particularly now when he's just lost his father, whose long life was shadowed by a congenital deformity. He doesn't speak English and knows nothing of life in America. His military experience is extensive, but it's all been in Central Europe. He's cautious, too, and he also doesn't quite trust this pipsqueak Lafayette, who thinks he's going to be the liaison between the general and Washington. Rochambeau quietly decides that this task will be given to the Chevalier de Chastellux, who's a real major general and knows what war is about.

Why has Vergennes made this somewhat unlikely choice? For one thing, Rochambeau is his own man, not allied with any of the court cliques and without partisans. News of his appointment reaches him in Paris, where he's been waiting to be sent against England. America instead? He could refuse politely and spend the remainder of his days in the family château, but he's not ready to leave the scene just yet.

Rochambeau has had a busy life. As Manceron describes him, "His style is slightly seventeenth-century, both at war and with his pen, which he prides himself on using well, albeit heavily, as he does all things. One of the army's quiet men. He ought to be able to get along with Washington and yet not let himself be pushed around. His ancestors on his father's side go back to the Crusades, and his mother's family is from the solid landowning bourgeoisie. (Michel Begon, an uncle on that side, colonizes Martinique and brings back the begonia.) He had one elder brother and was dutifully preparing to enter the Church, like any decently disciplined younger son, when the other's death shifted him into the army. It was a close shave. . . ." In the army, he's a veteran of the German wars; he knows his job.

As for Lafayette, he's disappointed (again) not to get what he desires, but by this time he's homesick for America, where they treat him like a general. He's so enthusiastic to be moving at last that he takes his own money, which he can't afford, and equips a division himself.

On March 18, Lafayette sails for America on the frigate *Hermione*, an armed three-master, but has to turn back briefly because of bad weather. After an otherwise uneventful voyage, he arrives in Boston on April 28, where he gets the kind of reception he has never enjoyed in France. "I was welcomed with cannon salutes and ringing of every bell," he writes home, "with music marching before me and the hurrahs of all the people around. Then I was conducted to the house which the Council and representatives' assembly of Boston had prepared for me. There were delegations of these bodies to welcome me. I asked permission to present my respects to the two chambers, which were meeting for that purpose, and I tried to resurrect my English during the hour I remained there. In the evening, the people gathered outside my door and made a great bonfire with much cheering, which went on until past midnight."

Buoyed up to no end by this adulation, he departs for the Morristown headquarters on May 1, and nine days later he arrives. Manceron describes his second triumphal entry: "Shouts of recognition run along the chain of sentries as the young man, slender under the plump curls of his powdered hair, dressed in his blue, white, and gold general's uniform, gracefully salutes these last-ditch soldiers. There they stand, hatchet-faced in their grayish uniforms, each with a sort of boiled leather helmet on his head, armed any-old-how with espontoons (a sort of half-pike) and assorted guns. The irreducible nucleus of the New World. No money, almost no ammunition, honor to spare, and, here at least, decent discipline."

Well, yes and no. Lafayette doesn't know it yet, but he's arrived in the middle of a near mutiny. Even the officers have voluntarily put themselves on bread and water because supplies are so low, but that doesn't pacify men so desperate for food that mass desertions seem imminent. The men are "growling like soreheaded dogs," as Joe Martin puts it, and they're insolent to the officers and disobey orders. A few days after Lafayette's arrival, an adjutant calls a soldier a "mutinous rascal," and the soldier slams down his musket, calling out, "Who will parade with me?" meaning who would defy authority and possibly desert. An entire regiment falls in with him, and they're joined by another. The original mutineer tries to get two more to join him but, in order to avoid a court-martial, he gives some signals to the drummers so that, as his rattling commands unfold, the two regiments fall in and march to join the others, fife and drums playing.

Alarmed officers come running. They order the remaining regiments to parade without their arms, and set up a guard between them and their huts so they can't get their muskets. This precipitates a scuffle in which Colonel Return Jonathan Meigs, of the 6th, suffers a severe bayonet wound in his side, possibly unintentional because darkness has fallen. The rebels pull back, the officers follow them. They remove a man from the ranks, thinking to make an example of him, but his comrades level their bayonets and it seems advisable to let him go. Then the officers try persuasion. A lieutenant colonel of the 4th thinks he's been successful at this until he orders the men to shoulder arms, which they refuse to do, and he "[falls] into a violent passion." He gives up and walks off; other officers follow him.

The Pennsylvania Line nearby is called up and told they're about to embark on a secret mission, but when they're ordered to surround the rebels, not knowing what's occurring, they hear about the mutiny and decide to join it. They obey an order to go back to quarters, however. After this the mutineers disperse, but they lie on their arms all night, "venting our spleen at our country and government," as one says, "then at our officers, and then at ourselves for our imbecility in staying there and starving . . . for an ungrateful people who did not care what became of us. . . ." A day later, provisions appear, the revolt dies down, a few men are arrested, but Washington pardons all except the most recalcitrant.

In such circumstances, it's no wonder that Washington greets Lafayette with overwhelming joy and can't wait to hear the news he brings from Paris. He gives Lafayette a fatherly embrace, and they immediately ride off together over snowy fields, the only way they can be sure of having a private conversation.

Lafayette is in a euphoric mood. He babbles on about his plan to recapture New York, take Canada simultaneously, seize Charleston, and before they know it, they'll be signing a peace treaty. When he gets down to the figures, however, Washington is completely dismayed. Rochambeau is coming, Lafayette says, with six thousand men and some warships. The commander was expecting three times as many men and a mighty French fleet to back them up. He says gloomily in a letter written after the meeting: "It will be impossible for us to undertake the intended cooperation with any reasonable prospect of success. Unless the States [General] should take extraordinary and effectual efforts now, the succor designed for our benefit will prove a serious misfortune."

He doesn't know the half of it, and neither does Lafayette. After he sailed, Rochambeau ran into considerable difficulty about getting his expedition together, so that many people believed it would never leave at all. The general was promised six thousand men, just as Lafayette told Washington, but in the end he had to be satisfied with a little less than five thousand. Not knowing about the delay, Lafayette has told Washington the expedition should be about halfway across, when in fact it never sailed until the day after the young advance man reached Boston.

However, facts are facts and there's nothing Washington can do but persevere. To that end, he gathers his strategists around him to see what's possible. Among them is Arnold, who's come up from Philadelphia; he takes careful notes. First question, what are the numbers? The officers think the British must have about thirteen thousand men in the North, and another twelve thousand in the South. We have a probable seven thousand—probable because no one knows how many of them are either fit or willing to fight. We'll just have to wait and see how many Rochambeau actually brings with him. Meanwhile, Lafayette, who by this time has grasped the seriousness of the situation, goes on a kind of personal crusade to revive America's confidence in itself, and to do whatever else he can. Up and down the coast from Philadelphia to Newport he goes, making inspirational speeches, putting the arm on governors and legislatures in an effort to squeeze money from them and, while he's at it, doing a lot of the detail work in preparation for Rochambeau's arrival.

Where is this French general? everyone wants to know. Not being aware of his late start, they're looking for him by the end of May, but there's no sign of him then. Maybe he's been shipwrecked. Or maybe he was blown off course and landed somewhere in the South, where he would probably fall into the hands of the British. An anxious June goes by with no answers, and then on July 19 the French sails appear at last off Newport. No one is happier than Rochambeau. He's carrying an army suffering from confinement and short rations, and he's in a state of anxiety over the whereabouts of the British fleet. For all he knows, they could be patrolling the coast.

They're not, however, and the ships sail into Newport Harbor, where the savior of America disembarks—into the empty streets of the town. Where is everybody? He's come to rescue the Americans but they're not here to welcome him. No one on the streets, shutters closed on the houses. In a way, it's Lafayette's fault. He hasn't told the inhabitants they are about to be saved, so they regard this foreign fleet as an invasion, possibly dangerous to property and female virginity. Consequently the only place Rochambeau can find to lay his head that night is the town's worst tavern. He's ready to believe they must all be Tories here.

Next day everything straightens out. As an old soldier, Rochambeau understands the Newporters' anxieties and hastens to reassure them that he'll hang the first soldier who gets out of line. This happy thought cheers up everyone, and when the general exhibits the charm that has carried him through a good many Parisian drawing rooms, the inhabitants melt. The shutters fly open, the girls come out to look at the soldiers who'll be hanged if they touch them, and Newport breathes again.

There are those who think Rochambeau has brought too many foreign troops with him, and more knowledgeable ones who are afraid they're too few, and to them Rochambeau offers the bland reassurance that this is only the vanguard. The thaw continues. People begin to cluster in little groups outside the meeting house, tavernkeepers bring out their best wine to toast the alliance. As night falls, the church bells start to toll, which is disconcerting to the French soldiers, who have never heard a Protestant bell in operation. To them it's the Catholic death knell.

That night the Whigs give Rochambeau and his officers a reception while fireworks explode, bonfires light up the squares, and skyrockets sail off into the night sky. Next day the troops disembark and make their camp outside of town. It's all very orderly, except that two thousand or so men suffering from scurvy, dysentery, or both are thrown on the mercies of the Newport hospital, which can't even begin to contain them. The least badly off cases have to be sheltered under canvas in the open street.

Peace doesn't last long. Rochambeau has no more than got all his troops ashore than his worst fears are suddenly realized. Twenty-one British ships appear offshore, and it's clear that what they're about to do is bottle him up in Newport. A few days later, Lafayette arrives and now *everyone* is unhappy: Rochambeau because he thinks the worst has happened, Lafayette because he finds out that, instead of 6,000 troops, Rochambeau has brought him fewer than 4,000 ready and willing.

Lafayette can scarcely believe it, but Rochambeau is in such an anguished state of mind that he's issuing an appeal for help to the people he came to save. That makes Lafayette even glummer than the general. He sees his grand design collapsing around his ears, and what is he going to tell Washington? He tells him the truth, and the commander responds with a call for local militia to be raised at once, and says he's taking his army north to Peekskill in case it's needed.

While it's easy to look askance at such an old hand as Rochambeau going into a panic, he has plenty of reason. He learns that Admiral Thomas Graves's fleet carries six thousand men, and if he can put them ashore, it's going to be Molly-bar-the-door for the French army, not to mention what will happen to the Americans. Rochambeau is also annoyed because he expected Washington to be there to meet him, not this *arriviste* Lafayette, who's so impulsive and quite possibly more American than he is French at this point. It doesn't help that Lafayette's first words of advice are to attack New York immediately. Who does this kid think he is? The only thing Rochambeau believes he himself can do is dig in and wait for an attack, certain that the first blow will probably be the last.

Lafayette watches, nearly in tears, as the French frantically reinforce the defenses built by the British when they had the place, and mount batteries on the headlands. In the summer heat and dust, they're using the butts of their guns to dig at the earth because they don't have shovels. If the attack comes within the next few days, there are only 3,600 men able to man these defenses.

Fortunately, the attack never comes. Rochambeau needn't have worried; the British are experts at blowing their chances to win this war. Clinton is in command of the troops in the British fleet and, on the brink of victory, he chokes up. From the water it looks to him as though the French have twice the force they actually possess, and he orders the fleet to sail back to New York. Graves and Admiral Arbuthnot, who are in command of the enlarged fleet, are furious at this chickenhearted retreat. But Clinton has also learned that Washington has moved his army up to Peekskill and that revives his perennial fear of an attack on New York, which he can't bear to think about even when he's there, where the living's been easy. "It's not the actual battle that scares them," Manceron observes, "it's the thought of attacking. Conservatism, like creeping obesity, has mounted into the very top loft of the armies, and is positively stifling this war."

After the British sail away, everyone is still unhappy. Clinton and his officers are quarreling among themselves, Rochambeau is mad at Washington for not immediately rushing to his aid with large forces he doesn't have, and not even paying him a personal visit of welcome. The French commander feels he's been humiliated.

It's damage control time again, and once more it's Lafayette's job to mend the alliance fences. He does so with more tact than his enemies would have given him credit for, and as a result, Washington proposes on September 20 that he and Rochambeau meet in a neutral corner, Hartford, to compose their differences and discuss strategy. He'll bring Lafayette with him, as well as Knox and some engineers. Rochambeau's entourage will include Admiral Charles Louis d'Arsac, Chevalier de Ternay, commander of the blockaded French fleet; the indispensable Mathieu Dumas, with his knowledge of fortifications and command of English; and Count Axel Fersen, the Swedish friend of Marie Antoinette, who's coming along to America for the exhilarating ride.

Traveling up to Hartford is a more or less routine excursion for the Americans, although Washington frequently expresses his low opinion of Connecticut roads, but for the French it's a penetration of the mysterious American interior, and it doesn't go well. Their coach suffers a broken axle on the way, leaving six dignitaries lost in the wilderness. Fersen and another man, the only ones on horseback, reconnoiter and find a blacksmith who comes to the door of his house. They offer him money to come and fix their carriage, but he says, "I'm sick abed with the fever. You won't make me get up this night, not if you fill my hat with guineas and give it to me."

Rochambeau and De Ternay appear on the scene to see what they can do. As Dumas interprets, the general explains who these wandering Frenchmen are, and why it's so vitally important for them to get to Hartford. The conference will fail if they don't, he says. The blacksmith agrees. "You're no liars," he says, "I can see that from your faces. It's been announced in the Hartford paper that Washington is coming. They've even got out the lanterns. Is it a public service you're wanting of me? Then why the devil are your men trying to give me gold? Smith's word, you'll have your coach by six tomorrow morning." This first contact with the peculiar American character so impresses Rochambeau that he sets it all down carefully in his memoirs.

The French have to sleep in their coach that night, but the blacksmith is as good as his word, and next morning they're ready to go on again. When they arrive in Hartford, the Americans are already there, and the two sides sit down for a first greeting, in an inn at a table hewn from an oak trunk, on which have been laid cakes, punch bowls, and jugs of cider. No wine? What kind of country is this? But the September sun is so bright and cheerful, and the company proves to be so agreeable, that no one really minds.

Everyone is charmed by everyone else. Fersen is eloquent about his meeting with Washington when he writes: "M. de Rochambeau sent me ahead to announce his arrival, and I had time to observe that illustrious, not to say unique, man of our century. His comely and majestic face, at the same time mild and dignified, perfectly matches his moral qualities. He has the air of a hero. He is very cold, speaks little, but is courteous and proper. His physiognomy is marked by sadness that does not ill become him, and indeed renders him all the more interesting. . . . In addition he had an escort of twenty-two dragoons, which was necessary, for he was riding through enemy country. . . .

"The repast was in the English fashion, consisting of eight or ten large dishes of butcher's meat and poultry, with vegetables of several sorts, followed by a second course of pastry, comprised under the denomination of pies and puddings. After this the cloth was taken off, and apples and a great quantity of nuts were served, which General Washington usually continues eating for two hours, toasting and conversing all the time. These nuts are small and dry, and have so hard a shell [they're hickory nuts] that they can only be broken by the hammer [Washington does it with his false teeth]; they are served half-open, and the company are never done picking and eating them. . . . There was more solemnity in the toasts at dinner; there were several ceremonious ones (to the King, Queen, Princes, Congress, etc.), others were suggested by the general. . . . After supper the guests are generally desired to give a *sentiment*; that is to say, a lady to whom they are attached by some sentiment, either of love or friendship, or perhaps from preference only."

When the conferees get down to business, they find themselves in perfect agreement. For the moment, they maintain, it's vitally necessary to do nothing. Any kind of offensive operation would be suicidal in the present condition of the two armies. It's better to wait until next spring, and if they survive the winter without any further disasters, that will be a much better time to fight. They also agree that both sides should try to get as much as they can in the way of supplies and money from their respective governments. Washington doesn't beat around the bush. He tells Rochambeau that it's absolutely essential for France to send more ships, more men, and more money if the war is to be won. Rochambeau promises to see what he can do.

They break up with great cordiality, and the French start off for Newport. On the way, unbelievably, the same axle breaks in the same place, near the home of the same blacksmith. Was there a warranty on this repair job? They find the smith and he's still shaking a little with fever but this time he's glad to see them. He gets out of bed again and goes to work. While he's doing it, he wants to know what they thought of Washington. The French sing a chorus of praise. Then he asks, "Was he pleased with *you*?" In his memoirs, Rochambeau writes: "His patriotism was satisfied, and he kept his word to us. I do not claim to give it out that every American is like this good wheelwright, but all the farmers in the interior, and nearly all the landowners of Connecticut, have such a public spirit that many another might take it as a model."

When he penned this, Rochambeau was doubtless thinking about the general character of the French peasant, but Washington could wish that the "landowners" in Connecticut and elsewhere were such models of civic virtue as the French general thinks they are. In fact, he's had a bad summer at Peekskill. Although the army is in a little better condition than it was in winter quarters, its situation is still just short of desperate.

A soldier named Sam Cogswell, returning to camp in July after a furlough at home in Massachusetts, reports to his father: "The most of the army I found destitute of tents and encamped in a wood with no other security from the inclemency of the weather than the boughs of trees, or now and then a bark hut. The evening after my arrival in camp a rain began which continued almost two days, the most of which time I was wet to my skin, as were all those with me.

"I find all the gentlemen, and indeed all the Lords of the Regiment to which I belong, very destitute of almost every inconvenience. . . . Besides being very ragged and very dirty (which, by the way, they were unable to prevent for want of a change of clothes) they were supplied with but half allowance of meat, bread, or rum. Whilst I pitied the poor fellows . . . my admiration was drawn forth at . . . the patience with which they bore it. Not a single complaint have I heard made by a soldier since I joined the army." Sam hasn't been in the army long.

During the rain Sam writes about, Lieutenant Colonel Ebenezer Huntington lies in rags on the ground for forty hours, "and only a hunk of fresh beef and that without salt to dine on," he reports. And he hasn't been paid since the previous December. Ebenezer is irate about it. He writes home to his brother: "The rascally stupidity which now prevails in the country at large is beyond all description. They patiently see our illustrious commander at the head of twenty-five hundred or three thousand ragged, though virtuous and good men and be obliged to put up with what no troops ever did before. . . . I despise my countrymen." He goes on in the same vein.

If there's anyone who is happy in camp, it's Lafayette. He has now what he wanted all along: "a charming command" of his own, the regiment for which he supplied the money himself before departing from France. They consist of 2,000 light infantry, with two brigadiers to lead them; 100 riflemen; another 300-man unit that is half infantry, half cavalry, all told, 2,400 men whose mission, it appears, is to act as—a scouting party! Lafayette doesn't care. He finds himself now in command of one-fifth of the entire American forces, and since he's fitted them out at his own expense, they look like peacocks set down in a meadow full of mourning doves. The soldiers wear cockades, the officers have proper swords, the battalions carry brave flags, and from their caps float long black and white plumes. And at their head is Major General Lafayette, a happy man, at least for the time being.

But what of our other hero, Arnold? Last we saw of him, he was entering Philadelphia as military commander of the regained city. It will prove to have been the turning point in his career. He came in triumph, riding at the head of a column of Massachusetts militia and a collection of town officials, crowds cheering him as he passed. He took command at once. All shops were ordered closed. Merchants were required to report their holdings, so the army could sign proper contracts with them for supplies.

Socially, he was a sensational success. The Tory girls flocked around this patriot hero, with his (to them) romantic limp. He couldn't dance with them, but he could flirt and enjoy their company. He'd always wanted luxury in his life, and now he was in a position to have it. Since he damn near lost his leg in the service of his ungrateful country, he felt he deserved whatever he could get. He discovered that living well is the best revenge, taking over the mansion Howe had occupied, with a staff that included a housekeeper, coachman, groom, a few other servants, and four horses in the stable. He entertained the best people, and you'd think he would be more than satisfied.

Arnold isn't able to get glory out of his mind, though. If he can't fight on land anymore, maybe he could do it on the water. He sends an urgent request to Washington to make him an admiral, and the embarrassed commander turns him down as gently as possible by saying that he, Washington, is "not a competent judge of marine matters."

One more rebuff, one more cause for deep resentment, and at this point Arnold begins to give up on the Americans. Now he pursues an entirely self-interested course, which involves first getting a piece of the black market action which is a growth industry in Philadelphia. Rumors circulate about what he's doing, and some patriots are furious about him, but he gets away with it.

Others aren't so lucky. The Pennsylvania Council can't stop the traffic, but it does convict two Quakers of collaborating with the enemy while the British were there, and sentences them to death, plunging the city into heated controversy. Conservatives consider this terrorism against men of property. Others say that, if these standards are applied generally, a good many other people should be in jail.

On the night before the Quakers are hanged, Arnold celebrates the event by giving a "public entertainment," to which he invites a number of Tory ladies, the wives and daughters of people the Council has proscribed—an odd act of defiance for a man who's supposed to be an American military governor. Among the guests are Edward Shippen and his daughter Peggy. She's got over the loss of the British officers who made Philadelphia so charming, and she's at least partly over John André, but what she can't stand in the new dispensation is austerity. That's why she's excited about going to Arnold's mansion. He notices her that night, and she's invited often. Soon he begins to single her out, and she responds to this man who's old enough to be her father, a widower with grown children.

Edward doesn't like Arnold, although it's clear the general is far from being a dyed-in-the-wool rebel. Shippen is reluctant to accept Arnold as Peggy's suitor and refuses permission at first, but they both press him. By this time, the hero of Saratoga has cast aside his crutches, needing only a cane and a high-heeled shoe to compensate for the bad leg.

Patriots in the city are beginning to think him a Tory, and they blame Peggy's influence, but it's really love, love, love. Just as the Council is about to charge him with what amounts to treason, he and Peggy are married on April 8, 1779. They have so much in common. Both of them love luxury; she's always had it until now, he's always aspired to it. Both think they have very little chance of getting it if the Americans win. In this fertile soil, treason is sure to flower, and it does.

Arnold isn't quite through with the Americans, however. For one thing, he claims that Congress owes him £2,500 for past salary and expenses. Moreover, he insists that the Council's attempts to convict him of improper conduct in office (that is, trafficking with the enemy through the black market) have stained his honor and he wants a court-martial to clear himself. He doesn't know it, but Joseph Reed and the Council are putting pressure on Washington to postpone any such event, and he does. That's the last straw. From the day he gets the letter advising him of the postponement, Arnold is resolved to sell himself to the British, and he has the willing cooperation of his new wife. It's Peggy who thinks of her dear friend André as a way to get to Clinton.

The man who did so much to give Howe such a magnificent send-off from Philadelphia has been living it up in New York as Clinton's aide, part of a corrupt administration ruling over a city even more corrupt. It's the class system at its worst. An embittered resident writes about how Clinton and his favorites are "regaling themselves in routs, dinners, little concerts, and small parties, over good, warm, comfortable fires, and enjoying all the ease and luxury in life, while the poor soldiers (for whom the wood was provided) were, with their wives and children, perishing in the barracks in the severity of winter for want of that fuel. . . ." Clinton and his friends! this disillusioned Tory snorts. The precious wood was "lavished away and distributed among strumpets, panderers, favorites, and pretty little misses."

Clinton and André have become the closest of friends. Some historians have speculated that there were sexual elements in this relationship, but proof is entirely lacking. In any case, there's no doubt that the general is crazy about his handsome, talented aide, putting him in charge of British intelligence the same month that Arnold and Peggy are married. One of André's orders is to see what he can do about encouraging disaffection among the Americans. Considering the possibilities, at that moment he has no thought of Arnold, but he does think of his friend Peggy Shippen. By an odd coincidence, Peggy is thinking of him.

She makes the first move. Looking for a go-between she can trust to make contact with André, she chooses Joseph Stansbury, a dealer in crockery and a social climber who would like to better himself. He takes Peggy's message to André, who is astonished by this concatenation of events. He replies cautiously. It wouldn't do, he says, for Arnold to make some kind of public switch, which would accomplish nothing but to get him hanged. What would be truly helpful, he says, would be if Arnold had some kind of command he could betray. Certainly not Philadelphia. The reply is sent directly to Arnold, not Peggy, and its tone is so arrogant that Arnold thinks momentarily he might be changing one kind of humiliation for another. He's angry enough so that negotiations are broken off.

Another and unexpected event, however, steers Arnold once more toward betrayal. In December 1779, he suddenly gets the court-martial he thought Washington had refused him. He limps into court at Morristown, brisk and confident of acquittal. He is acquitted on two of the charges, but is found guilty of two others. He's sentenced to a reprimand from Washington. Congress has to approve the verdict, and it does, with only three dissenting votes. For Arnold, this is the final blow. Washington, who's still a little embarrassed about the whole thing, tries to soften the disgrace with a reprimand that's not much more than a slap on the wrist, but for Arnold this is the end.

It's the end in other ways, too. Disgrace is bad enough, but he's also impoverished. He and Peggy have to move out of their mansion, and the French consul general promptly moves into it. Desperately, Arnold tries to find some way of making money. His mind is still set on the water, where his leg won't bother him so much, and he asks the Board of Admiralty for permission to command a fleet of privateers. The answer is no. All right, he'll take the command of a single privateer out of Boston. No again. Then he tries to sell his services to the French, but they treat him with complete contempt. And he has a new son to support, too.

In despair, he turns to his old friend, Philip Schuyler, who once thought so much of him, and asks if he can possibly find a command for him. Already he's plotting what to do if he gets it. He also swallows what's left of his pride and gets in touch with André again, sending him some sample information. Then, surprisingly, Schuyler gets him the American outpost at West Point to command, and now he has something to offer. He takes over his new post, and Peggy soon follows him.

Through it all, Arnold has been, understandably, in a terrible state of nerves, and he hopes his wife's arrival will quiet them, but she's exhibiting some of those symptoms of hysteria that once so worried her father. She's "subject to occasional paroxysms of physical indisposition, attended by nervous debility," one of Arnold's aides at West Point reports, "during which she would give utterance to anything and everything on her mind." Not exactly the kind of companion for a secret agent to have, even though Arnold loves her so passionately that his letters (and hers, as well) fairly scorch the paper.

As the aide says, her condition was "a fact well known among us of the general's family, so much so as to cause us to be scrupulous of what we told her or said within her hearing." True, she had never disclosed any secrets, but the strain she's now under as a potential traitor's wife is beginning to tell. Realizing the danger, Arnold appoints one of his aides, David Salisbury Franks, a dandy who's the son of a rich Philadelphia family and one of Peggy's old friends, to distract his wife and keep her away from headquarters as much as possible. Franks is happy to do it, and with proper chaperonage, they go on daylong picnics in the woods, among other devices.

That's the situation on September 23, 1780, the day the French get back to Newport from the Hartford meeting, and the day that Washington, riding back to camp with Lafayette, his aides, and an escort, plans to stop and inspect the West Point defenses. He's expected. When Washington last saw Arnold at Peekskill, before he set off for Hartford, this meeting had been agreed upon, although Arnold, his treasonous plans well advanced, is made more nervous than ever by this unexpected engagement. He has already told Clinton that a meeting with André, and only André, is essential. The general is reluctant to let his favorite go on what could be a dangerous mission, but Arnold is insistent. They finally meet at night, after innumerable complications with the intermediaries on both sides, and in utter blackness the two chief conspirators sit down on the banks of the Hudson, with their backs against fir trees.

Arnold is a no-nonsense seller of his services. He tells André at once that he wants a guaranteed £10,000 indemnity. André says he's empowered to offer only £6,000, and in the darkness Arnold begins a plaintive bargaining plea, arguing that his family situation is desperate, and if it wasn't for that, he wouldn't ask for money at all. Also his feelings are hurt that the British obviously don't think he's worth £10,000. He's so insistent that at last André can only get on with it by promising that he will do his best to get the full amount from Clinton. With that settled, they talk about the details of how the British will capture West Point. In the end, what Arnold actually gives the British is a copy of an important council of war, a complete account of the garrison and its works, and instructions on attack and defense, all of which Arnold later writes down.

In this original plan, the idea is that the British will come up the river stealthily while Washington is still there. (Or so it was argued for years by later historians.) That idea, in fact, tempting though it might be for the British to snare the commander himself, is a plan full of so many bear traps that it's quickly abandoned. It's one thing for Arnold to give up West Point by prearrangement, quite another if Washington is there. So they decide to postpone the attack until after Washington has left.

The next day, after the conspirators have ridden to a safe house (safe from Arnold's standpoint, but actually it's at an American strong point), Arnold gives André the written information he's gathered for him, and suggests he put it between his stockings and his feet. They part, André on his way back to New York, Arnold returning to West Point, where he finds the atmosphere tense. His aides don't like the company he's keeping; they don't know about André, of course, but they do know he's been with the villainous William Smith, a known Tory. His aides have even come to Peggy with their suspicions, but she calmed them down—somewhat.

In the end, it's Smith's carelessness as a fellow conspirator, not to say his foolishness, that gets André captured as he is escorting Clinton's wandering boy to New York. Taken first by soldiers who simply aren't sure about him, he winds up at South Salem in charge of Lieutenant James King, who has such well-founded suspicions that André realizes he's caught, admits who he is, and sits down to write an amazing letter to Washington in which he pleads that he wants to rescue himself "from an imputation of having assumed a mean character for treacherous purposes or self-interest"; he wants to vindicate his name as a spy. That's all. His excuse is that he was only trying to influence the Americans, "which is an advantage taken in war." He claims he was forced to enter the American lines, and therefore should be treated as a prisoner of war. In all this, he never mentions Arnold by name but it won't be hard to guess. After he sends off his letter, André is so relieved, he draws a picture of himself as a captive and goes to sleep.

Meanwhile, Washington's party rides in the morning light toward West Point, planning to have breakfast with the Arnolds. The commander wants to stop and inspect some fortifications on the river, and Lafayette protests that Mrs. Arnold will be waiting breakfast for them. Washington teases him a little. All his young officers are in love with Peggy, he says, but if Lafayette is worried, he'll send two of his aides on ahead to tell her they're coming.

When these aides, Majors Samuel Shaw and James McHenry, arrive, they find Peggy still in bed, but Arnold sits with them at the breakfast table briefly before he excuses himself and walks into the buttery, where he meets two messengers who hand him a letter from

André's captors, who have found the papers in his stockings and think they have "a very dangerous tendency," so they are to be forwarded to Washington.

Naturally, Arnold is aghast. He limps out into the yard, orders his horse brought up and his barge crew on the river alerted, goes back into the house and walks through the dining room, where McHenry observes, as he reports later, "an embarrassment and agitation" in him "so unusual that I knew not what to attribute it." He goes upstairs and bursts into the bedroom, where Peggy is sitting up in bed, happily awaiting the arrival of some peaches that young officers have promised to bring her from the orchard. Instead, she gets her husband, in a state of despair, who tells her that they're lost. She cries out, and then there's a knock on the door and they hear the voice of Franks, advising them that a servant has just brought word that Washington's arrival is imminent. At that, Peggy falls back in a faint.

All this takes place in the Robinson house, where Arnold has his headquarters, so it's reasonable when he dashes out past Franks that he should call back and say he's on his way to the fort itself to prepare a reception for the commander. Still, it's a near thing. He jumps on his horse, and as he comes around the corner of the house, there are four of Washington's light horsemen, who salute him respectfully and advise him that the general is close at hand. Stable your horses in the barn, he calls to them, and dashes off down the steep slope to the river.

At the barge, he does a strange thing, taking off the saddle with his pistols still in it and throwing it on board, after which he jumps on himself and tells the oarsmen to row away for Stony Point. Before they can do so, a boat from West Point appears, another advance guard from Washington. Arnold shouts to them that they're welcome to go up to the house and have breakfast. They should tell the commander that he will be back before dinner. Then he's off. His great plan has failed, but he still believes he has a lot to offer the British. He'll go to New York, Peggy can join him later, and they'll make a new life under the Crown.

Back at West Point, Washington has arrived, mildly surprised that Arnold hasn't waited, but ready to have a leisurely breakfast. At the Robinson house, however, Peggy has thrown one of her hysterical fits, which may well be real this time, for the benefit of Arnold's two aides, Colonel Richard Varick and Franks. They try to calm her by saying that Arnold will soon be coming back from West Point with Washington, but she cries, "No, General Arnold will never return. He's gone. He's gone forever . . . the spirits have carried him up there, they have put hot irons on his head."

In midafternoon, Washington returns from an inspection of the fort and Hamilton gives him some papers just arrived by messenger. He opens them, and a few minutes later, both Hamilton and Lafayette are summoned, to hear his cry that will go ringing down through the history books: "Arnold has betrayed us! Whom can we trust now?"

Great confusion. McHenry and Hamilton gallop off in the vain hope of catching up with Arnold. The doctor comes out of Peggy's room and begs someone to bring the absent husband home or his wife will die. Varick and Franks take the doctor aside and tell him what's happened. They think Peggy is completely innocent, that Arnold told her the truth just before he left and it has unsettled her mind. Either that, or she's the greatest actress of her day.

Peggy asks to see Washington. She says there's a hot iron on her head and only he can take it off. The general, who has other things on his mind, comes to her bedside and she refuses to believe he's really Washington; she thinks he and Varick are going to kill her child.

Peggy is left to the doctor's care, and the officers gather for a dismal dinner. Lafayette notes later: "Never was there a more melancholy dinner. The general was silent and reserved, and none of us spoke of what we were thinking about. . . . Gloom and distrust appeared to pervade every mind, and I have never seen General Washington so affected by any circumstances. . . ."

A messenger brings three letters sent back by Hamilton which had been put ashore downriver by the British sloop *Vulture*. One is a defense of Arnold by one of his conspirators, the other two are from Arnold to Peggy—and Washington. He begins the latter: "The heart that is conscious of its own rectitude cannot attempt to palliate a step which the world may censure as wrong. . . ." And then he tries hard to justify himself, charging that he has "too often experienced the ingratitude of my country." All he asks of Washington is that he protect Peggy, "as good and as innocent as an angel and . . . incapable of doing wrong." Except, of course, that she has been involved with the plot from the beginning.

What Arnold wrote to Peggy remains undisclosed. Washington

doesn't open the letter. He's now moving slowly and cautiously, so as not to alarm the entire garrison, which still doesn't know what's occurred, as he prepares for a possible attack.

Next day, Peggy appears somewhat more composed, and the young officers are there to console her. Hamilton writes to his fiancée that to hear her carrying on was "the most affecting sound I ever was witness to," and adds that she is "very apprehensive the resentment of her country will fall upon her. . . . I have tried to persuade her that her fears are ill founded, but she will not be convinced. . . ."

Everyone loves and pities poor Peggy and wants to do something for her. She asks to see Lafayette, and he rushes to her bedside. They've met several times before, in Philadelphia, and that's where she says she wants to go now. "It would be exceedingly painful to General Washington if she were not treated with the greatest kindness," Lafayette writes. "As for myself, you know that I have always been fond of her, and this moment she interests me intensely. We are certain that she knew nothing of the plot." Lafayette doesn't have the least sympathy for Arnold, although there are some ways in which they're much alike.

Now there's only one more act to be played out in this drama of lost hopes and betrayal. André may believe he's a prisoner of war, but the Americans consider him a spy and they mean to hang him. Clinton is distraught by Arnold's failure, not because of Arnold but because he's going to lose his favorite and get in exchange a limping traitor who has the gall to come and try to give him advice, to which he hardly listens. He's doing everything in his power to save André.

It's an ironic switch. Here's Arnold in New York, walking around in his new British brigadier general's uniform, but increasingly conscious that he's the object of sneers and glances of pure hatred. Everyone loved André, and in his prison cell everyone *still* loves André, even his American guards, who believe he's the victim of unfortunate circumstances. Washington declares that the captive is "a gallant and accomplished officer." Nevertheless, five days after his capture, he faces a trial before all the general officers at headquarters—except the commander. It's held in a small Dutch church. No witnesses are called; André confesses everything. The debate about his guilt may go on for the next two centuries, but at the moment there's no doubt. He's judged guilty and condemned to die by hanging.

Hamilton spends hours with the prisoner and reports that he never broke down but once. He thinks it is misfortune, not guilt, that has brought him to this end. He breaks down when he talks about Clinton, and asks permission to write him. In his letter, he tries to convince his beloved commander that the general is in no way responsible for his death, which is exactly what is tormenting Sir Henry.

André has just one request. He asks to be shot like a gentleman, not hanged like a peasant, and Hamilton urges Washington to agree, but the commander believes he has no choice. If André is convicted as a spy, he must die as a spy, which is by hanging. That's the law.

About the time Clinton gets his dear friend's farewell note, he has a letter from Washington explaining that André has confessed, that he was not operating under a flag, as first claimed, and that he will be hanged. The American colonel who brings this letter lingers after he delivers it, and lets Clinton know that if there's any way they can get their hands on Arnold, the Americans will release André. It's a temptation that twists Clinton's insides before he can refuse it. If he agrees, that will end any attempt to win over rebels. He can't do it. "A deserter is never given up," he says.

But Clinton himself isn't ready to give up. He sends a delegation of New York City officials to plead André's case, and then he co-opts Arnold, whom he's begun to hate, and instructs him to do what he can't do himself, that is, send Washington a threatening letter, declaring that, if the Americans don't release André, the British will feel free to retaliate on rebel captives. He notes that at the moment they hold forty gentlemen from South Carolina who are likely to lose their chances of clemency. If they die, Arnold concludes, the blood will be on Washington's hands.

Nothing works. Until the last minute, the Americans hope they'll get Arnold in exchange for André, but Clinton, under terrible pressure, simply can't bring himself to take such a step. On the day of the execution, André doesn't know it's going to be the noose and not the musket until he steps out in sight of the gallows. "Must I then die in this manner?" he pleads once more. Told that it is so, he says, "I am reconciled to my fate, but not to the mode."

Eli Jacobs, a boy from Killingly, Connecticut, is André's guard on execution day, and he describes the end of this man everyone loves, probably including Peggy Arnold. "When things were ready, André stepped into a wagon and, after he was fairly under the gallows, took from his pocket two white handkerchiefs, with one of which the marshal pinioned André's arms, and the other André hoodwinked his own eyes with, and put the noose of the rope around his own neck. After this, Colonel Scammell told André he might speak to the operators, at which André raised the handkerchief from his eyes and said, 'Bear me witness that I meet my fate like a brave man,' and the wagon was immediately moved from under him and he expired. His body was placed in a coffin, dressed in his royal regimentals, and buried at the foot of the gallows."

As the obituaries used to say, André is mourned by all. Count Fersen writes to his father: "They say Major André has been hanged; it is a pity. He's a young man of twenty-four who has such talent." And Lafayette writes to his "Dear One," his wife: "He was an interesting man, the confidant and friend of General Clinton, he conducted himself in a manner so frank, so noble, and so delicate, that I cannot help feeling for him with infinite sorrow."

Washington has the last word on both the spy and the traitor. "André has met his fate," he says, "and with that fortitude which was to be expected from an accomplished man and gallant officer." As for Arnold, "He wants feeling."

16

+   +   +

Two Roads to Yorktown: The Road from the South

C linton didn't spend all his time in New York during 1780, even though he had more than enough to occupy him there, as we've just seen. As 1779 dwindled down, he was nervous about the way his troops had become dispersed, with men in Florida, Georgia, the West Indies, and Canada. He'd like to recall the ones in the West Indies for service in the North, but he doesn't have enough convoy ships to get them there. And London isn't sending him nearly enough reinforcements.

All along, though, he's been obsessed with the idea that the war can be won in the South, where Tory strength is greatest. When he evacuated Rhode Island on October 7, 1779, it gave him an infusion of strength, enough to justify sailing for Charleston on December 26, with a strong force of 7,600 men. It's a wild voyage, bucking through heavy winter storms, so they don't arrive off Tybee until February 1, 1780.

Setting up a base, Clinton starts moving into South Carolina on April 12, and he sends his flamboyant cavalryman, Colonel Tarleton, on ahead. The defenders at Charleston get an idea of what's coming when British siege guns open up on them.

General Benjamin Lincoln is in command at Charleston, all several hundred pounds of him. He's no brilliant strategist, but he's steady and brave; like Arnold, he suffered a bad leg wound at Saratoga and was left with a permanent limp. "Solid" is the word for Lincoln, as one historian describes him. But not even the ablest commander in the army is likely to defend Charleston successfully, and his fleet with all its guns lies in the harbor. Lincoln understands that reason must prevail over valor. He opens negotiations, but the first proposals he sends over are curtly rejected.

That morning both armies are silent for an hour, waiting for peace or war after the rejection of surrender terms. Then, amazingly, Lincoln decides on at least a show of force, and as Colonel Moultrie described it, "At length, we fired the first gun and immediately followed a tremendous cannonade, and the mortars from both sides threw out an immense number of shells. It was a glorious sight to see them like meteors crossing each other and bursting in the air. It appeared as if the stars were tumbling down.

"The fire was incessant almost the whole night, cannon balls whizzing and shells hissing continually amongst us, ammunition chests and temporary magazines blowing up, great guns bursting, and wounded men groaning along the lines. It was a dreadful night! It was our last great effort, but availed us nothing. After this, our military ardor was much abated. We began to cool, and we ended gradually, and on the eleventh of May we capitulated."

For Moultrie, the old soldier who had already spent so much effort and blood to defend his city, the surrender was essential but nonetheless almost unbearable. Tears ran down his cheeks. A British observer wrote: "General Leslie with the Royal English Fusiliers and Hessian Grenadiers and some artillery took possession of the town and planted the British colors by the gate, on the ramparts, and Lincoln limped out at the head of the most ragged rabble I ever beheld. . . . They were indulged with beating a drum and to bring out their colors cased. They laid down their arms between their abatis and surrendered prisoners of war. . . . The militia, poor creatures, could not be prevailed upon to come out. They began to creep out of their holes the next day. By the capitulation they are allowed to go home and plow the ground. There only can they be useful."

In the end, though, it isn't all disgrace. When the British want to know where the American second division is, they're told that they are looking at the entire Continental force of defenders, except for the sick and wounded. Clinton and his officers are astonished by the fight this shadow of an army has put up against overwhelming odds, and call it a gallant defense. There's a shadow even on this, however.

Captain George Rochfort, one of the British officers, tells Moultrie what's getting to be an old and painful story: "You had a great many rascals among you who came out every night and gave us information of what was passing in your garrison."

No matter how you look at it, the fall of Charleston is a major defeat for the Americans, and knowing it would be, the fact may have impelled Lincoln to make a fight of it. He's going to go down in military history as the general who presided over the third largest surrender of American troops; his 5,500 will be exceeded only by General Julius White's surrender to the Confederate Army at Harpers Ferry in 1862, and General Jonathan Wainwright's to the Japanese at Bataan in 1942.

Lincoln himself is a casualty in some ways because he's now held by the British and has to wait until fall before he's exchanged for a pair of British generals, one of them Baron von Riedesel. The Baroness is thus enabled to go home at last, depriving us of any further entries in her entertaining diary. While Lincoln is waiting to be exchanged, he has to endure some harsh criticism but, as he points out, it would have been unthinkable to do otherwise than what he did. Most of the criticism comes from Congress; the public admires this general and doesn't put much blame on him for losing Charleston.

Politics are mixed up in the affair too. At one point in the siege, Lincoln had thought of retreating to the mainland, but he was visited by a body of irate South Carolinians who told him they would destroy his boats if he tried. Since most of his troops were Southerners, he had no choice but to give in to the argument that states' rights superseded anything Congress might order, and the South Carolinians were ordering him to stay and fight it out.

After the capture of Charleston, Clinton believes he's got the Southern campaign off to a good start, and he sails back to New York with a third of his army. The man he leaves behind to take charge is General Charles Cornwallis, who is going to be on center stage from now until Yorktown. We've seen him before, of course, from time to time, ever since he arrived to join Clinton in February 1776. This man who's fated to ring down the British curtain is the scion of an old and distinguished family, a man the historian George Trevelyan has called "an English aristocrat of the finest type, a living and most attractive example of unique and singleminded patriotism." Also possessing more military talent than most if not all of the other generals.

Yet he's about to make some highly debatable decisions in the Carolinas which will later temporarily tarnish his name, not to mention his later virtual defiance of Clinton and the climactic errors that will end in Yorktown. In spite of all that, however, after the war Cornwallis will come to be considered in England as one of the greatest generals in British history. Americans see him as "short and thickset, his hair somewhat gray, his face well formed and agreeable, his manners remarkably easy and affable—unless provoked." At the time of Charleston's fall, he's forty-two years old.

Before he left, Clinton held out a carrot and a stick to see if the Americans in the South wouldn't listen to reason. He issued a proclamation declaring that, if the rebels would return to the King's service, all, or nearly all, would be forgiven. If they didn't, their property would certainly be confiscated and probably they would be killed. No one is listening. The South is a hotbed of passions, on both sides.

A small example of what Cornwallis faces now as he vows to extinguish insurrection everywhere is the case of Josiah Culbertson, who lives in the South Carolina town called Ninety Six. Applying for his pension after the war, he told this story. Governor John Rutledge had sent ammunition for future rebel use to Ninety Six, as he said, "to keep the Tories in awe, who were plenty enough in that section." In fact, these Loyalists did more damage than the British in the region.

While the siege of Charleston was going on, 150 Tories, under a Colonel Moore, planned to attack Culbertson's house, where the ammunition was stored, and destroy it. There was a guard around the place but, knowing they were outnumbered, they retreated as the British approached. So there was no one left to defend this log house except Culbertson and his mother-in-law, Mrs. Thomas. Culbertson loaded his guns, while Mrs. Thomas kept passing him a supply of bullets, and he set up such a one-man fusillade that the Tories mistakenly believed the entire guard were inside and retreated ingloriously.

On a much larger scale, this is the kind of thing that's going on everywhere in the state after Charleston's fall. Of immediate concern to the army Clinton has left behind is a report that a force of three hundred Virginians under Colonel Abraham Buford had been on its way to reinforce the defenders but, hearing that the city had fallen, were retreating toward Hillsboro, and intelligence reports say they've halted near Waxhaw Creek, about nine miles from Lancaster Courthouse. If he's going to put down the rebels in South Carolina, Cornwallis figures, this is a logical place to start, and he sends a force of dragoons, mostly Tarleton's Loyal Legion, to search out and destroy them if possible.

Tarleton is the kind of hell-for-leather commander who spares no one, men or horses, and when his mount falls dead in the hot weather, he seizes others from the countryside and overtakes Buford. Surrender, he demands, and "if you are rash enough to reject the terms, the blood is on your head." If he had known how much blood was going to be lost, Buford might have thought twice before he replies: "I reject your proposals, and shall defend myself to the last extremity."

The extremity comes soon enough. With only three hundred yards between the two forces, Tarleton can hear the American officers telling their men to hold fire until the dragoons are only ten paces away. But the attack is just a few minutes old before the Americans have to ask for quarter. Buford hoists a white flag and negotiations begin, but under the pretext that he's been shot at while they were discussing terms, Tarleton signals his men to use their bayonets on the Americans who have already surrendered. It's a massacre which, in Henry Steele Commager's words, "for sheer savagery was unmatched in the entire war." Light Horse Harry Lee writes later: "This bloody day only wanted the war dance and the roasting fire to have placed it first in the records of torture and death in the West." It inspires a new American battle cry: "Tarleton's quarter!"

Some of the gory details are reported by Dr. Robert Brownsfield in a letter to his friend, William D. James. Writing about the attack on Buford's rear guard, in which every American was killed, Brownsfield relates that Lieutenant Pearson, who was in command, had his face mangled while he was lying on his back, helpless. "His nose and lip were bisected obliquely; several of his teeth were broken out in the upper jaw, and the under jaw completely divided on each side. These wounds were suffered after he had fallen, with several others on his head, shoulders and arms. . . . He lay for five weeks without uttering a single groan. His only nourishment was milk, drawn from a bottle through a quill. During that period he was totally deprived of speech, nor could he articulate distinctly after his wounds were healed."

Tarleton elaborates his excuse. The shot fired during the peace talks killed his horse under him, he says, and he calls it Buford's treachery. But the survivors agree, in the words of one of them, that "for fifteen minutes after every man was prostrate they went over the ground plunging their bayonets into everyone that exhibited any signs of life, and in some instances, where several had fallen one over the other, these monsters were seen to throw off on the point of the bayonet the uppermost, to come to those beneath."

There's one incredible escape. Captain John Stokes is stabbed twenty-three times and survives. His ordeal begins when a dragoon aims blows at his head, which he fends off with his short sword until a dragoon on his other side cuts his right hand. Both men attack him then, and he defends himself with his left arm until they cut off his forefinger and hack him in eight or ten places.

A witness writes: "His head was then laid open almost the whole length of the crown to the eyebrows. After he fell he received several cuts on the face and shoulders." The dragoons leave him for dead, but another soldier goes by and asks if he wants quarter. Stokes replies, "I have not, nor do I mean to ask quarter. Finish me as soon as possible." Obligingly, the soldier stabs him twice with his bayonet and walks on. Another soldier passes, asks the same question, and gets the same reply. He gives Stokes another two thrusts of the bayonet.

As he lies there, amazingly still conscious, the captain sees a wounded British officer nearby, and when a red-coated sergeant, risking his own neck, comes up and offers to protect him, Stokes says, "All I ask is to be laid by that officer that I may die in his presence." This humanitarian sergeant obliges, but while he's moving the captain, he has to put him down twice to defend him against the sergeant's own comrades.

Tarleton's surgeon, Dr. Stapleton, comes by and begins dressing the British officer's wounds, but when Stokes asks for the same succor, Stapleton refuses him scornfully until he's ordered to do so by the wounded officer. Stapleton's idea of dressing Stokes's wounds is to fill them with rough tow. Nevertheless, he survives the whole ordeal, and after the war will become a federal judge; he will even have a county named in his honor. His comrades are much less fortunate. The Americans lose a hundred officers and men in the massacre before Tarleton, his blood lust appeased, takes the two hundred others as prisoners.

"Perhaps it was Tarleton who started it with the slaughter of Buford's men at the Waxhaw," the historian John Pancake tells us, "and other depredations committed by the 'men clothed in green.'

Perhaps it was the Loyalists who were embittered by Whig oppression and anxious to avenge the recent executions. . . . The war that blazed up in the summer of 1780 took on an aspect of vindictiveness and cruelty that at times appalled even the participants themselves."

Among hundreds of examples is Colonel Elijah Clarke's assault on the British post at Augusta; Thomas Brown, a notorious Tory partisan, is in command there, and he is still full of hatred from the tarring and feathering the Committee of Safety gave him in 1775, and the torture he underwent the following year, when the Whigs burned his feet. He's organized a regiment in Florida called the Florida Rangers, and for five years he's been the terror of the Georgia–South Carolina border. Fearless as he is vindictive, Brown repulses Clarke's attack and takes thirteen prisoners who are hanged from the fort's staircase as their comrades retreat. It's said he turns some others over to the Indians supporting him.

Looting is a popular outdoor sport in this turbulent Southern theater. Bands roam around the country, saying they're on one side or the other, but actually interested primarily in robbing the populace. One leader, Samuel Brown, becomes notorious as Plundering Sam, whose partner is his sister Charity. Sam's a Tory, but he makes the mistake of terrorizing a Whig family while the man of the house is away. When he comes back, this man follows Brown to a Loyalist's house and kills him.

Some of these partisan guerrillas are no better than outlaws, a particularly vicious example being the Whig partisan Maurice Murphy. When his old uncle, Gideon Gibson, denounces him, Murphy kills him on his own doorstep while Gibson's two sons, who are members of Murphy's band, look on.

As Pancake says, it's hard to separate myth and legend from reality in this back-country war. An enduring legend is created by Nancy Hart, tall and muscular, redheaded and cross-eyed, "ungainly in figure and rude in speech," who settled with her husband Benjamin in Georgia early in the 1770s. Nancy is a Whig partisan and absolutely fearless. On occasion she serves as a spy, dressing as a man.

The climax of her career comes when she's suspected of hiding a fugitive Whig, escaped from a Tory raiding party. A half dozen Tories burst into her cabin one day, demanding food and drink, which she gives them to the accompaniment of pungent language and black looks, meanwhile secretly sending her daughter out to round up her husband and the neighbors. When they fail to get there immediately, she seizes one of the Tories' muskets and says she'll kill the first man who moves. She makes good on the threat when one of the Tories tries to disarm her. Another man makes the same attempt and she shoots him too. About that time, her husband and some friends arrive, and at her insistence, they hang the other four Tories.

Of all the Tory partisans, the one with the worst reputation is William Cunningham, a man so harassed by Whigs in his hometown that he has become a fugitive. Like so many of the others, Cunningham has a personal grudge. In Savannah, he learns that a Whig named Ritchie has killed his crippled and epileptic twin brother. Seeking quick revenge, Cunningham returns home just long enough to kill Ritchie and then organizes a partisan band that terrorizes the countryside as the notorious "Bloody Bill" gang.

Revenge is Cunningham's sole motivation, it appears, since he is not allied with anyone but devotes his time to killing Whigs wherever he finds them. He thinks of himself as an avenging angel. In one bloody slaughter at a blockhouse whose defenders have already surrendered, Bloody Bill swings his sword on them until he falls to the ground exhausted. He gets away with it, too. Nearly all his followers are eventually hunted down, but he escapes to Florida and his British friends see that he sails away to England, where Parliament votes him a major's half-pay pension.

In the South during these last years of the war, it's a tale of torture, whipping, tarring and feathering, hanging, sparing no one, man or woman, old or young. These are all incidents, mostly unrelated, in the larger movement of Cornwallis northward with the regular troops. From a tactical standpoint, he finds it a difficult job, with long lines of communications and outposts few and far between. It's almost impossible to hold down two states with such rugged terrain, especially since there are so many rivers,

Patriot guerrilla bands are also a constant problem. Some of their leaders become as well known as they are feared, especially Francis Marion, "the Swamp Fox," as they call him; Thomas Sumter; and Andrew Pickens. Sometimes these bands fight with the organized army, sometimes they don't. On July 12, for example, at Williamson's plantation in South Carolina, one of Sumter's lieutenants with a small force nearly exterminates a body of Loyalists and British dragoons.

Sumter himself attacks Rocky Mount, on the west bank of the

Catawba River, thirty miles from Camden. A detachment of British troops is occupying a loghouse fort there, under the command of Lieutenant Colonel George Turnbull. He's ready for Sumter because neighborhood Tories have warned him. Sumter charges the fort three times before he realizes he can't overcome it without artillery and falls back.

A week or so later, Sumter, joined by a detachment under Major William Davis, attacks a Tory camp at Hanging Rock, twelve miles from Rocky Mount, which is an easier proposition because it's an open camp. The Loyalists put up a fight but they're overcome, and Sumter's men plunder the stores, getting drunk in the process. The defenders, who have withdrawn only a short way, see that the rebels aren't in much of a condition to fight, so they re-form and manage to hold off Sumter's men until reinforcements arrive.

This skirmish, one of the most obstinately fought in the war, is typical of the way these partisan bands operate in the South. It's a fight between neighbors, often with no British soldiers or Continental troops involved. Sumter, however, is over his head when he encounters the real thing on August 18, as Tarleton surprises him at Fishing Creek and sends the Americans into panicky flight, leaving behind all the loot they had collected at Hanging Rock.

For the inhabitants of this rugged battleground, any day can be "the day of terror," as Eliza Wilkinson describes what happens to her and her family on June 3. Fifteen or sixteen horsemen come riding up to her house in the morning, and the family is terrified until the horsemen turn out to be rebels, as the Wilkinsons are. These men chat for a while, sitting their horses, then most of them ride off. Two linger, however, for a few minutes before they leave and, watching them go, Eliza sees one of them fall as the horses jump a ditch. She sends one of her boys to tell them to come to the house if they need help, and they do so. One has a bad wound behind the ear, and blood's flowing down his neck and chest.

While Eliza is examining the wound, a black girl runs in crying, "The King's people are coming! It must be them because they're all in red." Hearing this alarm, the two men take up their guns, mount their horses, and ride off, but they're seen and one of the approaching British soldiers fires a pistol at them, without visible result. They come charging up to the house, as Eliza tells it, "in such a furious manner that they seemed to tear up the earth, and the riders at the same time bellowing out the most horrid curses imaginable, oaths and imprecations, which chilled my whole frame."

They come bursting into the house with drawn swords and pistols, shouting, "Where are those women rebels?" Then they confront the Wilkinson women and begin by taking their caps, apparently to get the pins keeping them on. What follows, says Eliza, "was terrible to the last degree, and what augmented it, they had several armed Negroes with them, who threatened and abused us greatly."

The house is plundered of everything worth taking, trunks split open, clothes appropriated. Eliza pleads with the soldier who's taking her clothing, telling him times are so hard the family can't replace what's being taken from them; she begs him to spare a little, at least. But he curses her, and then, seeing her shoes, tells her, "I want them buckles," and starts to take them off. One of his comrades shouts, "Shares there! I say, shares!" and they divide the buckles. Eliza's sister has her earrings wrenched from her ears, and more buckles are taken. They want the sister's ring, too, and although she pleads that it's her wedding ring, they tell her that if she doesn't give it to them they'll kill her. Laden down with booty, the British ride off, as Eliza says, with "each wretch's bosom stuffed so full they appeared to be all afflicted with some dropsical disorder."

But skirmishes and looting don't conquer a country, and Cornwallis is far from conquering South Carolina. On August 6, he writes gloomily to Clinton that the entire country is in "an absolute state of rebellion, every friend of government has been carried off and his plantation destroyed."

Besides all this, Cornwallis now has to contend with a small force of Maryland and Delaware troops from the Continental Army, detached from the main forces in the North and brought down to South Carolina by Baron de Kalb but commanded after July 25 by Gates. Congress has given him command of the Southern Department without even consulting Washington. When Gates is reinforced by militia units from North Carolina and Virginia, he believes he's strong enough to move against the British fort at Camden, thus setting the stage for a battle on August 16 which the military historian Guy Perret calls the "most crushing battlefield success for the British in the war."

If Gates had listened to De Kalb, which he didn't, the outcome might have been different. The German has worked out a brilliant plan of tactical operations which calls for the Americans to take a western route to Camden. That will bring them into country where supplies are plentiful. But Gates ignores De Kalb and sends the army on a direct route to Camden. That's his first major mistake. The troops are already half-starving before they start out, and as they march along, conditions get worse by the day.

Otho Williams, deputy adjutant general, wrote later: "The distresses of the soldiery daily increased. Many . . . urged by necessity, plucked the green ears and boiled them with the lean beef which was collected in the woods, made for themselves a repast, not unpalatable to be sure, but which was attended with painful effects. Green peaches also were substituted for bread and had similar consequences.

"Some of the officers, aware of the risk of eating such vegetables in such a state, with poor fresh beef and without salt, restrained themselves from taking anything but the beef itself, boiled or roasted. It occurred to them that the hair powder, which remained in their bags, would thicken soup, and it was actually applied."

Lord Rawdon, in command at Camden, gets word of Gates's approach and is so alarmed that he sends word to Cornwallis in Charleston for help, and the general starts for Camden on the night of August 10. Both commanders have erroneous ideas of the numbers they're facing, and Gates doesn't even know how many are in his own force.

Cornwallis thinks the British have about 3,000 men, but hasn't been told that more than 800 of them are too ill to fight. He believes the Americans have 7,000, and that's what Gates believes too, but Williams, his adjutant, gives him more accurate figures—3,052 present and ready to fight, not enough to carry out a successful attack, in the adjutant's opinion. "These are enough for our purpose," Gates says grandly, in his usual fashion, and goes right on planning the attack, while his officers shudder at the idea of sending this little army, which is composed of more than two-thirds militia, most of whom have never fought a battle, against British regulars, although this isn't the first time it's been done by any means.

Coincidentally, both commanders decide on a night attack and start out at the same time, 10:00 P.M. on a sultry, moonless night. Before they start, the British troops get a ration of rum, following custom, but Gates has no rum and instead has to issue a gill of molasses, along with some quick-baked bread, half-cooked fresh meat, and corn meal. Gates apparently knows nothing of physiology and has no idea of what this dose of molasses will do. Its effect on the troops is explosive, further reducing the number able to fight.

The whole affair gets off to a bad start in another way when at 2:00 A.M. the Americans blunder into the British advance guard, nine miles north of Camden, and these militia flee in disorder. Cornwallis doesn't take advantage. Realizing the whole American force is marching toward him through a pine forest a mile wide, with marshes on either side, he concludes wisely that this is no kind of terrain on which to fight a battle in the dark.

During the initial encounter, a few redcoats are taken prisoner, and when he questions them, Williams learns for the first time that it's Cornwallis himself they're facing, with presumably three thousand regulars. On being informed, Gates is astonished and calls an immediate council of war. "Gentlemen, what is to be done?" he asks them, no doubt scenting disaster. A small silence falls and then General Edward Stevens, of the Virginia militia, brings them face-to-face with reality. "Gentlemen," he says, "is it not too late now to do anything but fight?"

Exactly. In the calm, hazy morning, the British begin their advance, but Gates, as at Saratoga, fails to give any immediate orders. Stevens orders his men to fix their bayonets and prepare to use them, but meanwhile the British are advancing. Williams advises Gates that General Stevens's brigade is ready to attack, Gates agrees, and the men advance perhaps forty or fifty yards. The British run straight at them, firing and huzzahing as they come, and the untried Virginians simply panic and run.

Garrett Watts, from Carolina County, Virginia, who later admits he was one of the first to flee, tells us what it was like. Although he and the others were under orders not to fire, he did so anyway. "I fired without thinking," he remembered after the war, "except that I might prevent the man opposite from killing me. The discharge and loud roar soon became general from one end of the line to the other. Amongst other things I confess that I was amongst the first to flee. The cause of that I cannot tell, except that everyone I saw was about to do the same. It was instantaneous. There was no effort to rally, to encourage to fight. Officers and men joined in the flight.

"I threw away my gun, and reflecting I might be punished for being found without arms, I picked up a drum, which gave forth such sounds when touched by the twigs I cast it away. When we had gone, we heard the roar of guns still, but we knew not why. Had we known, we might have returned. It was that portion of the army commanded by De Kalb fighting still. De Kalb was killed, General Dickson was wounded in the neck and a great many killed and wounded even on the first firing. After this defeat, many of the dispersed troops proceeded to Hillsboro in North Carolina."

It's nothing less than a rout. Tarleton pursues the Americans through woods and swamps for twenty miles. Gates himself flees precipitately on a horse reputed to be the fleetest in the army, sired by a famous racer named Fearnought, and it carries the flying general from Camden to Hillsboro, 180 miles, in three days.

After the battle, if it could be called that, several hundred dead and wounded Americans lie on the field. Among them is De Kalb, blood-soaked from eleven wounds, his gold-braided uniform coat stripped from him by a battlefield plunderer, and minus even his shirt, also taken. Gates's generals find themselves abandoned by their aides as well as their troops, and have to save themselves the best way they can. Among those who escape are the Virginia militiamen, who, not knowing the country, flee toward Hillsboro, but the North Carolina men disappear in various directions because they take whatever is the shortest way home.

Gates reaches Charlotte that night, along with his chief engineer, John Senf, and a pair of aides. Seeing no sign of any manpower that might be assembled on short notice, he goes on to Hillsboro, where there are both men and some artillery. But already word of his flight is spreading, and rightly or wrongly (but mostly rightly), he brings on a new torrent of criticism. Hamilton writes with contemptuous rage: "Was there ever such an instance of a general running away . . . from his whole army? And was there ever so precipitous a flight? It does admirable credit to the activity of a man at his time of life."

In his report to Congress, Gates blames the militia, not without reason, even though it was his fundamental mistake that sent these untried men against commanders like Cornwallis and Tarleton, with their regulars. Until then, Congress has been closing its ears to criticism of the militia, but many of the delegates now change their minds. Outside Congress, the public jumps on Gates with enthusiasm, but in the army there are few complaints among the soldiers. In the end, perhaps, he can justly be blamed more for fighting the battle at all than for running away.

In any case, it's a costly mistake. No accurate count is ever made, but Cornwallis estimates that nearly 900 Americans were killed and wounded, and 1,000 more captured, while the British have only 324 casualties. Loss of men is bad enough for the Americans, but they also lose guns, baggage, nearly all the wagons, and all but a few of their muskets. When the Continentals finally reassemble at Hillsboro, ten days later, there are no more than 700 of them.

At this point, Gates is trying to brazen it out. He didn't run away at all, he asserts; he just wanted to find a base where he could put together a new army. Some members of Congress greet this with hoots of skepticism, but there aren't enough of these doubters to carry a vote for an inquiry, and the general whose greatest talent may be to survive self-inflicted wounds will be back on top again by 1783, unfazed by his past. After all, he was the commander at Saratoga, wasn't he? And who believes that traitor Arnold ever had anything to do with the great victory?

After Camden, there's only one American force of consequence operating in the South, and that's Sumter's partisans. With four hundred reinforcements sent by Gates on August 15, he takes his men toward the Catawba country, in the northwest, and Cornwallis sends Tarleton after him.

Once more it's a story of that iron man, Tarleton, driving fiercely over the rough terrain, men dropping out, some dying from sunstroke and exhaustion, horses collapsing, but eventually 100 dragoons and 60 infantry of Tarleton's survivors catch up with Sumter on the eighteenth, at Fishing Creek, taking the Americans by surprise as they're resting at midday. The surprise is complete, and it's another massacre. Before he's through, Tarleton and his men have killed and wounded another 150 Americans, besides taking 300 prisoners and the usual haul of wagons and supplies. Sumter just barely escapes, without hat, coat, or boots.

There's even a bonus. Sumter was holding 100 British regulars and 150 Loyalists, who are now liberated. British losses are negligible—1 officer killed, 15 men wounded. If Cornwallis has set out to end resistance in the Carolinas, and he has, a good start has certainly been made with these two quick, easy victories. It's the low point for Americans in the South. With South Carolina subdued, what's to prevent Cornwallis from marching triumphantly up through North Carolina to Virginia?

By the irony of war, the only commander in his way at the moment is Gates, who by this time is convinced that Camden wasn't really his fault at all, that he was just unlucky. At his camp, behind the courthouse in Hillsboro, he looks around to see if there's anything available that will pass for an army. Not much, to be sure. No militia at all, and only a few units from the Maryland and Delaware regiments available. In mid-September, however, Colonel Buford rides into camp with a small force of 300 men, consisting of a few recruits and what remains of his regiment. Then slowly more help trickles in—50 militia, some more from Delaware freed by the Swamp Fox from British captivity. In all, about 1,200 men, or half of what Gates began with on this ill-fated campaign.

Cornwallis, meanwhile, is ready to go. He's thinking not only North Carolina and Virginia, but what's to stop him, if he gets that far, from invading Pennsylvania and Maryland? At the moment, his only problems are sickness among his troops and the constant annoyance of savage American guerrilla bands, who keep pecking away at him. It's incredible to him, the sheer gall of these Americans. As the army marches near Charlotte, a small band of partisans stands boldly in his way. As his commissary chief writes, in disbelief, "The whole of the British army was actually kept at bay for some minutes by a few mounted Americans, not exceeding twenty."

No matter where he goes now, Cornwallis is in hostile country. The best man he has to deal with these irregulars is Major Patrick Ferguson—"Bull Dog" Ferguson, his officers call him—a man "slight of build, long, oval, gentle-looking face, and affable disposition," as he's described, a Highlander who's a first-class professional soldier. A deadly marksman, Ferguson had invented a new kind of breech-loading rifle gun earlier in the war, and a special corps armed with it used this weapon to good effect at Brandywine. After that battle, Howe—was it jealousy or just carelessness?—disbanded the unit, saying he hadn't been consulted.

He adroitly keeps ahead of the army Gates sends out from the Hillsboro regrouping until the Americans finally catch up with him at King's Mountain in October 1780 and storm his positions, in one of the fiercest battles of this fierce back-country war.

One of the first casualties is Colonel James Williams, who had been with Gates through the whole campaign in the Carolinas. A sixteen-year-old private, Thomas Young, sees the end of the gallant colonel while he (Young) is limping along barefoot, having lost his shoes, but still managing to carry "a large old musket, charged with two balls.

"On the top of the mountain, in the thickest of the fight," Young reports later, "I saw Colonel Williams fall. . . . I had seen him but once before that day. It was at the beginning of the action, as he charged by me at full speed around the mountain. Toward the summit, a ball struck his horse under the jaw, when he commenced stamping as if he were in a nest of yellow jackets. The colonel threw his reins over the animal's neck, sprang to the ground, and dashed onward. The moment I heard the cry that Colonel Williams was shot, I ran to his assistance, for I loved him as a father. He had ever been so kind to me and almost always carried a cake in his pocket for me and his little son, Joseph. They . . . sprinkled some water on his face. He revived, and his first words were, 'For God's sake, boys, don't give up the hill! . . . I left him in the arms of his son, Daniel, and returned to the field to avenge his fate."

There's never any doubt about where Ferguson is during the battle. He moves his men around with signals from a silver whistle, whose shrill, penetrating sound can be heard above the clamor. Spurring a horse from side to side, Ferguson seems to be everywhere, highly visible in his checkered hunting shirt, his dress sword in his left hand and his whistle in his teeth. He's really asking for it, and suddenly it happens. The whistle stops in mid-signal, and he can no longer be seen. Captain Abraham De Peyster, his devoted second in command, whom everyone calls "the Bull Dog's pup," sees his commander fall, riddled by several bullets. When they reach Ferguson, one foot is still caught in the stirrup. They lift him down and prop him against a tree, but in a few minutes he's dead.

That event takes the heart out of the British. They wave the white flag, but the fighting has been so intense, it takes a little time to get the firing stopped. The man who bears the flag is shot down. The defenders raise another flag and call for quarter. Colonel Isaac Shelby, commanding the Americans, wants to know why they don't throw down their arms if they're surrendering, and they do. But the Americans keep on firing, and Shelby with another officer has to order them to stop. One still protesting soldier yells, "Give 'em Buford's ploy." The British, however, escape the fate of the Americans at the Waxhaw.

There's so much confusion that not everyone knows for a time that

Ferguson is dead and this is why the battle's over. One soldier, Robert Henry, says, "I had a desire to see him and went and found him . . . shot in the face and in the breast. . . . Samuel Talbot turned him over and got his pocket pistol." Ferguson is hurried off the field, wrapped in a raw beef hide.

As early autumn darkness settles over the gloomy woods on the mountain, both sides are so exhausted that they simply lie down on the contested ground "amid the dead and the groans of the dying, who had neither surgical aid nor water to quench their thirst," as one of the survivors writes.

In the morning, another dismal scene. Many of those under Ferguson in this battle were local Loyalist militia, and now, as James Collins tells us, "The wives and children of the poor Tories came in, in great numbers. Their husbands, fathers, and brothers lay dead in heaps, while others lay wounded or dying. . . . We proceeded to bury the dead, but it was badly done. They were thrown into convenient piles and covered with old logs, the bark of old trees and rocks, yet not so as to secure them from becoming a prey to the beasts of the forest, or the vultures of the air; and the wolves (later) became so plenty, that it was dangerous for anyone to be out at night for several miles around.

"Also the hogs in the neighborhood gathered into the place to devour the flesh of men, inasmuch as numbers chose to live on little meat rather than eat their hogs, though they were fat. Half of the dogs in the country were said to be mad and were put to death. I saw myself in passing the place, a few weeks after, all parts of the human frame . . . scattered in every direction. . . ."

Prisoners aren't even safe once they're captured and moved. Four days after King's Mountain, officers are still having to order their men to stop killing or torturing prisoners, as well as plundering the neighborhood, robbing Whigs and Tories indiscriminately. Before commanding officers can stop them, lesser ranks set up impromptu courts-martial and hang a number of prisoners.

Captured prisoners are taken to Gilbert Town, and there, in spite of everything the commanders can do, these helpless, unarmed men are fired on by American troops, others are beaten, others slashed with swords, others hanged. The charges against thirty-six prisoners who are tried by a committee of colonels tell why the fury persists. They are accused of breaking open houses, killing the men, turning the men and women out of doors, and burning the houses. Savagery is answered by more savagery. Nevertheless, some sense of justice remains. When the trial ends late at night, only nine of the thirty-six are found guilty and hanged.

King's Mountain is not a major battle, but it's an important one because this relatively minor victory makes the Americans believe that things aren't as hopeless as they thought, that Cornwallis isn't simply going to roll over them on his way to Virginia. And since those were mostly Loyalist militia who were devastated on the mountain, a chill goes through the Tory partisans and militiamen, who now think twice before they turn out to fight. That cuts off a source of supply for Cornwallis, who now finds himself retreating instead of advancing, with the American militia harassing him every step of the way. Autumn rains have made the roads a morass, wagons get lost, food supplies vanish, often the men are compelled to sleep on the wet ground. Sickness is rampant. Cornwallis himself is in a hospital wagon with a fever. Lying there, he realizes he's going to have to rethink his plans for a winter campaign.

17

+   +   +

Moving Toward the Climax:
The War in the South

Retreating as far as Winnsborough, North Carolina, Cornwallis considers what he's going to do next in the bright days of mid-October 1780. Tarleton, meanwhile, occupies himself with pursuing Sumter, whom he catches up with and attacks on November 20, at Blackstocks. This time the dashing horseman has his spurs clipped, not only being repulsed but losing more than a hundred men.

Is this another signal of things to come? The war may be looking up for the Americans. Gates, the old favorite of Congress, is now in their doghouse after his dismal failures, so the legislators have had to swallow their pride and ask Washington to appoint someone else. He immediately named Nathanael Greene, who only a few weeks ago had so few friends in Congress that some were talking about dismissing him from the service. At the end of 1780, Greene is off to his new command with Light Horse Harry Lee and Steuben. He leaves Steuben in Virginia to watch General Leslie, who seems to have designs on the territory.

In December, Clinton sends a raiding expedition to Virginia, testing the ground, and who's in command? None other than Arnold, the eminent traitor. He's anything but popular with the British, who still think he was a very bad exchange for André, but Clinton isn't blind to the turncoat's military talents. He entrusts 1,500 British provincials to him, and Arnold takes them down to Portsmouth; from there, he sweeps up the James to Jamestown. Leaving half his force in that village, Arnold hurries on to Richmond, where he destroys the place and seizes great quantities of stores. Steuben hurries to the rescue with a respectable force, and Arnold has to retreat to Portsmouth, but his first excursion for the British is an unqualified success.

As 1781 begins, and the war moves toward a climax, Cornwallis has made up his mind. With Gates gone, he's now confronting Greene, who has only 2,000 men available against 3,200 British troops. No sense in a head-on collision, Greene concludes, and divides his force into what amounts to two guerrilla armies.

Daniel Morgan has just rejoined the army, and Greene sends him with five hundred men to join up with Sumter in the West. Maybe they can move against Ninety Six then, or even Augusta. Greene himself establishes a base on the falls of the Pee Dee River. He's taking a big gamble by splitting his small army this way; his forces are separated by nearly 160 miles. Believing he's made the wrong decision and the risk is too great, Greene reunites himself with Morgan in North Carolina, and in January he sends Harry Lee's Legion down to help Marion.

These moves inspire Cornwallis to change his strategy. If most of the Americans are now in North Carolina, obviously that's the place to be and he decides to march there, destroying Morgan along the way if possible. He delegates Tarleton to make the first strike at Morgan, hoping to compel him to cross the Broad River, where Cornwallis can get at him.

When Morgan's intelligence tells him what the British are up to, he concludes that it would be better to confront Tarleton before Cornwallis can get there. At dusk on the evening of January 15, he falls back on a town called Cowpens, in the northwest corner of South Carolina, where Colonel Pickens, with two hundred more militia, joins him later that night, bringing the American total to about a thousand men. Morgan had hoped for more militia, but it turns out that many of them are on the frontier, fighting Indians.

Now the stage is set for one of the war's epic battles—Tarleton, the aristocrat, the brilliant leader of cavalry, against Daniel Morgan, the unlettered giant, the hero of Quebec and a number of other places. What a match-up! And not far away is Cornwallis, who is disobeying orders. Clinton has told him to stay in South Carolina and hold it at all costs because it's the key state in the British Southern strategy. But Cornwallis is equally convinced that Virginia is the theater where the fate of the South must be decided, and he's on his way there now. He means to cross the Dan River into North Carolina and then push on into Virginia, which he thinks will be a pushover.

Morgan means to stop him at Cowpens, or wherever he can. What a man, this Morgan! Born of Welsh parents who came to America in 1730 and settled on the New Jersey side of the Delaware River, Daniel grew up there and launched himself into the world at seventeen, unequipped to do anything substantial because he could scarcely read and had failed completely to master arithmetic. It was a wandering life for him, working at odd jobs, clearing land, becoming a wagoner, tough and unruly, with a quick temper. We've seen how he was nearly killed by British discipline, but survived to join the army and become a fighter with a formidable reputation.

After Saratoga, Morgan shared Arnold's feeling that he hadn't been given his due for what he'd done in the field. He was still a colonel and not well paid when he was paid at all. He was broke and heard from home that his farm was going to seed. Desperate, he asked Washington for a promotion, but the commander couldn't get him one, so he resigned in July 1779, went home, and stayed there until Gates's defeat at Camden. At that point, Washington asked him to return to service, and Morgan said he would if he was made a brigadier general. Now the promotion's been granted.

Oddly enough, in some respects Tarleton is not unlike Morgan, although they couldn't be further apart in background. This charming young man, with an Oxford education, was also a violent hellraiser when he was growing up, and he hasn't changed much. It was typical of him that when he heard about Concord and Lexington, he proclaimed: "To hell with the law! These miserable Americans must be taught their place." He's a man without mercy, as we've learned, and looking at him dashing and slashing his way on various battlefields, it's hard to believe that after the war he will be elected to Parliament and acquire as a mistress the beautiful actress-author, Mary Robinson. She had rehearsed her bedroom role with the nineteen-year-old Prince of Wales, who will become George VI. When he reaches the throne, the King will knight Tarleton. By 1812, Tarleton will be a full general and married to the Duke of Ancaster's daughter.

As they face each other at Cowpens, there's the usual disparity between the forces these two men command. Tarleton has his notorious legion, about 350 men, divided between dragoons and mounted infantry, along with a Royal Artillery unit carrying two three-pounders, and three battalions of British regulars, all veterans, with a sufficiency of food, clothes, and uniforms. Morgan, by contrast, has some detachments of Continentals, all lacking food, clothing, and uniforms, indifferently trained, along with militia troops who seem well above the average: they are marksmen and veterans.

When he gets to Cowpens at sundown, Morgan walks among the men and tells them they're about to fight Tarleton. Watching him with deep respect is Thomas Young, a volunteer attached to William Washington's cavalry, who reports: "He went among the volunteers, helped them fix their swords, joked with them about their sweethearts, told them to keep in good spirits, and the day would be ours. And long after I laid down, he was going about among the soldiers, encouraging them and telling them that the old wagoner would crack his whip over Ben [meaning Tarleton] in the morning, as sure as they lived. 'Just hold up your heads, boys,' he would say, 'three fires and you are free, and then when you return to your homes, how the old folks will bless you, and the girls kiss you for your gallant conduct!' I don't believe he slept a wink that night."

Morgan gives the men some idea of why he is unbeatable. Half-crippled with sciatica and rheumatism as he is, he lifts up his shirt and shows the troops what 499 British lashes did to his back, while they crowd around to see in the flickering campfire light. He tells them, "I'm going to put a line of North Carolina men way down front, and right alongside I'll put the same number from South Carolina. You're always blowing about how you can outshoot everyone else. All right. Here's your chance to prove it. Let's see you get mad and shoot straight. These damned British have burned your houses and killed your cattle and stolen your chickens and scared hell out of your womenfolks, and right here's the place to do something about it."

In the morning, with the men drawn up for battle, Morgan is still exhorting them. "Ease your joints," he calls out in the brisk January morning air.

Years later, military historians will still be disagreeing about whether Morgan has picked the proper place to fight, and whether his unorthodox disposal of his troops is wise. He chooses open woods to make a stand, with flanks unprotected, and with plenty of room for Tarleton's cavalry to operate. Behind him the Board River, effectively barring American retreat except at high cost. Before they can reach the river, though, the British will have to cross two small hills about five hundred yards apart.

Morgan disposes his troops in three lines. First come 150 riflemen from Georgia and South Carolina, a skirmish line. Behind them, 300 militia, also from Georgia and from both Carolinas, commanded by Pickens. The main line is at the crest of the first hill's slope, and it consists of 280 Maryland regulars, with Virginia militia on the left and Georgia militia on the right—all told, about 400 men. On the second hill are 80 cavalry and 40 volunteer horsemen under William Washington, another overweight officer but a valuable one.

Why doesn't he have a swamp to anchor his line? Morgan does not trust the militia. They've let him down before. He wouldn't have a swamp anywhere near the militia, he says later, because "they would have made for it, and nothing could have detained them from it." That's also why he deliberately closes off retreat by way of the river. "It was the very thing I wished to cut off all hope of," he says. "When men are forced to fight, they will sell their lives dearly. Had I crossed the river, one-half of the militia would immediately have abandoned me."

On the other hand, having been with them so often on so many battlefields, Morgan doesn't entirely discount the militia. He believes they'll do well if they don't have to do it too long; consequently he orders the first line to fire two blasts "at killing distance," then come back behind the main line, and he informs the other units about these orders so they won't think it's a retreat. His basic strategy is not to overwhelm Tarleton, just to discourage him enough so that Morgan can leave the field reasonably intact and hook up with Greene to create a more formidable army then he has now.

At dawn on the morning of January 16, Morgan's scouts rush in to report that Tarleton is only five miles away, after one of his famous all-night marches, this one five hours long. When these messengers arrive, Morgan has skipped breakfast and he's ready, but the troops are still eating. They rush to arms still chewing on half-cooked bacon, or with the last bite of oatmeal cake dribbling from their mouths.

Thomas Young writes: "About sunrise, the British line advanced at sort of a trot with a loud halloo. It was the most beautiful line I ever saw. When they shouted, I heard Morgan say, 'They give us the British halloo, boys. Give them the Indian halloo, by God!' and he galloped along the lines, cheering the men and telling them not to fire until we could see the white of their eyes [shades of Breed's Hill!]. Every officer was crying, 'Don't fire!' for it was a hard matter to keep us from it. . . . The militia fired first. It was for a time, pop-pop-pop, and then a whole volley; but when the regulars fired, it seemed like one sheet of flame from right to left. Oh! it was beautiful!"

One militia veteran out there, popping away, is James Collins, who fought at King's Mountain, and who rode into camp just before the battle. Collins has a small handicap: he gets sick when he sees blood. Nevertheless, he's fighting now on the right of this dismounted militia, fires once, then sees the morning sun flash on British bayonets and runs for his horse. By this time the dragoons have reached the militia and are trying to get behind them so they can conduct the customary slaughter.

Collins writes: " 'Now,' thought I, 'my hide is in the loft.' Just as we got to our horses, they overtook us and began to take a few hacks at some, however, without doing much injury. They, in their haste, had pretty much scattered, perhaps thinking they would have another Fishing Creek frolic [as they did when they destroyed Sumter's South Carolina partisans], but in a few moments, Colonel [William] Washington's cavalry was among them, like a whirlwind, and the poor fellows began to keel from their horses without being able to remount. The shock was so sudden and fierce they could not stand it, and immediately betook themselves in flight. There was no time to rally, and they appeared to be as hard to stop as a drove of wild Choctaw steers going to a Pennsylvania market. In a few minutes, the clashing of swords was out of hearing and quickly out of sight. . . . Morgan rode up and waving his sword cried out, 'Form, form, my brave fellows! Give them one more fire, and the day is ours. Old Morgan was never beaten!' "

Tarleton's men are more than a little weary after the long overnight march, guided by Loyalist backwoodsmen, who a British major asserts "are more savage than the Indians, and possess every one of their vices but not one of their virtues." This major says they'll "travel two hundred miles through woods, never keeping any road or path, guided by the sun by day and the stars by night, to kill a particular person belonging to the opposite party."

That's how Tarleton's men have found the Americans and, tired or not, they make a brave sight in that first assault, lines of scarlet and white, others in kilts and scarlet jackets, the horsemen in green, Royal Artillerymen in blue. It's the green-jacketed cavalrymen whose charge James Collins has described. When they retreat, Morgan's forward sharpshooters run back up the slope to the safety of Pickens's line, just as Morgan had instructed them to do ("they don't run away if they're ordered to run," the general says).

Now the British regulars advance in a bright mosaic of color. When they're about a hundred yards from the second line, the militia meet them with a devastating volley, backed up by another from sharp-shooters on the slope. The British are staggered. They halt, uncertain and angry, firing a volley of their own, but while they're reloading, the second line of militia gives them another round, killing or wounding half the British officers. Then, according to plan, these militia too retreat, and that looks like the usual panic the British expect from the Americans, so the cavalry swings in to pursue them.

As it happens, the British are at least partly right and Morgan's faith in the militia is shaken again as they fail to fall back in an orderly way, some of them jumping on their horses and galloping away, turning deaf ears to their officers. Thinking it's a rout, the British cheer and run after them, but the fleeing men get behind a clump of young pines on the slope and make a stand.

Again, Morgan orders his troops in the main line to hold their fire, and as the British run up the hill, bayonets at the ready to plunge into panicky Americans, he gives his regulars the order to fire. That stops the oncoming troops cold. Tarleton sees what's happening and sends in his reserves. The Highlanders charge the Virginia militia and the Maryland Continentals fighting together. Tarleton leads his dragoons in a flanking maneuver, but as he gets near the militia, William Washington's cavalry come galloping out of the swale. It's a head-on collision, and the dragoons fly apart. The Americans fall back to the swale, and there Pickens re-forms the militia.

In the next fifteen minutes, everything begins to disintegrate for Tarleton although, as always in war, chance decides much of what happens. When the Marylanders are ordered to turn at right angles and meet the oncoming Highlanders, they misunderstand, about-face instead, and start for the rear. Morgan sees this and rides across the line, instructing the officers to have their men ready to turn and fire when they're ordered. A moment later, William Washington observes Tarleton and his dragoons bearing down on the still retreating troops, and once more he comes out of the swale. Swords flashing, his men cut their way through the British charge and shatter it, then turn around and attack from the rear.

As Kenneth Roberts points out in his study of the battle, this event contains a good many "ifs": "If the Highlanders and the British line could have come to grips with the Continentals and Virginia militia, if Tarleton's cavalry could have hit the Continental right wing, as he anticipated, Morgan would have lost." But the old veteran's strategy of planned retreat gives Tarleton the illusion that the entire American infantry force is falling back, at least, and probably running way. Thinking they've won, the Highlanders and the British line, minus most of its officers, run after them up the hill in a disorderly mob. They have almost reached the rebel troops when, on Morgan's order, these troops turn suddenly and open a devastating point-blank fire, at thirty yards. Then the Americans run at the enemy with their bayonets, while Pickens's South Carolina militia charge out of the swale on the double to help them.

For once, Tarleton completely loses control of a battle. Why doesn't his cavalry obey orders? Later historians have offered fanciful reasons, but Tarleton himself says in his memoirs that there's no satisfactory explanation. Ordered to check the enemy on the right until Tarleton can rally the infantry, they simply refuse to do it, and neither threats nor promises move them. They either surrender or just fade away.

The most savage fighting takes place on the hilltop, where the Americans kill the Royal Artillerymen to the last man, with bayonets, sabers, and muskets. The British officers scream at them, waving their swords, but it's no good. Tarleton can't even persuade his cavalry to make a final, desperate charge, the kind he's noted for, and two hundred of his dragoons, the most feared troops in the British army, unbelievably just run away.

There's no help for it. Tarleton has to retreat toward the place where he believes Cornwallis is waiting with the main army, and if that had been true, he might yet have saved the day. But Cornwallis is twenty-five miles away, and no help at all.

The whole battle takes no more than an hour, and the British loss is heavy—110 killed, 200 wounded, more than 500 prisoners taken. Tarleton tries to burn his baggage, but Morgan manages to seize 800 muskets, 2 three-pound cannon, 60 black servants, 100 cavalry horses, 35 wagons loaded with the 7th Regiment's baggage, a traveling forge, and "all the enemy's music." Morgan's losses are light, only 12 killed and 61 wounded.

In the days after the battle, both Tarleton and Morgan have their critics. An American officer asks his British counterpart, one of the prisoners, why Tarleton's men were brought into action in such a desultory way. "Nothing better could be expected from troops commanded by a rash, foolish boy," the officer replies harshly.

Knowing that Cornwallis's arrival might be imminent, Morgan paroles the British officers and marches off to Catawba with his prisoners. It's his last action for the American cause. Twenty-three days after Cowpens, he retires from the army. It isn't the criticism of his tactics that inspires this move, but his sciatica and rheumatism, with malaria now added to the list. He can take great satisfaction, however, from the fact that his last blow was his best, and that when news of his victory reaches the North, it has a powerful effect on the morale of everyone, making people aware of how important it is to give Greene all the help he needs in the South.

Until now there's been considerable apathy about Cornwallis's march northward, but in the wake of Cowpens there's a general sense of the danger, and Morgan has demonstrated that the British and their best general aren't unbeatable. At last, Morgan gets his due, a gold medal voted by Congress, silver medals for other officers, and a ceremonial sword for Pickens. The Virginia House of Delegates, suddenly conscious of what they owe him, vote to give Morgan a house, "with furniture," and a sword.

So where is Cornwallis after this stunning American victory? Not brooding about it. When he gets the news, he sets off in pursuit of Morgan, but he realizes this old bird is likely to fly away without being caught, and he can't stand the prospect. He goes so far as to destroy his heavy baggage, tents, spare clothing, and supplies, even his rum, so that the army can move faster in the pursuit. He takes the wagon horses out of their traces and sets infantry on them. But then there's more frustration. For two days he can't cross the Catawba because heavy rains have swollen it.

Meanwhile, Greene is on the move. He sends Major General Isaac Huger, one of the celebrated Huger brothers of South Carolina, toward Salisbury, and with only a few men, he hurries over 150 miles of rain-soaked country alive with Loyalists to take command of Morgan's force. When he gets to Catawba, it isn't a triumphant army he sees but one beset with the usual troubles. The Virginia militiamen's time has expired, and they've already left for home, along with other militia from Georgia and South Carolina.

Greene changes his plans when he hears this, and sends a message to Huger that he'll meet him with what troops he can muster at Guilford Courthouse, not Salisbury. He's waiting, too, for Morgan's infantry and artillery, still on their way. He sends boats across the Yadkin River to get them, and they make it on February 3, with Cornwallis's advance guard so close that they can see the Americans' retreating backs. Cornwallis doesn't have any boats, so he has to go twenty-five miles upstream before he can find a ford.

Now it's a race for the Dan River, that gateway to Virginia. Cornwallis marches toward the upper Dan, believing Greene can't get across lower down. Greene at first planned on confronting the British at Guilford Courthouse, but when he finally gets his army together there, the deficiency of militia makes it too dangerous and he decides to push on toward the Dan.

By this time it's raw and blustery, the roads drowned by day in mud and water, freezing at night to make sharp ruts that cut the men's feet; many of them also have no shoes. However, the two armies do share some things; neither has tents nor enough food. The Americans, of course, are worse off. Their supply system is a mess in any case, but when field movements are so rapid, it gets worse. On the cold nights, three men are compelled to huddle under one blanket.

Greene's goal is to reach Boyd's Ferry, so he puts seven hundred men under the command of General Otho Williams, to keep Cornwallis at bay, if possible, until he can get to the ferry, where his quartermaster is already assembling boats for the crossing and Kosciuszko is erecting breastworks on the north bank to confront the British when they get there.

By this time, Greene's army is further depleted by the defection of the North Carolina militia, all but eighty of whom have simply quit the war. Nevertheless, Williams's little army is affording him more time as Cornwallis pursues him so closely that the general begins to wonder whether he'll have to sacrifice himself and his men to save the main army. But the maneuver works. Word comes that Greene has ferried the troops across, and they're next—cheering news for men who have been marching for four days with little chance to sleep. They hurry to the ford and get across, while Lee's cavalry delays Tarleton, who's now joined forces with Cornwallis. It's a close call. Lee's men swim the river with their horses just ahead of the enemy.

So it's an American retreat, all right, two hundred grueling miles of it, but it's a strategic one. An army is saved and Cornwallis is frustrated as he gets to the Dan and sees the campfires of the Americans blazing on the other side, with no way for him to cross the river. Moreover, he's extremely short of supplies because of his decision to junk them so he could move faster, and he's also a long way from home. At the moment, there's no way he can even think of invading Virginia, his ultimate goal, so he retreats to Hillsboro, where he hopes to acquire some Loyalist militia.

Greene has no intention of letting him off the hook so easily. Recrossing the Dan, he moves toward Cornwallis once more. An immediate reward occurs. Light Horse Harry Lee's cavalry encounters three hundred Loyalist militia who think erroneously that his cavalry is Tarleton's and suffer the consequences. When Cornwallis hears this bad news, he's moved to action at once. Both sides are eager for battle, but Greene is waiting for supplies from Virginia and they're late arriving, so for ten days he and the British maneuver about and make cautious feints at each other. At last Greene gets his supplies and decides to make his stand at Guilford Courthouse, with an army of about 4,500 men who vastly outnumber Cornwallis's scanty 1,900.

On a clear, cool March day, the fifteenth, the British attack soon after midday on a broken, hilly terrain where woodlands alternate with clearings. Greene's strategy emulates Morgan's at Cowpens. He places some North Carolina militia in the front line, under Generals John Butler and Pinketham Eaton, then forms a second line of Virginia militia three hundred yards back up a hill, commanded by Generals Edward Stevens and Robert Lawson. Four hundred yards farther back are the main force of Continentals under Huger and Williams—two Virginia regiments and the 1st and 2nd Maryland, the former of which is known to be one of the best available. Flanking the 1st in woods are William Washington's cavalry on the right and Lee's on the left. These lines are too far apart for support—a mistake. Greene apparently puts more faith in the militia than Morgan did.

The battle begins with a skirmish between Tarleton and Lee, and then the British attack the North Carolina militia on the first line. The Americans fire two or three rounds, turn, run for their lives from the battlefield, and are of no further use. That compels Washington's and Lee's men to fall back, but they do so in an orderly way. The Virginians in the second line are meanwhile moving down on the advancing enemy, but they're forced to fall back too, and that leaves the third American line, where the 1st Maryland is inflicting severe damage on the British line, first stopping it with heavy fire and then, having thinned it out, breaking up the remains with bayonets, mortally wounding their commander, Brigadier General James Webster, who had fought nearly the entire war with exceptional distinction—a severe loss to Cornwallis.

Greene fails to follow up this success as he might have done. Too risky, he thinks, and loses an opportunity. His failure gives the British a chance to launch another assault, this time by the Guards battalion, on the 2nd Maryland, who are green troops. They collapse under this pressure. But as the British pour through their lines, the 1st Maryland, with cool precision, swing around and catch the enemy's flank, while Washington's cavalry closes in on the other side to finish the job. The Guards flee, demoralized, with Washington in pursuit. Again, Greene is in a position to finish off the enemy, and again he decides it's too risky.

The fight goes on in a disorganized way, British and Americans, and their horses, swirling around in a confused mass. Cornwallis has his horse shot out from under him and, considering his situation a step away from disaster, orders up his artillery and instructs it to fire grapeshot into the maelstrom, which means that British as well as Americans are going to be killed. The grapeshot is devastating, and it does set back the Americans, giving Cornwallis the chance to regroup and send all the men he has remaining against the American left.

At this point, Greene decides enough is enough. He has visible evidence from the scarlet forms lying on the battleground that he has done considerable damage to the British, and he understands too that, if he persists and loses his own army, he won't get another one. So he decides to take the prudent course and, in an orderly retreat, brings his men by a night march to an ironworks on the opposite side of the Haw River, which he reaches by daybreak. Cornwallis doesn't follow; he's had enough too, for the time being. His losses are truly serious: 93 killed, 413 wounded, 26 missing. He'll lose some more as those wounded but still alive have to lie all night after the battle in a heavy rain. Greene says in a report to Jefferson that his losses are "very trifling," but just the same, the figures are 78 killed, 183 wounded.

As far as Greene is concerned, it's the defection of the North Carolina militia that sticks in his craw. He writes later: "The conflict was bloody and severe, and had the North Carolina militia done their duty, victory would have been certain and early. But they deserted the most advantageous post I ever saw, and without scarcely firing a gun. The Virginia militia behaved with great gallantry, and the fate of the day was long and doubtful. But finally we were obliged to give up the ground, and as all our artillery horses were killed before the retreat began, we were obliged to leave our artillery on the ground."

In this strange Southern war, the Americans both win and lose at Guilford Courthouse. People may criticize Greene for winning battles he seems to lose again by retreating, but in the end, it's the British who suffer most after these engagements, and Greene does what's vital, that is, keeps an army together without losing it. There's nothing more in the bottom of the barrel. A case in point is Cornwallis, who holds the field at Guilford Courthouse but nevertheless has to give up his planned campaign and retreat toward Wilmington with his battered troops. Greene follows him for a way, just to rub it in, but then lets him go.

Once in Wilmington, Cornwallis's spirits revive a bit and he decides the thing to do is give up on both the Carolinas and open a new theater in Virginia which he has intended to do all along. That leaves Greene free to advance into South Carolina and try to retrieve it from Lord Rawdon, who commands the forces Cornwallis has left there. Rawdon is young and half-sick, but he's a veteran, having been fighting more or less continuously since Breed's Hill. He's no amateur, with more than 8,000 men strung out across South Carolina and Georgia. However, he has only about 1,500 he can employ as a striking force, and they're at Camden.

If Greene thinks he's going to swallow up the British forts dotting the countryside all the way to Savannah, he's seriously mistaken, particularly since he has only a core force of 1,500 Continentals, plus whatever militia he can persuade to turn out, an always doubtful proposition. He can never be sure what these partisan guerrilla commanders—Pickens, Marion, Sumter—will do. They do what they feel like doing. Greene's dilemma is that he has to have their support to take over the state from the British, and that means he has to support them when they need it, but he can't guarantee they'll be there when *he* needs *them.*

Now that he's here, however, Greene has to do something, and obviously the first objective must be Rawdon's force at Camden; he'll need Sumter's assistance, if he can get it. Meanwhile, he sends Lee to join Marion for an attack on Fort Watson and dispatches a message to Pickens, telling him it would be a good time to attack Ninety Six.

Lee and Marion make the first move, laying siege to Fort Watson, which stands atop an old Indian burying mound, an evaluation that makes it difficult for besiegers who, in effect, have to shoot uphill sharply with their rifles. One of Marion's officers has an ingenious idea. Why not build a tower higher than the fort, a notion that goes right back to the Middle Ages? At night, the whole structure begins to take shape and by morning it's ready. Under cover of this elevated firing range, the Americans storm the walls and take the fort.

Greene isn't so successful, but it's his own fault. Trying to take Camden by surprise on April 19, he's betrayed by informers—will commanders never learn that there's no such thing as surprise in this war?—and Greene finds himself under attack on Hobkirk's Hill, two miles from the fort. Rawdon has only 900 men against Greene's 1,420, nearly all of them Continentals, but this advantage only makes Nathanael overreach himself. He tries a cute trick, waiting until the British are in range, then drawing aside the two regiments in front, like a curtain, revealing a battery of cannon. The blast certainly surprises the British and they fall back. The 1st Maryland and 2nd Virginia come at them with bayonets, while the 2nd Maryland and 1st Virginia try to execute a double flanking maneuver as William Washington's cavalry attacks the rear.

It seems like a plan designed for success, but Rawdon is a young man who knows what he's doing, and he extends his line so that it overlaps the American front. At that point, Greene's strategy begins to unravel. A 1st Maryland company loses its captain and falls back, and other companies follow. Trying to re-form, they fall into a hopeless tangle and leave the field, followed by the 2nd Maryland, leaving the 1st Virginia unsteady and the 2nd Virginia facing Rawdon alone.

Once more Greene has to order a retreat, and in his anxiety to save his guns nearly gets himself captured until he's saved by Washington's cavalry, who rescue the general and his guns after a brief charge. The 2nd Virginia holds firm and cuts off pursuit. Counting up the score, it's another loss-victory—270 casualties on the British side, 134 Americans killed and wounded—but Rawdon has the field.

After this, the war in the South will disintegrate into a series of guerrilla battles following Rawdon's withdrawal to a point about thirty miles from Charleston. Every kind of assault known in the history of warfare is employed. For instance, Marion takes Fort Motte by setting it afire with flaming arrows. Lee and Pickens attack Augusta, where the six-hundred-man garrison is commanded by Lieutenant Colonel Thomas Brown, the man, you'll remember, who has a personal grudge since rebels roasted his feet early on in the war. He's been hanging as many of them as he can find ever since. His defense of Augusta is valiant, the action characterized on both sides by an absolute abdication of mercy. It takes building another tower, like the one at Fort Watson, with a six-pounder mounted on it, to make the place surrender.

Greene, with Lee and Pickens, besiege the little fort at Ninety Six, which is the center of the ruthless struggle going on between Georgia Tories and Whigs—a cesspool of destruction, torture, rape, and assassination. Lieutenant Colonel John Harris Cruger, a New Yorker, commands this fort and his men are from first-rate Loyalist regiments in New York and New Jersey, so it seems his skillful defense with these troops might succeed. But the fall of the other forts has left him isolated, and when orders are sent to him to make a prudent withdrawal, he unfortunately never gets them.

In attacking Ninety Six, Greene uses every device in the guerrilla war book—the wooden tower, fire arrows, and finally a head-on assault. Cruger's troops are half-dead with thirst, but they repel this attack, and Greene loses another battle when Rawdon makes a forced march from Charleston to save the fort. Still another American defeat, with 147 casualties to 85 for the defenders, and Greene is much depressed by it. Ninety Six is evacuated a few weeks later, however, and Greene can console himself with the knowledge that, while he may have tactical defects, in the end he emerges with strategic successes.

At least he has Rawdon out of his hair. The young general retires to Charleston and soon sails for home, his health badly impaired by the impossible American climate. Before he goes, he takes a last shot at the rebels, ordering the execution of Colonel Isaac Hayne, but this death is avenged, in a way. Rawdon's ship is captured by a French privateer and he has to sit in a Brest prison for a year before he's exchanged, even though the war is unofficially over.

In the summer of 1781, when it's too hot to fight, Greene takes his army up into the High Hills of Santee. Just a little more altitude—no more than two hundred feet—is enough to purify the air and make it possible to recruit and train for new ventures in the fall. The British 3rd Foot (known as "the Buffs") are only sixteen miles away. Their commander, Lieutenant Colonel Alexander Stewart, is doing much the same thing; a drowned land safely separates the two forces.

On August 28, with the summer nearly over, Greene sets out with a force of 2,300 men, only about 1,000 of whom are militia, and prepares to descend on Stewart by a circuitous route but, as usual, the British know he's coming and slowly fall back toward Eutaw Springs, their supply depot. Stewart doesn't learn just how close the Americans are until a hundred unarmed men he's sent out to dig sweet potatoes, with a cavalry escort, are pounced on by Lee, who captures half of them. When the cavalry escort gallops back with the news, Stewart prepares to fight, deploying his force of 1,800 across a main road. Another 300 are at his rear. Facing him are North Carolina militia in the first line, under Marion and Pickens, and two regular regiments from the same state on the right.

When these forces meet on the sultry afternoon of September 8, the Battle of Eutaw Springs proves to be one of the most desperate small engagements of the war. Greene's militia for once fight with stubborn courage before they're pushed back. The Maryland and Virginia men charge with bayonets, and eventually the British line has to retreat, although William Washington, leading his cavalry too far, is captured.

Having won the battle, the Americans now proceed once again to lose it. They've pushed the British all the way back through their camp, and come upon the stores of food and rum. It's too much to resist for men who have had so little of these primary comforts. Many of them get roaring drunk, and while troops who are sober try vainly to rout out a British force barricaded in a brick house and garden (so like the Chew house incident at Germantown), the enemy cavalry sweep back into their plundered camp, and only after hard fighting are driven back again by Captain Wade Hampton's cavalry. (Later in the month, Hampton will declare himself a Loyalist and switch sides for a few months.) In the end, the British regroup and Stewart leads them back to claim the field.

Once more Greene's army isn't really beaten; it's not a resounding defeat, or a rout, since he retreats in good order. Nevertheless, the British occupy the ground and the Americans have lost 120 men killed, 375 wounded, with 8 missing, while Stewart loses 85 killed, 351 wounded, and 480 missing, mostly prisoners.

Stewart pursues Greene halfheartedly for five miles as he pulls back to the High Hills, but the British commander believes it's wiser not to press the issue and retires to Charleston after destroying his stores and leaving his most seriously wounded men behind.

Eutaw Springs is the last fighting in the South that year, at least with any considerable forces. The guerrillas continue to operate in the Carolinas and Georgia. Oddly enough, although the British seem to have won most of the battles, the Americans are in charge, except for Savannah and Charleston. It's another strategic victory for Greene, who's come a long way with not much to help him since Gates left the Americans in such a desperate condition after Camden.

It's hard sometimes to understand the complexity of this Southern war, until it comes down to individuals. Just before the Battle of Eutaw Springs, here's John Chaney, a Randolph County, North Carolina, boy who's served two years as a volunteer in the South Carolina infantry. Now he's with Colonel Washington's cavalry, camped no more than a hundred yards from the British picket line. Billy Lunsford, one of Washington's dragoons, requests permission to leave camp and go shoot himself a redcoat sentinel.

As Chaney tells the story later, "The captain told him it could not do the cause any good, and, as the sentinel was doing his duty, it was a pity to shoot him. Billy swore his time was out, and, as he was going home to Virginia, he would have it to tell that he had killed 'one damned British son of a bitch.' Accordingly, Billy commenced passing backwards and forwards with a pistol, creeping on his all fours and grunting like a hog. The sentinel was heard to slap his cartouche box and fired, and Billy changed his grunting to groaning, being shot through the body, entering his right and coming out his left side. It was as pretty a shot as could have been made in daylight. The British sentinel, being reinforced, carried Billy a prisoner into their camp, where, by the kind attention of a British surgeon who nursed him and had him nursed all night to prevent his bleeding inwardly and to make him bleed outwardly, he recovered."

As for the civilians, friends or foes, they all think God is on their side. When he's asked to pray at a meeting, John Miller, a Scottish farmer in western Carolina, first reviews the bloodshed round about the shattered South, then he thanks the Good Lord specifically for King's Mountain, as well as for the battles of Ramseur's and Williamson's mills, and most especially Cowpens. But he can't forbear a touch of reproof. "Good Lord," he prays, "if ye had na suffered cruel Tories to burn Billy Hill's Iron Works we would na have asked any mair favors at Thy hands. Amen."

The Good Lord is busy elsewhere, but certainly it's an argument for divine intervention that the Americans are about to be provided with a formidable and decisive tool in their struggle. On the day after Eutaw Springs, Admiral de Grasse and his French fleet appear off the Chesapeake and the final act is about to begin.

18

✛   ✛   ✛

Moving Toward the Climax:
The War in the North

W hile Greene has been bringing the South under some kind of shaky control and forcing Cornwallis out of it toward his promised land, Virginia, the North has been suffering through its worst hours of the war.

The condition of the army was so serious in January 1780 that Washington almost despaired of holding it together. Mutiny was in the air, as it had been for the past two years, the tension slowly building, building. At the bottom of it, besides the current shortages of everything, was the pay situation. Some of the veterans remembered how Congress told them in the glory days of 1775 that they would get "higher pay than any private soldiers ever met with in any war." A grim joke now.

Through no fault of their own, the Pennsylvanians were the worst off. Troops from other colonies enlisted for a year at a time, and then many reenlisted to get the bounty. Pennsylvania had a different enlistment clause: "For three years or during the war." They were cut off from bounty money while their pay, when they got it, steadily depreciated. In 1778, Pennsylvania gave new recruits $100, but a year later, New Jersey was giving them $250 to enlist, and in Virginia it was $750, even larger in some New England towns.

Short-changed as they were, the Pennsylvanians fought well and made no serious trouble until the terrible winter of 1779–80 at Morristown, when they joined others in plundering the countryside after supplies failed to reach them. By February, though, they were beginning to desert in large numbers.

Other outbreaks of mutinous behavior flared up. In January 1780, when a hundred Massachusetts men at West Point declared their enlistments were up and marched off, they were brought back forcibly and a few were punished. In June, thirty-one New Yorkers at Fort Schuyler left to join the British, nearly naked and without pay. A search party of Americans and Oneida Indians caught up with them and shot thirteen. For the first time, Indians were ordered to fire on soldiers they were supposed to be supporting.

In May, more trouble at Morristown as troops almost had to be whipped into joining the summer campaign. Eleven men were under death sentences, all but one deserters. No one believed the sentences would be carried out but, on the other hand, no one was certain they wouldn't be. The British took advantage of the situation. They sent out handbills from New York saying, "You are neither clothed, fed, nor paid. Your number is wasting away by sickness, famine, nakedness. . . . This is then the moment to fly from slavery and fraud." The Morristown camp was close to mutiny, and it broke out first in the Connecticut line.

These Connecticut soldiers had real grievances—no pay, no meat for days, convinced they were being discriminated against by the commissary. They assembled on the parade ground at dusk and announced that they were going out to get food. There was a scuffle, negotiations, and at last a Pennsylvania brigade, just as hungry but not as desperate, got them under control, and a few were arrested. A minor explosion that time.

Next day, however, when the three to be hanged and the eight to be shot were hauled out, and those to be shot saw that they would first have to watch the others hanged, there was a wave of angry unrest. At the last minute, reprieves for seven of those to be hanged were rushed in from Washington. That left one James Coleman, of the 12th Pennsylvania, who had just heard the names of ten other men read out. Coleman's crimes were serious enough. He's been in the business of forging discharges, providing a hundred or so of his fellow soldiers, and himself, with the means to escape the army.

On the other hand, he was a good soldier. Only a year before, when he was with Sullivan at Lake Canandaigua, he and another man got separated from the regiment and for seven days had nothing to put in their mouths except the hearts and livers of two dead horses they found. Yet he returned to fight again. On the scaffold, he gave a little speech to his comrades, telling them to obey their officers and love their country, advising the officers not to give the men good reason to desert. As the hangman adjusted the noose, Coleman gave it a professional examination and said he was too heavy for the rope, and anyway, the knot wasn't right. He fixed the knot himself and placed the noose. The trap was pulled, and he fell to the ground, still alive. As he climbed back up again, he said, "I told you the rope wasn't strong enough. Do get a stronger one." They did and this time he swung free.

All this sets the stage for December 1780, when 2,473 officers and men of the Pennsylvania Line are among those suffering again at Morristown. Other Pennsylvania regiments augment their number, so the total may be as high as 3,500. These men are the undeserving victims of the state's citizenry, who have never been much in favor of the war, have stingily failed to support it, and now seem to wish it would just go away. With some of them it's a matter of principle, as in the case of the Quakers and religious German immigrants, but with others it's simply conservative indifference to the whole idea of the Revolution, which they now regard as an expensive nuisance. The shivering, hungry Pennsylvanians hear stories of how their fellow colonists back home are living high on the hog in Philadelphia, well clothed, well fed, and warm. Apparently they expect Pennsylvania soldiers to live on patriotism. This is something for them to think about at night while trying to sleep in cold, crowded huts or to make a little food go as far as possible, with no rum or coffee to wash it down. On the twenty-fifth of December comes a final blow: Pennsylvania announces that they won't be paid, at least on any fixed date, if at all. Happy New Year!

On the holiday itself, there's a little cheer—more for the officers, who enjoy what one calls an "elegant regimental dinner and entertainment." For the men, it's a half pint of liquor each. Anyone with money can buy more outside camp.

At night, about eight o'clock, a sound of huzzahing rises from the 11th Regiment, but everyone thinks they're drunk. This regiment is a mixed bag, as the historian Carl Van Doren tells us, of "native and foreign town-bred men, skilled at trades. They were alert, hungry, angry, dressed in shabby odds and ends, some felt bullied, others near the bursting point, some determined for a settlement no matter at what cost."

About 10:00 P.M., there's another disturbance. Shots are heard. Someone shoots off a skyrocket. That seems to be a signal, and suddenly the night is filled with men running from their huts, arms ready. Officers try to quiet them, but that's hard to do because half the Line is now involved. Regimental groups begin to come together, and a lieutenant trying to stop them is shot in the thigh for his trouble. A captain strikes a soldier and gets a shot in the belly in return. Firing becomes so general that the officers think it's best to leave the scene.

For the moment, there's no discipline. The mutineers seize fieldpieces, and the firing becomes more general and indiscriminate; one soldier is shot, several others wounded.

General Wayne arrives with a few mounted field officers and tries to quiet the rebellion, but he gets a blast of fire over his head. "If you mean to kill me," he tells them, "shoot me at once, here's my breast," and he opens his coat. But they say they don't want to kill him or any of the other officers—well, maybe with a few exceptions.

At this point, only a minority of soldiers are keeping the mutiny alive, and some old grudges are being paid off. Lieutenant Colonel William Butler is chased by a soldier who finds a better target when he meets Captain Adam Bentin and kills him. Slowly, however, the affair takes on the general aspects of a mass movement by the Pennsylvanians to leave camp, taking as many horses, wagons, tents, baggage, provisions, and as much ammunition as they can lay hands on. Their numbers swell as they move along, protected by their captured fieldpieces.

This mutineer army is confronted once more by Wayne at a crossroads nearby. If they go one way, they'll be heading for the British by way of Chatham and Elizabethtown. If they take the other road, they're on their way to Philadelphia and that's the way Wayne wants them to go. The mutineers are surprised and hurt that Wayne would think they might want to join the British. They're not deserting, they tell him. If the British attack them, they're ready to fight, but they won't obey Wayne or any of the other officers until their wrongs are righted. It's like a labor dispute of our own time. What the striking soldiers want is to negotiate on equal terms with officers or civilian officials and arrive at a settlement of their grievances. But is mutiny negotiable? Pausing nearby for a day or so, they send emissaries back to camp to see if they can persuade the undecided, and they're successful. Most of what's left of the Pennsylvania Line join their comrades.

Wayne understands he has to settle this business if he can, otherwise he's going to be left with only half his command. He draws up what he thinks are some negotiable terms and sets out with his two brigade commanders, Richard Butler and Walter Stewart, to approach the mutineers. He's made good choices: Butler, a popular Irishman, has three younger brothers in the Pennsylvania Line, and Stewart, Irish but Pennsylvania born, is a persuasive young colonel and (not that it matters), as Van Doren notes, "reputed to be the handsomest man in the army."

When they left the main camp, the mutineers stopped first at Vealtown (now Bernardsville), and next day, with new recruits and in high spirits, they marched on, about 1,500 strong, and stopped the next night at Middlebrook, Washington's old winter quarters. Wayne's party catches up with them there, accepting the hospitality of patriot farmer Derrick Van Veghten, at whose house Kitty Greene entertained in 1779. Then Wayne sends a message requesting the mutineers to dispatch a delegation of sergeants to represent them. Several sergeants and twelve soldiers show up at the Dutchman's house next day, not knowing for sure whether they're going to be treated as negotiators or seized as prisoners.

Wayne means to bargain in good faith, however, and the talks begin. As in most such disputes, they get nowhere for a while, and the mutineers become more impatient and angry by the hour. The talks break off and the Pennsylvanians resume their march toward Philadelphia. Wayne needn't have worried, although now he doesn't want them to go that far. The two sides get together again at Princeton, where the mutineers enjoy a friendly welcome because they've strictly refrained from looting, in a place which has been successively robbed by everyone involved in the war. In these talks, the Pennsylvanians are represented by a Board of Sergeants; even then, the American solution is to form a committee.

For two days they talk in Nassau Hall, while the mutineers firmly control the town. The sergeants make proposals and the conversation is entirely civil, but Wayne has no authority to grant most of what the men are asking. As the second day advances, there's hope of a compromise, but the conference is attracting some unwanted visitors in the wings. A small force of eighty armed officers is on the way to nearby Cranberry (now Cranbury), to wait for the outcome. Ominous for the mutineers. Members of the New Jersey legislature also come up from Trenton to join the talks but they're rebuffed because there's a rumor that Jersey militia are being called out. A British messenger shows up from New York and tells the Pennsylvanians that, if they can get to South Amboy, a sloop-of-war and barges will be waiting to take them to a better world.

Three days after the talks begin, Lafayette and St. Clair come up from Philadelphia, with an escort of light horse, and are taken to Nassau Hall, where the sergeants treat them with due respect. As usual, Lafayette takes charge, but he quickly sees that, if the mutineers' grievances are legitimate and their demands are met, it's going to set a precedent that will wreck the army.

At this point, the mutineers become nervous over the presence of too many officers and order all but three to leave. St. Clair goes off to Morristown to take command of those who are still there, and Lafayette sets out for Windsor, Washington's camp. En route, he meets soldiers on their way to Princeton to join the revolt, and he tries to persuade them to go back, but they tell him: "We'll fight to the last man under your orders, but we intend to have justice from our country."

Meanwhile, as the talks continue in Nassau Hall, the atmosphere grows increasingly tense. More civilian officials come up from Philadelphia, and New Jersey legislators move to surround Princeton with militia. There's much sympathy for the mutineers from all hands, including the citizens of Princeton, who help to feed them as the negotiations drag on into a fifth day.

Now there are growing divisions among the Pennsylvanians. All kinds of fears and prejudices abound. The Protestants are still boiling because of the alliance with Catholic France. There are both English-and Irish-born men in the Line, and no love lost between them. Veterans don't think new recruits should get the same "rewards" they hope for. Most of the recent immigrants know where the liberty and rights they'd expected can be found. Certainly not in the army. Yet all can unite on one thing: If the country wants us to give our lives for independence, they should damn well pay what's promised.

A week after the start of the revolt, the mutineers assemble for roll call and the terms of a suggested compromise are read out to them, one devised by Joseph Reed and the sergeants. They are to march to Trenton and get their pay and some clothing, and then meet their officers. A general pardon is promised. There's a lingering fear that this is a trap, but the terms are accepted.

Next day, the committee and members of the Council meet in Trenton, where the sergeants stipulate that the men must remain under arms until the whole matter is settled. Reed says no. He gives them two hours to think it over, particularly his own stipulation that the men give up two British spies they're holding. The sergeants confer and agree to everything, and the spies are duly hanged. There's one last sticking point. The sergeants say the men won't disperse until they're discharged, and they still don't want to have anything to do with their old officers; they'll accept only regimental commanders who have come to Trenton.

The cause of peace is helped considerably at this crucial point when a shipment of clothes arrives from Philadelphia, including 1,200 shirts and pairs of shoes, 2,500 overalls, and 1,000 blankets. Each man is then promised fifty shillings, equal to a month's pay, and a sixty-day furlough. Anyone who wants to stay or reenlist will get £6 in new state currency and a guinea that's worth £9 in Pennsylvania.

All wrangle over the terms for another week or so, but things begin to move. About a hundred men choose to return to service. However, hitches in paying out the money develop because of bureaucratic mismanagement. Regimental records have to be used to determine how much each man gets and they're late in arriving. In the bargain, Philadelphia hasn't sent up enough money to pay off the men as fast as they're discharged.

Like the rest of the provincial governments, Trenton is in a financial crisis, and anyway, neither politicians nor citizens are deeply interested in what happens to these soldiers. So the revolt winds down in a miasma of disappointed men, bitter officers, and apparently endless confusion. Wayne reports to Washington that he's lost four regiments of artillery, although about two-thirds of the remaining regiments have reenlisted.

The revolt of the Pennsylvania Line is over, but it's having repercussions elsewhere, for the same reasons. At West Point, twenty-two Massachusetts regiments complain formally about their hardships; however, they don't mutiny. In New Jersey, Continental troops stage a smaller version of the Pennsylvania mutiny, but only two hundred men are involved and the revolt is quickly settled. Pennsylvania is in such a state that it has neither money nor soldiers, so that it has to sell Loyalist estates to get cash and pardon convicts to get soldiers. It's a small miracle that, by May, Wayne is able to take command of a thousand Pennsylvanians at York. Even then there's a brief flare-up, resulting in the conviction of six men, four of whom are shot.

Wayne takes these troops to Virginia, where Harry Lee assesses them as "bold and daring," but "impatient and refractory; and would always prefer an appeal to the bayonet to a toilsome march." Besides, they are "restless under the want of food and whisky" and Lee thinks they carry more baggage than they need. Not surprisingly, the Line continues its protests and a sergeant is shot as an example to the others.

In the midst of all this, Washington has to get on with the war, even though the army is now so reduced that in these months before Yorktown he can count on no more than two thousand men, most of them exhausted and discouraged, which is the condition of the entire South, while in the North apathy is king. No wonder he will write to Laurens in April, "We are at the end of our tether, and now or never our deliverance must come."

If there's any man remaining, aside from the French, who can produce deliverance, it's Washington. Somehow he must coordinate what troops he has with the French army in Newport, and they must move south and strike a final blow, if they can.

He begins with Lafayette. Who else? On February 20, he gives his unadopted son a force of 1,200 men with orders to take them to Virginia, toward which Cornwallis is hopefully moving. Their old friend Arnold is already there, a British brigadier general. This is the only move Washington can make immediately because everyone's waiting for reinforcements from France, for which Rochambeau has sent his son to negotiate after the meeting in Hartford.

While they wait, the French are bored and restless. Fersen, in Newport, writes to his father: "We vegetate, within range of the enemy's fire, in the most sinister and horrible idleness and inactivity, and because of our small numbers we are compelled to play the exhausting part of the defenders; we are no use at all to our allies, we cannot get off our island without exposing our fleet to capture or destruction; our fleet cannot go out without delivering us into the hands of our enemies who, with superior numbers in ships and men, would not fail to attack and cut off our retreat upon the mainland. . . .

"Far from being useful to the Americans, we are a burden to them, we are not reinforcing their army, for we are a twelve days' march from it, separated by estuaries which cannot be crossed in winter when they are filled with ice floes. They are having to pay for us, too, as by increasing consumption we are making supplies more scarce, and by paying coin we cause their paper money to fall, and in so doing we make it impossible for Washington's army to obtain supplies with ease, because the people will not sell for paper."

Just the same, Fersen wastes little sympathy on the Americans' financial woes. He thinks that money is the "premium mobile" of all their acts, and says they think of nothing but how to get it: "each is for himself, nobody for the public weal. The coastal inhabitants, even the best Whigs among them, bring every manner of supplies to the English fleet, because they are well paid, but they fleece us unmercifully, the price of everything is exorbitant, and in every agreement we have made with them, they have treated us more as enemies than as friends. Their curiosity is unequaled, money is their God, virtue, honor, all that is nothing to them, when measured against that precious silver metal." Fersen, of course, thinks a lot about money too because he has a valet and two grooms to support, so he dutifully thanks his father for keeping him in funds.

Rochambeau's son is having his own problems with money, trying to get reinforcements out of Vergennes, who's been warned by Admiral de Ternay that "the fate of North America is yet very uncertain, and the Revolution is not so far advanced as is believed in Europe." Having delivered this damper on American hopes for French help, De Ternay conveniently dies before doing any more damage.

In an attempt to move things along in Paris, Washington inadvertently confirms the admiral's gloomy view by writing to Vergennes from winter quarters that "without maritime superiority . . . there will be no certain operation in America. . . ." Congress sends Henry Laurens to Paris in February to see if he can speed up things, but that only makes Vergennes furious at what he thinks of as foreign intrusion into French affairs. He tells Laurens that the King has many troubles too, and he thinks it isn't unreasonable to expect that the Americans should provide for the expenses of their own army. Besides, the French are bored by the war, and they don't like Laurens. Franklin comes to the rescue and goes over Vergennes's head to the King, pointing out to Louis that, if the British scuttle the Americans and shift their forces into the larger war, it won't be very comfortable for the French.

If there's optimism anywhere in the entire scene, it's supplied by Lafayette, who couldn't be happier. He's got an army to command, he's off to confront Cornwallis and that bastard Arnold. Among his soldiers is a black regiment from Rhode Island, freedmen who are former slaves and willing to serve longer for less pay. They're a fine body of men, as a traveler reports who sees them marching to join Lafayette: "At the ferry crossing I met with a detachment of the R.I. regiment. . . . The majority of the enlisted men were Negroes or mulattoes, but they are strong, robust men, and those I saw made a very good appearance." They're highly successful as soldiers because they realize their freedom will be lost if the country loses, and no one in the army knows better than they how to survive.

It's not an easy march for Lafayette's little army. The roads are often awash in heavy rains and the horses founder. When that happens, he sets an example by getting off and going on foot through weeds and water. Moreover, like everyone else at the moment, he has an incipient mutiny in his ranks, most of whom come from New England, and all of whom could be considered unreliable.

Lafayette calls it (not to their faces, of course) his "dirty little army" as he delivers them at last to Head of Elk, Maryland, on March 3, where convoy ships are supposed to be waiting to take them to Virginia; if they aren't, he will have to make a long detour down the west side of Chesapeake Bay. Naturally, the ships aren't there. It's the fault of the French, since the craft were to come from Newport. Worse, it's also the result of pure haughtiness on the part of Chevalier Destouches, who has temporarily succeeded De Ternay. He isn't about to send troop ships such a distance just to please the pipsqueak general, and Rochambeau agrees with him.

Lafayette fires off an indignant letter to Washington, who doesn't understand what it's all about but requests Governor Jefferson to see that Lafayette's army is equipped if the boats don't arrive.

What's behind this petty French pique? Nothing very complicated.

According to Manceron, it's simply that all these senior French officers are so much older than Lafayette that they can't stand even the appearance of serving under him. After pressure from Washington, however, Destouches does set sail at last with the convoy fleet. Meanwhile, Lafayette has demonstrated his usual enterprise by getting together a fleet of small craft, arming them with cannon, and floating his men down the bay to Annapolis. While he's doing this, Destouches runs into Admiral Arbuthnot's fleet, loses two hundred men to British cannon, and limps back to Newport.

In Annapolis, Lafayette knows nothing of this disaster, but his spies inform him that Clinton is sending reinforcements to both Arnold and Cornwallis by sea, in preparation for the great invasion of Virginia.

When the army gets to Baltimore, the ladies want to hold a ball for the officers, but Lafayette tells them they would be much better occupied finding clothes for his men, so they turn to in a great flurry of sewing and produce overalls, hunting shirts, hats, and blouses. The city's merchants help by giving them a two-thousand-guinea loan in the form of linen from their warehouses.

Better prepared now for a hot climate, the army moves south again on April 10, just about the time Cornwallis is departing from Wilmington to join Arnold, who has two thousand men now sitting in Portsmouth. Arnold's intent is to march up the James toward Fredericksburg and Richmond. The only obstacle in his way, Lafayette, has landed at Yorktown, in a little dinghy, and he's about to enjoy the Virginia spring, complete with swamps and mosquitoes, offset by corn and tobacco. He determines to save this sacred land of Washington's.

By forced marches, impressing horses and wagons along the way, he moves rapidly with a thousand men, and it proves to be one of the worst marches any body of soldiers has had to endure. Virginia is crisscrossed with rivers flowing west to east, which means Lafayette has to cross all of them. Only the largest towns have bridges; the others have fords, if he can find them. Because it's high-water season, the Americans have to build rafts, seize ferrymen, use anything they can find for water transport.

This army, traveling now on not much more than honor, survives it all and on April 25 reaches Fredericksburg, where the inhabitants cheer them as they prepare to evacuate the place.

Making a short side trip to pay his respects to Washington's mother, the chronic complainer, he also stops at Mount Vernon, to see where God actually lives. While he's in Fredericksburg, Lafayette invites a young volunteer, James Johnston, a Pennsylvania boy who joined the army as it passed through Delaware, to have dinner with him. They dine in a small log house, just below the falls. As he sits at the dinner table, Johnston glances out the window and sees, to his astonishment, Generals Arnold and William Phillips walking along the beach, obviously making a reconnaissance with their glass while their servants hold the horses.

A few minutes later, five riflemen in hunting shirts and moccasins appear at the cabin door and report that they, too, have seen the generals. They earnestly request permission to move to a position from which they believe they can pick off these two prizes. Lafayette displays his humanity, if not his common sense. He's ready to meet the enemy in the field any time, he tells his soldiers, but he won't authorize assassination. The riflemen go away angry and dissatisfied, a feeling that soon extends all the way to Lafayette's aide, Major McPherson. But the boy is adamant. At least things are now all even. General Ferguson had the same opportunity to shoot Washington at Brandywine and refused to do it.

In April, Lafayette's reconnaissance without force ends when Washington orders him to join Greene, who's somewhere in the Carolinas, just where, no one at headquarters is quite sure. So the hope of France is off again; it's the kind of assignment he enjoys. He presses on, even though his New England soldiers are near open revolt at the prospect of spending the summer sweltering in the Carolinas. Lafayette has his own way of dealing with this, as he writes Washington: "Dissatisfaction and desertion are two greater evils than any other we have to fear. I am anxious to have rivers, other countries, and every kind of barrier to stop the inclination of the men to return home. . . ."

Even as he seals this letter comes the news that nine of the Rhode Island companies have deserted the night before, and they're the best he has, after the black regiment, whose members choose to stay. The deserters leave word that they'd rather take a hundred lashes than go south. They're "amazingly averse to the people and the climate," Lafayette says, considerably understating it, but he doesn't realize that, like so many soldiers in this war, these men are ready to defend only their own turf. Unfortunately, they're mostly indifferent to anybody else's.

Lafayette believes he can stem this revolt by sheer oratory. He lines up his remaining men, and with his red hair floating in the wind as he sits his horse, he gives them a Fourth of July sermon, covering the ground from Liberty to God, but the wind is blowing so hard that day, the men can't hear much of what he says. They do, however, hear his appeal to honor: "Anyone who wishes to leave may go," he tells them. "I shall force no one to remain. Soldiers desiring to return need but apply to me for a pass, and I shall send them back to their winter quarters." Not a man moves. Temporarily at least, honor prevails.

Back in Paris, Vergennes is still not listening. As Manceron tells us, "Whenever large sums of money are involved, this diplomat adopts the attitude of an estate manager. Franklin convinced him to part with some money, but not reinforcements. He's driving Rochambeau to distraction. Vergennes convinces the King not only not to send the ten thousand men Rochambeau wants, but not even to send over the second division that was to have left the year before."

At last sheer persistence wins out. Vergennes says that Admiral François Joseph Paul, Comte de Grasse, is about to sail from Brest for the Antilles, and sometime before winter sets in, he will be permitted to send part of his fleet north, under certain conditions. This is something less than half a loaf, but the Americans will take it. Vergennes tells them this is to be kept a dark secret, even from Washington, who hears about it when Rochambeau does.

Why is Vergennes taking this roundabout, halfhearted way to help the Americans? Because he knows that the French governing classes have no interest in the fate of America but they do want to protect their sugar plantations in the Caribbean, which is what De Grasse is going to do. If there's anything left over, the Americans can have it.

Not knowing yet that he's never going to see Destouches, Lafayette seizes Williamsburg, hoping to get oxen to draw the cannon he had to leave behind in Annapolis.

He pushes on to Richmond, arriving by April 29, and finds the town almost deserted, with Arnold only ten leagues away. By this time, Lafayette has forgotten all about Greene. Preparing to save Virginia, the first task is to keep the British from crossing the James to get at Richmond. Baron von Steuben has a small force nearby to help but he's being forced into a slow retreat.

Arnold is in his customary condition at this point—frustrated. It happens to him just as easily as when he was on the other side. He wouldn't be Arnold if he didn't want to do as much damage as possible before Cornwallis gets there, and so be credited for whatever's accomplished. However, he simply doesn't have enough arms and men to do what he'd like, so he has to content himself with burning everything in sight and hanging any Virginians he can capture, since they all seem to be stubborn Whigs.

Devastation follows Arnold wherever he goes. But while he's hanging Whigs, the civilian Americans are busy tarring and feathering Tories. Phillips writes a letter to Lafayette, saying he hopes this "gentleman of liberal principles" won't countenance "the barbarous spirit that appears to prevail," and gets an indignant reply. Who are the barbarians in this war? Sometimes it's a toss-up.

Arnold moves ahead on his path of destruction toward Richmond, where he hopes to eliminate a huge pile of stores. One morning his troops are so close they can see Lafayette's camp on the heights of the town. Phillips, with two thousand men, is the one who sees Lafayette first and, not knowing he has only nine hundred men there, decides not to attack—one more British mistake. If he had, it would have been the end of Lafayette, or at least of his army.

The two forces play a hide-and-seek game along the river, both trying to avoid combat in open terrain. For the first time, Lafayette demonstrates that he has the makings of a fine strategist. He plays the game cautiously, not coming too close, resisting the temptation to cross over even if he thinks Phillips is retreating. Each army is edging slowly down its own bank of the river toward the sea; both are waiting for reinforcements.

Along the way, Phillips dies suddenly of fever on May 13, and now Arnold is in complete charge until Cornwallis comes. Meanwhile, he digs in at Petersburg and waits. A captured American prisoner is brought before him and Arnold asks, as a particular point of interest, what the Americans would do to him if they captured him. "We should cut off the leg that was wounded in the country's service," the prisoner replies, "and we should hang the rest of you." Nothing to look forward to.

Everything begins to come to a climax on May 15. Cornwallis is expected imminently, and there is Lafayette with less than a thousand men, badly outnumbered, not enough arms, deficient in riflemen and cavalry. He sends several messages, the substance of which is, "Help!"

Before he gets a reply, Cornwallis arrives in Petersburg and now the British have a force of nearly four thousand. Lafayette is lucky to get eight hundred more men sent by Wayne. He is now officially commander of all American forces in Virginia, but where are the forces? He emits a groan of complaint in a letter to Hamilton: "I am just that much of a general as will make me a historian of misfortunes and nail my name upon the ruins of what good folks are pleased to call the army of Virginia." The odds are 5–1 infantry, 10–1 cavalry, he notes, and adds, "To speak truth, I am afraid of myself as much as of the enemy. . . ."

Falling back on Richmond, Lafayette sends a stream of frantic messages to Washington and Rochambeau, saying he doesn't dare go beyond a skirmish and, if he has to get involved with Cornwallis's cavalry, it will be the end because of the militia's great fear of these mounted warriors. At the moment they're mounted on eight hundred of Virginia's best horses, including two race horses. The Americans have forty to oppose them.

Cornwallis is confident that he's now sitting in the catbird seat. He writes to Clinton: "The boy cannot escape me." At that point the boy has just evacuated Richmond and is falling back, giving Cornwallis the opportunity to cross the river in force.

Only a few days before, the log jam in the North, frozen for so many months, had begun to move at last, and Cornwallis has contributed another mistake to the inevitable final disaster by failing to cross the river *above* Richmond, thus splitting the forces of Lafayette and Steuben apart, making it possible to destroy both. Why this hesitation? Cornwallis has a whole constellation of fears. He's afraid of getting too far away from his sea base, he fears the arrival of a French fleet (news gets around), and he hasn't read Lafayette's letter to Washington: "I am not strong enough even to get beaten."

Help is on the way, however distant. In May, Rochambeau's son returns from France with more promises from Vergennes; a new admiral for the Newport fleet, Jacques Melchior St. Laurent, Comte de Barras; and the "secret" information that De Grasse is sailing from Brest and may be available later on. That calls for another conference between Washington and Rochambeau. It takes place at Wethersfield, Connecticut, near Hartford. Washington travels there by way of the first covered bridge in Connecticut, then under construction. Floor planks haven't been laid, but Jacob Bull, whose bridge it is (it's the Bull's Bridge we know today), hurries out and lays down enough planks for the general to get across. He has breakfast next morning in Litchfield, dines in the afternoon at Farmington, and arrives at Joseph Webb's house in Wethersfield, where he'll spend the next five days conferring.

Washington hears with sharp dismay that no troops are coming, but Rochambeau assures him that De Grasse and his ships could be decisive. The two commanders agree to move south and join their armies at some point. Washington would like to attack New York along the way (his enduring hope), with the help of De Grasse's fleet, but Rochambeau assures him that the harbor channel there is too shallow, which is not true. So where can they strike? Slowly, during the conversation, it comes to seem that Virginia is the place to do it. If De Grasse can be persuaded to bring his fleet to Head of Elk, that would make a showdown possible. Rochambeau promises to write to the admiral and ask. Meanwhile, they agree that the two armies will make a feint at New York (maybe), then march on to Virginia.

Rochambeau has a small problem with his own admiral. He'll have to convince him to cooperate, since De Barras's orders are to take his eight ships into Boston if the French army moves inland. Rochambeau tells him not to worry, he'll leave 300 men to guard him, supported by 1,000 of the Rhode Island militia. If De Grasse arrives, De Barras is there to bring down the siege artillery as fast as possible.

De Barras listens but he isn't so sure of this plan. What if the British fleet closes in on him? It will be good-bye Barras. Rochambeau reminds him that it won't be much of an advertisement for French honor if he holes up in Boston. While the entire climax of the Revolution waits, these two old friends from Provence argue back and forth until May 20, when De Barras finally agrees that, if De Grasse shows up, he'll place himself under that admiral's orders and do what's expected.

Now that's settled, Rochambeau can sit down and write to De Grasse the extraordinary letter that will determine the outcome of this war. He puts all his cards on the table. "I must not conceal from you, sir," he writes, "that these people are at the end of their means; that Washington will not have the troops he counted upon, and that I believe, although he is reticent about it, that he has not now six thousand men, that M. de Lafayette has not one thousand regular soldiers with the militia to defend Virginia, and about that many who are on their way to unite with him; that General Greene was lately checked at Camden, upon which place he made an attempt, and that I do not know when or how he will join M. de Lafayette; that it is therefore of the greatest importance that you should take on board as many troops as possible; that four thousand or five thousand men would not be too many."

Rochambeau adds in a delicate way that he's broke and traveling in America on credit, consequently it would be a good thing if De Grasse brought some money with him—a lot of it. He suggests an equivalent of more than a million dollars. The letter is sent off, and now there's nothing to do but wait for a reply.

At least the two allies can make the start they agreed on, and on June 12, Rochambeau leaves Newport with five thousand men to join the American army of three thousand. They come together at Phillipsburg, near Kingsbridge, New York, on July 6 and the French camp a little to the left of Washington's force. Two days earlier, the Americans had celebrated the Fourth of July with hopeful bonfires.

Meanwhile, the cat-and-mouse game has been going on in Virginia between Cornwallis and Lafayette, in a state that's being torn apart by the contending armies. Wayne arrives with three regiments of the Pennsylvania Line, a thousand men, but they can't fight immediately because the march has exhausted them. While they're resting, the British move against Charlottesville, and Thomas Jefferson resigns as governor. He may be a towering intellectual, but he hates war and has no appetite for governing a state which has become the final pawn in the game.

Lafayette pens discouraging news to Washington. The ordinarily astute Von Steuben has let himself be surprised by British cavalry, with a loss of all his wagons, 2,500 pieces of arms, several casks of saltpeter and sulfur, flints, sailcloth, and, worst loss of all, more than sixty hogsheads of rum and brandy. Lafayette tells Washington he regards the baron's conduct as "unintelligible." But he rallies what remains of the German's army and they fight on. Cornwallis is a big help; he chooses this moment to waste a great deal of time reorganizing his own forces.

Lafayette gets further help with the arrival of six hundred tough mountaineers from the Shenandoah Valley, carrying their hunting guns and powder horns. That encourages him to pursue Cornwallis when he returns to Richmond, but then the British general does something inexplicable. He gives up Richmond without a fight and returns to Williamsburg. If there's any explanation, it must be that he has now given up his dream of a triumphant invasion of Virginia and has become convinced that the wisest thing to do is to control the James, his exit and escape route. He isn't going to go very far inland. This decision is confirmed when Clinton advises him that it may be necessary for him to get back to New York in a hurry because he expects, as he has from the beginning, that Washington means to attack the city. No more reinforcements for Virginia can be expected now. Cornwallis is on his own with what he has in stock.

Still, he's in greater strength and in better position than the Americans, so why doesn't he attack? His own officers can't understand it. A colonel writes: "His Lordship has not thought proper to attack; though to my knowledge he has had it in his power several times, and to advantage."

The Duc de Lauzun, with Rochambeau's army, has been in America long enough to study what's going on, and he has his own view. "Throughout the entire course of this war," he writes, "the English have appeared to be struck blind. They always do what should not be done, always refuse to take the most obvious and certain advantages. Once the army was gone [from Newport] all they needed to do, to destroy the entire scheme, was attack the French squadron in Rhode Island, but it never occurred to them. The French army marched across America in perfect order and discipline, a wonder for which neither the English nor the American army had ever set an example. . . . General Washington was well out in front of both armies."

The two armies rest side by side momentarily at Phillipsburg, the first time that the Americans have ever seen their allies, and they're awed by the appearance and size of these French regulars. Units of both armies skirmish with the outposts Clinton has set up around New York. Washington himself does what he's wanted to do for so long: reconnoiter New York from close up. With Lauzun and a hundred hussars, he inspects the perimeter, drawing some gunfire from muskets and cannon as he makes a three-day examination, marching day and night with only fruit to eat.

Clinton doesn't know it, but the Americans are absolutely incapable of storming New York, even with French help. They have enough powder to last no more than three days, and while they're waiting for word from De Grasse, there's really nothing to do but forage for food or, in the case of some soldiers, warm female bodies.

The French are fascinated, or possibly merely bewildered, by sex in America, although even then they have an undeserved reputation for knowing everything about love. Jean-François-Louis de Clermont-Crèvecoeur, with Rochambeau, keeps a campaign journal (it will be discovered in 1923 in a Providence attic) and, while he's waiting, records some observations on the subject.

"In a country so new where vice should not be deeply rooted," he notes, "why should there be such a large number of prostitutes? Only one reason seems to me to be the cause. Although the fathers and mothers keep an eye on their daughters during their childhood, once they reach the age when human nature demands that they know everything, they become their own mistresses and are free to keep company with anyone they wish. Among the common people (for today in the towns education has corrected the abuses of which I shall speak) the girls enjoy so much freedom that a Frenchman or an Englishman, unaccustomed to such a situation, straightaway seeks the final favors.

"The women are generally very faithful to their husbands. . . . Yet some girls lead a most licentious life before they marry, though once married, they, too, become good. The men are not fussy in this respect; they believe a girl should be free and do not despise her unless she is unfaithful after marriage. It is rare to find a woman committing adultery here, although it does happen. In this instance the husband announces the deliverance of his wife and publishes it in the papers. No dishonor falls upon the husband. . . ." Crèvecoeur will never qualify as a sociologist.

While the French are musing about sex in America, the British are taking a serious view of this combined army of ten thousand men now at Dobbs Ferry, who are obviously preparing for something major. Clinton's reports to Cornwallis alarm him so much that he's convinced his new policy of withdrawal is correct, maybe overdue. Lafayette still pursues him cautiously, passing once more through Richmond, that "poor little bruised town, like a child battered in a fight between adults," in Manceron's vivid metaphor, "with the pink bricks forming low mounds of coagulated blood."

As Washington did so long ago when he fell back through New

Jersey, Cornwallis is experiencing the same situation in reverse as Lafayette nips at his heels all the way to Williamsburg. Each side now has about 4,600 men, but they're not risking battle, even though it's British regulars against American militia again.

On July 4, Cornwallis evacuates Williamsburg, where he could have held out for a long time in case of siege, and retreats back toward Portsmouth. He executes this move so skillfully that it leaves Lafayette nowhere, besides narrowly escaping a clever British trap. It's a classic maneuver, a tribute to Cornwallis's standing as the best British field general. He manages to conceal his entire army from Lafayette, using the Queen's Rangers as a decoy. If Lafayette bites on this one, it's all over for him. Tarleton helps by sending false information into his camp via two supposed deserters.

Just in time. While Wayne's men are exchanging shots with the British pickets, Lafayette notices that the redcoats seem to be displaying unusual care in replacing the pickets immediately, and it occurs to him that they may be decoys. He decides to go alone to a point of land and make a personal observation.

Through his glass he sees at a distance that the main British army is waiting for him on open ground near the river, where enemy ships and guns are waiting too. Immediately, he gives the order to fall back, but it comes too late for Wayne, whose regiments are encircled. They manage to save themselves, however. Wayne has his horse shot out from under him, and Lafayette himself has a narrow escape as two of his own mounts suffer the same fate. One of his officers says of Lafayette afterward that "his native bravery rendered him deaf to the admonition" not to take chances. But he takes them, and this time it costs him forty-two dead men. He retires to Williamsburg.

Soon thereafter, it's Arnold who's taking one more chance, one more shot at glory. Returning to New York in August, he convinces Clinton that, with the French and American armies out of New England, now would be a splendid time to invade his native Connecticut and destroy whatever American forces remain. This territory—southwestern Connecticut and the Long Island shoreline—is in fact still being ravaged by guerrilla warfare, as it has been since 1776. Already it's produced a legendary force, the Tory cowboys. They're actually rustlers who harass the Whig farmers by stealing their cattle for the benefit of British troops as well as themselves. The Americans have satirized these cowboys in a print titled *British Heroism*, depicting soldiers moving toward a herd of cattle with bayonets leveled. Nevertheless, these roving bands of cowboys, other Tories, British soldiers, and American guerrillas have made most of Westchester County and much of Fairfield uninhabitable, a virtual no man's land.

Arnold's plan is to attack New London, and he does so on the morning of September 6, in a raid that goes down as one of the most ferocious of the war. He first drives the defenders out of Fort Trumbull on the west side of the Thames River and then moves against Fort Griswold on the opposite shore, whose garrison is commanded by Lieutenant Colonel William Ledyard. After a brief defense, Ledyard has to surrender because the odds are overwhelming. Arnold's army, composed of Tories, Hessians, and British regulars, then slaughter the garrison indiscriminately, between seventy and eighty men.

Historians still argue about the tragedy that occurs at the moment of surrender, when Ledyard hands his sword to the British commander at the scene, Lieutenant Colonel Abram Van Buskirk, of the New Jersey Volunteers. Some say it was all a misunderstanding, others that no one knows who performed the despicable act, but Joseph Wood, a young Scituate boy who was there, testifies that before he escaped he saw the British commander enter the fort and inquire, "Who commands this fort?" Ledyard answers, "I did, but you do now," and hands him his sword. Van Buskirk takes it and runs Ledyard through without a word. "This I heard and saw," Wood will testify years later when he's applying for a pension. Ledyard's aide, Captain Allen, standing nearby and about to present his own sword, draws it back and thrusts it through Van Buskirk, who dies immediately. "This I also saw," Wood swears. "I then leaped the walls and made my escape."

Afterward, Arnold sets fire to New London. Climbing into a church belfry, from which he can almost see his birthplace, Norwich, twelve miles away, he watches the town burn with great satisfaction—one more act of revenge against what he believes the American establishment did to him. While the troops are plundering, he stays in a house whose owner asks him politely if his home and property will be safe. Arnold promises that it will be safe as long as he's there, but before he can leave, the place is already on fire. His troops are stacking their arms against trees and fences so they can have both hands and arms free to carry off plunder.

In his report to Clinton, Arnold claims burning the town was accidental. He says nothing about Ledyard's death, and writes coolly that eighty-five men "were found dead in Fort Griswold, and sixty wounded, most of them mortally." One of his most brazen lies. In his memoirs, he further whitewashes himself by asserting that, when the American stores were burned, they contained a large quantity of powder, "unknown to us," and the resulting explosion, along with a change of wind, burned "a part of the town, which was, notwithstanding every effort to prevent, unfortunately destroyed." Unfortunate, indeed. This is Arnold's last exploit in America, and he fades away with the war to his eventual English exile.

Affairs are moving rapidly now toward a climax. Cornwallis has spent most of July in a tedious correspondence with Clinton. All the old animosities between them become nearly impossible. It ends with an order from Clinton that Cornwallis should have refused, as he's done before when he thinks his superior's demands are unwise. On August 1, at Clinton's command, he moves back across the river and fortifies himself at Yorktown. A historic mistake. If he'd refused and stayed in Portsmouth, he would have had an exit route to the sea. Now he's trapped at the peninsula's foot because Clinton says he wants to retain Chesapeake Bay. Meanwhile Washington informs Lafayette that he and the French are on their way, and on August 21 bugles and drums herald the start of their march to Virginia.

All this has been set in motion by the incredible act of one man, Admiral de Grasse, who makes the crucial decision of the war. This bad-tempered giant of a man, six feet seven inches tall, is notorious in the French navy. On the voyage out to the Antilles, his conduct was so savage that both officers and men were ready to revolt. When he gets Rochambeau's urgent letter, he's sitting in the islands with his fleet, under instructions from Vergennes, and therefore the King, to protect them until the summer is over. After that, but only if he gets further orders, he can proceed north to help the Americans—that is, if he thinks there's no danger from the British fleet. Not much encouragement to action for a man on whom America's fate, as Rochambeau correctly surmises, now depends.

Reading Rochambeau's almost desperate plea for help, De Grasse understands that he's being asked not only to disregard his orders and take his ships north in support of a cause for which he has no particular sympathy one way or the other, but to take with him French troops who are now protecting French soil in the Antilles. Even more than that, he's expected to bring money.

What's De Grasse thinking about as he reads Rochambeau's letter? God only knows, and historians can do no more than speculate. Certainly he has options. He can do nothing, and that's certainly his wisest course. If the Americans lose their war, the blame will be on them, Lafayette, and Rochambeau, not him. If he does what his compatriot is desperately imploring him to do, he will be far exceeding his orders, indeed disobeying them, and will face the possible loss of ships, men, and money, not to mention his own career, if he loses the gamble. For French officers of his class, to act is a mortal sin; to do nothing is considered by far the safest course.

Nonetheless, on July 28, 1781, De Grasse dictates his reply to Rochambeau, a letter that Manceron, among others, believes founded the United States as surely as the Declaration. For reasons still obscure, but no doubt having their origin in old, unsettled scores at home, De Grasse decides to do what every instinct tells him *not* to do. He will borrow the money on his own signature from Spanish bankers in Havana, using as part security his valuable properties in Santo Domingo, because the French moneylenders in the Antilles are not interested in America's fate. Furthermore, he decides on his own authority to embark about three thousand men and a hundred artillery pieces from the French garrisons, leaving the Antilles relatively unprotected.

Perhaps most astonishing of all, De Grasse understands exactly what he's doing. "As this whole expedition has been undertaken at your request," he writes to Rochambeau, "and without consulting the ministers of France or of Spain, I have felt myself authorized to assume certain responsibilities in the interest of the common cause." That's the first and last time De Grasse will ever indicate he thinks there *is* a common cause.

On the morning of August 4, he weighs anchor on his flagship, the *Ville de Paris*, and leads twenty-six ships of the line plus a few transports, with more than three thousand troops aboard, northward. The British have already made a fatal error. Instead of concentrating their fleet, they've split it up into two squadrons, one to guard New York, which has never needed guarding, and the other to sit in the Antilles and watch De Grasse, which it's been doing.

That's how Vice-Admiral George Rodney has been occupying himself when he sees the French fleet pull up anchor and begin to move northward. Rodney then carries out the orders left him by his superior, Admiral Samuel Hood, when he departed for England a little earlier, suffering from gout and rheumatism. If De Grasse sailed, these orders had presumed, he would be heading for New York, and Rodney was instructed to beat him to it. So he crams on sail and starts off on a somewhat different course.

Washington is in Chester, Pennsylvania, on his way south when he gets the news that De Grasse has arrived off the coast. As Rochambeau approaches him to learn what's happening, he sees the austere Washington in a virtual transport of joy, of a kind no one has ever seen before, waving his hat in the air and shouting as he stands on the riverbank. He tells Rochambeau the good news "with many demonstrations of uncontrollable happiness."

Until that day, the march south had not been an easy one, crossing New Jersey for the last time, possibly, and marching through Philadelphia to raucous huzzahs, as the inhabitants turned out to see an international army marching through its streets.

In his journal, Crèvecoeur gives us a graphic account of the hardships on the way. "One cannot imagine," he writes, "how many afflictions we had to endure during the six days it took us to march from Phillipsburg to King's Ferry on the Hudson River, a distance of forty miles. It took us six days because of the terrible weather and incredible roads. We slept every night in bivouac. There was a terrific storm on August 30. I floundered in the mud and in a horrible marsh with all the wagons and the artillery train, not knowing where I was or how I could get out of it. Not until daybreak was I able, with great difficulty, to extricate myself."

Later, in his memoirs, he wrote of the march through Philadelphia: "The Continental 'Army' with which General Washington was thus setting out upon an expedition of greater magnitude and far wider military importance, from the boldness of execution and influence of its results, than any other in the war, was composed of but two thousand men. So far had the tide of the Revolution ebbed in the summer of 1781, and to such an extent was the country exhausted by the incessant demands of the preceding years of struggle, that the Commander-in-Chief could bring together, in the face of this impending crisis, only what naturally enough seemed to General de Rochambeau a mere 'handful of men.' Accompanying this force were the well-equipped and thoroughly disciplined French troops, four thousand men. . . ."

Now that he's on the brink, Washington is seized with gloomy thoughts of impending disaster. Lafayette reassures him; there's nothing more to worry about now, "the boy" is certain. We'll see.

1781

19

✛   ✛   ✛

Yorktown

When Rodney gets to the waters off Yorktown and sees no Frenchmen in sight, he concludes the French fleet must have outsailed him and is already threatening New York, while in fact De Grasse is still coming up the coast, delayed by bad weather. Sailing into the Chesapeake a little later, he's astonished— and relieved as well—to find himself alone. He lands his troops immediately on September 2. Rodney, meanwhile, has arrived off New York, realizes his mistake, and, with all sails set, starts south.

Graves and Hood, coming down from New York with the Northern British fleet, are already ahead of him, and on September 5 they sail up the mouth of the Chesapeake just in time, so they anticipate, to enclose and destroy De Grasse. One immediate obstacle stands in the way: Graves. He's in command, not Hood, who is much the better admiral. The French have about a thousand sailors and ninety officers busy at the moment helping to land the troops brought up from the Antilles. De Grasse can either wait awhile, or he can sail out and give battle at once, leaving the landing operations until later. He makes the right decision. Do it now.

The British have been sighted just after dawn on September 5. By 10:00 A.M., De Grasse has every man at his post, and in another hour he's leaving the bay, having saved a great deal of time by slipping the cables on his anchors, marking them with large buoys. This leaves the forces he's just landed without their artillery or their means of communication, but they won't be needing them right away and the French admiral has no intention of being bottled up.

It isn't easy to get out to sea, however. The tide's coming in and the onshore winds are still, making it necessary to tack back and forth. The ships also have to be careful to avoid a perilous sandbank in the middle of the passage between Capes Charles and Henry.

By the practice of those days, De Grasse isn't leading the parade. He'll be the last to emerge. At the head of the line is the *Auguste*, commanded by Louis de Bougainville, a fifty-two-year-old veteran who got married in January and whose wife is expecting a baby. Perhaps with his mind on domestic affairs, he nearly runs aground. Six ships known as "the blue and white squadron" follow him. Then come nine ships of the main battle corps. By one forty-five, the entire French fleet is through the channel, the *Ville de Paris* taking up its command post in the last line. Facing them is a British line out-numbering them three to one, with Graves at the center and Captain Drake, a descendant of Sir Francis, in the rear.

At this climactic moment, Graves is holding all the cards. Any experienced naval commander would bless his patron saint forever if he found himself in so fortunate a position. But Graves becomes another victim of the British disease. He blows it. No one knows why. Perhaps because he's too cautious, or maybe he believes the French fleet is so small he can crush it at his leisure.

De Grasse certainly doesn't look like a man to be easily overcome. As Manceron describes him, "Standing head and shoulders above everybody else at the poop, visible from afar to the naked eye in his dress uniform with a wide scarlet band across his chest, De Grasse looks like some sort of seaborne ogre." There's reason for his confidence. He has 1,800 cannon as against 1,400 for the British, but on the other hand, he left shore so hurriedly he had to leave men behind and he's so shorthanded there aren't enough sailors to serve all the pieces. Besides, the British fleet has the advantage of being copper-sheathed.

At two-thirty in the afternoon, Graves makes his first major error, although it's not entirely his fault. Through a signaling mistake, he inadvertently sends Hood's squadron so far out of reach that it takes two hours to get it back into the battle, and by that time it's too late. The fight begins at 3:00 P.M., when the French vanguard and the British rear guard exchange volleys, the first one killing a French commander. Four French vessels find themselves fighting off a larger number of Graves's ships, and one of them is set afire. But when the

Princessa moves in to sink her, the *Saint Esprit* comes to the rescue and cripples the British ship.

Casualties begin to mount on the British side. The captain of the *Shrewsbury* loses his leg and two masts. French shells carry away two topsail yards off the *Intrepid* and damage her lower masts. The *Montague* is so badly damaged that she has to take in sail, begins to leak, and starts to heel. The *Auguste* gets the *Terrible* under her guns and does such damage that she will sink four days later, although the French ship has its foresail bowline torn off. When two sailors try to rerig it, sharpshooters from the *Princessa* pick them off. Bougainville, in command, cries, "My purse to whoever rigs that bowline!" A third man, going to undertake the job, tells him, "Admiral, we don't do this for money."

By 5:00 P.M., the wind has dropped and the French line is in much better condition in spite of its being outnumbered, a tribute to De Grasse, who is regarded as one of the eighteenth century's great naval commanders, despite his personal faults. At this stage, no ships have been actually lost on either side, with an hour of daylight remaining.

But an intramural war is going on in the British fleet. Graves, described as "a bowed little man with a complexion so red it's almost blue," keeps getting testy, even insulting messages from Hood, sent over by corvette. Obviously, Hood thinks he could have managed things much better. Without wind or light at six-thirty, both sides have to signal a cease-fire for the night.

After that it's a standoff over the next five days as the fleets face each other, weathering gales, riding in calms. Several times they come so close it looks as though hostilities will break out again, but on September 9, Graves suddenly runs up the signal for retreat and the fleet sets sail for New York. By the rules of eighteenth-century warfare, De Grasse has won because the other side left the field first. Hood may think it's disgraceful, but Graves concludes that he has several extremely sick ships, and a quantity of sick men aboard them. Since he can't get what he needs for both in Yorktown, and having failed to force an entrance to the harbor in any case, there doesn't seem much else to do but sail back home. When the British are out of sight, De Grasse goes back to his unloading.

The British have no more than gone when another French fleet comes creeping along the coast to safety. It's Admiral de Barras, keeping his word, bringing twelve more ships of the line and eighteen transports, full of men and the siege artillery taken from Newport.

After the battle at sea, Cornwallis tries to set fire to the French fleet by sending out fire ships at two in the morning. They're manned by suicide squads whose job is to ram the ships, then set them afire. They have some success. First the night sky lights up with the flames from the 64-gun *Vaillant*, setting her drifting toward the *Réflèche*, whose sleepy commander bounds out of his cabin believing that the *Vaillant* itself is a fire ship and starts cannonading her. But they manage to sort it out before they sink each other, and that's the extent of the damage. De Grasse is eight miles away downstream.

Now all the actors are coming together for the final scene. Washington and Rochambeau arrive in Williamsburg on September 14, well ahead of their armies, having ridden sixty miles a day on horseback, conscious of how important every day can be. They're met with an elegant supper, not to mention universal joy.

Three days later Washington is taken out to the *Ville de Paris*, where De Grasse greets him on the quarterdeck with a French hug and kiss on both cheeks as De Grasse exclaims, "My dear little general!" For once the commander has met someone who's not only taller than he is (he's six foot three and a half himself), but who succeeds in making him lose his cool. Seeing how embarrassed he is, all the others around them try hard not to laugh out loud at the spectacle, but Knox, who's come aboard with the party, can't contain himself and explodes in helpless laughter.

On the outskirts of this celebration, which quickly becomes a council of war, there's Lafayette, back in second class and not enjoying it. Only a few days ago *he* was the one hugging Washington when the commanders arrived in Williamsburg, and he got up from a sickbed to do it. Told that Washington was coming, he hoisted himself on a horse and galloped off to meet his hero as the drums began beating behind him on this warm autumn afternoon. Several Americans were waiting to be introduced as Lafayette arrived, but he paid no attention to them, jumped off, and rushed forward with his arms outstretched.

Among the amazed spectators of this scene was Major General St. George Tucker, a fellow Virginian, who reported: "He caught the general round his body, hugged him as close as it was possible, and absolutely kissed him from ear to ear once or twice with as much ardor as ever an absent lover kissed his mistress on his return." And Tucker went on to his wife: "The whole army and all the town were presently in motion ... men, women, and children seemed to vie with each other in demonstrations of joy and eagerness to see these beloved countrymen."

Lafayette has gone out with Washington to meet De Grasse on the *Charlotte*, a trim little captured English ship, but when he gets there and the greetings are over, he's just one of the boys again, and it rankles. The conference takes longer than planned because the weather turns cool and squally, and Washington can't get back to the mainland for four days. He hasn't been seasick since he went down to Barbados with his half brother Lawrence as a young man. This is only his second time on a heaving ocean and he's queasy.

Nevertheless, the talks are held in complete unity. Then, a week later, all is tension again when De Grasse announces he's sailing for the Antilles. He's heard that the British are coming back (that would be Rodney) and he wants to quit while he's ahead. He has taken a monumental risk to his career, and he isn't about to have it threatened any further. "I'm going to put out to sea as soon as the weather permits," he tells Rochambeau, "and remain outside the bay to prohibit the enemy from entering." Once out there, who knows what he'll do?

Lafayette is sent to negotiate, carrying a letter, presumably from Washington. In effect, the commander suggests that De Grasse really can't do this to him and Rochambeau. De Grasse knows he can, but for the time being he's content to sulk. Thus a rift has opened in the high command, Washington and Rochambeau standing together against the reluctant admiral. In the end, the generals win, at least temporarily. They even persuade De Grasse to give them eight hundred more men for the coming battle.

At five in the morning on September 28, the two armies begin to move toward Yorktown, to the beating of drums and the music of fifes. The Americans may not look like the French regulars, but they're certainly colorful. There goes the light infantry commanded by Peter Muhlenberg, the fighting parson as they call him, followed by Moses Hazen's non-Loyalists in their tattered brown-and-red uniforms. After them, Wayne's Pennsylvania Line, a fieldpiece, regiments of Marylanders, and so on. However, they're overshadowed completely by the overwhelming mass of the resplendent French, moving up behind.

At last the British and Americans confront each other, for almost the last time. Yorktown, the goal for one and the prospective graveyard of the other, is a little village of only sixty houses. Before the Revolution, it was a sleepy tobacco port, but having lost that trade, it's seemed so unimportant until now that the British haven't even raided it.

Captain Samuel Graham, of the 76th Regiment of Foot, sitting in Yorktown with his British comrades, writes later: "The two armies remained some time in this position observing each other. In ours there was but one wish, that they would advance. While standing with a brother captain . . . we overheard a soliloquy of an old Highland gentleman, a lieutenant who, drawing his sword, said to himself, 'Come on, Master Washington, I am unco glad to see you. I've been offered money for my commission, but I could na think of gangin' hame without a sight of you. Come on!'"

The Americans, surveying the enemy, are in excellent spirits, seeing the end of their long ordeal. They joke with each other, and do some bragging about past exploits. In his diary, Captain James Duncan writes: "A militia man this day, possessed of more bravery than prudence, stood constantly on the parapet and damned his soul if he would budge for the buggers. He had escaped longer than could have been expected, and growing foolhardy, brandished his spade at every ball that was fired till, unfortunately, a ball came and put an end to his capers."

While the siege lines are being laid, British guns fill the air with a subdued roar. There's a little public relations going on here, too. Washington takes a pickax and strikes a few blows where the lines are being dug, so it can be said (not by him, of course) that "General Washington with his own hands first broke ground at the siege of Yorktown." In one respect, digging the lines isn't particularly hard work, since the ground is sandy and soft.

The besiegers are further cheered by the news they get from a few British deserters. Two thousand men are sick in the hospital, they say, supplies are in a "naked state," and the cavalry is without enough forage. The deserters also report that Cornwallis has advised his men not to be afraid of the Americans because they have no heavy ordnance, with the exception of a few fieldpieces—an incredibly erroneous estimate. Is it possible he doesn't know about the heavy siege guns supplied by Newport and De Grasse? Cornwallis also remarks that the French fleet is inferior, has no idea of attacking, and only came this way to get tobacco, with which they would sail off in a few days. He must be hallucinating.

Disillusionment begins on an October afternoon, the ninth, when the French and Americans finally get some of their big guns in position, with flags of the two nations flying over them and, as one observer says, "Forty-one mouths of fire were suddenly unmasked." Washington himself touches off the first cannon fired from an American battery. Colonel Philip Van Cortlandt, of the 2nd New York, writes of this initial bombardment: "The first which was fired I could distinctly hear pass through the town. . . . I could hear the ball strike from house to house, and I was afterwards informed that it went through the one where many of the officers were at dinner, and other tables, discomposing the dishes, and either killed or wounded the one at the head of the table." (In fact, it killed a British officer and wounded three others.)

On into the night the bombardment continues, and as Ebenezer Denny observes, "the scene viewed from the camp now was grand... a number of shells from the works of both parties passing high in the air and descending in a curve, each with a long train of fire, exhibited a brilliant spectacle."

Over in the British camp, Stephen Popp records the effect: "The heavy fire forced us to throw our tents in the ditches. The enemy threw bombs. We could find no refuge in or out of the town. The people fled to the waterside and hid in hastily contrived shelters on the banks, but many of them were killed by bursting bombs. More than eighty were thus lost, besides many wounded, and their houses utterly destroyed. Our ships, too, suffered under the heavy fire, for the enemy fired in one day 3,600 shot from their heavy guns and batteries. Soldiers and sailors deserted in great numbers. The Hessian regiment of Von Bose lost heavily, although it was in our rear in the second line, but in full range of the enemy's fire." Under this incessant bombardment, Popp says, the British can scarcely get to fire their own fieldpieces, "guns and gunners being all pounded together in a mass."

The situation is almost as bad at Cornwallis's headquarters, the house of Thomas Nelson, former Secretary of the Virginia Council. Nelson is the general's unwilling host and suffers while he sees his fine old house battered until Cornwallis sends the old man, who is suffering from gout, hobbling out of town under a flag of truce. St. George Tucker records the human damage: "Two officers were killed and one wounded by a bomb the evening we opened. Lord Chewton's cane was struck out of his hand by a cannon ball. Lord Cornwallis has built a kind of grotto at the foot of the Secretary's garden where he lives underground. A Negro of the Secretary's was killed in his house."

This becomes a classic case of how to besiege a town. For four days the allied troops dig zigzagging trenches, one after the other, closer and closer to the enemy lines, until they're only three hundred yards away at the most advanced point. Then the guns are mounted and the tremendous barrage begins.

Dr. James Thacher, a Barnstable surgeon in the light infantry, records in his *Diary of the American Revolution*, published years later, what it's like behind the lines. On October 8 and 9, he writes: "The duty of our troops has been for several days extremely severe. Our regiment labors in the trenches every other day and night, where I find it difficult to avoid suffering by the cold, having no other covering than a single blanket in the open field." Two days later, he's writing of the "tremendous and incessant firing" from the American and French batteries, and the enemy returns the fire, but with little effect.

Thacher sees the *Charon*, a British 44-gun ship, and two or three smaller vessels struck and set aflame, all of them wrapped in "a torrent of fire. . . . Some of the shells, overreaching the town, are seen to fall into the river and, bursting, threw up columns of water like the spouting of the monsters of the deep. . . . The bomb shells from the besiegers and the besieged are incessantly crossing each other's paths in the air. They are clearly visible in the form of a black ball in the day, but in the night they appear like a fiery meteor with a blazing tail, most beautifully brilliant, ascending majestically from the mortar to a certain altitude, and gradually descending to the spot where they are destined to execute their work of destruction. . . . I have more than once witnessed fragments of the mangled bodies and limbs of the British soldiers thrown into the air by the bursting of our shells. . . . About twelve or fourteen men (of ours) have been killed or wounded within twenty-four hours, and assisted in dressing a number of wounds."

The allies begin to assault the British redoubts. Taking the first of these costs eight men killed and thirty wounded, but the position falls and Major Campbell, its commander, is taken prisoner with about fifty soldiers. Revenge is still in the air, old scores are about to be settled. A New Hampshire infantry captain wants to kill Campbell in revenge for Colonel Scammell's death. Alexander Hamilton, his superior officer, refuses, and no redcoat is killed once he surrenders.

Washington, with Lincoln and Knox, rides up to inspect, and Colonel David Cobb, one of Washington's aides, says to him with great solicitude, "Sir, you are too much exposed here; had you not better step back a little?" The commander gives him a sharp look and replies, "Colonel Cobb, if you're afraid, you have liberty to step back." Cobb stays.

Washington, in fact, shows himself to be an extremely cool customer (or a foolhardy one, in the opinion of some) on various occasions. John Sudderth, a Virginian from Amherst County, observes and reports one of them.

"During a tremendous cannonade from the British in order to demolish our breastworks," he recalled many years later, when applying for his pension, "a few days prior to the surrender, General Washington visited that part of our fortifications behind which [I] was posted and, whilst there, discovered that the enemy were destroying their property and drowning their horses, etc.

"Not, however, entirely assured of what they were doing, he took his glass and mounted the highest, most prominent, and most exposed point of our fortifications, and there stood exposed to the enemy's fire, where shot seemed flying almost as thick as hail and were instantly demolishing portions of the embankment around him, for ten or fifteen minutes, until he had completely satisfied himself of the purposes of the enemy.

"During this time his aides, etc., were remonstrating with him with all their earnestness against this exposure of his person and once or twice drew him down. He severely reprimanded them and resumed his position. When satisfied, he dispatched a flag to the enemy and they desisted from their purpose."

Amid the thunder of the cannonading day after day, life goes on behind the lines, as though the armies were encamped in a peaceful field. An unsung heroine is Sarah Osborn, from Blooming Grove, New York, who began life as a servant in the house of an Albany blacksmith and married another blacksmith, a veteran who reenlisted and took Sarah with him. She becomes one of those indispensable women traveling with the army who cook and do the washing.

Part of the time she travels on horseback or in a wagon, and some-times she walks. At Yorktown, she sees several dead blacks lying near the camp, victims of the siege, whom the British have driven out of town and left to starve when food became scarce.

Sarah can't do anything for these unfortunates, but about a mile from town, behind the American camp, she sets up shop and, with the help of other women, begins the daily round of washing, cooking, and mending. The roar of the bombardment is in their ears day and night as Sarah cooks and carries up beef, bread, and coffee in a gallon pot to the soldiers in their entrenchments. Once she encounters Washington, who asks her if she's afraid of the cannonballs. She answers, "No, the bullets won't cheat the gallows. It wouldn't do for the men to fight and starve too." It's Sarah who will carry breakfast to her men in the entrenchments on the day the firing stops as the British surrender.

There's still a way to go, however, before she performs that merci-ful act. In the midst of the firing, there's time for officers to carry on like officers. In a captured redoubt, Aeneas Monson, a Connecticut soldier, overhears a conversation between Hamilton and Knox. They're looking at a system of blinds, hogsheads and pipes filled with sand, set up to protect soldiers when shells are flying in. These shells lie on the ground burning for several seconds before they explode and the commanders believe that lives can be saved if there's something to duck behind. Strict orders govern this kind of thing, however. Men are permitted to cry, "A shell! A shell!" if they see or hear one, but never "A shot!" if it's something else, since only the shell can be avoided.

The two officers are discussing whether it's soldierly or not to call out "A shell!" Hamilton thinks it isn't, but Knox doesn't agree. While they're talking, a practical example occurs as shells begin to fall near them. Cries of "A shell! A shell!" come from every quarter. Both Hamilton and Knox stop philosophizing and dive for shelter. The blind they've chosen isn't quite large enough for Knox's substantial bulk, so Hamilton has to squeeze in behind and hold on. Thinking he's in danger of being shoved out, Knox gives a powerful heave and Hamilton is thrown out toward where the shells are smoldering on the ground. Just in time, Hamilton dives back behind another blind. Two minutes later, the shells burst, killing no one. The two generals climb out and Knox says, "Now, Mr. Hamilton, what do you think about crying 'shell'? But let me tell you, don't make a breastwork of me again."

Another kind of argument is going on in New York. Clinton has for some time been getting desperate pleas for help, brought up from Yorktown in small ships slipped by night through the French blockade. He calls a council of war, and his officers tell him he should be prepared for the worst, but they neglect to acquaint him with what they believe the worst is, and he thinks they mean nothing more than a retreat. More councils, and the decision is made to send down a fleet carrying five thousand reinforcements, if the ships can be refitted in shipyards not up to the job. There's also the rather large question of how, once they get there, these ships are going to break through the French blockade.

Delay follows delay and it's October 12 before the fleet is scheduled to depart. But it is delayed yet again, and Clinton is frantic. New York simply doesn't have enough dockyard space and workers, and there are shortages of powder and other stores. Everyone also has to take time out to welcome the arrival of Prince William, who has chosen this most inopportune time to pay a royal visit. So it's the seventeenth before the troops embark, and even then the ships have to wait off the Hook for favorable winds and tide. They're not at sea until the nineteenth, and already we can hear that old refrain which could well be the theme song of this year, "Too late." They arrive off Cape Charles five days later, just in time to meet refugees from Yorktown and learn that the party's over.

On the same day that Clinton's relief expedition finally sails into the open sea, Cornwallis has decided he can't wait any longer. He's desperate enough to try anything. The allied cannonading has almost silenced his batteries with the weight of more than a hundred heavy guns, the American and French sorties against the redoubts have not gone well for the British, and conditions in the army and town are frightful.

Word is sent to Tarleton, lying at nearby Gloucester, to prepare for an attempt at a breakthrough. Cornwallis hopes he can get his troops out into the country, leaving his sick and baggage behind, then cross over to Gloucester Point, destroy the French legion that's camped there, and use their horses to push his infantry in the direction of New York. Tarleton thinks it's worth the gamble.

Before he leaves, on a dark and windy night, Cornwallis writes a letter which Washington will get later, asking mercy for the sick and wounded and others left behind to carry out the surrender. The problem now is to get the troops over to Gloucester Point with an inadequate supply of small craft. Cornwallis figures it will take three trips. The first division makes the passage by midnight, but the second is struck by a fierce squall and it has to give up. By 2:00 A.M., with the weather moderating, they try again. Now, however, the allied batteries have taken notice and the shells begin to fall, sending everybody back to Yorktown. There's no escape.

While the bombardment is going on, bitter contests have been taking place around the periphery, particularly at Gloucester, where Tarleton has been trying to establish an escape route. The Duc de Lauzun moves on this place with eight hundred men borrowed from De Grasse, and writes: "I was not a hundred paces from there when I heard my vanguard letting off their pistols. I galloped away to find a piece of ground on which I could fight. As I came up, I saw the English cavalry bearing down on me, three times more numerous than my own; I charged without pausing, and we joined.

"Tarleton picked me out and came toward me with raised gun. We were about to fight in single combat when his horse was thrown by one of his dragoons pursued by one of my lancers. I rushed over to take him, a body of English dragoons thrust between us and protected his retreat, his horse was left with me. He charged me a second time but did not break me; I charged him a third, overran part of his cavalry, and chased him back to his entrenchments. . . . He lost one officer and fifty men, and I took a fair number of prisoners."

Behind the allied lines, in Williamsburg, dead and wounded lie on tent sheets spread on the ground. In their voluminous white aprons, the surgeons are busy, working without help, drugs, bandages, or much of anything else except their instruments. An officer may get nursing from his servants and live to tell about it and be decorated, but the other ranks have only one another. They try. Some urinate into comrades' wounds to keep them from festering, or so they believe. Infirmaries in the field are jammed, as is the Williamsburg hospital. Equipment and staff coming down from Newport haven't arrived yet; there's nothing with which to bind the wounds.

And where is our boy Lafayette? Right in the thick of it, naturally. He and Laurens lead a bayonet charge on a British redoubt and take it. Lafayette contrives to let the Baron de Viomenil, on Rochambeau's staff, know about this heroic sally. The baron, a rabid anti-American, has frequently questioned whether Lafayette could take *anything*, much less a British redoubt. In reporting his success, "the boy," with a straight face, offers to help the baron if he requires it.

The British make a last sortie at night on the fifteenth, with six hundred men disguised as Americans. They get close enough to spike four guns and capture a French captain, but then the reserves come in and chase them back.

From a firing step on the British lines, a Hessian named Johann Dohla gives us a view of what the British are enduring: "Early on the break of day the bombardment began again from the enemy side even more horribly than before. They fired from all redoubts without stopping. Our detachment, which stood in the hornwork, could scarcely avoid the enemy's bombs, howitzer shot, and cannonballs anymore. One saw nothing but bombs and balls raining on our whole line. . . . General Cornwallis came into the hornwork and observed the enemy and his works. As soon as he had gone back to his quarters, he immediately sent a flag of truce with a white standard over to the enemy. The light infantry began to cut their new tents in the hornwork to pieces."

Cornwallis has just made the hardest decision of his life. He's nearly out of both food and shells, there are only two days' worth of cartridges, his men have had no biscuits for forty-eight hours, he can't even bury his dead. His visit to the hornwork that Dohla describes convinces him there's no hope. On the seventeenth, exactly four years from the day of Burgoyne's surrender, the flag of truce is sent out.

A drummer boy stands on the British parapet, beating a parley. An officer appears, waving a white handkerchief, and the two advance toward the allied lines, drum still beating. The guns are suddenly stilled, and in the profound silence that follows, Ebenezer Denny remembers later, "I never heard a drum equal to it—the most delightful music to us all." When this two-man delegation reaches the allied lines, a handkerchief is tried over the officer's eyes, the drummer is sent back, and the officer is taken to a house in the rear where he delivers Cornwallis's letter to Washington.

"Sir," it begins, "I propose a cessation of hostilities for twenty-four hours, and that two officers may be appointed by each side, to meet at Mr. Moore's house, to settle terms for the surrender of the ports of

York and Gloucester." He has chosen the Moore house because it's one of the few still standing in Yorktown, miraculously spared since it sits on one of the highest points. No doubt Cornwallis hopes that by the time the delegation gets there he can have removed the soldiers lying on the lawns at this house and elsewhere, exhausted and waiting for someone to give them food. Washington sends back a message to Cornwallis, asking him to set down a formal proposal for terms, and gives him two hours to do it.

In the chilly October night, a silence that seems almost unnatural envelops both camps. St. George Tucker writes in his diary: "A solemn stillness prevailed. The night was remarkably clear, and the sky decorated with ten thousand stars. Numberless meteors gleaming through the atmosphere afforded a pleasing resemblance to the bombs which had exhibited a noble fireworks the night before, but happily divested of all their horror. At dawn of day the British gave us a serenade with the bagpipe . . . and were answered by the French with the band of the Regiment of Deux-Ponts. As soon as the sun rose, one of the most striking pictures of war was displayed. . . . From the Point of Rock the battery on one side of our lines was completely manned and our works crowded with soldiers were exhibited to view.

"Opposite these at a distance of two hundred yards, you were presented with a sight of the British works, their parapets crowded with officers looking at those who are assembled at the top of our works. The Secretary's [Thomas Nelson's] house with one of the corners broke off and many large holes through the roof and walls, part of which seemed tottering . . . afforded a striking instance of the destruction occasioned by war. Many other houses in the vicinity contributed to accomplish the scene."

The actual surrender is giving everyone trouble. Cornwallis can scarcely bring himself to do it, and Washington has never once, in his long career, had the opportunity to dictate terms. That's why he gave Cornwallis only two hours, not knowing that in practice such things take more time, so a whole day is spent with flags of truce carried back and forth between the lines while negotiations continue. When the commissioners sit down to talk in the Moore house, they have their own difficulties—Major Alexander Ross for the British, Colonel Laurens for the allies.

"This is a harsh article," Ross remarks at one point.

"Which article?" Laurens inquires.

"The troops shall march out with colors cased and drums beating a British or a German march."

"Yes, sir, it's a harsh article," Laurens agrees.

"Then, Colonel Laurens, if that is your opinion, why is it here?" Ross asks.

"Your question," says Laurens, "compels an observation which I would have gladly suppressed. You seem to forget, sir, that I was a capitulant at Charleston, where General Lincoln, after a brave defense of six weeks in open trenches by a very inconsiderable garrison against the British army and fleet . . . and when your lines of approach were within pistol shot of the field works, was refused any other terms for his gallant garrison than marching out with colors cased and drums *not* beating a German or a British march."

"But Lord Cornwallis did not command at Charleston," Ross protests.

"There, sir, you extort another declaration," Laurens answers. "It is not the individual that is here considered. It is the nation. That remains an article or I cease to be a commissioner." It remains.

With such arguments, the negotiations drag on through the night so that the truce has to be extended until nine the next morning. The completed document is taken back to Washington for review, and he accepts most of the terms, denying a few, and sends them back with a note saying he expects them to be signed by 11:00, and by 2:00 P.M. the garrison should march out. The final document is duly returned and the commander adds a line in his own handwriting. "Done in the trenches before Yorktown in Virginia, October 19, 1781." Then he signs it, followed by Rochambeau and Barras for the French.

Now comes the formal surrender ceremony, and promptly at 2:00 P.M. the British begin marching out, first the Yorktown garrison, with arms shouldered and colors cased, and the Gloucester men an hour later. Watching them, Ebenezer Denny writes later, he thinks that "the British prisoners appeared much in liquor."

Conspicuously absent is Cornwallis. At the last minute, he can't face it and, pleading illness, sends his second in command, General Charles O'Hara. As the defeated troops advance, an officer of the New Jersey Line reports: "The British officers in general behaved like boys who had been whipped in school. Some bit their lips, some pouted, others cried. Their round, broad-brimmed hats were well adapted to the occasion, hiding those faces they were ashamed to show."

Later, Captain Graham, of the Highlanders, writes: "It is a sorry reminiscence this. Yet the scene made a deep impression at the moment, for the mortification and unfeigned sorrow of the soldiers will never fade from my memory. Some went so far as to shed tears, while one man, a corporal, who stood near me, embraced his firelock, and then threw it on the ground, exclaiming, 'May you never get so good a soldier again!' Nevertheless, to do them justice, the Americans behaved with great delicacy and forbearance, while the French, by what motive actuated I will not pretend to say, were profuse in their protestations of sympathy. . . . When I visited their lines immediately after our parade had been dismissed, I was overwhelmed with the civility of my late enemies."

As for the Americans, they're already giddy with joy at the prospect that the war might be over. Observing them that night, a colonel writes: "I noticed that the officers and soldiers could scarcely talk for laughing, and they could scarcely walk for jumping and dancing and singing as they went about."

On the surrender field, however, the allied soldiers are restrained, and it's the British who nearly break down. Once more, there's the contrast in appearance. The British, wearing brilliant new scarlet uniforms, march between long lines of the French regulars, resplendent in the shining black gaiters around their white broadcloth legs, brought out for the occasion. Then the lines of Americans, most still in their hunting shirts and motley collection of what passes for uniforms, mended as best they could for the great day, representing years of incredible courage and persistence no American army would ever be called upon to display again.

Looking at the ranks of these men who had endured and beaten them at last, it's small wonder the British music is so aptly titled, "The World Turn'd Upside Down," and no wonder too that many of the losers are tearful and some throw down their arms in rage and frustration.

How hard it is for these British, both officers and men, to give in to the Americans is apparent to everyone. In his diary, Dr. Thacher writes: "In their line of march we remarked a disorderly and unsoldierly conduct, their step was irregular, and their ranks frequently broken. But it was in the field where they came to the last act of the drama that the spirit and pride of the British soldier was put to the severest test; here their mortification could not be concealed. Some of the plateau officers appeared to be exceedingly chagrined when giving the word, 'Ground arms,' and I am a witness that they performed this duty in a very unofficerlike manner, and that many of the soldiers manifested a sullen temper, throwing their arms on the pile with violence, as if determined to render them useless. This irregularity, however, was checked by the authority of General Lincoln."

The climax comes when the surrender sword is presented. General O'Hara, displaying the insolence and haughtiness toward the Americans that the British officers still feel, first tried to give it to Rochambeau, as though he's saying, "Well, my old enemy, let us just consider this another incident in the thousand years of war between our countries." By doing this, he's also refusing to admit, even now, that the British have been beaten by the American rebels. But Mathieu Dumas, standing beside Rochambeau, won't permit O'Hara to get away with it.

"You are mistaken, sir," he says, "the commander-in-chief of our army is on your right." With reluctance, and wincing a little, O'Hara is forced to offer the sword to Washington, who delivers the final blow. "Never from such a good hand," he says politely, and indicates that this British second in command should give the sword to General Lincoln, his second in command, the man who was humiliated at the surrender of Charleston. Revenge at last!

It's all over. Next day, Lafayette writes to Maurepas, whose reluctant release of the purse strings set these events in motion: "The play is over . . . the fifth act has just come to an end." Lauzun carries this letter to him after a stormy twenty-two-day crossing of the Atlantic, and Maurepas just has time to read it. He's on his deathbed and dies two days later.

Was Cornwallis really too ill to surrender in person? One of his officers speculates: "Indeed, there were grounds for sickness unto death, for a general of his quality to have allowed himself to be trapped in such a way after being abandoned by his own and held at the mercy of the man he had chased across New Jersey and pursued everywhere in vain five years before." Translation: "No, he isn't sick, but you can hardly blame him for feeling as though he's at death's door."

For that matter, De Grasse, whose extraordinary decision in the

Antilles has, in effect, given the Americans their freedom, is not present at the ceremony either. He's lying abed, suffering from fatigue and gout, "the admirals' affliction," and already thinking of a gentler climate.

Nothing matches the allies' consideration for their defeated enemy after the surrender is over. British staff officers, in spite of their arrogance, are dined lavishly for days afterward. Rochambeau even gives Cornwallis a personal loan so he can get back to New York. The general is broke as well as defeated.

What's amazing are the actual casualties of the battle, after so many days of fierce cannonading and hand-to-hand fighting. The Americans have lost only 20 killed, 56 wounded; the French, 52 killed, 134 wounded; the British, 156 killed, 326 wounded. But the statistics that count are those that record a staggering British loss: 7,157 soldiers surrendered, along with 840 seamen, and 80 camp followers, not including 2,000 more men sick in hospitals.

Most of the British officers are granted paroles, to New York or England; the other ranks are sent to prison camps in Virginia, Maryland, and Pennsylvania. They're given the same rations as American troops, which gives them some idea of how their enemies have been existing. And there's mopping up to do. Lieutenant Reuben Sanderson, of the 5th Connecticut, reports that he's spent two days in Yorktown "collecting tents . . . and collecting Nigars till five o'clock." He means the hungry blacks Cornwallis has turned loose after promising them freedom if they stayed with him.

Small human dramas are enacted. A Mr. Day arrives from the countryside looking for a splendid horse Tarleton liberated along his way. Surprisingly, he finds Tarleton, who happens to be holding a sweet gum stick in his hand "as thick as a man's wrist." Even more surprisingly, Tarleton still has Day's horse, having had no opportunity to ride it to death, and the recent scourge of the South meekly surrenders the animal as a street crowd gathers to watch this exchange laughs and roars approval.

News of Yorktown reverberates through America like some tremendous explosion. There's rejoicing enough in Connecticut, where the inhabitants are still in a state of anger and shock over Arnold's September raid on New London. But the greatest joy is reserved for Philadelphia, the seat of what remains of America's government. Tench Tilghman gallops into town with the news at two in the morning, and the old German watchman takes him at once to the house of the president of Congress, Thomas McKean, and then wakes up everybody as he passes through the streets calling out, "Past three o'clock, and Cornwallis is taken."

Candles light up in windows everywhere. People put their heads out of open casements to confirm the news, and soon the streets are filled with cheering crowds. Next day, divine services are held, the air resounds with salutes, everybody wants to give a banquet, the whole city is illuminated that night, and there's dancing in the streets as well as in many houses. It's been a very long time since Americans had something to cheer about, and now, so it seems, the war is over.

A wry footnote to the celebration. When the bearer of the great news, Tench Tilghman, has to ask Congress for hard money to pay his expenses, it appears that there isn't enough cash in the Treasury to supply his need, so the members of Congress have to pass the hat among themselves, each putting in a dollar.

When the news reaches the Hudson Highlands at Newburgh, there's a reminder of the war's savagery, as General Heath, in command of the small garrison there, reports later: "The company collected and determined to burn General Arnold in effigy. . . . Just as they were going to commit the effigy to the flames, one of the company observed that one of Arnold's legs was wounded when he was fighting bravely for America, that this leg ought not to be burnt, but amputated; in which the whole company agreed, and this leg was taken off and safely laid by," accomplishing in imagery what Arnold so resolutely refused to do in reality.

In time, the news reaches London, and when Germain is asked how Prime Minister Lord North took it, he replies, "As he would have taken a ball in his breast. . . . For, he opened his arms, exclaiming wildly, as he paced up and down the apartment during a few minutes, 'Oh, God! It is all over!' Words which he repeated many times, under emotions of the deepest consternation and distress."

As for George III, he takes the news in his pigheaded stride, remarking that he hopes no one will think it "makes the smallest alteration in those principles of my conduct which have sustained me in past time."

For a moment, America lies happy but exhausted after Yorktown. Some of those who still suffer most, not surprisingly, are the blacks, abandoned when they're no longer useful, as Cornwallis did. To their shame, the British have even used them for an early version of germ warfare. General Alexander Leslie wrote to Cornwallis before York-town: "About seven hundred Negroes are come down the river in the smallpox. I shall distribute them about the rebel plantations." (Americans won't feel quite so self-righteous, however, if they recall how their commanders spread blankets from smallpox-ridden hospitals to Indian villages during the French and Indian War.)

In this war for democracy, the rank and file have failed to learn much about it in any practical way, emerging with the same old prejudices and bigotries they brought into it. Here's our old friend, Joe Martin, who's fought the whole bloody war, and now, in the wake of Yorktown, is on his way to Philadelphia after the victory, having already been given a large sum of money as a reward for helping to round up blacks. He's spent most of it on rum, and drunk all of that by now, so he stops at a house where he hears they sell liquor.

Entering, he sees a young woman "in decent morning deshabille," as he elegantly puts it, and goes on: "I asked her if I could have any liquor there. She told me that her husband just stepped out and would be in directly, and very politely desired me to be seated. I had sat but a minute or two when there came in from the back yard a great potbellied Negro man, rigged off in his superfine broadcloth, ruffled shirt, bows, and flat foot and as black and shining as a junk bottle. 'My dear,' said the lady, 'this soldier wishes for a quart of rum.' I was thunderstruck. . . . I took my canteen and hastened off as fast as possible, being fearful that I might hear or see more of their 'dearing' for had I, I am sure it would have given me the ague."

That's the last we'll see of Massachusetts Joe; his descendants at home will someday get around to helping free the slaves.

The lesson of Yorktown, however, as the lesson appears to be for the entire war, is not to be found in the cerebrations of great men, or even in the actions of men in the field alone. We don't have to agree with Karl Marx's politics or his program to understand the truth of what he'll write in an 1871 letter: "Coincidence plays a great part in the history of the world. The acceleration or delay of events depends to a large degree upon such accidents, which also include the personalities of those at the head of the movement."

20

✦ ✦ ✦

Winding Down

When the cheering stops, some are asking, "Is it really over?" Among those who aren't so sure is Washington. After all, the British are still holding on in New York and Charleston. He'd like to persuade De Grasse to join in an assault on the latter, but the gouty admiral is off to the West Indies, where his career is much less at risk.

The rest of the French are about to take up pleasant winter quarters in Williamsburg. The officers plan to do some serious drinking in the Raleigh Tavern, and the other ranks hope to find willing, or at least companionable, American ladies. Washington sends St. Clair off to the Carolinas, with regiments from Pennsylvania, Maryland, and Virginia, to help Greene, who will now turn his attention to Charleston.

The commander himself manages to take a few days off to visit his neglected Mount Vernon plantation, the subject of constant correspondence between him and his overseer. Then he must go to Philadelphia and make his report to Congress. It takes him fifteen weeks, most of the winter, in endless conferences and paperwork to get everything done, so it's nearly the end of March 1782 before he can go up to Newburgh, where the troops have been spending the winter in sullen grumbling.

If everything's over, Washington may well be thinking, then what am I doing with the same dreary round of problems—the perennial difficulty of how to supply the army, the rising disaffection of the officers, the continuing greed of contractors, and the apathy of fellow citizens, which appears to be increasing again in the aftermath of

Yorktown? There's peace, or at least a cessation of most hostilities, and there are rumors of real peace to come, but meanwhile there are the tag ends of war. Clinton is not a problem now. He's sitting in New York, depressed and sour, thinking only of going home.

Reports trickle in from the ongoing great war between Britain and France, in which the Revolution has been not much more than a sideshow as far as the British are concerned. De Grasse has scored striking successes in the West Indies. The British have lost Minorca, and Gibraltar is under siege, while there's a major revolt in far-off India. Rumors abound that the British people are so sick of having their dead sons lying in American graves that they've petitioned Parliament and the King himself to stop doing whatever it is they've been doing in the colonies.

Two months after Washington reaches Newburgh, Sir Guy Carleton arrives in New York to take the command from Clinton, who will at last soon be on his way home, leaving the city in far better hands, since Carleton has not only been one of the war's best unsung generals but he's an accomplished administrator as well.

After hours of unrealistic debate, the House of Commons authorizes the Crown to make peace, and on August 4, Carleton writes Washington, informing him that the negotiators will sit down in Paris soon, and that the British commissioners have been authorized to offer independence to the Americans, which of course is all they've wanted from the beginning. There's a new government now in England. Lord North has resigned, the Whigs are in power, and there are more friends of America in Parliament.

Washington remains cautious about George III. He thinks the King will try to put down his former colonies just as soon as he can find enough men and money to do it. As though to underscore his feeling that even now the war isn't over, Tory and Indian frontier fighters are still harassing settlers.

In Ohio, frontier leader Colonel William Crawford takes five hundred volunteers on what will prove to be a semifinal event in the frontier war. Only about a hundred of Crawford's men have ever fought Indians before, and they display an overwhelming fear when they encounter those braves who sally from their villages. This fight goes on for two days, until the Americans break ranks and flee in considerable disorder. Crawford and some others try to fight on, but they are overwhelmed and captured.

One of these captives, a Dr. John Knight, reaches Fort Pitt in July, "in the most deplorable condition a man could be in and be alive," as someone describes his arrival. Knight has a tale of horror to tell. The prisoners were taken to an Indian town, he relates, stripped, and compelled to walk between lines of men, women, and children who beat them unmercifully with clubs, sticks, and flats. On the following day, Crawford and Knight were brought out with their hands tied behind them. Crawford was fastened to a stake by a rope long enough so that he could be made to walk barefoot on beds of hot coals. At the same time, Knight says, the Indians fired squibs of powder at him, "while others poked burning sticks on every part of his body, thus they continued torturing him for about two hours, when he begged of Simon Girty, a white renegade who was standing by, to kill him."

"Don't you see I have no gun?" Girty says.

After a while, the Indians scalped Crawford, then beat him on his bare skull with sticks. Exhausted and almost fainting, the colonel fell back on the burning embers and squaws shoved hot coals on him.

After the colonel was scalped, the Indians slapped the grisly token over Knight's face, telling him, "This is your great captain's scalp, tomorrow we will serve you so." Next day, he was taken to another town and, on the way there, saw what remained of Crawford's body, mostly bones, lying on the ground. The Indian who was transporting Knight seemed more kindly disposed than the others, and on the way untied the doctor and ordered him to make a fire.

While collecting wood, Knight concocted an escape plan. Taking a heavy piece of wood in his hand, he dealt the Indian a severe blow that knocked him down. He got up again, but by that time the doctor had his gun and the brave ran off. The doctor plunged into the woods, and twenty-one days later, walked nude into Fort Pitt. He'd abandoned the gun along the way.

A number of Pennsylvania militia organize an expedition, ostensibly against any pockets of British or Loyalist resistance in the area, "but instead of going against the enemies of the country," as one observer explains, "they turned their thoughts to a robbing, plundering, murdering scheme, on our well-known friends, the Moravian Indians," many of whom had, indeed, helped the Americans in their struggle.

After the expedition, ostensibly on a friendly visit, living with them in a peaceful manner for three days, the militiamen suddenly fall on the village and kill ninety-three people—men, women, and children. They tomahawk, scalp, and burn, exactly the atrocities they've always accused the Indians of committing. One boy escapes after being scalped and finds sanctuary with the Delawares, who take the hint and thereafter display exceptional cruelty to white prisoners.

In August, the Indians make a sally of their own at Blue Lick, Virginia, killing seventy-five of a militia force that's making its way toward their village. This is the last gasp, however—for a while. Frontier warfare will far outlast the Revolution.

Meanwhile, the last major British bastions outside New York have fallen in the year since Yorktown. Savannah is evacuated in July, but it's December before the redcoats leave Charleston, just as Greene's army is marching into the city. No shots are exchanged.

In the fall, the French army comes together again with the Americans at Verplanck's Point. Rochambeau has orders from Paris to take his troops down to Santo Domingo and join Spanish forces against the British in the Caribbean. He hopes to depart from New York, but it hasn't been evacuated yet. After consulting with Washington, he agrees to give the appearance that he's going into winter quarters to deceive the British. Washington still can't believe the war is over. So the French army sets out over the Connecticut hills once more, along the route they traveled to victory only last year. This time their objective is Boston, and as soon as ships are available, they can sail from there.

At Newburgh, Washington hears nothing but bad news. John Laurens is killed in "a trifling skirmish" in South Carolina, where the war isn't over either. On October 2, General Charles Lee, that remarkable soldier of fortune who's been fighting in America off and on since the French and Indian War, including traitorously allying himself with the British in this one, dies in Philadelphia. Appropriately, death comes to him in a tavern, the Sign of the Conestoga Wagon.

Postmaster General Ebenezer Hazard reports this news to his friend Jeremy Belknap, saying that Lee died after only a few days' illness, "in some degree his own physician and but badly attended, except by two faithful dogs, who frequently attempted in vain to awaken their dead master." (Lee always said dogs were better than any humans he ever knew.) "They laid themselves down by his corpse for a considerable time, so long that it became necessary for new masters to remove them. He lies buried in Christ's Church yard. No stone marks his bed. Indeed, those who saw his open grave can scarcely mark the site, as it is continually trodden by persons going into and coming out of the church. Behold the honor of the Great!"

Few people have any reason to mourn Lee. He had remained unregenerate to the last. Only a few weeks before his death, he told his sister that Washington was "a puffed-up charlatan. . . . Extremely prodigal of other men's blood and a great economist of his own." In his will, he instructed that he not be buried in a church or churchyard, or indeed within a mile of any Presbyterian or Anabaptist meetinghouse, "for since I have resided in this country, I have had so much bad company when living that I do not choose to continue it when dead." Lee's final wish is disregarded, like so many other things he demanded in his lifetime. He's buried with full honors in an Anglican churchyard. A large crowd turns out for the ceremony, but there must have been a minimal number of sincere mourners.

Another questionable character has his name cleared, at least officially. Congress repeals its earlier order for a court of inquiry to look into the conduct of Gates, and he's returned to the army as a senior major general.

Oddly enough, in this strange interlude between Yorktown and the actual signing of a peace treaty, recruiting for a Loyalist army goes on in the four months after Cornwallis's surrender as though nothing had happened. The King's American Dragoons were organized as early as February 1780 by Benjamin Thompson, a Massachusetts scientist who will become much better known later on as Count Rumford. The motive now is not so much military as a means of giving employment to young Loyalist aristocrats who have nothing to do since they left the British regiments in which they served. There are American Loyalists who keep on recruiting as late as August 1782, when Prince William Henry delivers standards to the new regiment in a ceremony witnessed by what remains of Tory society.

Such activities are more or less controlled from New York by something called the Board of Associated Loyalists. In April 1782, this body, through one of its members, Captain Richard Lippincott, asks for permission to take three American prisoners out of the notorious provost jail in New York and return them to Monmouth County for exchange. Permission is granted. One of the prisoners selected is a patriot named Joshua Huddy, captured early by Loyalist irregulars.

Lippincott's idea of an exchange, it turns out, is to make Huddy an object of revenge, "exchanging" him for a man already dead, a Loyalist named White who Lippincott claims has been executed by the Americans. The Associators, as they're called, take Huddy up into the hills near Middletown and hang him. On his chest, they leave a placard reading: "We, the Refugees, having long with grief beheld the cruel murders of our brethren, and finding nothing but such measures daily carried into execution, therefore determined not to suffer without taking vengeance for the numerous cruelties; and thus begin, having made use of Captain Huddy as the first object to present to your view; and we further determine to hang man for man while there is a Refugee existing."

Consternation at headquarters. Washington sends off a sharp letter to Clinton, demanding that Lippincott be handed over. Clinton replies that he had nothing to do with this act, and he doesn't intend to turn over one of his own officers. However, he does have Lippincott put in jail, charged with murder (he's later acquitted), which infuriates the Loyalists. But that's not enough for Washington. He decides on an unusual form of retaliation. Lots are to be drawn among British prisoners, and the loser will be elected to hang as high as poor Huddy.

Unfortunately, this loser proves to be no ordinary officer but Captain Charles Asgill, among those surrendered at Yorktown and therefore presumably protected by the terms of the capitulation from any punishment of this kind. And that's not the worst of it. Asgill, a mere boy of twenty, is the only and beloved son of Sir Charles Asgill, who had been Lord Mayor of London and had risked his reputation to defend the American cause, for which he could be counted an old friend. The younger Asgill has a good many friends of his own in America, including three South Carolinians who were his classmates at Westminster School.

This charming young man with such impressive connections is obviously not someone to be executed with impunity in any case, particularly since he hasn't committed any crime. The story quickly becomes public and arouses almost as much outrage among Americans as it does abroad. Strong pressure is brought to bear on Washington, but he won't hear of a release and will agree only to a stay of execution. Protests continue to come in—from Rochambeau, from Richard Oswald (who's in Paris leading peace negotiations for the

British), and from Hamilton. It's now becoming an international incident, with potent political overtones for a not-quite-yet nation that's going to need all the diplomatic support and help it can get from other countries.

The stay of execution gives Lady Asgill time to make an extraordinary effort to save her son. Distraught with grief as she is, she hurries off to Paris and makes a personal plea to Vergennes, who is touched by it and takes up the matter with Louis XVI and Marie. They instruct him to appeal directly to Washington and tell him, in effect, to think twice about it, which Washington is more than willing to do. He has no taste for this affair, and blames it on Moses Hazen, the man who ran the lottery and didn't remember that the loser had to be someone who wasn't guaranteed protection.

Still, Washington doesn't think he should make the decision himself, since the appeal has come from the French government, so he hands the matter over to Congress, which tactfully votes that Asgill's life shall be given as a compliment to the King of France.

This isn't quite as tactful as it sounds, however, as Elias Boudinot tells us. There was "a very large majority of Congress," he writes later, who were determined to execute Asgill. The question was argued for three days before vital documents came to them—an exculpatory letter from Washington, another from the King and Queen of France, and a heart-wrenching missive from Asgill's mother. All these were "enough to turn the heart of a savage," Boudinot says, but there were still paranoid savages in Congress who thought the whole thing was a scheme of the minority.

These dissidents called for a cover of the letters, and the President of Congress himself was interrogated. They even scrutinized Washington's signature as a possible forgery. Eventually a motion was unanimously moved to let the original verdict stand, and ordering Asgill to be remanded to quarters at Lancaster. Why? Boudinot wants to know. If Congress's motion meant anything, he argues, it means that Asgill is now a free man, free to go to New York without an exchange. Somewhat shamefacedly, Congress agrees—unanimously.

One unexpected result of this affair is the dissolution of the Associated Loyalists. They're so outraged by the decision that they declare themselves not willing "to serve in future under persons [they mean Clinton and Carleton] in whom they can place no reliance." But if the Loyalists have lost confidence in their British masters, most people in

Great Britain as well as New York have lost any confidence in *them*. The unregenerate Loyalists are now men almost literally without a country. They're angry, too, believing their King has deserted them.

In New York, during this interim year, tensions are high as Loyalists and rebels begin coming face-to-face. Hundreds of people who had lived in the city before the British occupation pour in to see if their houses are still standing and whether they can get them back. This situation is further complicated by the fact that many have given up the houses they had been living in outside of town and now have nowhere to go if they can't reoccupy their former homes.

Carleton orders that they can "visit their estates, take inventories," and will not be molested or insulted. But there's a Catch-22. These two thousand or so returning citizens can't get their property back immediately in any case. That means they have to find whatever space they can to lay their heads, unless they're lucky enough to have relatives still in residence.

It also means that Tories and patriots are coming face-to-face on the streets every day, and naturally there's no love lost, particularly when some rebel recognizes a man who's done him particular harm, as in the case of Captain Tilton, a well-known burner of gristmills and meetinghouses, who has to carry a spear cane when he walks abroad to protect himself. The British post sentries every hundred yards, and under the circumstances, there's surprisingly little violence. The British soldiers themselves are "tolerably civil and polite." They've had enough war.

Outside the city, however, where the damage has been greater, it's a different situation. People want to drive out every Loyalist they can find, particularly those who were most active. As the historian Thomas Wertenbaker tells us, organized mobs called Levellers (not necessarily New Englanders this time) are organizing to carry out forced evacuations. Their tactics are quick and brutal. In Goshen, New York, they seize Joshua Booth and take him off to Ward's Bridge. There they cut his hair off and shave his eyebrows with a penknife, after which they tar and feather his head and place a sheepskin cap over it. They hang a cowbell around his neck and paste a paper on his head reading, "Look ye Tory crew/and see what George/ your King can do." Booth is made to walk four miles, drum and fife following him, until he gets to the next town, where he's paraded through the streets until nearly midnight while the populace mocks and insults him. At last they put him on a New York-bound sloop, where he's released.

Cavalier Jouett, a prisoner on parole in Woodbridge, New Jersey, thinks he's safe there because the citizens have treated him kindly up to now, but they tell him things have changed and he hasn't any right to be there. A mob carrying sticks and whips surrounds him. Jouett asks whether he's ever injured any one of them, but they aren't listening. He's a traitor to his country, they say, and "no such damned rascal should ever enjoy the benefits of the country again." With great difficulty, he escapes.

For many Loyalists, particularly the young, the main hope is Nova Scotia; they see it as a place not too far from America where they can make a fresh start. But to older people, it's a *terra incognita*, and they're afraid. One of them writes: "I can't bear the idea, and it is distressing to me to think I should be drove with my wife in our old age and my two dear daughters to begin a settlement in a cold climate, and in the woods where we are to cut down the first tree. I can hardly expect to live to see the settlement so far advanced as to be in a tolerably comfortable way and then what situation shall I leave my dear wife and daughters in?"

But the Loyalists have to go, whether to Nova Scotia or elsewhere, and as transports begin to line up at the piers in New York, the whole city seems ready to board them. It takes a long time, but on April 27, 1783, a vast flotilla of transports sets sail, carrying seven thousand of these refugees to Nova Scotia and elsewhere. By that time American officers are present to check them out on the piers, making sure that no American property is carried away. These guards see scores of blacks boarding the ships and protest that this is a breach of the treaty. Not at all, says Carleton, who's now in charge: "The Negroes I found free when I arrived at New York. I had therefore no right, as I thought, to prevent their going to any part of the world I thought proper." All he's willing to do is register them and find out who their previous owners were in case compensation money is asked. And that's how hundreds of former slaves are unexpectedly emancipated.

These and other transports continue to converge on Nova Scotia, and six months later, a refugee city has grown up at Port Roseway, with nine thousand residents, who have already developed a slum called Black Town, where a thousand blacks who had served during the war now live. One fleet of transports follows another in this exodus, carrying more civilians, many of them prisoners taken at Burgoyne's surrender, and whole provincial regiments—the British Legion, the Queen's Rangers, the King's American Regiment, the New York Volunteers, De Lancey's Volunteers, the Loyal Americans, the American Legion, and other names now rapidly fading into history.

Through part of 1782 and nearly all of 1783, the great exodus continues as the time when it's still possible to leave draws to a close. New York harbor is filled with ships of every description, and boarding them now are fewer soldiers or former guerrilla fighters than the kind of people who are going to be needed in a new land—civil officers, laborers, seafarers, merchants, farmers, mechanics, and, as always, mixed in with them some of the former rich who have contrived to remain rich. British and American ships lie side by side at the piers to transport these displaced people on transports brought up from as far away as the West Indies.

From the decks, these departing former citizens can see triumphant Americans crowding the New York streets, particularly pleased because they're buying up Loyalist properties dirt cheap at sales, providing numerous business opportunities. On the docks, army commissaries are selling their surplus stock—cattle, wagons, horses, firewood. Auctions are the biggest business in town as merchants about to sail away sell everything except what they can take with them.

All told, at least 2,900 former American citizens (the inclusive total is much higher) are exiled, to settle in Nova Scotia, St. John's, islands in the Caribbean, Canada, and other places, where those lucky enough to survive will write new chapters in their lives.

Some historians have wondered whether this exodus wasn't premature. After all, one major victory on the field doesn't guarantee a war is over, particularly when it's only the second major victory the victors can boast in eight years. After Yorktown, the British still have plenty of troops, and it's not impossible to reinforce them. What they don't have is the will, either in London or America, to carry on a conflict that has become too expensive and burdensome.

Yet the Americans at this point, some insist, would have been pushovers, or nearly so. The army could hardly be dignified by that name, and in May 1782, Congress recognizes this fact when the Secretary of War tells its members that the country is so broke it would be absolutely impossible to carry on another campaign. The Secretary has even had to tell Daniel Morgan that the medal he's been promised will have to wait a little while because whatever money is available (and it's not much) has to buy food for men still under arms. It will be seven years before Morgan gets his decoration. Knox goes up to Rhode Island to plead with the legislature for money to support the army, but he has to borrow money himself in order to get to Providence and back.

At this point, the troops are owed more than six million dollars in back pay, and a paradox has arisen. The government doesn't have enough money to keep the army going, but it doesn't have enough to let it go either, and the debt grows every day. No individual is safe from this pinch. Timothy Pickering is about to hand Martha Washington into a carriage when a process server gives him a writ that would make him personally responsible for the debts his quartermaster general's department has contracted. He's only saved from jail by the New York legislature, which passes a bill absolving public officials from such responsibility. Until it's passed, however, he has to lie low at home.

Things in Pickering's department, in fact, are so bad that Greene has to mortgage himself as surety in order to get a little food for the troops, and then he's caught in an unholy mess of bankrupt contractors and hostile creditors so that he has to sell the beautiful estate in South Carolina which a grateful legislature had given him for his services to the state.

In short, America is bankrupt, it has no army to speak of and no possibility of raising another one. Large parts of the country have been devastated by the war. It isn't so much that the Americans have won as that the British have lost, and don't even care since France now occupies all their attention.

Historians today hate such "iffy" questions, but some have speculated about what would have happened if the British, understanding the condition America was in after Yorktown, had pulled up their boots, mobilized their still considerable resources, and won a military victory that would arguably have not been too difficult to accomplish.

The answer, according to those who have grudgingly taken the time to examine the possibility, is that to have a bankrupt America on its hands would have been the worst disaster the British had ever faced.

The American future, whatever the outcome of the war and however uncertain its present might be, was assured. In time, these historians speculate, the United Kingdom would be an American colony, clinging to the opposite shore of the Atlantic, and subservient to Washington. Understandably, this view is not popular in Great Britain.

Fortunately for them, the British aren't tempted to reverse their fortunes in 1782. While they're waiting to go home, those who remain can sit back and watch the Americans struggle to survive.

Much as the trumpeters of democracy might deplore it, America is dividing along class lines now that the war that brought them together is all but over. It begins in the army. Soldiers who have endured the conflict's terrible privations, and who still don't know what's going to happen to them, believe correctly that their fellow citizens should pay attention and give them the kind of treatment they deserve. But somehow, as they begin to mix with the civilian population again, they find little sympathy or understanding (or even interest) in either them or the Revolution itself.

The officers are particular victims. When they visit Philadelphia, it isn't like the old days when everyone wanted to give them parties, and society offered its best food and daughters for their enjoyment. These officers now find something in common with the soldiers. One of them observes that soldiers "seem to be a people left of themselves, and are evidently . . . considered as the fag end of creation."

Another writes bleakly: "We poor dogs shall return with broken constitutions and empty purses, and the cursed sin of ingratitude has taken such deep hold of our virtuous countrymen that I expect a chosen few only will know us." Ironically, the morale of these soldiers wavered badly during the war but the hard core of them held firm and survived the worst times; now it appears that morale won't survive peace.

By 1783, tensions are so high in the army that, when Washington suggests soldiers ought to be allowed to keep their guns and pass them on down to their children as heirlooms, he's advised not to alert them because these muskets could be used for other purposes and "become a great terror to the inhabitants." These objectors fear that men who have such deep grievances can hardly be trusted with guns when they get home. Many in Congress agree, but they're afraid of becoming the first victims if they refuse the muskets and vote to let the soldiers keep them.

The center of dissatisfaction remains the officer corps. Many of them are already living on their own financial resources, which are worth increasingly less as Continental currency depreciates. The entire class of officers is rapidly becoming impoverished. In December 1782, they send a committee to Congress to demand back pay, and the assurance that they'll also get what's coming to them before they leave the army, besides the half pay for life Congress promised them back in 1779. Instead, Congress debates a motion that half pay for life be changed to six years of full pay. The motion loses, but the damage is done.

Utterly disgusted, the officers' delegation goes back to Newburgh, where Washington and the remnants of the army have just gone through their last painful winter, replete with all the problems they've had every other winter.

In March, the officers issue two brilliantly written but anonymous papers (probably the work of John Armstrong, Jr., of the Continental Army, according to John Miller) which have come to be known as the Newburgh Addresses. The first of these is a call for a summit meeting to be attended by representatives of all branches of the army, to consider how to redress their grievances. Until that happens, they suggest, the army should resist letting itself be disbanded. The Addresses remind army personnel that they have the power to make Congress come to terms with them because they can turn their bayonets against civil authority—in short, armed rebellion against the government is suggested as an ultimate weapon.

For those who think the war has established democracy and overthrown despotism, the Addresses declare that men who have just fought to end tyranny by a monarch might reasonably oppose the tyranny of a republic. They end with a call for the army to seize power, and Washington is invited to be a dictator, an idea that fills him with horror.

It's obvious that the officers, and the soldiers as well, have been treated badly, inexcusably badly, but what they don't understand is that their government is stony broke and can't help them even if it wanted to. One difficulty about ruling in the kind of republic the war has just established is that it's almost impossible at this point to get the states to cooperate, making national government virtually impossible. Even if they understood this, however, the officers are in no mood for tolerance. Washington is understandably apprehensive. He calls a meeting of the officers on March 15 to hear the report of their committee that went to Congress (already old news), and to discuss the matter.

A great deal depends on this meeting, because the Addresses have made it clear that, if nothing is done, the army is prepared to move to some point in the western part of the country and set up its own government, defying Congress to destroy it. In a word, this is mutiny on a potentially national scale.

As senior officer, Gates would nominally be the chairman of this meeting, so the officers are surprised when Washington appears in the chair and asks to speak. He makes the speech of his life, a masterpiece of diplomacy—and theater. He offers praise for the Addresses, but he has to tell them that he finds their content both unmilitary and unreasonable. They may not believe it, he tells them, but Congress has no doubt of the justice of their cause and fully intends to do everything it can to help them. Then Washington appeals to their patriotism, and draws from his pocket a private letter from a congressman outlining some of the difficulties that he and his colleagues are confronting.

At the same time, in order to read, he slowly pulls out a pair of spectacles, in a gesture right out of the Williamsburg theater, and says: "Gentlemen, you will permit me to put on my spectacles, for I have not only grown gray but almost blind in the service of my country." Until then, most of these officers haven't heard that Washington was suffering from impaired sight, and this gesture and those words have far more effect than anything the congressman has written. A wave of genuine emotion sweeps the meeting; some weep. Washington thanks them and leaves, after which they vote to entrust their problems to the commander.

So the perilous moment passes, and Congress is so shaken when it hears about the episode that it promises what it still has no money to implement—that is, full pay for officers for five years, either in cash or 6 percent securities, and full pay for four months for enlisted men.

On April 15 comes the news that the provisional peace treaty has been ratified, and the war is truly over. Everybody can go home now, but no actual cash has come from Congress. Washington tells it that the least it can do is to provide three months' pay before the army disbands. Congress is more than willing to do so, and they're putting all the heat they can on the states to come through with their tax collections. France is even asked for another loan. Over Vergennes's dead body! As a quick fix, Congress decides to furlough the troops at once, with a written promise for each man, and assurance of discharge just as soon as the treaty is actually signed. They're buying time, of course.

The impasse persists. On June 7, another group of officers gets off a petition to Congress to *please* give them some financial relief so they can get home. Congress can't do anything but forward their petition, with a supporting letter from Washington, to the states, pleading with them to honor the notes they've issued.

It's not enough. On June 17, the Maryland Line, nearly all native-born Americans by this time, are furloughed and march home through Philadelphia, intending to stop long enough to stand outside the State House and threaten Congress. About the same time, there's a revolt among the troops garrisoning Philadelphia, and instead of controlling these unhappy soldiers, as they might have been called on to do, the Marylanders join them. While Congress looks out the window to see what's going on, they're surrounded by soldiers with drawn bayonets. The President and Council of Philadelphia are in the same building, and both of these government bodies are now prisoners of their own army.

The irony is that most of the besiegers from the garrison are short-term recruits, who have never had to endure the hardships of the past eight years. They are, says one congressman, "fellows who had never been in action, the off-scouring and filth of the earth." It's true that most of these men have never learned anything about suffering patiently. Most have been spending their army careers in guarding prisoners. Nevertheless, they have guns, and temporarily they have power.

Led by a troublemaking lieutenant, and a captain said to be mentally deranged, they seize the Philadelphia arsenals before they march on the State House, where they send in a message demanding redress of grievances, giving the legislators fifteen minutes to answer, or else the soldiers will come in. Some of these mutineers are too drunk to enter anything but a tavern.

Ignoring the fifteen-minute ultimatum, Congress sits and debates the matter for three hours, and they then decide to face down the soldiers by leaving the building, an act of considerable courage in the circumstances. At 3:00 P.M., they call the soldiers' bluff and leave.

Surprisingly, beyond catcalls and insults, no one harms them, and they depart at once for Princeton, a much safer place.

With their departure, Philadelphia is in a state of anarchy. St. Clair appears and gets the troops back into their quarters temporarily, but they break out again and, in effect, control the city. The Pennsylvania authorities briefly consider calling out the militia but decide this might well add more sympathizers to the disaffected. Stronger measures are obviously necessary and Washington takes them. He orders Continental troops into the city and, confronted by these veteran regulars, the mutinous soldiers lay down their arms. The ringleaders hide out until they find a ship that will take them to England.

In Princeton, Congress tries to retrieve some shreds of its lost dignity by denouncing Philadelphia as "the sink of America, in which is huddled and collected villains and vermin from every quarter." It is also, they say, a center of vice and politics, snobbish, corrupt, and expensive. One congressman calls it "the most inhospitable scandalous place I ever was in. If I once more can return to my family, all the devils in hell shall not separate us."

These denunciations don't attract much attention except from Southerners, who take the occasion to propose moving the capital farther south, say, along the Potomac. There are other offers, too. Come live beside the Hudson, New Yorkers say. Why not Annapolis? the Marylanders want to know. If you're comfortable in Princeton, why not stay there? the New Jerseyans suggest. In fact, all Congress needs is a quiet place to die in, and they've found it.

Reports of more mutinous soldiers come up from the South. Hungry, ragged, and unpaid, like all the others, they've been told they must live off the land, but most of the land is desolated and exhausted. Greene reports that "our beef was perfect carrion, and even bad as it was, we were often without any." Wayne has the same complaint. "Our regimen is rice, poor beef, and alligator water," he writes while hostilities are still going on, "which in addition to the British bullet and bayonet, the tommyhack, and scalping knife of other less savage allies . . . affords no very flattering prospects of seeing Pennsylvania in health and safety."

These Southern soldiers have another common complaint: "Have you all forgot us to the Northward?" they inquire plaintively, and with anger as well. "We have not had a drop of spirits in camp for more than a month." While Yorktown was being fought, Greene reported that nearly half his men in North Carolina were "entirely naked, with nothing but a breech cloth about them, and never came out of their tents, and the rest were ragged as wolves."

The suspicion of these Southern soldiers is correct. They have been forgotten "Northward by all but their families and Washington, who agonizes over their situation as he does everybody else's. As the historian Charles Royster reminds us, there was an underlying fear of the military among the population, an irrational fear that this disaffected army would turn against civil government.

Officers bear the brunt of much of that feeling, for another reason. These shopkeepers and artisans and ordinary citizens have been elevated to positions of power and prestige they had never known before. They have become "gentlemen," as officers are presumed to be in the social context of the times, even though the British officers have been alternately aghast and amused by such pretensions. Now they're going back to their former lives, shorn of that same power and prestige, and it's a hard transition for many. They've been free about denouncing civilians for their apathy and other sins; now they're out of uniform and the citizens are free to cut them down to local size.

At Fort Pitt, Colonel Stephen Bayard reports: "The soldiers have said, as soon as peace was concluded, they would immediately go home, as they then considered themselves free men." As free men, they can start over again with their lives, but the officers have come to consider themselves professionals, commanders of men, and now their profession is no longer required. They're about to lose everything—their commands, the friends they've made over eight years, and the feeling that they're doing a highly responsible and patriotic service. Worst of all, no one is now going to treat them as "gentlemen."

An officer in the 1st Virginia speaks for them: "I may now go where I please, but where to go or what to do I am at a loss. The pay etc. that the country gives us is not sufficient to live genteelly on, and poor me, unfortunately, have spent all I had in the army, so that it's out of my power to commence trade, which I was brought up to. To work I never did, and to go a-begging I can never consent to."

This Virginian doesn't mention it, but he's also going to miss the life of an officer, with its camaraderie and privileges and status. What can peacetime offer to compare with it? Later, a former officer will confess that it took him a year after the war before he could feel like a farmer again. Some are so depressed by the harsh transition that they commit suicide after their discharge. In his suicide note, one writes: "I march off as gaily and almost as eagerly as when my friend Genl. Wayne sent me to attack Lord Cornwallis."

For a time, there's a fierce argument over the officers who demand compensation and aid in returning to civilian life, which results in an agreement by Congress to pay commutation fees, setting off a flood of civilian abuse, particularly in New England. These officers, say the citizens, were nobodies before the Revolution began and now they expect people who are having a hard enough time to subsidize them with their earnings through pensions. There are those among the civilians who sympathize more with the soldiers. Why should the officers get pensions and the other veterans nothing?

James Morris, who returns from the war to his farm near Litch-field, Connecticut, after serving as a captain, tells us what it's like to suffer from a mean-spirited citizenry who begrudge him any money at all, especially a pension. "I became obnoxious to the mass of people," he writes. "When I had any severe sickness they hoped I would die. One noisy old man said he hoped I would die and that they would take my skin for a drumhead to drum other officers out of town."

Steuben, the old soldier, proposes that the formal discharge of the army take place with an elaborate ceremony, but there's no possibility of any such thing. Regiments are simply leaving camp one by one, the officers too. Steuben writes later: "This disbandment of the army was so thoroughly comic that you would have laughed yourself sick had you seen it." (He means it ironically, of course).

Nothing so marks the difference between military and civilian life after eight years of bloodshed as the way Americans celebrate on the day peace is finally declared, with the treaty duly signed. The civilians eat. Orations, to be sure, are heard everywhere, along with salutes of various kinds, but mostly it's eating.

In some places, there's roasted ox. The Southerners barbecue. Everybody, everywhere brings out cold hams, bacon, tongue, fowl, veal, and every other kind of food. Many of the celebrants have been eating this way while the army was starving. And after the meal is over, they congratulate themselves. As Royster puts it succinctly, "On the festive day, instead of musters, parades, prayers, tears, and fast days, people got fireworks, a prayer of thanksgiving, a speech of self-praise, and a good meal."

The last scene of the military drama is played out in New York, on November 25, 1783, the day designated for the British to evacuate the city officially. The last of the troops and refugees are still boarding ships as the advance guard of Americans arrives from Newburgh, with Washington and his aides close behind.

It's a clear, bright day and it begins with one last outburst of hatred. William Cunningham, the brutal provost marshal, who was responsible for the horrors of the city's prisons, is still in town, and when he sees an American flag hoisted over Day's Tavern, on Murray Street, he runs toward it, hurling choice curses, and attempts to enter the tavern to tear it down. His way is blocked by a formidable figure, Mrs. Day, the wife of the tavern keeper, who bashes him so hard on the head with a blunt instrument that it makes the powder fly. There are no more attempts to remove the flag.

The streets are filled with people who have come to welcome the advance guard, under Henry Knox, as it moves down as far as the Bowery, where it breaks ranks and rests on its arms until the last British regiment is ready to leave. At 1:00 P.M., these redcoats march to their ships on the East River.

One piece of Loyalist spite remains. When it comes time to raise the flag at Fort St. George on the Battery, it's discovered that someone has taken the cleats and halyards and greased the pole. New cleats are hurriedly sawed up and tacked on, a sailor climbs to the top, grease and all, and unfurls the flag amid cheers from the onlookers and the booming salute of the fort's guns.

Afterward, Washington and Governor Clinton enter the city to take it over officially. They, along with a company of officers and civilians, dine that night at Fraunces Tavern. Next day, on the second floor of this historic spot, Washington bids an emotional farewell to his officers, then leaves for Annapolis to resign his commission, and hurries on to arrive in time for Christmas at Mount Vernon.

As the new year begins, the entire Revolutionary army has simply melted away, and the defense of the country is in the hands of a single infantry regiment and a few companies of artillery. Six months later, even those are disbanded except for a few officers and eighty enlisted men charged with guarding military property at West Point and Fort Pitt.

As the military historian Geoffrey Perret reminds us, "The men of the Continental Army simply made their way home as best they could, penniless as usual, in rags, ditto, begging for food at farm-houses along the way. All they had to show for what they had done was a free musket. . . . These Continentals, trudging down the dirt road, were both an embarrassment and a source of pride. That heritage of mixed feelings would be handed down to generations yet unborn."

So the American Revolution ends, not with a bang or a whimper, but with a silence that still resonates in our time.

SELECTED BIBLIOGRAPHY

Bailyn, Bernard. *The Ordeal of Thomas Hutchinson*. Cambridge, 1974.
———. *Faces of Revolution: Personalities and Themes in the Struggle for American Independence*. New York, 1990.
Bakeless, John. *Turncoats, Traitors and Heroes*. Philadelphia, 1959.
Bernier, Olivier. *Lafayette: Hero of Two Worlds*. New York, 1983.
Bill, Alfred Hoyt. *The Campaign of Princeton, 1776–1777*. Princeton, N.J., 1948.
Bolton, Charles. *The Private Soldier Under Washington*. Boston, 1902.
Brown, Wallace. *The Good Americans*. New York, 1969.
Busch, Noel F. *Winter Quarters: George Washington and the Continental Army at Valley Forge*. Paper. New York, 1974.
Carp, E. Wayne. *To Starve the Army at Pleasure: Continental Army Administration and American Political Culture, 1775–1783*. Chapel Hill, N.C., 1984.
Chinard, Gilbert, ed. and trans. *George Washington as the French Knew Him: A Collection of Texts*. New York, 1940.
Commager, Henry Steele, and Richard B. Morris, eds. *The Spirit of 'Seventy-Six*. 2 vols. Boston, 1958.
Dann, John C., ed. *The Revolution Remembered*. Chicago, 1980.
Davis, Burke. *George Washington and the American Revolution*. New York, 1975.
Dorson, Richard M., ed. *America Rebels: Narratives of the Patriots*. New York, 1953.
Flexner, James Thomas. *The Traitor and the Spy*. New York, 1953.
Forbes, Esther. *Paul Revere and the World He Lived In*. Boston, 1942.
Fowler, William. *Rebels Under Sail*. New York, 1976.
Freeman, Douglas Southall. *George Washington*. Vols. III, IV, V. New York, 1951, 1952.
Gelb, Norman. *Less Than Glory: A Revisionist View of the American Revolution*. New York, 1984.
Gross, Robert A. *The Minutemen and Their World*. Paper. New York, 1958.
Higginbotham, Don. *The War of American Independence: Military Attitudes, Policies, and Practice, 1763–1789*. New York, 1971.
———. *War and Society in Revolutionary America: The Wider Dimensions of Conflict*. Columbia, S.C., 1988.
Jensen, Merrill. *The Founding of a Nation: A History of the American Revolution, 1763–1776*. New York, 1968.
Lee, Henry. *Memoirs of War in the Southern Department*. Philadelphia, 1812.

Lossing, Benjamin. *Pictorial Field-Book of the American Revolution.* New York, 1850.

Manceron, Claude. *Twilight of the Old Order* New York, 1977.

———. *The Wind from America.* New York, 1978.

Metzger, Charles. *The Prisoner in the American Revolution.* Chicago, 1971.

Miller, John C. *Triumph of Freedom.* Boston, 1948.

Montross, Lynn. *Rag, Tag and Bobtail.* New York, 1952.

Moore, Frank. *Diary of the American Revolution.* 2 vols. New York, 1858.

Pancake, John. *This Destructive War.* Tuscaloosa, Ala., 1985.

Perret, Geoffrey. *A Country Made by War.* New York, 1989.

Roberts, Kenneth. *The Battle of Cowpens.* New York, 1958.

Royster, Charles A. *A Revolutionary People at War: The Continental Army and American Character, 1775–1783.* Chapel Hill, N.C., 1979.

Ryan, Dennis P. *A Salute to Courage: The American Revolution as Seen Through Wartime Writings of Officers of the Continental Army and Navy.* New York, 1979.

Scheer, George, ed. *Private Yankee Doodle: Being a Narrative of Some of the Adventures, Dangers, and Sufferings of a Revolutionary Soldier*, by Joseph Plumb Martin. Boston, 1962.

———. and Hugh F. Rankin, eds. *Rebels and Redcoats.* New York, 1957.

Shy, John. *A People Numerous and Armed.* New York, 1976.

———, ed. *Winding Down: The Revolutionary War Letters of Lieutenant Benjamin Gilbert of Massachusetts, 1780–1783.* Ann Arbor, Mich., 1989.

Tebbel, John. *George Washington's America.* New York, 1954.

Thacher, James. *A Military Journal of the American Revolutionary War.* Boston, 1827.

Tilghman, Lieut. Col. Tench. *Memoirs.* New York, 1974.

Treacy, M. F. *Prelude to Yorktown: The Southern Campaigns of General Nathanael Greene.* Chapel Hill, N.C., 1963.

Underdall, Stanley F., Major. USAF, Air Force Academy, ed. *Military History of the American Revolution: Proceedings of the 6th Military History Symposium, USAF Academy.* Washington, D.C., 1976.

Van Doren, Carl. *Mutiny in January.* New York, 1943.

———. *Secret History of the American Revolution.* New York, 1951.

Van Every, Dale. *A Company of Heroes: The American Frontier, 1775–1783.* New York, 1962.

Wallace, Willard. *Appeal to Arms.* New York, 1951.

Ward, Christopher. *The War of the Revolution*, John Richard Alden, ed. New York, 1952.

Wertenbaker, Thomas J. *Father Knickerbocker Rebels.* New York, 1948.

Young, Philip. *Revolutionary Ladies.* New York, 1977.

Index